John Wood

A Journey to the Source of the River Oxus

John Wood

A Journey to the Source of the River Oxus

ISBN/EAN: 9783744799966

Printed in Europe, USA, Canada, Australia, Japan

Cover: Foto ©Andreas Hilbeck / pixelio.de

More available books at **www.hansebooks.com**

A JOURNEY

TO THE

SOURCE OF THE RIVER OXUS.

By CAPTAIN JOHN WOOD,

INDIAN NAVY.

NEW EDITION, EDITED BY HIS SON.

WITH AN ESSAY ON THE

GEOGRAPHY OF THE VALLEY OF THE OXUS.

By COLONEL HENRY YULE, C.B.

WITH MAPS.

LONDON:
JOHN MURRAY, ALBEMARLE STREET.
1872.

[The right of Translation is reserved.]

PREFACE TO THE SECOND EDITION.

In bringing a Second Edition of "A Personal Narrative of a Journey to the Source of the River Oxus" before the Public, I have avoided any great change in the text; for although the years that have elapsed since its first appearance have brought with them vast changes, and although many, ay, most of the actors have passed away, still great interest cannot but attach itself to an early explorer's description of men and things, and I have on this account refrained from expunging passages that may be familiar to some of my readers. I have thus been enabled to preserve the continuity of the story throughout, and where I have been able to collect later information of a nature likely to interest those who take up the book the reader is referred to notes.

The attention that has of late been directed to Central Asia has induced Mr. Murray to publish the present work (the first edition having been out of print); and it is no small source of gratification to me to be able to point out that my father's reports have been fully confirmed by later travellers.

Thanks principally to the Russian forgeries attributed to Klaproth, the geography of that portion of Central Asia treated of in the following pages was for a considerable number of years shrouded in mystery, and Wood's account was subjected to doubt and suspicion of inaccuracy. Fortunately however the labours of the Mirza, of Pundit Manphúl, and of other Eastern travellers, have poured a flood of light upon the question, and the truth and reliability of Wood's drawings and reports are now fully established. The "Edinburgh review" for January, 1872, contains an able and exhaustive article on this subject, tracing the origin and course of the so-called Klaproth forgeries and their complete refutation by later travellers.

The following remarks briefly show the causes which led to the Expedition, and the estimation in which the work accomplished by it was held by Government.

After Sir Alexander Burnes' voyage up the Indus to Lahore, in 1830, the Indian Government never relaxed its efforts to procure the fullest details respecting that stream and the adjacent countries. The information collected by that officer led to negotiations with every State which bordered on the Indus and its affluents between Lahore and the sea, the enlightened object of which was to confer a boon on Asia by permitting commerce again to circulate through an artery which barbarism had closed. This desirable arrangement was effected by treaty in April, 1832. It was further necessary to have the seaboard of Sind surveyed; but the expediency of this measure was not at first apparent to its suspicious rulers, nor was the point conceded until the close of 1835. This survey was no easy task; and for the excellent map of the "Mouths of the Indus" which resulted from it Government were indebted to Lieutenant Carless, I.N.

Aga Mahomed Rahim, a Persian merchant of Bombay, was the first to take advantage of the opening of the Indus for the purposes of trade; and with a view of outstripping all competitors, and reaping largely of the profits which might be expected in this new field of commercial enterprise, he purchased a steamer for the navigation of the river. At his request, and with the permission of Government, Lieutenant Wood took command of this vessel; and on Saturday, the 31st October, 1835, he, with Dr. Heddle, had the proud satisfaction of unfurling their country's flag on the Indus from the first steamboat that ever floated

PREFACE TO THE SECOND EDITION.

upon its celebrated waters.¹ In February, 1836, the steamer returned to Bombay, leaving Lieutenant Wood on the river to ascertain its periodical rise and fall, to note the spread of the inundation, and to record such other phenomena as might hereafter be useful for its navigation. Having performed this service, failing health, the result of hard work, compelled Lieutenant Wood to leave for Kutch, whence as soon as he was convalescent he proceeded to Bombay. On arrival he found Alexander Burnes engaged in preparing the commercial mission to Affghanistan by the Indus, to which he had been nominated by the Governor-General.

On the 9th November, Lieutenant Wood was appointed an assistant to this mission by Sir Robert Grant's Government, and on the 26th November, 1836, the mission left the harbour of Bombay.

On nearing the Sind coast, Burnes gave written instructions to his coadjutors. The following extracts are from the instructions given to Lieutenant Wood:—"You are aware that one of the objects of this expedition is to ascend the Indus from its mouth to Attock, that a more perfect knowledge of the river may be procured, as well for the purposes of commerce as of war, and this important examination I am instructed by the Government of India to entrust entirely to you. In doing so, I am sure that the experience which you have gained by nearly a year's residence on the banks of the Indus, added to your professional skill and well-known assiduity, will be certain to secure the accomplishment of every object contemplated by the Governor-General in Council. . . . . . . The instructions which I have received from the Government of India draw my

---

¹ The boat was named after the river, and was of ten-horse power. Thirty-four years later Captain Wood, as superintendent of the Indus steam flotilla, reports the existence on the river of a fleet of first-class steamers in the highest state of efficiency, earning for their owners, in 1870, a net profit of 22,673l. 10s. for the first six months of the year. No guaranteed undertaking in India has done more than this in proportion to its capital, or been more successful in a commercial sense. And this eminent success of the Indus flotilla is attributed entirely to Captain Wood's management.

attention to the facility which the country in the neighbourhood of the river affords for the supply of coal, as a most important point, and this I also beg of you to keep in view.[1] . . . . . . I have confined myself to sketching out the general nature of your duties; but you will of course note particularly the breadth and depth of the stream, the strength of its current, the means of crossing it by boats, the number which may be found on it, and its canals, &c., &c. : but besides these there are many subjects of interest in a country that is in part so little explored to which you might turn your attention with advantage. Your own turn of mind can only suggest such inquiries to you, and while we perform the duty which has been entrusted to us, it is still to be borne in mind that we have it in our power to combine with the correct discharge of that duty the advancement of general knowledge."

(Signed) "A. BURNES.
"*On a mission to Cabûl.*"

The following extracts from reports by Sir A. Burnes, wherein that officer does full justice to the perseverance and zeal of Lieutenant Wood, will best show how these instructions were carried out. Writing from Cabool, under date 30th October, 1837, he says :—" I have the honour to transmit, for the purpose of being laid before the right honourable the Governor-General in Council, a geographical notice of the Valley of the Cabool river, by Lieutenant John Wood, Indian Navy. The valuable and interesting account now given of the physical geography of this tract of country, correcting as it does the position of several places on the earth's surface, will, I respectfully believe, procure for the labours of Lieutenant Wood the approval of his Lordship in Council."

[1] Burnes writes from Simla under date August, 1838:—" I have the extreme satisfaction to forward for the information of the right honourable the Governor-General an original letter from Lieut. Wood, announcing the discovery of coal on the eastern bank of the Indus. The specimens accompany this letter."

Unfortunately these beds of coal proved of such small depth as to render their profitable working impracticable.

PREFACE TO THE SECOND EDITION.

Again, under date 4th April, 1838, Burnes thus reports the discovery of the source of the Oxus:—"It is with extreme satisfaction I report that Lieutenant Wood has successfully accomplished his explorations and discovery of the source of the Oxus, and, having overcome the many difficulties that beset him, returned in safety to Kunduz." And in October, 1838, Wood's services are particularly brought forward in these terms:—
"The unremitting attention of this officer throughout will be apparent to his Lordship in Council in the perusal of his clear and practical report, while his own zeal and assiduity appear in the precision, variety, and extent of the information. A most important subject, the successful navigation of the Indus, is finally settled. Under these circumstances, I beg respectfully to submit, for the consideration of the right honourable the Governor-General, the advisability of making this report known without delay, that the widest circulation may be given to facts which have only been determined after two years' labour, and which it cannot be doubted will shortly lead the merchant and trader to the Indus."

It is unfortunate that so promising a career should so soon have been checked, and that the services of an officer whose merit was of no ordinary standard, and whose experience and devotion had been fully tried, should not have been further utilized in the same field. But having, as it were, been a mouthpiece for British assurances to the semi-barbarians of Affghanistan, his conscientious nature could not approve the later action of the Indian Government towards them, and a rupture with those whom he had assured of his countrymen's good-will left him no alternative but to retire. In connection with this subject, extracts from letters of the late Sir A. Burnes, now in my possession, and hitherto unpublished, may not prove uninteresting, especially in view of the sad conclusion of that distinguished man's intercourse with the Affghans. He writes from Cabool in February, 1841:—"We had a hard struggle for our existence here, but all went well, and Dost Mahomed surrendered, and I had the singular honour of being the man 'who mainly influenced it,' as the public despatch says. We followed the poor man everywhere, and there was no rest for the sole of his foot. His interview with me was very affecting; he said that Russia had misled him, that his ignorance never laid bare to him what we meant (a delicate way of saying we meant nothing), that the Persians at Herat started the Kuzzilbashes at Cabool, &c. &c.; but neither to me personally, nor in my absence, did he use a disparaging word, and on our departure he gave me his sword, his all indeed that was left, and bade me keep it as the remembrance of a man who regarded me. I hardly know how we shall ultimately end here. Many of them say we must take the country, and set the king aside; to me this seems pure folly, but clever fellows think otherwise. Of our coming here at all I say nothing now. Our connection should have been diplomatic, and not military; but the more I said, the less the great men believed; they thought I was favouring Dost Mahomed, forgetting it was the good of my masters I sought. For two or three lacs I could have made all square, and after spending five or six millions we are nearer the beginning than the end. But, in truth, Shah Mirza will do well and prosper if we will but let him alone and do as his countrymen wish, but we won't. Every man comes here and makes a Barataria of his own; one man even proposed a constitution, another has gone to form a society for the suppression of vice amongst the Uzbecks! Truly common sense is very uncommon sense. The Envoy and I are great friends, we understand each other; he is tired of the business, and wants to get away."

It is not my intention to treat of what is now a matter of history, and the above has only been inserted as an interesting relic of its author.

After leaving the service Captain Wood emigrated to New Zealand, in connection with the then newly formed New Zealand Company; but finding the advantages derivable from his association with this undertaking greatly over-estimated, he returned to Europe, and by his representations on the subject was greatly instrumental in furthering the interests of the settlers in that colony and increasing her prosperity.

Between the years 1843 and 1849, Captain Wood's attention was mainly given to mercantile pursuits; but in the latter year we find his name again brought forward in connection with his early sphere of usefulness, by Sir Charles Napier, then proceeding to assume command of the army in India. Knowing Wood from his book, and hearing much of him from Lord Ellenborough, Sir Charles was anxious to have him with him in Sind and the Punjab; feeling that his intimate knowledge of the rivers of these provinces might be of incalculable service in the face of what was then to all appearance certain, a protracted war in the Punjab. On Wood's consenting to return, application for his services was made. Both the Duke of Wellington and Sir Charles considered the matter of great importance, but, strange to say, the request was curtly refused by the Court of Directors, whose inimical spirit to the new commander-in-chief denied him any assistance they were in a position to afford. It appears strange that, supported by such men as the Duke, Lord Ellenborough, and Lord Fitzroy Somerset, Sir Charles's request should have been denied; but so it was, and in after years when bitterly complaining of the opposition he had encountered, we find the old general citing Wood's case as one of the most marked rebuffs he had experienced.

A natural fondness for a settler's life led my father again to turn his attention to the colonies, and in 1852 he embarked for Australia. Here he was greatly solicited to take a prominent part in the politics of the then rising colony of Victoria; but that retiring disposition which was in him second nature, would not allow of his doing more than suggesting improvements, and all efforts on the part of his friends to induce him to accept a seat in the Legislative Council were unavailing.

Returning to Europe in 1857, his co-operation was sought by an eminent engineer, whose scheme for the navigation of Indian rivers by a train of articulated barges was at the time attracting much attention. Once more Sind was the field chosen, and in 1858 he proceeded to Kurrachee as manager of the Oriental Inland Steam Navigation Company. Finding the project practically a failure, he with characteristic energy suggested alterations which would have rendered the vessels suitable for the peculiarly rapid current of the Indus; but the shareholders were not guided by his counsels, and the result was the ruin and wind-up of the concern.

In 1861, Mr. W. P. Andrew, the spirited projector of railway and river communication in Western India, secured Captain Wood's services for the Indus steam flotilla, and he continued to superintend this undertaking with great success until his death on the 13th of November last. An oft-repeated wish of my honoured father's was "rather to wear than to rust out;" and those who knew him of late years can understand how thoroughly this has been so to the last. Fatigue consequent upon a hurried journey to Simla, undertaken in the interest of his employers, at the height of the hot season, brought about his last illness, and the numerous marks of respect for his memory and regard for his character received by his family, are pleasing though most melancholy proofs that his career of usefulness and large-heartedness has left its mark for good upon those with whom he was throughout life for the most part associated.

ALEXANDER WOOD.

HEATH LODGE, ABBEYWOOD, KENT.

CONTENTS.

	PAGE
Preface to the Second Edition	v
Essay on the Geography of the Valley of the Oxus	xxi

CHAPTER I.

Embarkation on the Indus.—Seaports of Sind.—A Dutch gun-brig.—Changes in the course of the Indus.—Present to the Amirs.—Pír Putta.—Site and Shrine.—T'hat'hah.—Manufactures.—Antiquity.—Falling banks.—Fishing on Kínjor Lake.—Sonda.—Aspect of the country.—Alligators.—Alligator feast.—Beluches.—Arabs.—A shooting match.—Jírk.—Arts in Sind.—Haïderábád Mausoléa.—Lakkat.—Shooting.—Hawking.—Archery.   1

CHAPTER II.

Halla.—Manufacture of earthenware.—Chunniah.—Ruins of Khodábád.—Altars of Alexander.—Otters.—Black partridge.—Castle at Sihwan.—River and Crops.—Absence of trees.—Pulla-fish.—Fisheries.—Dur-myaní.—Wullí Mohamed Laghari.—Arrival of Dr. Lord.—Arore.—Mulala.—Importunity of fakírs.—Anecdote.—B'hkur, Rorí, Sukur.—Sand storm.—Battle of Sukur.—A Mohamedan's beard   18

CHAPTER III.

Shikárpúr.—A fair.—Shoes.—Sindí ignorance.—Bad roads.—Wheeled vehicles.—Predatory tribes.—Unsettled country.—Remarks.—Tigerprints.—Buffaloes.—Swimming the Indus.—Horned Cattle.—Herdsmen.—Plundered village.—Journey to Ahmedpúr.—Bullock-hackeries.—Nawab's Palace.—Guards.—Followers.—Warlike appearance.—Interview with Bhawul Khán.—Bhawulpúr.—A French adventurer.—Uch.—A drunken Afghan.—Arrival at Mittun-Kote.—Indus.—Accounts of the river by ancient and modern authors   30

CHAPTER IV.

Mittun-Kote.—Trial by ordeal.—Departure from Mittun-Kote.—Character of the country.—Kalórás.—Arrival at Dhera Ghazí Khán.—A trading mart.—Wrestling matches.—Alteration in the river.—Departure for Dhera Ismael Khán.—Aspect of the country.—Irrigating dams.—Earthquake of 1819.—Charitable feeling.—A water echo.—Takht-i-Suliman .   45

CONTENTS.

CHAPTER V.

Dhera Ismael Khán.—Old and new town.—Peasantry in the Dherajāt.—Departure from Dhera Ismael Khán.—The wild palm.—Difficult tracking-ground.—Kaffir-Kote.—Country of the Esaw Kyl.—Khán Beg Khán.—Ahmed Khán, chief of the Esaw Kyl.—Interview with the chieftain.—Dislike to the Seiks.—Kurum river.—Pebbles in the bed of the Indus.—Arrival at Kalabagh.—The Indus during its swell.—Submerged island.—Unceremonious removals.—Pendant nests.—Mirage.—Bulrush-gatherers 54

CHAPTER VI.

Town of Kalabagh.—High temperature.—River bathing.—Amphibious population.—Hindú Sunday's amusement.—Their general character.—Alum works.—Arrival of a Seik army.—Instructions.—Departure for Attock by the river.—The Duggah.—Swan river.—Dinghot.—Mukkud.—Author's mishap.—Town of Mukkud.—Influence of rain on the Indus.—Bundewan rivulet.—Mountain torrents.—Dead bodies.—Ascent of the river abandoned.—Success of the Seiks.—Departure for Attock by land.—Guide.—Sagrí Patans.—Seik bad faith.—Jats and Awans.—Arrival at Attock 63

CHAPTER VII.

Embarkation at Attock.—Berrí island.—An open plain.—Hurrú river.—Mountains.—Character of the Navigation.—Nilúb.—Ghori-Tarap whirlpool.—Dangerous eddies.—Great depth of the river.—A Kuttock outwitted.—Muncú.—Dangers off the Toe river and Soheilí rocks.—Dubber mountains.—Fearful eddies.—The Indus among mountains.—In the plain.—Characteristics of both.—Great velocity of the stream.—Dreadful when confined.—Upward navigation impracticable.—Villages on the river 75

CHAPTER VIII.

Escort.—Salt range.—A benevolent fakír.—Water-stored shed.—Pass of Shukur Durah.—Village.—Bungí Kyl.—Agha Maheide.—Start for Kohat.—Country improves.—Banks of the Toe River.—Frontier lines.—Superstitions.—Fine valleys.—Shadí Kyl.—Kohat.—Plain.—Town.—Fort.—Seik soldiers.—A love-sick youth 82

CHAPTER IX.

An Excursion in the Kuttock country.—Misfortunes at starting.—Sulphur mines and Naphtha springs.—Reflections.—A warm bivouac.—A Kuttock chief.—Gumut village.—Religious and social character of Mohamedans.—Prayers for rain.—Murdered travellers.—A horse exorcised.—Return to Kohat.—Notice of the Kuttocks.—Bungush.—Kheirulah Khán's durbar.—Quit Kohat.—Reach Peshawúr.—Agha Maheide.—Kabul river. Visit Attock.—Return to Peshawúr.—Town.—A Seik review.—Quit Peshawúr.—Jamrud.—Murdered grass-cutters 90

CHAPTER X.

Wah gurují ka fatteh.—Wussulam Alaikum.—Grinth.—Koran.—Rival nations and creeds.—Enter Khyber.—Seik scalps.—Ali Masjíd.—A character.—A mountain torrent.—"Topes."—Presents to the Khyberies.—Height of mountains.—Sufeid Koh.—Pine forests.—Supply of ice.—Province of Nanjhnehar.—Surkh Rúd or Red river.—Range and Pass of Karkatcha.—Enter Kabul.—Mohamed Akbar Khán.—Amír Dost Mohamed Khán 99

CONTENTS. xv

CHAPTER XI.

PAGE

Map of Afghanistan.—Province of Koh Daman.—Kabul race-course.—Skukur Durah.—A noble prospect.—Beauty of the scenery.—Gardens of Danow and Istalaf.—Baber's description of Istalaf.—Great abundance of fruit.—Plain of Begram.—Coins.—Turkish settlers.—Reig Rawan, or the moving sand.—Ziarats.—Dost Mohamed Khán's belief 110

CHAPTER XII.

An Uzbek Ambassador arrives in Kabul.—Object of his Mission.—His success.—Mirzá Buddi.—The Passes of Hindú Kosh.—Make choice of Parwan.—Start for Turkistan.—Afghan Elchi.—A mistake of the Kafila Bashi.—Deserted by the Afghan Elchi.—Bad roads.—Dangers among the Mountains.—Enter the Parwan valley.—Encamp at the foot of the Pass.—Guides.—Ascend the Pass.—Its dangers.—Forced to return.—Death of the Afghan Elchi.—Hindustanies among the snow.—Return to Kabul . . 117

CHAPTER XIII.

Start by Bamian for Turkistan.—A hen-pecked husband.—River Helmand.—Immigrant Hazaras.—Tribes.—Allegiance.—Hucksters.—Hazara females.—Depraved hospitality.—Hazara family.—Anecdote.—Pass of Hajikak.—Fuel.—Pass of Kalu.—Pimuri defile.—Ruins of Zohawk.—Akrobat.—Ungracious reception.—A ringing stone.—Sykan.—Assafœtida.—Slave tribute.—Kamrud.—Reflections.—Mirzá Buddi's tenantry.—Mazar ziarat of Hazrat Ali.—Arrival in Kunduz 125

CHAPTER XIV.

Murad Beg in Durbar.—Kunduz.—Character of the chief.—Uzbeks.—Tribes of Tartary.—Tajiks.—Uzbek intolerance.—Influence of the Mullahs.—Predestination.—Meals.—Salutations.—Horses.—Dogs.—Uzbek ladies.—Cemeteries.—Mohamed Beg's case.—Consultations.—Obtain leave to trace the Oxus. 137

CHAPTER XV.

Start on an exploratory expedition.—Fellow travellers.—Gholam Hussein, Abdul Ghuní Yesawal.—Servants.—Marco Polo.—Kunduz Plain.—Phenomena.—Khana-a-bad.—Hospitable students.—Snug quarters.—Reflections.—Badakhshies.—Colleges of Khana-a-bad.—The town.—Journey to Talikhan.—Character of the road.—Nature of the mountains.—Koh Umber.—Eagles and crows.—An embarrassed interview.—Reach Talikhan . 146

CHAPTER XVI.

Ataluk Khán.—A descendant of Alexander the Great.—Talikhan sparrows.—Kirghis slaves.—Market days.—Mohamed Cassim Khojah.—Pass of Latta-band.—Mountain scenery.—Superstitions.—Kila Afghan.—Wolves.—Earthquake.—Karabolak.—Meshid valley.—Legend.—Agurdurah.—Nahwi.—Taishkhan.—Junasdurah.—Wild hogs.—Vale of Duraim.—Plain of Argu.—Reishkhan.—Khojah of Kashgar.—Chittah.—Aspect of country from Latta-band to Chittah.—Absence of inhabitants.—Dreary appearance.—Fyzabad.—Reflections.—Glen of Kash.—Arrival in Jerm . . 155

CHAPTER XVII.

Interview with the governor of Jerm.—Start for the Lapis-lazuli mines.—A crazy guide.—Partridge hunting.—An unwelcome reception.—The Kokcha river.—An iron mine.—Shrine of Shah Nasr.—Firgamu.—Preparations for visiting the mines.—A description of the mines.—A village sacked by Kaffirs.—Anecdote of Abdul Ghuní.—Re-enter Jerm 165

CHAPTER XVIII.

Badakhshies surprised by winter.—Their dwellings.—Advantages and disadvantages.—Expenses of housekeeping.—Domestic utensils.—Light from reeds.—Dress of the Badakhshies.—Their character.—Winter's employment.—Starved partridges.—Ahmed Shah.—Chinese.—A Jew traveller.—Novel punishment for theft.—An Alchemist outwitted.—A partridge hunt on the banks of the Kokcha.—Earthquakes.—Kaffirs.—Dinner party.—Marriage customs.—The independent Mirza.—The intrepid ironmonger.—A faithful dog.—Register of the weather 174

CHAPTER XIX.

Inhabitants of Badakhshan.—Tajiks.—Kaffirs.—Mullahs.—Good breeding of the lower classes.—Grave deportment of Mohamedan children.—Arrival of Messengers from Shagnan.—Obtain permission to visit the Ruby Mines.—Religious discussion.—Slave-dealing.—Reflections.—Start for the Ruby Mines.—Execution of Criminals.—Kokcha river.—Khyrabad.—Kosh Darow.—Keen air.—Yowl.—Thieving Donkeys.—A suspicious death.—Robat.—Zé-bak.—Preparations from milk.—Pass of Ish-kashm.—Plains of Ish-kashm.—A way-worn traveller.—Misfortunes of a tribute-levying party.—Fail to reach the Ruby Mines.—Some account of them . . 191

CHAPTER XX.

Fall out with Abdal Ghaní.—Make up the quarrel.—A mounted Kirghiz matron.—Her steed.—The Yak, or kash-gow.—Ishtrakh.—Shah Turai of Kundut.—A Kirghiz encampment.—Kila Panj.—Mineral spring.—Issar.—Streams from Mastuch and Pamir.—Vestiges of the ancient Fire-worshippers.—The Wakhan chief.—Difficulties.—A Kirghiz escort.—Some account of that people.—The Kazaks 207

CHAPTER XXI.

Quit Langer Kish.—Enter Durah Sir-i-kol.—Cold bivouac.—March on the frozen river.—A meeting.—Willows.—Snow encampment.—Horns of the wild sheep.—Snug quarters.—A mutiny.—Difficult travelling.—Accident upon the river.—Kirghiz at prayers.—Source of the river Oxus.—Lake Sir-i-kol.—Height of Mountains.—Sources of many streams.—Sounding the Lake.—Effects of a rarefied atmosphere.—Pulsations upon Pamir.—Snow line.—Scarcity of wood.—Himalaya and Hindú Kosh chains.—The Kutchkar, or wild sheep.—The Rass.—Return to Langer Kish . . 226

CHAPTER XXII.

Wakhan.—Population.—Mohamed Rahim Khán.—Sources of revenue.—Slave dealing.—Its evil tendencies.—Descendants of Alexander the Great.—Physical characteristics of the Wakhanis.—Their dress and appearance.—Vanity of the sex.—Domestic Animals.—Crops and seasons.—Houses.—Stoves.—Fires.—Pine slips.—Matrimonial squalls.—Roshan.—Shagnan.—Darwaz.—Wandering fakír.—A singing entertainment.—Spring.—Changed aspect of the landscape.—The Edd.—Arrival at Kunduz . . 243

CHAPTER XXIII.

Start for Hazrat Imam.—Marching.—Hazrat Imam.—Patients.—Dogs.—Hunting of pheasants.—Murder of the Wakhan chief.—Fertility of the banks of the Oxus.—Mortality of Kunduz and Hazrat Imam.—Uzbek females.—Sharwan.—Kila Chap.—Ford the Kokcha.—Site of Barbarrah.—Plain of Turghi-i-Tippa.—Jan Kila.—Ford the Oxus.—Said.—Return towards Hazrat Imam.—Inhospitable reception.—Find shelter in an old shed.—Arrive in Hazrat Imam.—Death of the Mír's son.—Death of the Mír.—Kunduz.—Philanthropy of Moghul emperors.—Robbers.—Khulm—Samarcand.—Export of skins.—Furs.—Mohamedan saint.—Moorcroft.—Kunduz. 254

CHAPTER XXIV.

Quit Kunduz.—Death of Mirza Badi.—Shor-Ab rivulet.—Plain of Narin.—Hindú Kosh.—Inderab.—Patriarchal manners of a Tajik chief.—Reflections.—Movements of pastoral tribes.—Arrangement for entering Afghanistan.—Thermal springs.—Crossing the Pass of Khawak.—Khawak fort.—Panchshir valley.—Scenery and inhabitants.—Uzbek dislike of pistols.—Arrive in Kabul.—Friendly reception by Nawab Jabar Khán.—Public feeling.—Dost Mohamed Khán.—A new acquaintance.—Conclusion . 269

LIST OF ILLUSTRATIONS.

VIEW OF ALLIGATOR TANK . . . . . *Frontispiece.*

MAP OF THE COURSE OF THE INDUS . . . . *At the end of volume.*

MAP OF THE SOURCES OF THE OXUS, BY COLONEL YULE, C.B.
At the end of Introduction.

AN ESSAY

ON THE

GEOGRAPHY AND HISTORY OF THE REGIONS ON THE UPPER WATERS OF THE OXUS.

CONTENTS OF ESSAY.

	PAGE
1. Interest attaching to the region—The Rivers of Paradise—The names Jaihún and Saihún—*Historical Notices*—Vast antiquity of some surviving geographical terms—Names of the Oxus—Ancient Iranian populations	xxi
2. The Greco-Bactrian monarchy—Movements leading to its overthrow—Yuéchi, Tochari, Kusháns, Yetha, Haiúthalah, Ephthalites or White Huns—Tokháristán, and its principalities . . .	xxiv
3. Buddhism in Bactria—Christianity—The last Sassanidæ—Chinese intervention and influence; cut short by Mahomedan conquest .	xxix
4. Early spread of Mahomedan power, and early Mahomedan notices of the Upper Oxus countries—Princes claiming descent from Alexander—Successive empires on the Oxus—The Mongol invasion .	xxxiii
5. Marco Polo's Notices—Notices in the Life of Taimúr—Badakhshán under his successors—Present Dynasty of Mírs . . .	xxxv
6. Chinese dealings with Badakhshán—The Khojas—Uzbek oppression, and depopulation under it—Restoration of the Mírs under Afghan supremacy	xxxix
7. *Further notes on the geographical history*—Aristotle's conception of the mountain mass of Pámír—Ptolemy's account of the Seric caravan route—The valley of the *Comedæ*, and its identification—The Stone Tower	xli
8. Hwen Thsang and other Chinese Pilgrims—The mission of Zemarchus—"The thousand springs"—Marco Polo's Notices, as illustrated by Captain Wood—Clavijo's mission to Samarkand—A. Jenkinson—B. Goës	xliv
9. Works of Elphinstone and W. Erskine—Work of A. Burnes, and of his assistants—Captain JOHN WOOD	xlix
10. Later geographical work and travels—Khanikoff—Ferrier—The Punjáb Trade Report of 1862—Explorations organized by Major Montgomerie—Journeys of Shaw, Hayward, Forsyth . . .	li
11. The Mirza and his work—Great expansion of longitude between the Oxus and Kasghar basins; a result from recent surveys—The Principality of Sarikol—Faiz Bakhsh and latest Indian explorers—Russian work; Severtzoff and Fedchenko . . .	liii

		PAGE
12.	Apocrypha of Central Asian geography—Gardiner—The anonymous German and Chinese Itineraries of St. Petersburg—Klaproth the probable author—Origin of the false geography which these documents appeared to corroborate—Injustice done to Captain Wood—Bolor and Karchu	lvii
13.	*Geographical Sketch*—Pamir or Tsungling mountain knot, and its relation to the Himalya—Grounds for geographical distinction between them—The Pámír Plateau and its characteristics . .	lxiii
14.	The northern boundary of the Oxus basin—The mountains of Fán; the Iskandar-kúl—Mountains south of Samarkand—River of Shahr Sabz—The Iron Gate—Koh-i-tan—Termedh—Hissár . . .	lxvii
15.	Southern boundary of the Oxus basin—Hindú' Kúsh—Objections to recent opinions as to there being no proper range to claim this title—Its offshoots towards Badakhshán—List of Passes of western Hindú Kúsh	lxxi
16.	Koh-i-bábá—Road from Bámián to Khulm—Character of the hill country south of Balkh and Khulm—Balkh—Khulm—The Oxus plains	lxxv
17.	Rivers forming the Oxus—Old Arab account (Istakhri's) of the five confluents	lxxviii
18.	Sketch of the chief confluents—The SURKHAB, or river of Karátigín—Its true source only now made known by Fedchenko—Karátigín—The Pul-i-Sangin—Stories of subterranean channel—Misrepresentation in maps of the confluence of the Surkháb and Panja .	lxxix
19.	The PANJA—Its two branches—Wakhán—Shighnán—Possible trace of the *Sacæ*—Roshán and Darwáz unknown . . .	lxxxiii
20.	The KOKCHA and districts on its banks—Faizábád—Tributary streams —Kishm—Rusták—Chaáb—Provinces acknowledging the Mír of Badakhshán—Peculiar character and beauty of the country .	lxxxvii
21.	The SOUTHERN SURKHAB, or AKSARAI river—Its course and tributaries traced	xciii
22.	The Oxus, and the few data as to its size and levels . . .	xcv
23.	Notes on the topography and drainage of Pámír—The different lakes and their positions—"Dysame Lake," probably a mistake—Extract from "Lettres Edifiantes" regarding the Chinese march across Pámír in 1759—Names mentioned therein—Problem as to the drainage of Karákúl, and contradictory evidence on the subject—Aktásh	xcvii

N.B. For Oriental names in this Essay, the vowels are used according to the system generally called Sir W. Jones's, and recently adopted officially in India. But, in revising for the press, it has not been thought needful to insist on repetition of the vowel marks in words which frequently recur, such as *Bámián, Badakhshán, Pámír* (or *Pámer*), *Amú, Tájik, Ferghána* (more strictly *Farghánah*), *Hindú Kúsh, Khorásán, Hissár, Herát* (*Hirát* or *Harát*), *Tokháristán, Tásh-Kurghán, Kábul.*

ERRATA IN "INTRODUCTION."

Page lxi. Second paragraph, line 7, *for* "Boolor" *read* "Bolor."
,, lxi. note 2, *for* "Royal Geographical Society's Proceedings" *read* "Royal Geographical Society's Journal" (vol. xlii.).
,, lxvi. line 15, *for* "second slope" *read* "general slope."
,, lxvi. line 25, *for* "This is perhaps" *read* "This seems to be distinct from."
,, lxx. line 19, *for* "we know more" *read* "we know no more."
,, lxxxiv. line 10, *for* "Sarhad *Wakhát*," *read* "Sarhad *Wakhán*."
,, lxxxv. line 25, *for* "no less than 1000 souls" *read* "no more than 1000 souls."
,, xcii. line 12, remove the remark attached to xv. and xvi. ("These appear to lie," &c.).
,, cv. line 2, put note to "knowledge," * as follows:

* "Since this was first published, Mr. Shaw has satisfied me that these two places named as Aktash, if not identical, are closely adjacent, and that the Mirza must have made the mistake suggested —not surprising under the circumstances of his journey."

N.B. These and a few other corrections introduced in the text have been forwarded by the Author of the Essay; but he has not had an opportunity of seeing the proofs of the present Edition.

THE
GEOGRAPHY AND HISTORY

OF THE

UPPER WATERS OF THE OXUS.[1]

1. FEW regions can present claims to interest and just curiosity so strong and various as that heart of Asia which gives birth to the Oxus. Forming the great physical and political watershed of the Old Continent, it has been through difficulty of access long shrouded in mist that has darkened and distorted a variety of ethnological and geographical problems, mist which only now begins to lift; it is a centre of primeval tradition as well as of modern theory regarding the primitive history of mankind; its past history is interwoven with that of all the great Asiatic conquerors, whilst its coming history looms on the horizon rife with all the possibilities suggested by its position on the rapidly narrowing border-land between two great empires, one of them our own.

Here is the one locality on the earth's surface to which, if some interpretations be just, the Mosaic narrative points, in

---

[1] The knowledge of a particular region, after advancing rapidly for some years, sometimes comes to a standstill for a very long time. This does not seem likely to be the case with the geography of these regions; and it is therefore well to state that before these sheets went to press, the writer had seen the extracts from M. Fedchenko's letters in "*Petermann's Mittheilungen*," for June, 1872, but no map or further detail of his journey. Neither has he yet seen any copy of Mr. Arrowsmith's new map of Central Asia. Neither, I may as well add, have I ever seen Sir Henry Rawlinson's paper on the Oxus, read at the Liverpool meeting of the British Association in 1870, though I have read with diligence whatever of his connected with this subject is accessible to me. I trust that before long we shall have the advantage of seeing, in a complete form, his treatise on the Oxus, and the translations from Mír Haidar which he has promised.

unison with the traditions of Aryan nations, as the cradle of our common race. If Oxus and Jaxartes be not in truth rivers of the Adamic paradise, the names of Jaihún and Saihún show at least that they have been so regarded of old.[1] The old pictures of Eden figure the four rivers as literally diverging from a central lake to the four quarters of the earth; and no spot so nearly realizes this idea as the high table-land of Pamir in the centre of the Asiatic world; upon whose lofty plains a tussock of grass decides the course of the waters, whether with the Oxus to the frontier of Europe, or with the Yarkand river to the verge of China; whilst the feeders of Jaxartes and Indus from the borders of the same treasury of waters complete the square number, and the lakes that spot the lofty surface lend themselves to round the resemblance.

Looking back as far as written history will carry us, we find the regions on both sides of the Oxus subject or tributary to the Persian monarchy. Among the many races whom Darius, still speaking from the cliffs of Behistún, claims as his subjects, and whom Herodotus has catalogued as contributing their contingents to the treasuries and the armies of the great king, we find Bactrians, Chorasmians, Sogdians, and Sacæ, all of them nations dwelling by or beyond the Oxus.

Nor is it a little remarkable that after all the manifold floods of conquest or migration that have poured across those plains since the days of Darius the son of Hystaspes, three at least of those four names remain unobliterated from living memory.[2]

---

[1] The translator of Istakhri's "Geography" cites *Jaihún* as an example of the enduring vitality of Oriental names. But there is, I believe, no trace of the application of *Jaihún* to the Oxus, or of *Saihún* to the Jaxartes, before Mahomedan times. The name *Saihún* (often applied by Mahomedan writers to the Indus also) is probably *Phison* corrupted to a jingle by the Arabs. As they made Cain and Abel into *Kábil* and *Hábil*, Saul and Goliah into *Tálút* and *Jálút*, Gog and Magog into *Yájúj* and *Májúj*, so from Gihon and Phison, *Jaihún* and *Saihún*. M. Garrez supposes that the river was called Jaihún by the Arabs, because "it encompassed the Land of Kush;" *i.e.*, of the Kushán, or Haiáthalah, confounded with the Kush of Scripture.—"Jour. Asiat.," ser. vi., tom. 13, p. 181.

[2] The names of *Bakhtar, Khwarizm, Soghd* would all be intelligible on the banks of the Oxus now, in something closely approaching to their ancient application, though not denoting political divisions that now exist. Of *Sacæ*, also, there is perhaps still a surviving trace, as will be noticed hereafter.

Nay, in traditions which may be far earlier than the Achæmenian kings, and which seem to set in the Oxian highlands the primitive and goodly land of the Iranians, two of those three names appear as attaching to the earliest settlements of the race. Another class of Persian legends refers to Kaiomurs, the first of the primitive Peshdadian kings, the foundation of Balkh. This city has always been regarded in the East, probably with truth, as one of the oldest in existence, insomuch that Múrád Beg of Kunduz, an Uzbek ruffian who figures in Captain Wood's narrative, and who possessed Balkh for a brief interval some forty years ago, was ever after proud to stamp upon his coin its venerable title, "the Mother of Cities."

The Oxus appears in the traditions of the Parsi books under the name of VEH-*Rúd*, in some form of which originates the classical name which we find it most convenient to use, and also it may be presumed that of the names of territories and tribes on the banks of its upper waters, such as *Wakh*-an, *Wakhsh*, and *Wash*jird, names also no doubt identical in formation, if not in application, with the classical *Oxiani, Oxii*, and *Oxi-Petra*.[1] *Jaihún*, the name by which the river is most commonly known to Oriental writers of the middle ages, is, as we have seen, one arbitrarily given. In earlier Mahomedan history, the usual title of the Oxus would seem to be *Al-Nahr*, "the River," whence *Máwaralnahr*, or "Transamnia," or, as it has been happily rendered in modern use, *Transoxiana*. *Ámú* is the name now most commonly used in the East, a name apparently of no great antiquity and of uncertain origin.[2]

---

[1] Properly these names in question express two forms, one, *Wakh* and *Wakhán*, belonging to the Panja or southern branch of the great river, the other, *Wakhsh*, to the northern or Karátigín branch, in which the affix *sh* seems to represent some distinctive particle, qu. the "smaller" or "northern" Wakh? This latter form, *Wakhsh*, seems to have originated *Oxus*, whilst *Wakh* seems better represented by *Ochus*. And the evident confusions in classical geographers about the Ochus, which seems at one time to be a river of Aria, and at another time a great confluent of the Oxus, may have relation to these circumstances.—See Strabo, xi., c. xi., 5; and Pliny, vi., 16.

[2] Some derive it from the city of *Ámol*, or *Ámúyah*, which stood near its western bank, on the road between Bokhara and Khwarizm, called by Abulfeda *Ámol-ul-Shatt* ("on the river"), to distinguish it from Amol in Mazandarán ("Annal. Moslem.," ii., 581); but it seems as likely that the town took

The great river figures in Persian romantic history, as the limit between Iran and Turan. Yet there are grounds besides the older forms of tradition already referred to, for supposing that from remote antiquity the substratum of settled population in Transoxiana may have been of Iranian lineage. The fact that the mass of traders in the cities appears to be of Persian race and speech would not alone have great weight, but there is evidence of a large basis of Tajik blood among the agricultural population of Khiva, Sogdiana, and even Ferghana. The inhabitants of secluded mountain districts generally represent the earlier population, driven by intruders from the easier life of the plains. Now we find that the inhabitants of such inaccessible regions as Karátigín and Mácha are Persian in speech; and such evidence as we have, confirmed by the general report of the nations round, ascribes a Tajik (*i.e.*, an Iranian) origin to the people of Badakhshan, Wakhan, Shighnan, Roshan, Darwáz, and even of Sarikol beyond Pamir.

Meagre as is the ethnological information to be derived from the lists of nations and characteristics of their equipment detailed by Herodotus, it is more than can be extracted from the vague statements of the historians of Alexander. Between the time of that conqueror and the Christian era vast changes occurred.

2. Bactriana, after an interval of uncertain allegiance during the struggles that followed the death of Alexander, was recovered effectually by Seleucus, and remained a province of the empire which he left to his successors. But, under his grandson the second Antiochus, Theodotus, who is termed "Governor of the thousand cities of Bactria," threw off his allegiance and declared himself king, a revolution accomplished between B.C. 250 and 256, and nearly simultaneous with the revolt of Arsaces, which laid the foundation of the Parthian

its name from the river. General Cunningham supposes *Amú* to have been taken from *Hieuma*, one of the five great clans of the Yuèchi, whom he believes to have occupied Wakhán. This seems hazardous. *Hámún* appears as a popular form of the name in Badakhshan; and Raverty seems to imply that the Kafirs call it *Aemán* ("Jour. Asiat. Soc. Ben.," xxviii., 324). The Turkish Admiral Sidi Ali calls it *Umm*.—"Jour. Asiat.," ser. i., tom. 9, p. 204.

monarchy. The Greco-Bactrian dominion, which began with Theodotus, is alleged to have extended at one time or another not only over Bactriana, but over Sogdiana to the Jaxartes, nay, even to the confines of the Seres,[1] as well as over the countries now called Herat, Segistan, and Afghanistan, besides some substantial part of north-western India, and the valley of the Indus to the coasts of the Delta and Guzerat.[2]

It is, however, quite uncertain what may have been its widest limits at any one time or under any one sovereign, as there are many proofs of divided rule and contemporary dynasties, insomuch that the seven princes, among whom the chronologists of the last century had distributed the brief duration of the empire, on the basis of the scanty data afforded by classic writers, have been multiplied by the discovery of coins to more than five-and-twenty.[3]

The empire north of the Indian Caucasus suffered first from Parthian encroachment, and then was overwhelmed entirely, about B.C. 126, by the results of a great movement originating in the far East. The Greek dynasties south of the mountains continued to endure, and perhaps even to extend their dominions in the direction of India for a few years longer, but ceased to exist about a century before our era.

The classic notices of the movements which destroyed the empire in Bactria are meagre and obscure. Chinese historical collections have preserved accounts in greater detail, and with an appearance of fuller knowledge, to which it is both natural and just to give credit.

The Chinese story, much compressed, is this. In the third century B.C., a numerous people called Yuéchi, alleged to have been of Tibetan race, occupied pastures outside the north-western boundary of China, between Shachau and the mountains on the Tibetan frontier. About 162 B.C. the

---

[1] Strabo, xi. 1. Old Arab writers speak of towns close to Jaxartes as being in the "Lands of China." And compare Capt. Wood's own expressions, at p. 180, where *China* is used for Yarkand. Such expressions throw light on the ancient applications of *Seres*.

[2] The chief direct authority for the extent of the Greek dominion appears to be Strabo, in the passage just referred to. This and the other scanty notices of the kingdom in classic authors, are collected by Mr. Edward Thomas in "Jour. Roy. Asiat. Soc.," vol. xx., p. 109, *seqq*.

[3] Mr. Thomas says fifty; but this must include the barbaric kings, who imitated Greek coinage.

Hiongnu (the Huns of Deguignes), who were then in great predominance on all the northern frontier of China, attacked the Yuéchi and drove them from their settlements. They made a long migration, reaching the valley of the Ili, and dislodging in turn a people called *Szu* or *Szé*, who moved onward to the steppes bordering the Jaxartes. Before many years another swarm alighted on the Ili, that of the *Usún*, driven also before the resistless Hiongnu. The Yuéchi and Szé were thus precipitated upon Sogdiana. The date of this inundation of nomads, as recounted by the Chinese, agrees well with that assigned by chronologists on purely classical data to the destruction of Bactria.

Strabo names as the nations which achieved this destruction the Asii, Pasiani, *Tochari* and Sakarauli; Trogus Pompeius, the Asii and Saranci. But the Tochari are named also by both Trogus and Justin in a manner which connects them with these events, and this name of Tochari assumes afterwards a prominence in connection with Bactriana, not quite easy to explain.

The Yuéchi are said to have divided their new territory into five governments, corresponding apparently to five great clans of the nation. But about the Christian era the prince of Kueishwang,[1] named by the Chinese *Kyutsyukho*, subdued the other four princes, and extended his conquests over the countries south of Hindu Kush, including Afghanistan and Sind, thus establishing a great dominion of which we hear from Greek writers as that of the Indo-Scythians.

I am not aware of any information regarding the history of these dynasties to the north of the Hindu Kush for several centuries after our era, with the exception of some vague references, cited from the Chinese, to a kingdom of *Ho* or *Hoa*, apparently in Sogdiana, which is said to have made in the second century great conquests in Persia, India, and the countries east of Pamir.[2] To the fourth century, however, the Chinese books

---

[1] The position of the Kueishwang, or *Kushán* state, probably survived in *Kusháníah*, mentioned by Istakhri (tenth century) as a flourishing city of Sogdiana. It lay about one-third of the distance from Samarkand towards Bokhara on the north side of the valley.

—See Sprenger, "Post und Reise Routen," and his Map No. 2, and V. de St. Martin in "Pèlerins Bouddhistes," iii. 281.

[2] Rémusat, "Nouvelles Mélanges Asiat." i. 244.

ascribe a revival of the Yuéchi under the title of *Yetha*, said to have been the family name of those conquering kings of Hoa. A great warrior-king of the Yetha, *Kitol* or *Kitaur* by name,[1] crosses the mountains, conquers five kingdoms to the north of Gandhára, or the country of Pesháwar, and establishes his son as king in the latter city.

These kingdoms north of Gandhára must have embraced Swát and the adjoining Hill-states (now inhabited by an unruly Mahomedan population, from whom the country has taken the popular name of *Yághistan* or "Rebellia"), with the Dard districts and Chitrál, probably including also the Káfiristan of our day. And it is remarkable that the name *Kitaur* is not only recorded by a celebrated Mahomedan writer (Al-Birúni) as that of the Pagan dynasty of Kabul,[2] but presents itself also in the account of Taimúr's campaign against the Kafirs, and seems to have survived to our own day as a title affected by the ruler of Chitral.[3]

The Yuéchi in this revival as *Yetha* are, according to the view ably maintained by M. Vivien de St. Martin, the same as the *Haiáthalah*, Ephthalites or White Huns, who appear prominently in the history of the Sassanian kings during the fifth and sixth centuries, and who are known to some of the Armenian writers as *Kushán*, a term apparently identical with the *Kueishwang* of the Chinese notices.[4] In the early part of

[1] *Kitolo* in the Chinese form.

[2] See "Dowson's Elliot," vol. ii., pp. 403—407.

[3] *Sháh Kataur*. Kataur, or Kitolo, has perhaps something to do with that singularly Teutonic-looking name *Katulphus*, which appears in Menander as that of an Ephthalite (see Müller's "Fragm. Hist. Gr.," iv. 235). *Kotulo* is, however, a name that frequently occurs in the old Turkish dynastic lists (from the Chinese) given by Deguignes.

[4] The term *Kushán* occurs also in Firdusí. Instances of its use will be found in V. de St. Martin's paper, "N. Ann. des Voyages," 1849, vol. iii., p. 49, *seqq.*, and in one by M. Garrez, already cited. The latter supposes *Tálikán* on the Murgháb to have derived its name from the Haiáthalah, whose name appears in one Armenian writer as *Idálagán*. Tálikán, on the borders of Badakhshan, probably had the same origin. And the valley and pass of Kushán, over the Hindu Kush, preserves their other name; likewise perhaps Kushán, or Kabushán, in Khorásán.

Ibn Khurdádbah says that the title of the king of Transoxiana was *Kushán Sháh*.—"Jour. Asiat.," ser. vi., tom. v., p. 257.

Theophanes, in a curious passage ("Müller's Fragm.," iv. 270), calls a prominent king of the Haiáthalah in the fifth century, "Ephthalanus, king of the Ephthalites, from whom indeed the

the sixth century their power extended over Western India, and Cosmas tells us of their king Gollas, who domineered there with a thousand elephants, and a vast force of horsemen. But the Haiáthalah, of the Oxus, were weakened by the defeats they suffered at the hands of Khosru Naoshirwan; and in 571 their kingdom was shattered by the invasion of the Turkish Khakan. In the early part of the next century they still held Herat and Badghís; but when the Chinese pilgrim, Hwen Thsang, passed through the Oxus valley on his way to India in 630, and on his return in 644, he found the former empire of the Haiáthalah broken up into a great number of small states, of which he enumerates twenty-seven, all acknowledging the supremacy of the Turkish Khakan. These states extended from the frontier of Persia, almost to the head waters of the Oxus; on the north of that river they reached to the Iron-gate, and included Hissar with Karátigín, or part of it; on the south of that river, they reached to the Hindu Kush. In studying the brief, but tolerably precise notices of Hwen Thsang, it is not a little remarkable how many of the political divisions, and even of the names are substantially identical with those which still exist. In fact, this is the case with so large a proportion of these states, that we feel, in reading this part of Hwen Thsang's memoirs, that we have already opened the chapter of modern geography.

To the whole group of states, as fragments of the extinct kingdom, Hwen Thsang gives the remarkable name of *Tukhára*. And either by this name in the form *Tokháristan* or by that of Haiáthalah, the country continued for centuries to be known to the Mahomedans; the former name surviving the latter, but also becoming obsolete about the time of the Mongol domination, in the thirteenth century. There can be no doubt that the name *Tukhára* is the same as that of the Tochari, whom we have seen to be mentioned by Greek and Roman writers among the nations that overthrew the Bactrian kingdom; and the name is evidently used by Hwen Thsang as

race derived that name." This is a highly improbable statement; but it may be that the usual title of the king was *Haiáthalán Sháh*, which was taken for a proper name. We find *Khottolán* *Khodah, Kábulán Sháh, Kashmírán Sháh*, &c., given by Ibn Khurdádbah as the proper titles of various Gentile kings.

synonymous with that of *Yetha*, though he does not employ the latter. There are, however, some curious obstacles to the identification of the Tochari and the Yetha, into which we cannot here enter.[1].

Early Mahomedan writers tell us that, previous to the Arabian conquests, the frontier of Khorasan, under the Sassanian kings, was ruled by a great officer, called the *Sipahbed*, who had under his orders four *Marzbáns*, or Margraves, viz., one governing in Merv, one in Balkh and Tokharistan, a third in Herat, Púshang, and Badghís, and a fourth in Transoxiana. It would be difficult, however, to name a period during which such an organization could have completely applied, unless, perhaps, during the reign of Naoshirwan, who is alleged to have ruled as far as Ferghana.

3. During the time of the Ephthalites, Buddhism had spread wide in the Oxus countries, and seems almost entirely to have displaced the religion of Zoroaster in its very cradle. The prevalence of Buddhism, and the connexion with India through the extension of the Ephthalite rule over the valley of the Indus, must have more or less Indianized Bactria.[2] Hwen Thsang found Termedh, Khulm, Balkh, and other cities of Tokharistan, but above all these Bamian, amply provided with the convents, *Stupas*, and colossal images which are the striking characteristics of prevalent Buddhism: even the secluded valleys of Andaráb and Khost, and Wakhan, in the bosom of lofty Pamir, were not without their convents. To this Indianized

---

[1] See a paper by the present writer in the coming No. of the "Jour. Roy. Asiat. Society." I have omitted there to notice the fact that *Thogar* is stated to be a title applied by the Tibetans to the Turks of Eastern Turkestan (Koeppen, "Die Religion des Buddha," ii. 42), a circumstance, so far as it bears, not favourable to the theory of the Tibetan origin of the Yuéchi. On the other hand, if they *were* recognized as of Tibetan race, this would help to account for their being called *Huns*, as *Huna* appears to be an ancient Hindu name for certain races of Tibet. The name of *Hun-des* applied to Tibet has indeed sometimes been explained as *Hiun-des*, or Snow-land. And it is remarkable that *Tukhára* is explained by Lassen to mean *snow* or *cold*.

[2] The bilingual inscriptions of the Greco-Bactrian coins show that an Indian language was prevalent in the dominions of the Greek kings, though we do not know what was the northern limit of that language.

character of Bactria, in the Sassanian age, a late writer refers the frequent confusion in the Parsi traditions between the Oxus and the Indus; and to this period also, he refers the introduction of the name of Balkh, into Sanskrit literature, and of the *Vanxu*, or Oxus, into Hindu cosmogony.[1]

Christianity also penetrated to Khorasan and Bactria, at a somewhat early date. In A.D. 334 an episcopal see existed at Merv and Tús; and Samarkand is alleged to have become also the seat of a bishop, or even of a Metropolitan, by the beginning of the sixth century. Cosmas (*circa* 545) testifies to the spread of Christianity among the Bactrians and Huns, *i.e.* the Ephthalites; and it was apparently from Balkh that went forth that Rabban or Nestorian monk, who in 635 founded in China, under the protection of the great Emperor Taitsung of the Thsang dynasty, a Christian Church, which has been long swallowed up in the sea of Paganism, leaving as its almost solitary relic and evidence, that famous and wonderful monumental inscription which still stands in the suburbs of the great city of Singanfu.

This missionary movement was doubtless intimately connected with the fact, that under the first emperors of the dynasty just mentioned, there was a great revival and extension of the conquests and influence of China towards the West, and that the whole of the territory, up to the base of the Tsungling, or mountains of Pamir, was then organized into regular Chinese order of government. Chinese influence, if not conquest, also passed the mountains into Transoxiana and Tokharistan, so that many of the princes of those regions adopted the custom of sending complimentary embassies to the Chinese court. But at this time a power of harder temper, and moved by more ardent fires, was rising in the West. In 638, Yezdegird, the last of the Sassanian kings, when defeated and hard pressed by the Saracens, sent to ask aid from the Emperor Taitsung, and after his flight across the Oxus is said to have encountered in Sogdiana his messenger bringing back the emperor's prudent refusal.[2]

[1] M. Garrez in "Jour. Asiat.," as before quoted.

[2] It is remarkable that Hwen Thsang, who returned through Tokharistan in 645, nowhere makes any allusion to the rising power of the Mahomedans.

Tokharistan was one of the last strongholds of fidelity to the Persian kings. Here, after the death of Yezdegird (651), his son Feroz maintained himself for some twenty years, but was finally compelled to take refuge at the Chinese court. The son of Feroz, like a prototype of Charles Edward Stuart, came back some years later to Tokharistan, where he was hospitably received, and struggled on for twenty years longer. By that time, we are told, the tribes that had served him were scattered by the Arab sword, and he too returned to end his days in China.[1]

It is during the efforts of Feroz to maintain himself in Tokharistan, that we find the Chinese emperor making an extraordinary, though futile, display of his claim to sovereignty almost up to the shores of the Caspian, and by edict organizing the whole country, from Ferghana to the borders of Persia, into Chinese administrative districts (*Fu, Chau, Hien*).

It is scarcely possible to suppose that this organization ever took effect except on paper, or that the hundred and twenty-six military cantonments for Chinese garrisons, which the scheme embraced, ever had any actual existence; still the measure is a very remarkable and characteristic one. The list of sixteen *Fu*, which were thus constituted, has been published by Rémusat. It is difficult, perhaps impossible, to identify all the localities, but some of them cannot be mistaken, and one such, which bore the name of *Persia* itself, was apparently intended to embrace territory, as near the lion's jaws as Segistan. And the first of these, *Fu*, is Tokharistan, with its capital at *Ahwan*, a city which obtained the official Chinese title of *Yuéchi-fu*. We cannot identify it with certainty, but it is evidently the same with the *Hwo* of Hwen Thsang, and must have been near modern Kunduz; probably the same with *Wawálin*, which figures as a place of importance in the early Mahomedan times. The province was divided into twenty-four *chau* or districts, no doubt corresponding, more or less exactly, with the twenty-seven principalities, of which we have already spoken.

The struggles of the last Sassanidæ in Tokharistan, for half a

[1] Rémusat, in "Mém. de l'Académie Roy. des Inscr.," tom. viii., 103, 104.

century after the death of Yezdegird, illustrate the fact that though the leader of the troops that pursued the fugitive king may have " neither halted nor reposed till his foaming cavalry had tasted the waters of the Oxus,"[1] yet the effective conquest of the country, even south of that river, was by no means rapid. It was in 675-6, that Saad, the governor of Khorasan, passed the Oxus and advanced to Samarkand, which opened its gates to him. But, as in the parallel case of Northern India, this and similar raids were often repeated before a lasting lodgment was effected in the land beyond the river; and it was not till the time of Kotaiba Ibn Moslem, who entered Transoxiana in 706, that the Arabs permanently established themselves in that region. Even then their dominion must for many years have been but a partial occupation, leaving the native princes in nominal possession of authority. This, at least, may be gathered from the Chinese records, which show that till far on in the eighth century various states of Transoxiana and the Upper Oxus continued from time to time to send missions of homage to the court of Singanfu, as if retaining a lingering hope that help and deliverance from the Arab robber might yet come to them from that quarter. One of the latest of these missions was from the king of Ferghana in 754, probably in near anticipation of being swallowed up by the black-robed followers of the Abbasid Khalifs, and it was accompanied by a young prince whom the king, his father, commended to the emperor for education in Chinese manners and learning. Of the Yuéchi in Tokharistan, we are told that their chief was, in 755, raised by the emperor to the rank of king, and received the aid of a Chinese force against the Tibetans, who were threatening invasion. But five years later nine of the western states are recorded to have finally thrown off their allegiance to China, and among these was Tokharistan. Vague statements are made in later years of tribute coming from the Hill principalities to the east of Tukhara, but probably the last date (760) marks the time when all the more accessible regions of the Upper Oxus became thoroughly amalgamated with the Khalif's dominions.

    I have dwelt, perhaps unduly, on these details, because they

[1] Gibbon, chap. li.

exhibit an unfamiliar phase of Asiatic history, in which we discern that China, with all its peculiarities, was not always that hive apart—*penitus divisus orbe*—which we are apt to consider it, but had at that remote date, before Islam transformed the face of the continent, relations somewhat close and frequent with the nations of Western Asia. More than once since then the Chinese power has touched the foot of Imaus, but it has never again passed that natural barrier.

4. Abulfeda speaks of the splendid remains of the palaces of the kings of Wakhsh, and refers to the wars waged in that region on the first introduction of Mahomedanism;[1] but no details on this subject are accessible to me, nor indeed regarding the conquest of Badakhshan, or any other of the Hill-states. In the year 793 Fadhl Ibn Yahya, the Barmecide, was invested with the government of all countries from Kermán to the frontier of the Turks; and he, we are told, caused a barrier with two castles to be erected in a defile beyond Khotl, by which the Turk marauders used to come down on their forays. It is believed that the memory of this barrier, which was known to the Arabs as *Al-Báb*, or "the Gate,"[2] survives in the name of the state of *Darwáz* ("Gate"), which still exists upon the Panja, or Upper Oxus, and into which debouche some of the passes from Pamir, though they are as yet utterly unknown. The fact shows that, by the end of the eighth century, the Mahomedan power was established almost up to the verge of Pamir.[3] And in the revenue rolls of Abdallah Ibn Táhir, quasi-independent ruler of Khorasan, in 836, we find not only Tokharistan and Termedh, but Chaghánián, Khotlán, and its mountains.[4]

Not much information regarding Badakhshan and the adjoining valleys is to be got from the old Arab geographers. The

---

[1] Hudson, "Geog. Gr. Min." iii. 75, 77.

[2] *Reinaud*, "Mém. sur l'Inde," p. 161. M. Reinaud takes the gate for that above Termedh (p. xlviii. *infrà*), but this is a mistake.

[3] Kataiba's troops are said to have reached Kashgar, probably by way of Ferghana and the Terek Pass; but no occupation seems then to have ensued.

[4] *Dakhán* also appears with a reported revenue of 40,000 dirhems. The name looks very like a mistake for *Wakhan*; and yet it is difficult to suppose that state to have come so early under Mahomedan rule.—See Ibn Khurdádbah, in "Jour. Asiat.," ser. vi., tom. 5, pp. 245, 246.

books of Istakhri and Ibn Haukal, written in the middle of the tenth century, speak of the chief town of that province as belonging to one Abu 'l Fatteh, whence we may conclude that for some time before they wrote it had been subject to Mahomedan rule. The town is described as situated on the banks of the *Khariáb*, a circumstance difficult to understand, as other dates compel us to identify this river with the Panja. The mines of ruby and azure were already famous, and Badakhshan was a mart for the musk of Tibet, which was brought thither by way of Wakhan. In the more open country below, Táikán (or Túlikán), and Balkh, are described as the chief places south of the Oxus; Termedh, Kobádián, and Chaghánián north of it. Panjhir, beyond the ridge of Hindu Kush, is already famous for its silver mines, and infamous for its miscreant population.[1] In Wakhsh and Khotl, regions now so dark to us, and presumably so barbarous, we find notices of flourishing commerce and handsome towns; but to none of them can we assign a position.[2]

That the Mahomedan conquerors generally left the old princely families in some authority, we may here also reasonably conclude, from that singular circumstance that so many of the petty dynasties claim, or have claimed, descent from Alexander of Macedon, a circumstance several times alluded to by Captain Wood in the course of his work. Some of these princes have no doubt merely followed a fashion in making this claim, but with a few of them it would seem really to have been an old tradition. As a general rule, Asiatic traditions connected with the name of Alexander, are of no more historical value than traditions of Arthur or Brian Boru, in Great Britain and Ireland, or of Pandus in India. They attach to the popular Mahomedan view of Alexander as a hero of the faith, or to the wide cycle of the Alexander romances. But here the tradition was possibly connected with memories of the Bactrian kingdom, and may have had some such origin as the

---

[1] Andaráb, a singularly secluded position for a mint, furnishes upwards of twenty separate coins of the Samanid sovereigns, between A.H. 292 and 366 (A.D. 904—976). This was probably owing to the vicinity of the Panjhir silver mines.—See Erdmann's "Numi Asiatici."

[2] See "Edrisi," i. 479, 480, whose authorities are evidently some two centuries at least older than his own day.

Grand Turk's claim to be "Cæsar of Rome." For the real ancestry of the oldest dynasties was probably to be sought among the Yuéchi, or Tochari, rather than among the Greeks whom they had overthrown.[1]

Tokharistan in general formed a part successively of the empires of the Sassanian dynasty of Bokhara (terminated A.D. 999), of the Ghaznavi dynasty, of the Seljukian princes of Persia, and of Khorasan, of the Ghori or Shansabanya kings, of whom one branch reigned specially over Bamian and Tokharistan for about half a century, and of the sultans of Khwarizm, whose rule was ended by the invasion of Chinghiz Khán. How far the authority of these successive dynasties extended to the remote provinces there is little information available. The campaigns of Chinghiz, in Tokharistan, were prolonged by the vigorous resistance he met with before its fortresses; and marked by massacres in the true Mongol fashion, from which probably the country has never thoroughly recovered. Balkh was the victim of one of these, and a garrison in the district of Tálikán, which held out against him for six months, was another. Bamian followed. Here a favourite grandson of the Khán's was killed by an arrow, and Chinghiz, in his wrath, when the city fell, ordered, not merely that all life should be extinguished, but that all property should be annihilated, and no booty taken. The city received from the Mongols the name of *Mau-Bligh*, "The City of Woe." But it was the end of Bamian, which has never since been a city, though its caves and its colossal idols remain.

5. Fifty years later (1272-3) Marco Polo, with his kinsmen, tarried some time in Badakhshan, before proceeding by the high valleys of Vardoj and Wakhan to Pamir and Káshgar on their way to Cathay. Meagre as his information may seem, it is more than any Eastern author yet translated has afforded us on the subject of that interesting province. He speaks of the

---

[1] The princes who have made the claim are, as far as I can collect:— 1. the kings of Badakhshan, long extinct; 2. Wakhan; 3. Shighnan; 4. Roshán; 5. Darwáz; 6. Karátigín; 7. Kuláb (?); 8. Chitrál; 9. Khapolor in Balti; 10. Gilghít; 11. Swát. The last, however, was in that position at least a modern intruder (Yuzufzai).

difficult passes which made the country so strong, and paints, with a few touches of force and colour unusual with him, the charming character of the climate and landscape in the high plateaus, frequented, as he tells us, by the sick, as sanitaria, and of whose healing influence he speaks from pleasant experience.[1] He notices the vast flocks of wild sheep on the uplands; the valuable falcons; the huskless (or Tibetan) barley; the almonds, pistachios, walnuts, and abundant wine. He speaks, also, of the mineral riches of the country; of the silver and the rock salt, the azure and the rubies, which had already made the name of this remote province familiar to Europe in the form of *Balas*. He commends the sure-footed horses of the country, and heard stories of a breed descended from Bucephalus, that had not been long extinct; another curious fragment of Alexandrian tradition. It is, perhaps, another version of the story regarding the same famous blood, which is related by the Chinese many centuries earlier, when speaking of this same country of Tokharistan. A cave on a mountain, north of the capital, was said to be 'frequented by a wonderful stallion of supernatural origin. Hither the people every year brought their mares, and the famous breed of horses called *Ku* was derived from the foals so produced.[2]

Such particulars as Polo affords of the inhabitants of the various districts, from Tálikán upwards to the verge of Pamir, show that, though all professed Mahomedanism, they were as yet but rough converts to its doctrine and civilization. They are depicted as rude hunters clothed in skins, and very fond of wine. They appear to have been, in fact, very much in the condition at this day of the people of such districts, professing Mahomedanism, as Gilghit and Chitral.

In the life of Taimúr we begin to hear more frequently of Badakhshan and the countries adjoining it; and one of his early campaigns there, as described by his biographer, Sharífuddin, was full of peril to him, and would be full of interest were the

[1] On M. Fedchenko's journey to the Alai steppe (1871), he found in the brooks running into the Kizil-su, or upper stream of the Karátigín river, a small kind of trout, which he mentions as the first discovery of a *salmo* in Turkestan. Let me point out that Marco Polo mentions trout (*temali*) in the mountain brooks of Badakhshan.

[2] Rémusat, "Nouv. Mélanges Asiat.," i. 245.

geography more intelligible.[1] His march to India, at a later date, is more easily traced. He crossed the Oxus by a bridge of boats at Termedh, and then advanced by Khùlm, Ghazniyak, Samanján, Baghlán, and Andaráb. Here, at the immediate base of Hindu Kush, he heard bitter complaints regarding the exactions and kidnapping inroads of the Black-coat Kafirs from beyond the mountains, and crossing by a branch of the Khawák Pass, by which Captain Wood returned to Cabul in 1838, he made a resolute and successful invasion of the Kafirs in their mountains, and inflicted terrible punishment.

In the time of the successors of Taimúr the rule over Balkh, Kunduz, and Hissár, often changed hands among the princes of his family, or the adventurers who rose to power amidst their feuds; but as long as the old royal house of Badakhshán, claiming descent from Alexander, endured, the actual rule of that province seems to have been left in their hands. Thus, under Shah Rukh, in 1411, we find Beháuddin, king of Badakhshan, endeavouring to establish independence of the House of Taimúr; but Mirza Ibrahim Sultán, who was in charge of the Balkh country, suppresses the attempt, and gives the kingdom to Behauddin's brother, Shah Mahmúd.[2] An envoy from the king of Badakhshan also takes part in the mission sent to the court of Peking by Shah Rukh in 1419.[3] In the time of Abusaid, great-grandson of Taimúr (1449—1469), the male line of the old house expired with Shah Sultán Mahomed, one of whose

---

[1] See "Pétis de la Croix," i. 167-170. Taikan (or Tálikán), Kalaogan, Kishm, and Jerm are all well known; but Mount *Kerkes, Ortondye, Tenknaï,* and *Conghoralenk* are dark, and some no doubt corrupted. The latter name is *Mongol,* and was applied to a variety of open pasture lands. Some of the names still extant in Badakhshan and the adjoining countries appear to be of Mongol origin, a thing not very easy to account for. Thus *Aulang* ("a meadow"), the last part of the name written *Congoralenk* by Pétis de la Croix, is found in the *Sal-aulang* Pass of Hindu Kush, and in the *Yeke-aulang* ("great meadow") near the source of the Balkh river. *Shibrtú,* the name of the pass commonly used by Baber, is a name also in Zungaria, and is said to mean "*muddy.*" *Sirgholan,* which is the name of at least two streams in Badakhshan and Wakhán, appears to be the same as *Dsirgalang,* the name of a river in the Ili country (said to mean "*prosperity*").— See "Journal Asiat.," ser. iv., tom. viii., 399, 401, 440.

[2] "Notices et Extraits," vol. xiv., pt. I., pp. 222, 224.

[3] "Notices et Extraits," vol. xiv., pt. I., p. 387, *seqq.*

daughters was married to Abusaid, and another to Yúnus, khan of the Mongols of the eastern branch of Chaghatai.[1] In the early part of Baber's history we find Badakhshan, with Kunduz, Balkh, and Hissár, in fact, the whole of ancient Tukhára, in the hands of Khosru Sháh, a worthless and unscrupulous Turk of Kipchak.

The first years of the sixteenth century were marked by the rise of that Uzbek rule in Turkestan, which has ever since retained its hold, though it is now rapidly dwindling before the growth of Russian power. The Uzbeks were no one race, but an aggregation of fragments from nearly all the great tribes, Turk, Mongol, and what not, that had figured among the hosts of Chinghiz and Batu; and the names of many of these tribes are still preserved in the list of the numerous clans into which the Uzbeks are divided. Shaibáni, their great chief, before he fell at Merv (1510) in a disastrous battle with Sháh Ismael of Persia, had conquered all the country, from the Saihún to the Jaihún, with Kunduz, Balkh, Khwarizm, and Khorasan. At one time, Badakhshan also was subject to him; but in 1505 a general rising of the people took place, which effected the expulsion of the Uzbeks. Nasir Mirza, a younger brother of Baber, was invited to come and reign over them, but after about two years, the chiefs becoming dissatisfied with him, defeated him at Khimchán in the Kokcha valley, and expelled him in his turn (1507). About a year later Baber's cousin Wais, commonly styled the Khan Mirza, whose grandmother, the widow of the Mongol Khan Yúnus, was a daughter of the last of the old kings, was instigated by her to try his fortunes in Badakhshan. At this time Mirza Abubakr, king of Kashgar, had seized the high valleys (Wakhan, &c.), then known as the *Upper Hazáras;*[2] the lowlands of Kunduz were held by the Uzbeks: and Raziuddin, a heretic leader, had got possession of a large tract on the side of Khotl. The Khan Mirza, however, succeeded in establishing a footing, making his residence at the Fort of Zafar on the Kokcha, a place famous in the history of Baber's successors, and maintained his position till his death in 1520. Baber then bestowed Badakhshan on his son Humayún, who ruled it for eight or nine years, and resided much in the province. When

---

[1] See "Baber," p. 13.   [2] *Hazáraját Bálidast.*

Humayún, in 1529, left the country to join his father in Hindustan, the chiefs invited Sultán Said Khan of Kashgar, another descendant of their old kings by the female line. The Sultan of Kashgar came, but soon abandoned the enterprise, and Baber then put the kingdom into the hands of Suliman, son of the deceased Khan Mirza. This prince eventually transmitted the kingdom to his descendants with almost independent authority. In 1555, we find Suliman ruling not only over Badakhshan, but also over Talikán and Kishm, Kunduz, Ishkimish, and Andaráb. He appears to have made Kishm his capital.[1] Akbar appears to have withdrawn early from interference with the country north of Hindu Kush; but in 1646, Shah Jahán revived his claim, and sent thither in succession his sons, Murád and Mahomed (Aurangzib), and the erection of a bridge, which still exists over the southern Surkháb, between Ghori and Baghlan, is ascribed to the latter. Balkh was captured, and Badakhshan overrun, but the emperor, seeing the difficulty of maintaining such a frontier, made over the country to Nazar Mahomed, the expelled prince of Balkh, apparently an Uzbek. The Mogul emperors never again interfered in those provinces. Materials for the latter history of Badakhshan are scanty in the extreme, and I have not been able to learn when or how the descendants of the Khan Mirza, who represented, through the female line, the ancient dynasty of Badakhshan, became extinct. It appears to have been about the middle of the seventeenth century that the present dynasty of Mírs, descended from a Syad of Samarkand, were called to power, and some time in the last century they fixed their seat at Faizábád, the present capital.

6. When the Chinese conquered Kashgar, in 1759, they pursued two of the Khojas, who had been the recent rulers of that country, to the heights of Pamir, where they attacked and routed them. The Khojas took refuge in Shighnán, and when the Mír, or king, of Badakhshan, declined to surrender them, the Chinese general advanced into Badakhshan, and, indeed, if one Chinese account can be trusted, to the capital itself.[2]

[1] See the narrative of Sidi 'Ali, who calls it *Kishmis*.—" Jour. Asiat.," ser. i., tom. ix., p. 204.

[2] See "Magasin Asiatique," i. 92. From the Chinese maps the place meant would appear to be the old

One of the Khojas had by this time died of his wounds, and the Badakhshan prince found a paltry pretext for the condemnation and execution of the other. The bodies were demanded by the Chinese, and eventually one head was given up and transmitted to Peking.

The Chinese profess to have obtained at this time the formal submission of the King of Badakhshan as a vassal of the empire, and during the succeeding year several missions of compliment from him reached Peking. Wilford[1] states (about 1790) that the Chinese were then in possession of Badakhshan as far as Baghlán. I do not think this can mean more than that Badakhshan owned itself tributary to China; but I have little doubt that this passage of Wilford's was the basis of an apocryphal statement noticed further on.

The Khoja, who was a Syad, and a spiritual personage, as well as a prince, is popularly reported in his dying moments to have invoked curses on Badakhshan, and to have prayed that it might be three times depopulated; a malediction which found ample accomplishment. A few years after the outrage (in 1765, according to Manphúl) Shah Wali Khán, the Wazir of Ahmed Shah Abdali of Kabul, invaded the country, and carried off from Faizábád a certain holy relic, the shirt of Mahomed, which had been the pretext of aggression. Early in the present century, Kokan Beg, a Kataghan Uzbek adventurer, again ravaged the country, and its misery came to a climax in 1829, when Murad Beg, the Kataghan chief of Kunduz, again overran Badakhshan, and swept away a large part of the inhabitants, whom he sold into slavery, or set down to perish of fever in the swampy plains of Kunduz. It was when still languishing under this tremendous infliction, that Badakhshan was visited by Captain Wood. The impression of silence and depopulation which his narrative leaves upon the mind is alleviated in the reports of later (native) travellers, which indicate some considerable revival of life, and even of something like prosperity.

capital, further east than Faizábád, which appears as a distinct place; but the account in the "Lettres Edifiantes" gives no reason to suppose that the Chinese advanced into Badakhshan, though they were on Pamir, and perhaps in Wakhán.

[1] 'Asiatic Researches,' vi. 457.

Murad Beg died some years after Wood's journey,[1] having made himself master of the whole country from Wakhán to Balkh inclusive, and from the Hindu Kush to the borders of Karátigín. On his death, and even before it, power fell into the hands of another Uzbek, Mahomed Amír Khán, the Wali of Khulm. In 1850 the Afghans recovered possession of Balkh, and in 1859 they conquered Kunduz from the Kataghans. The chiefs of Badakhshan had succeeded in reinstating themselves at Faizábád some years before, and they now acknowledged the Afghan supremacy to avoid invasion. Their prince, Mír Jahándár Sháh, was in 1867 expelled by the Afghans, but Mír Mahmúd Sháh, another of the family, took his place. A tribute of 50,000 rupees is paid by him to the Amír of Kabul, who receives also additional payment for the feudatory province of Rusták.[2]

7. Something of the history of geographical knowledge of the Upper Oxus regions has appeared incidentally in the foregoing sketch; but I will now notice a few points in that history that have been omitted.

Aristotle, even it is supposed before the expedition of his great pupil, had heard of "the Mountain Parnassus, the greatest of all that exist towards the winter sunrise," from which flowed down the Indus, the Bactrus, the Choaspes, the Araxes, and other rivers of the largest size; a description doubtless applying to the mountain mass formed by Pamir, and the ranges diverging immediately therefrom.[3]

I cannot find in Strabo any indication of a knowledge of this great feature, of which Ptolemy, though erring greatly in some

---

[1] Ferrier, p. 210, puts his death in 1836, which is of course a mistake, probably a misprint.

[2] Faiz Bakhsh.

[3] In the seventeenth century, Father Henry Roth, who had belonged to the Jesuit Missions in India, told Kircher, that among the snowy mountains of Tibet, there was a vast lake, from which the Ganges, Indus, Ravi, and Athek (*Attock*, *i.e.* the Indus in duplicate, or perhaps the Kabul river) derived their sources. This idea of great rivers radiating from a central lake constantly recurs. The Hindus had the story applied sometimes apparently to Manasarowar, sometimes vaguely to Pamir. The Arabs applied it to a great lake of Central Africa, perhaps Baker's lake, or Tanganyika, whence flowed the three Niles, viz., Nile of Egypt, Nile of Sudán (Niger), and Nile of Zanj (the Jabb).

details of this region (*e. g.* placing *Maracanda,* or Samarkand, in Bactriana south of the Oxus), has a very just conception under the name of Imaus. By far the most interesting notice to be derived from him regarding these regions, is his brief and incidental statement about the route of the Seric caravan, when discussing the extent of the known world in longitude. Having carried the merchants to Hyrcania (or Jorján), near the S.W. angle of the Caspian, he proceeds:—"Then the route runs on through Aria (the Herat territory), to Margiana Antiochia (Merv), first declining to the south, for Aria lies in the same latitude with the Caspian gates, and then to the north, Antiochia being somewhere near the parallel of the Hellespont. Thence the road proceeds eastward to Bactra (Balkh), and from that northward, up the ascent of the hill country of the Comedæ, and then inclining somewhat south through the hill country itself, as far as the gorge in which the plain terminates. For the western end of the hill country is more to the north also, being (as Marinus puts it) in the latitude of Byzantium, the eastern end more to the south, in the latitude of Hellespont. Hence [the hills running thus from south of east, to north of west] the road runs, as he describes, in the opposite direction, *i.e.* towards the east, with an inclination south, and then for a distance of 50 schœni [say 150 miles], extending to the Stone Tower, would seem to tend northwards. The Stone Tower stands in the way of those who ascend the gorge, and from it the mountains extend eastward to join the chain of Imaus, which runs north to this from (the territory of) Palimbothra."

It has long been considered almost a settled fact, that the Stone Tower, which is the key to this route, is the ruin or rock excavation near Úsh, in Ferghana, known by the often recurring names of the *Chihil-Sitún* (forty pillars), and *Takht-i-Suleimán* (Solomon's throne). This identification seems to have been first propounded by Wilford; it was adopted by Heeren and Ritter, only doubtfully by Humboldt. The location of the ancient route across the mountains so far north, may have been the more easily accepted, because the statement of Ptolemy does carry the Itinerary *north* from Bactra; whilst the route by Úsh and the Terek Pass, was the one best known in Europe, and the only one to which such a direction from Balkh, strictly interpreted, could point. The identification of the Stone Tower with *Tashkand*, by Al-Biruni, shows that a similar view had been entertained by him, and the position of the Comedæ being totally unknown, might be at any point of the broad sweep of Imaus. The amount of comparative light that has come to us since the days of Wilford and Heeren, first from Chinese sources, and secondly from actual exploration, enables us to discern that the route probably lay in another direction.[1]

General Alexander Cunningham, in his early studies on the geography of Hwen Thsang's Itinerary, first (I believe) pointed out the identity of the *Comedæ* of Ptolemy with the *Kumidha* which Hwen Thsang describes as one of the Hill-states to the east of Tokharistan.[2] The geographical definition which the Chinese memoirs give of this state leave no room for doubt as to its position. It lay to the east of Khotl; it was enveloped by the Tsungling or mountains of Pamir; it had the Oxus to the south-west, and Shighnán to the south. This is as perfect a definition of the state of Darwáz, or of the states of Darwáz and Roshan taken together, as our present knowledge would enable us to lay down. The direction from Balkh is not indeed *north*, though it has some *northing;* but this is just the direction intended by Ptolemy, as his tables show.[3]

From Darwáz the Seric route may have led either by one of those passes across Central Pamir, of which we know nothing, or up the valley of the Panj, and so by Wakhán and the sources of

---

[1] The great traveller Fedchenko has recently been at Úsh, so we ought at last to have a true account of the Takht-i-Suleimán. It is not mentioned in the extracts from his letters published by Petermann (June, 1872).

[2] See "Jour. Asiat. Soc. Bengal" (1848), vol. xvii., pt. 2, p. 15. Kiepert, in his Ptolemaic map to Lassen (vol. ii. 1852), adopted this position for the *Comedæ*, but in his "Asia," 1864, seems to indicate their locality north of Karátigín.

[3] The name of *Kumidha* has not been, I believe, traced in any Mahomedan geographer, but may have continued in local use till the erection of the barrier mentioned at p. xxxiii., after which the valley probably acquired the name of *Darah-i-Darwáz*, or Valley of the Gate. It is possible that we have a surviving trace of *Kumidha* in the name of Kila' *Kúm*, the chief place of Darwáz. (From Sir H. Rawlinson's annual address to the Roy. Geog. Soc. for 1872, it would seem that an Arab geographer, Ibn Dasta, *does* mention Kumidha.)

the Panj to Tásh Kurghán. This is the route which we find in use by Hwen Thsang, on his way home from Tokharistan, within five centuries of Ptolemy's time; and it would suit fairly with the latter's indication if we suppose the Stone Tower to have been somewhere about Panja, or Langar Wakhan. Sir H. Rawlinson seems inclined to accept Tash Kurghan itself as the Stone Tower,[1] and the antiquity popularly ascribed to that fortress favours such an identification. But the name of *Tásh Kurghán* ("Stone Fort") is too common in Turkestan to be of importance in itself, and Ptolemy's words, surely, lead us to look for the station at the western ascent to the great pass, rather than at the eastern descent from it. I doubt if a solid conclusion can be reached until we know more of Darwáz and the passes leading thence across Pamir.

8. We have just referred to Hwen Thsang's route on his return to China. This appears to have passed up the valley of Wakhan and across the little Pamir to Tash Kurghan, and thence to Kashgar, exactly by the route recently followed by the Mirza. And he gives on the way a striking account of the lofty and desolate steppe of Pamir. On his outward travels he arrived on the Oxus from the north, having on his journey crossed the Thian Shan, and passed by the margin of lake Issikul as far north as Taraz, and then travelled southward through the cities of the Jaxartes valley to Samarkand. His route, especially with the aid of M. Vivien de St. Martin's Commentary, is clear enough. We have, however, translations of two earlier travellers of the same class, whose indications are not so lucid. Fahian, the first of these, started on his travels in A.D. 400. From Khotan he seems to have advanced to the vicinity of Yarkand, and then to have gone south across the Karakorum mountains to *Kiecha* or Ladak, whence he goes down the Indus valley to Darail, Udyána (now Swát and the adjoining districts), and Pesháwar. He thus did not enter on the Oxus basin at all.[2]

---

[1] "Proc. Roy. Geog. Soc.," xv. 201.

[2] This is clearly shown by Cunningham at the beginning of his "Ladak." Mr. Beal has unfortunately overlooked the passage, and has thus missed the key to this part of Fahian's route (see his "Travels of Fah-hian and Sung-yun," p. 14, *seqq.*) The term *Tsung-ling* is by Fahian extended to the Karakorum and adjoining mountains.

The next pilgrim, Sungyun, also travels by Khotan and Yarkand, and thence, as well as can be understood, by Tash Kurghán across Pamir to Wakhán, and the territory of the Yetha or Tukhára. The name of Wakhá or Wakhán, which does not occur in Hwen Thsang, appears in this narrative under the Chinese form *Poh-ho*. "To the south of that country," he observes, "are the great snowy mountains, which in the morning and evening vapours rise up opposite one like gem-spires."[1] The Yetha were then (A.D. 518) still in unbroken power. Forty countries were tributary to them, including (the traveller says) *Tich-lo* in the south (in which we may probably recognise the famous port of Diul or Daibal, on the coast of the Indus Delta), and the whole country of *Laeleh* in the north, which extended from Khotan to the frontiers of Persia. The traveller gives a few curious particulars of the manners of the Yetha, but without specifying the custom of polyandry, which other Chinese writers ascribe to them. The ladies of the court wore long trains which required the attendance of train bearers, and, as a head-dress, horns of great length suspending veils.[2] The king, on state occasions, sat upon a gilt couch, supported by four golden phœnixes, a description which (reading peacocks for phœnixes) exactly agrees with that of the Turkish Khan Dizabulus when visited by a Byzantine envoy half a century later. And the peacocks, transferred to the canopy, survived to a very recent date in the celebrated throne of Delhi. At Pesháwar the Chinese pilgrims fell in with another king, of the Yetha race, a rough warrior who had small respect for the law or priests of

General Cunningham justifies the name, which in Chinese means (according to one interpretation) "Onion Mountains," by the fact that the Karakorum abounds in wild leeks. Izrat Ullah notices the wild onions on the mountains between Drás and Ladak. And according to Klaproth, the term *Túrtásh Dabán* having the same meaning (*Túrtásh* being the wild onion), is applied in Turkestan to the Tsungling or some part of it ("Ritter," vii. 411). But we do not find this name in any of the recent documents.

[1] "Beal," p. 184.
[2] Hwen Thsang also describes these horns, but as peculiar to one of the Tukhara states, Himotala (*Daraim*). The coincidence with the head-dress of the Druze women of Syria (a fashion which the Crusades seem to have sent home to England) is remarkable, especially when we take note of the Druze tradition that their ancestors came from China, and of the quasi-Buddhist elements ascribed to the Druze religion.—See C. Graham in "Jour. Roy. Geog. Soc.," xxviii., pp. 262, 263.

Buddha, and who kept seven hundred elephants of war. He was possibly the *Gollas*, with his thousand elephants of war, of whom Cosmas tells us.

Between the journey of Sungyun and that of Hwen Thsang occurred a remarkable mission to Transoxiana from the Imperial Court at Constantinople, to which we have just alluded. In the year 568 an embassy from Dizabulus, Khan of the Turks, arrived at Court. The Turks had by this time thoroughly beaten the Ephthalites and expelled them from Sogdiana. The troubles of the time had interrupted the trade in silk, which the people of Soghd carried on to their great profit, no doubt as intermediaries in the trade from China and Khotan. Naoshirwan, then king of Persia, alarmed at the rise of the new power in Transoxiana, and disinclined to make Turks free of his frontier, checked all attempts to open intimacy, and is even said to have poisoned a whole batch of the Turk's ambassadors. On this the Sogdians, through Maniakh their prince, prevailed on Dizabulus to open communication with Byzantium, in order that a direct trade might be initiated with the great Western consumers of silk.

These Sogdians, so readily transferring their allegiance from Hun to Turk, we may suppose to have been the forefathers of the present unwarlike and trafficking Tajiks of Bokhara. It must be said, indeed, that the name of their prince pertains rather to Turan than Iran. Yet he may easily have been of different race from his people.[1]

The embassy was well received by the Emperor Justin, and a return mission despatched under Zemarchus, "Prefect of the cities of the East." After many days they arrived in Sogdiana, where they and their baggage were subjected to a symbolical purification by fire, which it is singular to find preserved not only in the etiquettes of the Mongol camps of the thirteenth century, but even in the Bokhara superstitions of our own day.[2]

They were conducted to the Khan's camp, in a valley among

---

[1] *Maniak* is a Tartar name, and was that of a prince who invaded Poland in 1468.—See Hammer's "Gold Horde," p. 403.

[2] See "Cathay," p. clxiii. Khanikoff's "Bokhara," p. 271.

the mountains called *Ak-tagh* ("White Mountain"), a name too trivial to enable us to identify the position. But the mention of *Talas* as a position, afterwards passed by the party in company with the Khan, seems to indicate that his camp lay beyond the Jaxartes, perhaps in the rich and watered basin still known by the Turco-Mongol name of *Ming-bulák* or "Thousand Springs," where the successor of this same sovereign was accustomed to spend the summer heats. The Byzantine ambassadors on their return to Europe came, we are told, to the river *Oech*, in which we probably have the latest mention of the Oxus, by its name in the primeval form (*Veh* or *Wakh*),[1] and then to "the great and wide lagoon," no doubt the Aral. Their course then lay across the steppes to the Volga, and so by Caucasus and the Phasis to Trebizond. This circuitous route was compelled by the jealous hostility of the Persians, who tried to intercept them even north of Caucasus. The fragmentary narrative which alone survives does not describe the outward route, but, from the same motive, it must also have lain north of the Caspian.

We have already quoted scanty notices from the early Arabian geographers, and from the book of Marco Polo. The journey of the latter extended not only through Balkh, Tálikán, and Badakhshan, but by the borders of Shighnan and through Wakhan and Pamir, all of them names which occur in his story.

This old traveller has never met with elucidation of a more

---

[1] For this identification I am indebted to a learned article in the "Edinburgh Review," for January, 1872. I venture to differ from the distinguished reviewer in believing *Talas* to be the place still so called beyond the Jaxartes. The place of the great Khan's summer encampment is thus described in A.D. 630 by Hwon Thsang: "After having travelled four days' journey west of the river Chu, he arrived at the Thousand Springs. The district so called ... is bounded on the south by the Snowy Mountains (Aktagh?), and on three other sides by level plains. The soil is abundantly watered, and richly adorned with forest trees. In the latter months of spring the soil is richly carpeted with flowers of every hue.... The Khan of the Turks comes hither every year to escape the summer heats.... After proceeding (one day and a half) to the westward of the Thousand Springs, *the traveller arrived at the city of Talas*," &c. ("Pèlerins Boud.," ii. 14; and see iii. 268. Some notice of the Ming-bulák tract will be found in the journey of M. Severtzoff, who visited a part of it in 1864. The Kirghiz still regard it as the best place for summer encampment in all that region.—"Jour. Roy. Geog. Soc.," vol. xl., p. 367.

striking and interesting kind than in the narrative of Captain Wood, when following in his footsteps. Nor was there ever a better example of the manner in which a genuine but obscure narrative becomes more and more clear and intelligible under the tests of advancing knowledge, just as the veins of fine wood or marble come out under polish, than we find in this part of Marco's notices. Little more than a year ago I published an elaborate commentary on it, from all the sources then available; but even since then, the journey of Major Montgomerie's "Mirza" has thrown a new light on the subject, and we can see now, as it was not possible to see then, the *exact* route (in all probability) by which the Venetians travelled from Pamir to Kashgar. Perfectly true and accurate as Marco Polo's Oxus geography was, it was far beyond the digestion of his own or the following ages. Information so far in advance of an author's own time is like prophecy, which only becomes clear in the light of its fulfilment.

In 1405 Ruy Gonzales de Clavijo with his brother envoys from Castille, after passing through Balkh, crossed the Oxus by a bridge of boats, on his way to the court of Taimúr at Samarkand. He saw Transoxiana flourishing as no traveller has had a chance of seeing it since, and he was the first and last European traveller whom we know to have passed through the famous Iron Gate above Termedh. But he was not higher up the great river than that city; and of Badakhshan he saw nothing, though he found the prince of that country (*Balaxia*) at Taimúr's court, and paid him a visit, eager with questions as to the manner of finding the rubies which had carried the name of his country into regions so remote.

In 1558-59 our countryman Anthony Jenkinson succeeded in reaching Bokhara, travelling as an explorer on behalf of the Muscovy Company by Astrakan, the Caspian, and the Turkman desert. He found no commercial promise in Bokhara under the Uzbeks, but brought back among other observations one of the latitude of the capital, which was by no means accurate, though perhaps a better approximation than the map makers of his time were prepared to turn to account.[1]

---

[1] Jenkinson's observations make the atitude of Bokhara 39° 10′. Burnes made it 39° 43′, and Khanikoff 39° 46′. Ulugh Beg's table gives 39° 50′.

It was more than three hundred and thirty years from the time of Polo's journey, ere he had a European follower through Badakhshan, and across Pamir. This was the Lay-Jesuit Benedict Goës, a truly noble character, and a man whose name would have occupied one of the brightest places in the history of geography, had he survived to tell his story in a complete and intelligible shape. His object was the exploration of Cathay, the determination of its whereabouts, and the reconnoissance of its capabilities as a mission field. He started from Agra in the latter part of 1602, and travelled by Lahore, Attock, and Pesháwar to Kabul. After long detention here he proceeded by Parwán across the Hindu Kush, and so by Badakhshan and Pamir to Sarikol, and thence by the Chichiklik Pass and the Tangitár valley to Yarkand. This latter part of his route is perfectly clear in the light of recent exploration, but in Badakhshan the obscurities of the narrative, as we have it, are great.[1]

9. The material available is too defective, nor would it be of interest to trace the growth of juster conceptions of the geography of *Bucharia* (as it was termed) during the seventeenth and eighteenth centuries. The translation of Edrisi and the Arabian tables, utilized especially by the great French cartographers, assisted this, as did the information that gradually began to come from the Russian side, and that which was gathered by Rennell in India. The amount of material collected by Elphinstone and Macartney during the Pesháwar mission of 1809 was very large, but greatly needed to be bound together by actual travel and survey. Still it added much new detail to the maps; and that of Macartney is still, *on certain points*, truer than later ones.[2] The publication of Sultán Baber's autobiography followed (1826), with an admirable introduction by the principal translator, Mr. W. Erskine, who

---

[1] One of his stages is recorded as Serpanil, probably *Sir-Pamir* "top of Pamir." *Pamil* is the Alai Kirghiz pronunciation, as we learn from Fedchenko. It comes close to Hwen Thsang's *Pomilo*.

[2] It is to be regretted that Mr. Elphinstone did not print the Itineraries used by Macartney in preparing his map. He appears to have possessed some of which I can find no details now, and which now could be better utilized than was the case sixty years ago.

possessed a remarkable knowledge of the geography of those countries.

The memorable journey of Alexander Burnes (published by Mr. Murray in 1834) formed an era in Central Asian geography. Apart from the singular charm of his narrative, he for the first time afforded a chain of observations tying together the Indus, the Oxus, Bokhara, and the frontier of Persia, which formed the chief basis of Mr. John Arrowsmith's long unrivalled map of Central Asia, originally published as an accompaniment to Burnes's work.[1]

Burnes deserved well, not only for what he did himself, but for what he stimulated others to do. His assistants during his second journey to Kabul, Leech, Lord, and Wood,[2] all contributed valuable matter to the stock of knowledge.

Of these, Wood's services were by far the most memorable. And we cannot doubt that his name will live in the select list of eminent explorers. He was the first, as this book relates, to trace the Oxus to one of its chief sources; the first European in modern times—first and last as yet, five-and-thirty years after his journey—to stand on the table-land of Pamir; and it is still on his book and survey that we have to rely for the backbone of our Oxus geography. The book, in its clear manly and cheerful narrative is, in many respects, a pattern book of travels. Its almost only fault, it seems to me, is that the author seems scarcely aware of the importance of his own

---

[1] M. Khanikoff has criticised Burnes severely, as well as the body of Anglo-Indian travellers. I have made some remarks on the subject elsewhere, not inconsistent, I trust, with the sincere respect which I feel for M. Khanikoff (see "Ocean Highways," edited by Mr. C. R. Markham, C.B., for July, 1872). M. Khanikoff does not notice the labours of Elphinstone and Macartney. But I may point out that they corrected two of the most serious errors to which he alludes, viz., as to the true direction of the flow of the Herat river, and as to the position of *Khabis* (see "Caubul," 3rd ed., i. 155 and ii. 396). Macartney assigns to the latter lat. 30° 40′ and long. 58° 18′, a surprising approximation to the truth, all things considered. It is true, and not creditable, that our maps continued for many years afterwards, some of them even after the publication of Mr. Abbott's excellent diary, and till that of M. Khanikoff's own survey, to misrepresent the position of Khabis.

[2] Major Leech, of the Bombay Engineers, died in 1845. Dr. Percival Lord was killed at the fight of Parwándarah, at the base of Hindu Kush, in 1840.

researches and of their full record, and thus it does not contain so much detail as a geographical student desires. Indeed, his original preface alludes to the omissions which had been forced on him by the fear of passing into a second volume; no doubt an essential consideration when a traveller has to find a publisher to take the risk of putting forth his narrative. Among the details omitted on that ground he specifies: " Vocabularies of the dialects spoken among the mountain tribes to the north of Hindu Kush." The loss of these is deeply to be regretted, for, so far as I know, we are still without any vocabularies of the districts of the Upper Oxus, such as Wakhan, Shighnan, Zebák, Roshan, &c., full of interest as such a series would be. It is strange to find, years after Wood's explicit statements as to the elevated plain of Pamir, doubts expressed as to its existence, just as if (to say nothing of Marco Polo) Wood's journey never had been made, or his narrative, from every line of which truth shines, had never been published.[1] Even in M. Fedchenko's recent letters describing his successful visit to the Alai steppe, he speaks of his own firm belief in the real existence of the high plain of Pamir as if it were quite exceptional.

10. In the year or two immediately following Captain Wood's journey there seemed reason to look for the erection of a large superstructure on the foundation he had laid. British outposts reached as far as Saighán and Haibak (or Samangán, the birthplace of Rustum,) in the valley of Khulm; and British shrapnel rattled about the ears of the gigantic Buddhas in the gorge of old Bamian. But the dark days came speedily, and our knowledge of the Oxus region stood still. Khanikoff's able work on Bokhara (1843) dealt with the valley of the Soghd, and scarcely touched on that of the Oxus. A wall of iron seemed to separate us from that region, and it was with surprise that we received General Ferrier's narrative (1856), embracing among his extensive travels a rapid journey from Herat to Balkh and Khulm, and back to Herat by untrodden routes through the country of the Eimáks and western Hazáras,

[1] See note in vol. xxi. of the "Journal of the Roy. Geog. Soc.," p. 65.

and the valley of Ghúr, the cradle of the Ghurid dynasty. But no substantial addition to our knowledge of the Oxus countries was made for twenty years after Wood's publication. Abdul Mejíd's mission to Kokan then gave us the first modern account of a journey across the latitude of the Pamir plateau. The Punjab trade Report (1862), compiled by Mr. Davies, now Lieutenant-Governor of that province, was accompanied by numerous appendices containing a mass of new and valuable information, chiefly supplied by Mahomed Amín, formerly the guide of Adolphus Schlagintweit, and by Pandit Manphúl, a well-educated Hindu gentleman in the service of the Punjab Government.[1] In 1868 we began to reap the fruits of systematic exploration by trained Asiatics beyond our frontier, a system originated by Col. J. T. Walker, R.E., and matured and carried out with singular perseverance, tact, and success by Major T. G. Montgomerie. The first of these journeys was that of Munshi Mahomed Hamíd, who in 1865 succeeded in bringing back a highly satisfactory survey of the route from Ladak to Yarkand, and many observations for the latitude of the latter city. This meritorious man died on the journey just after recrossing the Karakorum Range. His achievement was followed by that which is the most memorable and successful of these explorations, that of "the Pandit," who, in 1866, reached Lhassa, and determined the position of that famous and inaccessible city, connecting it by a route survey up the whole length of the Sanpu valley, with the holy lakes of Kailás and the valley of the Upper Indus, a chain of entirely new work stretching through 11° of longitude. In the meantime (1866) Mr. Johnson of the Indian Survey had succeeded in reaching Khotan, and making observations there, bringing back not only his own head upon his shoulders, but the first notices of that region that we possess by a visitor since the days of Benedict Goës.

The spirited journeys of Mr. R. Shaw and Lieut. Hayward to Yarkand and Kashgar followed (1868-9), and then the mission of Mr. Douglas Forsyth, C.B., accompanied by Mr. Shaw,

---

[1] The geographical information was extracted with admirable skill and patience from Mahomed Amín, chiefly, I believe, by Col. P. Lumsden, the present Quartermaster-General of the Army in India.

to the former city (1870). We have already had much valuable geographical information from Mr. Shaw, and a great deal more may be looked for, in the position which he now holds at Ladak.

11 Another emissary of Major Montgomerie's, the Mirza,[1] reached Kashgar from Kabul by way of Badakhshan and Pamir during the detention of Messrs. Shaw and Hayward at that city (winter of 1868-69). This worthy has been the first to tie together the basins of the Oxus and the Tarim by a chain of route measurements and compass bearings, with several determinations of latitude. Had we not been prepared for his results by the labours of Mahomed Hamíd, corroborated by Messrs. Shaw and Hayward, which showed how erroneous were the longitudes heretofore assigned to the great cities of Eastern Turkestan, there can be little doubt that the accuracy of the Mirza's work would have been subject to general misgiving. But a main result of the longitudes deduced from the former explorations had been the great enlargement of the width of the unknown mountain-country between the Upper Oxus valley and the basin of Eastern Turkestan. The amount of this reform may be best appreciated from the fact, that the distance from Faizábád of Badakhshan to Kashgar, as the crow flies, which in Kiepert's "Asia" (of 1864) amounts to two hundred English miles, extends by Colonel Walker's Map of 1867 to three hundred and twelve miles, and by a more recent compilation since the Mirza's journey to three hundred and sixty-four. This at once threw light on a matter which had always caused perplexity, viz., the great number of days assigned by Marco Polo, Goës, and all the Oriental Itineraries, to the passage between Eastern and Western Turkestan. Between Yarkand and Pamir, again, our maps had nothing to show that implied human occupancy beyond one or two names resting on questionable authority, and representing one knew not what, of which *Karchu* was the most prominent.[2] Nor had we any

---

[1] Major Montgomerie's emissaries are like the emperors of China, whose true names, according to M. Pauthier, are not known till they are dead.

[2] This will-o'-the-wisp, which has bogged so many commentators, has been identified by the venerable Ritter with the *Chárchunár* of Goës, and by Mr. Beal with the *Kiesha* of Fahian, whilst in fact it never had any exist-

knowledge of settled towns and villages in those mountain recesses. Yet the old Chinese pilgrims to India, whose route lay this way, speak of principalities that must have lain in this region. Such was the state of *Uchcha* (of which a trace seems to survive in the name of the Uch or *Vachcha* valley), and especially that of Kabandha, visited by Hwen Thsang in descending from Pamir in A.D. 645. The population of this state was indeed small, and the people rude; but they had attained some degree of civilization, for they had a considerable cultivation of wheat and pulse; they possessed a written character, and they had some half-score of Buddhist convents. We now know this state, which was reckoned an ancient kingdom in the seventh century, to be identical with the modern territory of Sarikol, otherwise called Tash Kurghan from its chief town. The foundation of this place is ascribed to the ancient Turanian king Afrasiáb, *i.e.*, it is of legendary antiquity. It is of oblong or oval form, is stated to be more than a mile and a half in circumference, with walls built of great blocks of stone now in dilapidation,[1] and stands in the middle of an extensive plain between two rivers. The people are generally alleged to be (or rather, as we must now say, to have been) of Tájik race; whether from the first a solitary outlying *enclave* of that race which had settled beyond Imaus, or, as Mr. Shaw has recently maintained, a last surviving relic of a Tajik population which anciently occupied the whole Kashgar basin.[2] Though the population had been much reduced by the kidnapping forays of their neighbours, and the emigrations which these pro-

ence. From what concourse of atoms it grew will be indicated hereafter.

[1] Manphúl says of *hewn* stone, the Mirza of *rough* stone. It should be noticed that Faiz Bakhsh does not think the fortress of great antiquity.

[2] Manphúl gives a small list of sixty-four Sarikoli words ("Punjáb Report," App., p. cccliii. a). Of this number, some ten are plainly Turki, about twelve are Persian, seven or eight Sanskrit or Hindu; of the rest I cannot trace connection. Faiz Bakhsh calls the people of Sarikol *Hazdras*, a term which he extends to those of Wakhan and Kanjúd also, identifying them with the tribes so called to the westward. I suppose this to be a mistake. Those Hill-states were called, as we have seen, in the sixteenth century, the *Hazdrajút Báládast*, or Upper Hazáras, but it is not likely that this had any ethnological bearing. In fact, the Hazáras of the Perso-Afghan frontier seem to be themselves of very various race.

voked, they did survive here down to 1869, when the valley was harried by the Atalik Gházi, the new sovereign of Kashgar, and the whole of the inhabitants swept away, to be replaced by Kirghiz.

The "Mirza's" work, as a line binding the two sides of Imaus, is invaluable, but it conveys no such mass of information as did the work of the original immortal "Pandit." It is a mere skeleton. But recollecting the extraordinary treatment that Captain Wood's data have met with in recent years from various Continental geographers, perverted *ad libitum*, or shoved aside altogether to make room for the Gulliverian geography of the Freiherr Georg Ludwig von (Weissnichtwo), it is highly satisfactory to find the entire general and often closely detailed agreement of the Mirza's work with Wood's.[1] We must not lay any stress on the Mirza's thermometrical observations for height. Faizábád is set down by Wood (p. 164) at 3,500 feet above the sea, whilst the Mirza makes it 5,100. Ish Kashm is reckoned by Wood 8,700, whilst the Mirza makes it 10,800. At the head of the Wakhan valley they come back to a better agreement. But these wide discrepancies shake our faith in the deduction which has been made by Major Montgomerie, from the comparison of their observations of altitude, as to the relative height of the two Oxus sources in the lakes of Great and Little Pamir; and the fact must still rest rather on the general considerations urged by Wood himself (p. 217).

The absence of collateral detail in the Mirza's survey leaves us on various points in darkness, which a word or two recorded on the spot would have dispelled. But justice cannot be done to his work without attention to the hardships and difficulties under which his observations were made on those high lands

---

[1] It is right, however, to observe that this agreement is not so close as one might gather from the instance of *Panja*, quoted by Major Montgomerie, in which the differences are in latitude 3', in longitude only 2'. Though the same longitude is assumed for Kabul, the common starting-point, and the same longitude within two miles is obtained for Panja, the last common point of their surveys,—there is along the whole interval between Kunduz and Faizábád (inclusive) a difference of 10' in their longitudes. I have no doubt that the preference is to be given to Wood.

in the depth of winter, superadded to the absolute necessity of secrecy in accomplishing them.[1]

Faiz Bakhsh was employed by Mr. Douglas Forsyth, in 1870, to travel viâ Badakhshan and Pamir to meet him at Yarkand, when on his recent mission to the Atalik Ghází. He mentions having previously travelled twice to Samarkand and Bokhara. He is not a surveyor, but is evidently a clever, intelligent, active person, and his journal seems to have been kept with exemplary diligence, recording at frequent intervals the direction of march and time occupied, besides a number of facts in the collateral geography of his route. I have found it a very useful aid in forming some approach to a connected idea of the Pamir topography, and generally in supplying new names to the blank spaces on our maps of Badakhshan. Faiz Bakhsh's journey coincides with Captain Wood's somewhat further than the Mirza's. He leaves Wood's route to Lake Victoria at the Zerzamín stream (see Wood, p. 217), striking off to the left there, and following for some distance the track of Abdul Mejíd on his way to Kokan. He seems to quit this on the plain of Khargoshi, and strikes the *eastern* end of Lake Victoria, to which he gives the new name of Lake *Sikandari*, a title which he applies also to the river which issues from it, Wood's Oxus. From this point he goes eastward by the Aktash and Shindi Passes to Tash Kurghan, joining (I apprehend) the Mirza's route to that place in its latter part. He then crosses the Chichiklik spur of Pamir by the high Pass of Yámbulák, and for the rest of his journey to Yanghisár his route is that of the Mirza. Faiz Bakhsh evidently took great pains with the task assigned him, and deserves high commendation.

The last explorer to whom I can refer is a havildar or native

---

[1] In the map accompanying this essay I have ventured in two or three points to deviate from the data afforded by the Mirza. The chief of these is, that I have placed the fort of Panja on the south instead of the north side of the river. It seems to me to be represented implicitly, if not explicitly, by both Wood and Faiz Bakhsh as on the south bank; and Major Montgomerie, in his Report on the Mirza's work (Indian ed., p. lxix.), says that it is on the *left* bank, *i.e.*, the south. Wood's map omits it, strange to say. Major Montgomerie himself is not disposed summarily to reject this correction.

sergeant of Sappers, who, under Major Montgomerie's instructions, accomplished in 1870 a route survey, from Pesháwar to Faizábád, by way of Dhír, Chitral, and the Doráh Pass over the Hindu Kush range, coming down upon Captain Wood's route at Zebák (see Wood, p. 202). The map supplies a valuable and interesting additional link; but the report is very brief.

It is only recently that the Russian explorers have begun to trench on the geographical field of this review. M. Severtzoff's actual journey in the Thian Shan does not come within it, though his excellent remarks on the relation of the Tsungling or Pamir mass to the Thian Shan and Himalya, are suggested by that journey. But M. Fedchenko's recent journey (1871) to the Dasht-i-Alai (as well as to the upper waters of the Jaxartes) is an era not only in Central Asian geography, but in that specially of Pamir and the Upper Oxus.[1] Now that the Russian travellers have found admission to Kokan, we may look to a rapid advance in the exploration of Pamir, &c., from the north. And we shall hear no more of the Klaprothian geography, of which a few words must be said.

12. Geography, like Divinity, has its Apocrypha, and no sketch like this would be complete without some notice of that curious branch of the subject. We have both apocryphal narratives and apocryphal localities.

I am sorry to be obliged to include under this head those extracts from the diary of Colonel Gardiner, which appeared in the twenty-second volume of the Journal of the Asiatic Society of Bengal; for Colonel Gardiner is not only a real person, and one who has had real personal acquaintance with the regions of which we are treating, to a degree, it is believed, far surpassing that of any European or native traveller whose narrative has been published, but he appears to have acquired the esteem of men like the late Sir Henry Durand, whose good opinion was of unusual worth. But I know not how else to classify the paper. I have read it some half-dozen times at considerable intervals, on each occasion hoping that increased acquaintance with the

[1] And I regret that this essay must be printed before I can see any map of his, or any further detail than is contained in "Petermann," for June, 1872.

topography would at last enable me to trace some fraction of the writer's journeys, and to draw out some new facts on which one could rely. But every trial has ended in disappointment and mystification. When we read the narratives or incidental notices of other travellers, however far removed from us in date, and however fragmentary, we can generally trace their direction by known landmarks, and connect their new localities with old names. Marco Polo and John Wood, Hwen Thsang and the Mirza, throw a flood of light upon each other, though separated by intervals of 600 and 1200 years. But in trying to follow Colonel Gardiner, it is very different: well-known names now and then occur in the diary, such as Kunduz, Badakhshan, Darah Darwáz, Yarkand, Gilghit. But amid the phantasmagoria of antres vast and deserts idle, of weird scenery and uncouth nomenclature, which flashes past us in the diary till our heads go round, we alight upon those familiar names as if from the clouds; they link to nothing before or behind; and the traveller's tracks remind us of that *uncanny* creature which is said to haunt the eternal snows of the Sikkim Himalya, and whose footsteps are found only at intervals of forty or fifty yards!

With surprise and delighted curiosity like my own, many must have read in the valuable collection of translations by the Messrs. Michell, called "The Russians in Central Asia," an extract from M. Veniukhoff's account of the existence in the military archives of St. Petersburg, of two unpublished records of exploration, one German and the other Chinese, among the obscurest and most interesting portions of Central Asia. Kashgar, Tashbalik, Bolor, Badakhshan, Wakhan, Kokan, and other names were there, the mere enumeration of which was enough as M. Veniukhoff observed, to excite the irresistible curiosity of all who had made a study of the geography of that region. The particulars which afterwards became accessible to English readers, through papers by MM. Veniukhoff and Khanikoff, showed that one of these documents consisted of the journals of a German traveller, Georg Ludwig von —— (the name carefully erased in the original), who had been employed by the Anglo-Indian Government at some date (not stated), in the latter part of last century, to purchase horses in Turkestan. The journal was accompanied by elaborate maps, and by a series of thirty astronomical determinations of position. The papers were asserted to have been deposited in the archives of the Russian War Office on the 14th August, 1806.

This traveller's journey extends from Kashmir across the Indus, and northwards to Kashgar, then up the Yapnyar or Yamanyar river to Lake Karákúl, and southward by the river and town of *Bolor,* and across a river *Duvan* to the "town of Badakhshan." Both Bolor and Badakhshan were found in the occupation of Chinese garrisons. From Badakhshan the traveller proceeds *due north,* and arrives, strange to say, at *Vochan* (Wakhan), and after that travels by Lake Riang Kúl and over a mountain range to Kokan. Thence he is stated to have returned through Samarkand and Yarkand to Kashmir, but I have seen no extracts from this part of his journey.

The other document is the Itinerary of a Chinese traveller, translated by Klaproth in 1821. It leads from Kashgar to Yarkand and the valley of the Indus, and thence in a northwesterly direction into Badakhshan, Bolor, Wakhan, and Kokan.

There is no need to dwell on the controversy which arose upon these documents. Their fictitious character had been essentially established by Sir Henry Rawlinson, even before the lamented Lord Strangford's discovery that a parallel mass of papers, embodying much of the same peculiar geography and nomenclature, existed in the London Foreign Office, purporting to be the Report of a Russian expedition sent through Central Asia to the frontiers of India, in the beginning of this century. The papers having been purchased from the celebrated Julius Henry von Klaproth in 1824, there can be little doubt, it is to be feared, that the acute and brilliant linguist and geographer was himself the author of all three sets of papers; nor perhaps was there any contemporary capable of accomplishing a fraud of the kind so successfully.[1]

[1] I am not aware if the officials of the Russian War Department have ever explained on what grounds M. Khanikoff was led to suppose that the date of the entry of these documents into their office was 14th August, 1806. That date is really the date of the letter of the pretended traveller, which is attached to the series; *i.e.,* it is an organic part of the fiction (see "Proc. Roy. Geog. Soc.," vol. x., pp. 304 and 310). We know that the real date of

Not on this occasion only has Klaproth, living or dead, been a leader of gross geographical heresy. He too it was, who, by dint of Chinese learning and considerable distortion of ascertained geography, argued the waters of the great Tibetan Sanpu into the Irawadi, and in that matter corrupted the geographical sense, not only of his own countrymen, but of some eminent French cartographers, so that the false doctrine is scarcely dead and buried to this day.

Apart from detailed analysis and Lord Strangford's discovery, one fact is notable and fatal. If, leaving out these three documents, we take the whole series of Itineraries from Hwen Thsang (I might say from Ptolemy's Seric traders) to the Mirza, we shall find a common core in all, enabling us easily to recognise the same geographical facts, and in great measure the same names. But when we take up the extracts or abstracts of this German or this Chinese traveller, we find nothing that fits in with this consistent and gradual growth of knowledge. Take, for example, the localities Badakhshan, Shighnan, Wakhan, and Pamir. We find these with the same order of place, first in Hwen Thsang, again in Marco Polo, again in Elphinstone's work, and in Burnes's, till Wood, in his ascent of the Oxus, defined their position by actual observations, with which all the later reports are in entire accordance. But in the Russian documents the relative position is entirely misrepresented.[1] Or take an Oriental history, such as the Autobiography of Baber, or the History of Mír Haidar, so often quoted by Quatremère and by Sir Henry Rawlinson. Here we find a variety of names and incidental notices of places in these regions, an ever increasing number of which we are enabled to assign to their proper positions with more or less of certainty. Thus, take names (I give them without election) like Yamgán, Khwája Changal, Kalaogán,

composition, and of course of entry into the office, must have been *subsequent* to the publication of Elphinstone's "Caubul" (1815). And we may be certain also that it was previous to the knowledge of Izzet Ullah's Itinerary, first published, I believe, in the Calcutta "Oriental Quarterly Magazine," about 1824.

[1] To be exact, I note that Shighnan does not occur in the Russian documents; Wakhan does not occur *by name* in Hwen Thsang, though accurately described; and Pamir is omitted from Elphinstone's *map*, though frequently mentioned in the text of Macartney's Geographical Paper.

Kila' Zafar, Kilkai, Amber Koh, Rágh, Yaftal, Kishm, Rusták, Khimchán, Nárín, Siráb, Tághdumbásh, Raskam, Sárigh Chaupán. All these are mentioned by one or other of the writers just named;[1] but no one of them, I believe, except Kishm, appeared in any of the maps that preceded Elphinstone's, though now we can locate them all with tolerable accuracy, as the names reappear in the gradual accumulation of detail by modern travellers. But in turning to the Russian documents we find no such coincidences. The only coincidences in these are with the representations of a Chinese Missionary map, *which we can prove to have been accidentally inverted!*[2] On the other hand, they present a variety of names unknown to historians or to other travellers, such as river Duvan and Sharud, Namzir and Birlagul, mountains of Nola, Vadig, and Sozna, with dense forests, stone bridges, cherry brandy, and horses for sale by the thousand, in the heart of Pamir.

It is lamentable to think that so estimable and zealous a geographer as M. Veniukhoff's papers indicate him to be, should have been led to waste so much labour and ingenuity as have been expended by him on utter fictions like these. In consequence, his papers *On the Pamir and Sources of the Amu-Darya, On the Belors and their Country,* and *Additional Remarks on the Boolor Highlands,* as they appear translated in the Journal of the Royal Geographical Society, are with scanty deduction utterly baseless and futile; shadows of smoke. M. Veniukhoff was biassed by the natural partiality of a discoverer

---

[1] With the exception of *Yamgán*, which Quatremère cites (without knowing its position) from another Persian authority.

[2] This matter involves detail too long for insertion here, but which has been made the subject of a paper for the Royal Geographical Society's Proceedings. The series of Chinese maps in question were in Klaproth's possession, and used by him in the construction of his published map of Central Asia. But, strange to say, he omitted to use that part which embraces Pamir and Badakhshan, leaving it blank upon his map. I have shown, in the paper alluded to, that the part of the Chinese map embracing the perverted geography of Bolor, Wakhan, Badakhshan, the Pamir lakes, Shighnan, and Roshan, has really by some accident been turned through an angle of 90°, and it is the map thus deranged with which the Russian documents agree. When the proper adjustment is made, the Chinese map represents Wakhan, Shighnan, and the course of the Panja, etc., in remarkable agreement with our more recent knowledge.

of new documents, but it is more surprising that Dr. Kiepert should go so far astray. He had before him, on the one hand, the sober and unquestionable narrative and map of Captain Wood, a genuine living English naval officer, whose work unmistakably expresses the author's truth, candour, and good sense, consistent as steps in the growth of knowledge, with all that had preceded in that growth; on the other hand he had these maps and journals ascribed to the German traveller, without name, without date, directly contradictory to Wood and to all that preceding gradual growth of knowledge. He preferred his imaginary countryman, and thus did his best to throw back the geography of the Upper Oxus to a worse position than it was in when Mr. Elphinstone's work had first been published.[1]

As regards apocryphal topography, we can only briefly notice *Bolor* and *Karchu*, which have haunted the map of Central Asia for the greater part of this century, but neither of which, *as applied therein*, have any corresponding localities *in rerum naturâ*. The details of this subject are set forth in the paper alluded to in a recent note: and with regard to Bolor, I will only state here the conclusion that there is no real evidence for the existence of a state, town, or river called *Bolor* on the western side of Pamir; and my opinion, that the name has now become so tainted, first by mistake and next by fiction, that it would be well rigidly to exclude it from geography for the future.[2] As for *Karchu*, which in so many maps occupies a position on the upper waters of the Yarkand river, it was an erroneous transliteration of the name *Hatchút* or *Ketchút*, which appeared in the (Chinese) tables of the later Jesuit surveyors to the south of Sarikol, and was by them apparently intended as a loose approximation to the position of the frontier of the

[1] Arrowsmith's Map of Central Asia (1834) contains some portion of the imaginary geography. This was derived from the Klaproth documents in the Foreign Office, to which no suspicion then attached, *and which Wood's work did not exist to contradict.* The present writer was led by well-founded confidence in Mr. Arrowsmith to use some of these fictitious data with an expression of doubt (?), *where not in contradiction to Wood*, in a map published in "Cathay" (1866).

[2] M. Severtzoff's suggestion that the Chinese name of Tsungling should be adopted by geographers for the mountain mass in question, is well worthy of attention.—See "Jour. Roy. Asiat. Soc.," vol. xl., pp. 345, 398.

Dard state of *Kanjút* or Hunza. But *Karchu*, I fear, will appear in many a map yet!

13. We limit our geographical sketch to the regions of the Upper Oxus, and we have no intention of entering on the highly interesting but difficult questions touching the physical history of the Lower Oxus, and the changes, or even alternations, in its discharge between the Caspian Sea and the Aral.

The chief and governing geographical feature in this field is the great mountain mass, so often already spoken of, which divides the basin of the Oxus from that of the Yarkand river and its confluents—the northern Imaus of Ptolemy, the Tsungling of the Chinese.

Several recent travellers and geographers, of deserved reputation, insist much that this mountain mass should be regarded merely as a prolongation of the Himalya; and this will probably prove to be a just view as regards physical character, though I am unable to see either that its direction is so truly, as has been urged, that of the Himalya, or, that any one can yet possess absolute knowledge sufficient to pronounce finally on identity of physical character. The fact adduced by Mr. Shaw that certain of the most prominent chains of eminences on this mass appear to run from east to west, which seems to apply specially to the Kizil Yart, or Trans-Alai mountains of Fedchenko, might be taken as an argument for a closer relation to the Thian Shan than to the Himalya. Indeed, M. Severtzoff, whose remarks on the subject appear to be the weightiest, desires, as we have just mentioned, to restore to the mass the distinctive name of Tsungling, claiming for it a special character as the convergence of the two systems of Himalya and Thian Shan. The divergence of the Hindu Kush, I may also remark, which coincides with some change of direction, be that greater or less, would in itself be a physical feature of importance, marking a boundary between the Himalya and this Tsungling. But independent of geognostic structure, and whatever be the precise direction of the watershed and the culminating ridges of Tsungling, as regards mankind and their history, the Himalya is, and has ever been, a barrier between south and north, the Tsungling a barrier between east and west. The one has been the great division between Tartary and India, with its influences, chiefly religious; the other, the great division between Western Asia and China, with its influences, chiefly political.[1]

Fragmentary as our knowledge still is, we know, with something like certainty now, that the core of this mountain mass forms a great elevated plateau, extending at least one hundred and eighty miles from north to south, and something like one hundred miles from east to west. The greater part of this plateau of Pamir appears to consist of stretches of tolerably level steppe, broken and divided by low rounded hills, much of it covered with saline exudations, but interspersed with patches of willow and thorny shrubs, and in summer with extensive tracts of grass, two or three feet in height, the fattening properties of which have been extolled by travellers, from Marco Polo to Faiz Bakhsh. Many lakes are scattered over the surface of the plateau from which streams flow. Wild-fowl abound upon these lakes in summer to an extraordinary degree; and in the vicinity of water deer of some kind are very numerous, and the great sheep *(ovis Poli)* apparently all over the plateau. In 1869 a murrain among these latter is said to have killed them off in multitudes. A goat called *Rang*, affording a fine shawl wool, is found on the steppe; also a kind of lynx, whose fur is valued. Foxes and wolves frequent Pamir; bears and tigers are occasional visitors. The wild yak, according to Faiz Bakhsh, is also found there; if this be true, Pamir is its western and northern limit.[2] Pamir was at one time the summer haunt of a large nomad population of Kirghiz with their

---

[1] Exceptions may be cited, but not sufficient to upset the general truth of this view. We have noticed the brief existence of the political influence of China west of the Tsungling. The prevalence of Indian religion at one time in Khotan and the adjoining states *may* have crossed the Himalya by Tibet, but it is more probable that it travelled, as the Chinese pilgrims did, by way of Kabul and Turkestan.

[2] The Yak is not mentioned by Manphúl in his list of Pamir quadrupeds. But in Quatremère's extracts will be found a notice of a huge yak, which was killed apparently on Pamir in the sixteenth century ("Notices et Extraits," xiv., pt. I., p. 478). Tame yaks were kept by the pastoral tribes of the Upper Jaxartes in Baber's time (p. 352). I know not if the Kokan Kirghiz still keep them.

numerous flocks; but the depredations of the Shighnis (regarded also with horror by the Kirghiz as Shíah heretics) and other kidnapping neighbours, are said to have driven them to the eastern valleys, or to the Kokan territory, and the only summer visitors now are about one thousand families, who frequent the shores of Rang-Kúl on Little Pamir.

Mountains in some places lift themselves out of the steppe; one group between the two southern Oxus sources being estimated by Wood to rise three thousand four hundred feet above Lake Victoria, or nineteen thousand feet above the sea-level; and either a branch of this group, or another of not much inferior height, would appear to be crossed on the direct route between that lake and the valley of Tash Kurghan over a pass called Shindi Kotal. The difficulty of respiration is experienced all across Pamir, though more severely on these higher passes; and the Kirghiz of the less elevated Alai steppe gave this as a reason to Fedchenko for their being unable to live on Pamir.[1]

A belt of lofty mountains, of considerable but uncertain breadth, forms the eastern border of the plateau, rising occasionally into peaks, which Hayward sets down approximately at 20,000 and 21,000 feet. The steep and rugged eastern spurs of this mountain belt form the buttresses of Pamir towards Eastern Turkestan. The same belt, or an offshoot, called from one of its passes Kizil Yart, traverses the plateau to the north of Lake Karakúl, separating Pamir from another and a narrower plain called the *Dasht*, or steppe, of Alai. As it goes west it seems to rise higher and higher; for Fedchenko, who

---

[1] The suffering from attenuated atmosphere is called by the Badakhshis and Wakhis *Tunk*, by the Turkis *Esh*, signifying an odour or miasm, by the Indian population of the Himalya *Bish-ká-hawa*, or "poison-air." In fact, Asiatics generally refer the uneasiness produced by this cause to local miasm. Huc and Gabet suffered greatly from it in crossing the Burkhan Bota mountain to the south-west of Koko-núr; but the true nature of the mischief did not occur to them. They talk learnedly of carbonic acid gas, and tell how, this being heavier than atmospheric air, when they got on horseback they suffered less than on foot. No doubt; but the horse, I apprehend, suffered more. They were taught to use garlic as an antidote. Benedict Goës mentions the custom of using garlic, leeks, and dried fruits in this way. The Mirza and Faiz Bakhsh speak of dried fruits. The custom is alluded to by Mr. Matthew Arnold in one of his poems.

recently saw it from the western part of the Alai steppe, and gave it the name of *Trans-Alai*, states that the medium height of the ridge could not be less than 18,000 or 19,000 feet, whilst the summits of the highest peaks even reached to at least 25,000. For grandeur of aspect, he says, nothing in the scenery of Turkestan can rival this view of these mountains. The Alai steppe runs in length from west to east, with a decided tendency north, and is drained, as M. Fedchenko has discovered, by the upper course of the Surkh-áb of Káratigín. It is, by native report, about forty miles in length, and from seven to fourteen miles in width. In the west, where Fedchenko was, its height above the sea is 8,000 feet; but it is believed to rise to about 12,000 at the eastern end, and this is probably about the height of the adjoining part of Pamir; for the second slope of this appears to be, as Wood was aware,[1] from south to north. Fedchenko was told that the few passes across the intervening range were exceedingly difficult. But Mahomed Amín represents the Kizil Yart Pass, leading from near Karakúl into the Alai, as "not very difficult."[2] From the head of the Alai passes lead northward to Ush and Kokan over the watershed between the basins of the Oxus and Jaxartes, and are used by a detour in summer, when the *Terek*, the principal pass between Kashgar and Ush, is impracticable. A pass, called *Taimurum*, leads from the Alai north-eastward into the Terek road and the Kashgar river valley. This is perhaps the *Dina Davàn Etizek*, or "Twin Mountain Pass" of 'Izzat Ullah.

Among the hills immediately south of the Terek Pass are, it would seem, the sources of the river of Kashgar. Others of the rivers that flow down into Eastern Turkestan, and eventually join the Kashgar river to form the *Tarim-gol* of our maps, appear to have their sources far back in the Pamir steppe, such as the river which our maps of the last age have taught us to call Yamanyar, and the Karású, which is one of the chief contributors to the river of Sarikol.[3] We do not know whether

---

[1] See p. 224. The vicinity of Wood's Lake (15,600 feet) is probably the culmination of the steppe land. Hence perhaps the title of *Great* Pamir.

[2] "Punjab Report," App., p. xxii. o.

[3] The hydrography of the Kashgar plain is exceedingly perplexed, by the manner in which the rivers are broken

any of these streams, in their course through the high plain, exhibit anything approaching to the stupendous ravines which characterise the high plain of Tibet, on which lie the holy lakes of Kailás.

To the drainage and obscure topography of Pamir I shall recur in the conclusion of this essay; but I will now say something of the frontier of our geographical field on the north and south.

14. On the north our boundary begins with that rugged country which intervenes between Karátigín and Kokan, in which are said to lie the Tajik states of Mácha and Ignao, counting among the most unknown regions of Asia, and in which the Zarafshán or Polytimetus has its remotest sources. An offshoot from this highland, which was known to the old Arabian geographers as *al-Botm*, runs westward, forming the separation between the basins of Sogdiana and Bactria. To this great offshoot we find various names applied, such as *Fántágh* and *Karátagh*.[1] It is said to reach far into the region of perpetual snow. The wild mountains to the eastward of Sarvadi are said to contain rich copper and coal mines. A "burning mountain" in this vicinity is mentioned by Lehmann, but explained by him as a coal-bed on fire.[2] From about longitude 68° to 69°, the Fántágh seems to be singularly impenetrable. One pass leads southward into the province of Hissar by the lake

up artificially into parallel streams for irrigation; and there are considerable discrepancies among our recent travellers as to their names and exact positions, which it seems impossible yet to determine. The ancient city of Kashgar stood to the north of the present (old) city, and the river Taman flowed through the middle of it. The present city (not the Yanghi-hisar) was built by Sultan Abubakr in the beginning of the sixteenth century.—"Notices et Extraits," xiv. pt. 1., p. 474.

[1] The name *Karátagh* is applied to this range both by Macartney and by Khanikoff. Burnes says no one knew it; and I do not find it in Fedchenko's sketch of the topography of the Zaraf- shán valley, translated in the "Jour. Roy. Geog. Soc.," vol. xl., p. 448. The fact is, that names applied to extensive mountain ranges are, in a great proportion of cases, the creation of geographers.

[2] Fedchenko however mentions sal-ammoniac as a product of this region; and this the old Arab geographers describe as collected from *fumaroles* in the mountain of Botm (see "Notices et Extraits," xiii., 256; "Edrisi," i., 486). Mas'udi relates how he had seen from a distance of 100 parasangs the fires burning in the mountains of Soghd, from which sal-ammoniac was extracted (i. 347).

called *Iskander Kúl* (lake of Alexander), and the crest of this can be crossed only by pedestrians, so that travellers have to dispose of their horses before crossing, and to procure fresh animals on the other side. This is probably the pass called by Baber *Sir-i-Túk*, which was traversed by him in 1500, just before his daring and brief recovery of Samarkand from the Uzbeks. From Hissar, he ascended a branch of the Hissar river called the *Kám Rúd*, descending by the lake through the *Fán* and *Khshtút* territories into Sogdiana; and he gives a most formidable description of the road, which must have been indeed a bad one to make such an impression on Baber with all his experience.[1] The lake of Iskander was visited by General Abramoff in 1870, but I have yet seen no account of the expedition.

The branches which this range throws off towards the Zarafshán are still of great height. One called *Mázár Tágh*, to the west of Khshtút, is reckoned approximately at 12,000 feet, whilst that to the eastward of the same place seems to be still higher. The main range divides near Maghián, one branch passing north and west round the head of the Shahr Sabz territory, forms the southern wall of the valley of Samarkand, under the name of *Ak-sai*. This rises to a height of about 7,000 feet, and has but one pass, that of *Kará-Tappah*. The mountains however, can be turned by the defile of *Jám*, some twenty-five miles further west, which is passable by wheel carriages.[2]

The valley principality of Shahr Sabz, the old Kesh, the country of Taimúr, is well watered and fertilized by the snow-fed streams which descend from the mountains south of Maghián, the confluence of which forms the river of Shahr Sabz. It flows on to Karshi, the old Nakhshab, and is generally exhausted in irrigating an oasis round that city, a mass of fruitful verdure; but its bed can be traced turning thence to the northward, and terminating in a lake bed called *Kúl-Máhi*, usually dry, but which in the spring is said to fill with water, and abound with

---

[1] See "Baber," p. 85. *Fán* is read *Kán* by Erskine; but there can be no doubt of the true reading—a question of a dot.

[2] Fedchenko, in "Petermann" for June, 1872, p. 460.

fish, whence its name ("the Fish Lake"). Here, as elsewhere in the Oxus basin, vegetation is confined to the irrigated tract; all outside that is sandy and utterly sterile.

From the range south of Maghián another ramification of the highlands extends south and south-west. One branch of this reaches a much greater height than the Aksai, and is covered with perpetual snow.[1] In the heart of it is the once famous pass of *Kohluga*, or the Iron Gate. The usual modern route from Bokhara, and even I believe from Samarkand to Balkh, goes by Karshi, turning the mountain; and of this celebrated pass we have, so far as I know, no recent account. It is thus described by Hwen Thsang, in A.D. 630. On leaving Kesh, this traveller after two days' journey to the south-west entered the mountains. "The journey was rugged and stony; the paths up the gorges ran along the verge of precipices; no village was met with, nor was there water or any green thing. After three days' journey among these mountains in a south-west direction, the traveller entered the pass called the *Iron Gate*. This is a gorge between two mountains, which rise parallel to each other, right and left, to a prodigious height. Nothing divides them but the path, which is extremely narrow and precipitous. The two mountains form on either hand mighty walls of stone, of an iron hue. The pass is closed by folding gates clamped with iron, and to the gates are attached a number of iron bells. From these circumstances, and from the difficulty and strength of the pass, it has got the name it bears."[2]

I know no notice of any pass from Sogdiana into the Oxus basin between this and Iskander-kúl, a distance of about eighty miles. Other branches of the Karátágh (or Fán Tágh) are sent

---

[1] Burnes saw these mountains from Karshi, and was told they were six marches distant. In June they were "entirely enveloped in snow." Fedchenko apparently saw them from the top of the Aksai.—"Jour. Roy. Geog. Soc.," vol. xl., p. 460.

[2] II. 23. The gates themselves had ceased to exist eight centuries later, when Clavijo passed this way: "This hill is very high, and there is a pass leading up by a ravine, which looks as if it had been artificially cut; the hills rise to a great height on either side, and the pass is smooth and very deep. . . . This pass is called the *Gate of Iron*, and in all the mountain range there is no other pass, so that it guards the land of Samarkand towards India. . . . In former times they say that there were great gates covered with iron placed across the pass."—Markham's "Clavijo," p. 122.

off southwards, which, in the longitude of Termedh, do not altogether die away till within half a day's march of the Oxus.[1] But we know nothing of them in detail. One branch, which runs down through Hissár, is called by Burnes *Koh-i-tan*, and appears to subside into the plain about half a degree north of Hazrat Imán. Burnes says it is about 4,000 feet high, which is, I presume, but an estimate from a distant view. The name which he gives it appears to be the same with the *Kotin* of Baber (p. 29), though the king's use of the name rather applies generally to the mass of mountains closing in Hissar on the north.[2] *Termedh* was a very ancient and once famous city which stood upon the verge of the Oxus, and disappeared for some time from existence after its destruction by Chinghiz. The city was rebuilt in the following century about two miles from the river, and had already greatly recovered its prosperity when visited by Ibn Batuta, about 1334. It still exists, but we hear nothing of it now, and still less of *Kobádián*, which barely retains a doubtful place in modern geography. Of Hissar itself we know more than the late General Waddington could learn fifty-six years ago, when compiling the map for Erskine's Baber.[3] Of the *Tupalak* or *Tuflang* river, which enters the Oxus near Termedh, and of the *Káfir-nihán*, which comes down from the vicinity of the Fán district, we know little more than the names and general direction. This province, in old times, bore the name of *Chaghadián*—perhaps from some tribe of Mongol affinity which found its way hither in the movements that led to the fall of the Bactrian monarchy;[4] and under the Arabic form of *Saghánián*, it is famous in early Mussulman history and geography. From the *Hissár* or fortress called *Hissár Shadmán*, said to lie a few miles to the east of the Káfir-nihán, and which was, in the later middle ages, the chief place of the kingdom, the latter derives the name which still adheres

---

[1] Dr. Gerard, writing from Khulm, speaks of seeing mountains, "at the base of which rolled the Oxus;" but perhaps this is not to be taken quite literally.—"Journal Asiat. Soc. Bengal," ii., p. 11.

[2] The maps of Waddington (in Baber) and of Khanikoff, on the other hand, show Koh-i-tan as the name of a station on the road between Kesh and the Iron Gate.

[3] See Introd., p. lxviii.

[4] Referring to the Mongol *chaghán*, "white."

to it, though *Deh-i-nao* ("New Town"), some fifty miles farther west, has been for many years the capital. Hissar, a country in the main hilly, but not rugged, except in its northern portion, well watered, and producing rice, extends eastward to the valley of the Surkháb or river of Karátigín.

15. We pass now to the southern limit of our field, which is the Hindu Kush.

The name properly applies to the lofty mountain tract immediately north of the Kabul valley, and perhaps especially to one particular pass over that tract. But it has been fairly and conveniently extended to the whole line of mountain watershed stretching eastward to the southern end of Pamir, and represents the Caucasus of Alexander's historians. At that eastern extremity perhaps the watershed ceases to have prominence, and, like the Karakorum range of the Himalya farther eastward, almost merges in the elevated plateau, for the most easterly pass which crosses it, leading out of the Mastoj or Upper Chitral valley to the Sarhad Wakhán and Pamir, is described as of singularly easy and gentle slope on both sides, and practicable even for laden carts. But for all the remainder of its length westward to Bamian this mountain tract, to which we give the name of Hindu Kush, appears to me to correspond to the popular conception of a mountain chain much better than some high authorities are disposed to admit.

Colonel Walker has more than once expressed his opinion that there is no well-defined range where the Hindu Kush is represented on our maps. This of course applies only to the eastern half of what we style by that name; for, as regards the western portion—from the Bamian Passes to that of Khawák, at the head of the Panjshír valley—nothing can more perfectly typify a mountain range or chain, for we have there an unpierced watershed with *cols* never sinking below twelve thousand or thirteen thousand feet, and with no room for any great dislocation between the true watershed and the line of highest peaks. But even in regard to the more easterly half of the tract, my impression is that Colonel Walker's words are far too strong. I ground this impression, first, on Wood's incidental

f 2

notices. From Ishkashm he says, "Behind it rise, though not abruptly, the towering mountains of Chitral" (p. 204); on his first march from the same station, again, "The mountains . . . . of Chitral on our right . . . . rising to a vast height, and bearing far below their summits the snow of ages" (p. 208); and once more at Issar, "The mountains forming the valley had decreased in height . . . . those on the Chitral side were, however, still lofty" (p. 216). Mahomed Amín ("Punjab Trade Report," App., p. ccclxii) says that the Kharteza, Nuksán, and Agram Passes are covered with perpetual snow; and so is the Sad-Ishtrákh Pass to the eastward. This carries the lofty watershed within fifty or sixty miles of the Ab-i-garm Pass, at the head of Mastoj. And since the preceding sentences were written we have the Havildar's narrative of his journey across the Nuksán and Doráh Passes, which seem entirely corroborative of the view I have expressed; the former crossing a great glacier as well as large beds of snow, whilst on the latter a snowstorm and intense cold were experienced on the 6th November.

The Panja branch of the Oxus runs parallel to the watershed for sixty or seventy miles (between Kila' Panj and Ishkashm) at so short an interval as to preclude any considerable spurs. The first great one is that which strikes northwestward to the west of Ishkashm, separating the Panja valley from the upper waters of the Kokcha. The valleys themselves are lofty; Ishkashm, on the Panji or Wakhán side, being reckoned by Wood 8,700 feet above the sea, whilst Zebák, in the Vardoj valley, is probably not less, so that the relative height of the *kotal* or *col* is not more than some 2,000 feet, though its absolute height is 10,900 feet. This spur runs far to the north, expanding into the mountain tract north of Faizábád, to which Wood's map gives the name of the Khoja Mahomed range.

Of the offshoots of Hindu Kush west of this we know almost nothing. One of the most prominent peaks on these of which we hear is the mountain of Khastak, between the Vardoj and Kurán branches of the Kokcha, rising into the region of perpetual snow. This is perhaps the *Astánah* mountain mentioned by Wood (p. 161), without indication of its position, as it rises not far from the mazár or shrine (*Astánah*) of Shah Nasr Khusro. And, in the country south-west of Faizábád, Wood names as eminent the peaks of Argu, Takht-i-Suleiman, and Kishm, but without any estimate of altitude. Of the mountains of Eshk Mushk also, to the north of Andaráb,[1] he speaks in terms implying very considerable height (pp. 136, 270).

Of the main chain itself, or what we suppose to be such, between the longitude of Ishkashm and the Pass of Khawák, at the head of Panjshir, we know absolutely nothing. Here it is the frontier between Badakhshan and the Kafir country, a frontier constantly violated by fierce inroads for slaughter and man-stealing from one side and the other.

At Khawák the range becomes within more definite knowledge, thanks mainly to Captain Wood, the only modern traveller who has crossed this pass.[2] If there be any virtue in the current identification of *Adrapsa* with Andaráb, which, however, seems to me very uncertain, this should be the pass by which Alexander returned to the south after his campaign in Bactria, and his march to the Jaxartes. It is more surely that traversed by Hwen Thsang on his return from India; and by one branch of it (the Túl) Taimur passed to the conquest of Hindustan.

Between the head of the Panjshir and the passes of Hajjiyak, leading to Bamian, we have notices of some nineteen passes, which may be thus grouped:—

UPPER PANJSHIR PASSES—

1. *Anjumán*.—This leads from Paryán at the head of the Panjshir valley, by the border of the Kafir country, into the high district of Anjumán pertaining to the Jerm province of Badakhshan.
2. *Khawák*.[3]—This is also near the head of the Panjshir, and on the northern side descends by the head waters of the Andaráb river to the town of that name.
3. *Túl*.—A loop line to the last, which it rejoins at Siráb in the descent to Andaráb.

---

[1] Though the name *Eshkmushk* appears in the same form in the memoirs of Humáyún (p. 92), I imagine that it is the same name that we have otherwise in the shape of *Ishkimish*.

[2] With his companion Dr. Lord.

[3] I see that Fedchenko mentions a Pass of Khawák also in the Kokan mountains; but I do not know the meaning of the name.

4. *Zarya.*—This ascends from Safed Chír on the Panjshir, some miles below Túl, and joins the last pass before reaching Siráb.

LOWER PANJSHIR PASSES—

5, 6, 7. From Umraz (or Murz of Wood's survey), three bad passes called Shwá, Urza, and Uratimak lead over the mountains, joining No. 8 on the other side of the *cols.* The two last of the three are seldom free from snow.

8. *Bazárak.*—This quits the Panjshir river at the village of Bazárak (probably the *Barzaura* of Ptolemy's Tables), and descends upon Khinján in the Andaráb valley.

9. *Shatpál.*—This starts from Gulbchár at the entrance of the valley, and joins No. 8 on the other side at Kishnábád or Kistábád, twenty-one miles from Khinján.

PARWÁN PASSES—

10. Pass of *Parwán*, from the town of that name, descends upon Bájgáh in the Andaráb valley. Baber describes this as a very difficult pass, and says that between Parwán and the great *col* there are seven minor passes, called the *Haft-bachah* (seven young ones).

11. Pass of *Sal-aulang*, or *Sirilung*, of Wood. This starts from Tutan-darah, six miles north-west of Chárekár, and descends, like the last, not far from Khinján. This was attempted, unsuccessfully, by Wood and Lord (see p. 121 *seqq.*).

GHORBAND PASSES—

12. *Kúshán.*—This is the pass which leads under the great peak specially known as that of Hindu Kush. It starts from a point in the valley about ten miles above Tutan-darah, and descends upon Khinján. It seems to be the Yangi-Yuli, or "New Road," of Sultán Baber.

13. The *Gwálián* Pass leaves the valley some twenty miles from Tutan-darah, and descends upon Gozan on the Andaráb river.

14. *Gwázyár.*—This pass leaves the valley near the ruins of the old town of Ghorband, about twenty-four miles

from Tutan-darah, and leads to Kilagai, a small town on the way from Khinján to Ghori.

15. *Char-darya.*—Leaves the Ghorband valley about twenty-nine miles from Tutan-darah, and apparently descends into the upper valley of the Surkháb, from which it reaches Ghori. It is the *Kipchák* Pass of Baber, and the historians of his successors.

16. *Pass of Shibr.*—This is at the extremity of the axis of the Ghorband valley, at the head of the territory of the Sheikh'ali Hazáras. It descends upon the Bamian branch of the Surkháb at the ruins of Zohák. This seems to be the pass that was traversed by Hwen Thsang on his way to India, and it was crossed by Taimúr on his return from Delhi. It was the pass most commonly used by Baber, who calls it *Shibrtu.* According to him it was the only pass never closed in winter; and in that season, when the waters were low, it was possible to go from it direct to Madr on the Khulm road by the *Abdarah*, which I take to be the upper valley of the Surkháb, below Zohák.

HAJJIYAK PASSES—
17. Pass of Irák.
18. Hajjiyak.
19. Pusht-i-Hajjiyak.

Though these are the passes into Bactriana with which we are most familiar, it is curious that there is no allusion to them, as far as I can find, in Baber's memoirs. They are approached from Kabul, not by the Ghorband valley, but by the upper vale of the Kabul river, and the Unai Pass, to the south of the Paghman hill country. The Hajjiyak was crossed by Burnes on his journey, and by Wood and Lord on theirs, as well as by a variety of other officers, during the British occupation of Kabul. The Irak Pass was that by which Brigadier Dennie crossed to Bamian in 1840, before fighting his action with Dost Mahomed on that famous site.

16. These three latter passes are popularly considered to cross, not the Hindu Kush, but the *Koh-i-bábá*. This distinction,

which seems to be founded on a somewhat sudden change of direction (from S.S.W. to W., and that to the westward of the Hajjiyak Passes), but with no breach of continuity, from the shape it took in native reports, led Elphinstone and Macartney to regard the Koh-i-baba as a separate parallel ridge, and to represent Bamian erroneously as lying to the *south* of the watershed. Burnes, indeed, says that beyond the lofty peak of Hindu Kush, of the absolute height of which I find no estimate, the range dwindles into comparative insignificance. Yet he estimates the peaks of Koh-i-baba to reach a height of 18,000 feet, and the route over Hajjiyak and Kalu to Bamian, by which he travelled, mounts to 13,000, or nearly the height of the Pass of Khawák at the head of the Panjshir.

The Koh-i-baba, with its ramifications about the sources of the rivers of Balkh, Merv, and Herat (otherwise Dehás, Murgháb, and Heri-rúd), forms the head-quarters of the nomadic or semi-nomadic Hazara and Eimák tribes, the nucleus of a considerable part of which appears to be a standing relic of the Mongol invasions of the thirteenth century. The mountains near the head of the Balkh river are described as lofty and woodless, but to some extent clothed with grass and with various shrubs and herbs, affording pasture and fodder. The valleys are inhabited up to a height of ten thousand feet, the highest of them producing late in the year crops of the naked Tibetan barley.

The road by Bamian to Khulm in the Oxus valley crosses three great ridges beyond the former place, called, respectively, *Akrobát* ("White-station"), *Dandán Shikan* ("Toothbreaker"), and *Kará-Kotal* ("Col-Noir"). Beyond these ridges the traveller plunges into a chain of narrow defiles, walled in by stupendous cliffs, which he follows for some six days' march. At Khulm he issues from a narrow gorge upon the plain of the Oxus, some twenty miles from the river itself, leaving the mountains suddenly, as one leaves the gates of a fortress, rising behind him in a bold and precipitous rampart, bare, black, and polished, and still reaching to a height of two thousand five hundred feet.

The mass of mountains extending from the Koh-i-baba to

Khulm and Balkh, presents as a general characteristic an utter rocky aridity, broken in those sudden trench-like valleys to the north of Kará-Kotal by an exuberant vigour of vegetation.[1] As far north as the latitude of Khurm the mountains to the west of the Khulm defile must reach a height of 11,000 or 12,000 feet; for here General Ferrier, the only traveller who has crossed the mountains between the rivers of Khulm and of Balkh, found bitter cold, and the summit of the pass covered with snow on the 7th of July.[2] Beyond these loftier mountains some of the hills towards the Balkh river have a thin clothing of wood, and the *darahs* or valleys opening on that river are wide and not unfertile. The valley of the Dehás itself expands into level tracts of pasture, covered with long grass and intersected by artificial watercourses, but the gorge by which the river issues on the plains of the Oxus is narrow and walled in by very high hills on either side.[3] Immediately below the gorge the river begins to be drawn off for irrigation, and its waters are in this process exhausted in fertilizing, by numerous canals, the plain in which still stand, some six miles from the hills, the ruins and gardens of ancient Balkh, and no part of its waters appears to reach the Oxus in a running stream; nor, indeed, does any part of the river itself reach the site of the city in its natural bed. Balkh, though it would seem never to have absolutely ceased to be inhabited, has never recovered from the heel of Chinghiz, which was set so heavily upon it; it has never since been a city of importance. The chief collection of population now appears to be at a place called Takht-i-pul, to the eastward of the old site.

Old Khulm occupies a position similar to that of Balkh, but the modern seat of population is Tash Kurghan, at the very mouth of the gorge. The river of Khulm is also consumed in irrigation before reaching the Oxus.

[1] Of the Bamian valley itself, we read (in May):—" Desolation is not the word for this place ; the surface of the hills is actually dead ; no vegetable trace is to be seen ; all is parched up, and, as it were, baked white and scoriated by the sun's rays. Such is the horrid aspect."—Dr. Gerard in " Jour. Asiat. Soc. Beng.," ii., p. 8.

[2] On the 24th May, Burnes apparently found no snow on the Akrobát ridge, which Wood calculates to be 10,200 feet above the sea.

[3] Ferrier, 223, 224; "Notes (by Conolly?) on the Calcutta Staff Map."

The plains that slope gently from the gardens of Balkh and Khulm to the Oxus, are naturally white hard steppes, destitute of all spontaneous verdure, save sparse and meagre bushes of tamarisk and the like, but responding richly to irrigation wherever it is bestowed. This continues eastward to the bed of the Kunduz or Aksarai river, beyond which the plains stretching (not unbroken) towards Hazrat Imám are covered in part with rich cultivation, thick with groves and hamlets, and in part with a splendid pasturage; the latter extending up the Oxus as far as Wood, still our only traveller in this direction, attained. Immediately round Kunduz itself, and as far up the valley of the Aksarai or Surkháb as Baghlan, the country is positively swampy, with tracts of tall and dense jungle grass. It recalled to Wood the Delta of the Indus; and near the town of Kunduz the roads have to pass over piles amid the rank vegetation. The Palm is mentioned by Baber incidentally within the Oxus basin;[1] but I do not find it noticed in our modern narratives. To the Kunduz river we shall return, but it is time now to take up the great contributaries to the Oxus in succession.

17. The old Arab geographers reckon these as *Five*, and hence according to some the name of Panj or Panja (*Five* in Persian) given to the Oxus in its upper course.[2] These five are thus detailed by Istakhri:—

"The Jaihún rises under the name of Jari-áb (or Khari-áb) in the land of Wakhan which belongs to Badakhshan. In Khotl and Wakhsh it receives several tributaries, which swell it to a great river. The first tributary of the Khariáb is called Akhás or Halbak; the next is the river Bartán; the third is the river Faraghi; the fourth is the river Andijárá; the fifth is the Wakhsháb, which is the greatest of all these rivers. These all unite with the Jaihún."[3]

The readings are very uncertain, and we have so little trace of most of the names occurring here that we cannot be certain as to the geographer's view. But there seems no room for

---

[1] See p. 131.
[2] Wood gives a different origin for the name of the fort of Panja in Wakhan, which it is difficult to disconnect from that of the river.—See p. 215.
[3] "Mordtmann's Transl.," p. 125.

question as to the identity of the Kbariáb[1] itself with the Panja of Wakhan, and of the Wakhsháb with the northern Surkháb coming from Karátigín. We are thus led to seek the intermediate tributaries also on the right or northern bank, a scheme suggested also by the rude maps inserted in the books of Istakhri and Ibn Haukal.[2] We shall then be induced to identify the Akhás with the river of Shakh or Shaghnán, and the Bartan with that large branch from Pamir which the information of Wood (see Walker's map) and of Manphúl concurs in exhibiting as entering the Panja at Bartang on the borders of Darwáz. For the rivers of Faraghi and Andijárá we must be content to wait till we are better acquainted with the territories of Kuláb and Darwáz.

The fictitious geography which has so much perplexed our maps of the Oxus regions has thrown needless difficulties in the way of a just conception of the main contributaries. The "Bolor branch" has been very persistent, but may now be finally discarded.

Whatever may be the true view as to the five traditional confluents, if we consider the Oxus or Amu to have attained maturity at Kobadián, we may regard the main contributaries as four, viz. the northern Surkháb, the Panja (embracing the rivers of Shaghnán and Bartán as too obscure to be separately dealt with, however important they may eventually prove), the Kokcha, and the Aksarai or Kunduz river.

18. The most northerly branch, and in the bulk of its contribution probably second only to the Panja, is the SURKHÁB,

---

[1] Or Jari-áb. If *Khari-áb* be the correct reading, we have in it perhaps the *Icarus* of Pliny, a confluent of the Oxus, which was only seven days' journey from India.—vi. 17.

[2] Moreover, the Itineraries in Khotl given by the old geographers, dark as they are, seem to me to show clearly that the rivers of Andijára, Faraghi, and Bartán (all with very various readings, but recognizable identity) were regarded as lying on the Khotl side of the Khari-áb.—See "Mordtmann," p. 135; Sprenger's "Post und Reise-Routen," p. 45; "Edrisi," i., p. 472. The text was written long before the issue of Sir Henry Rawlinson's notice of the Oxus hydrography of Ibn Dastah, in his address to the Geographical Society for this year. The details as they appear there are to me very perplexing; but they are as yet given too briefly for discussion.

Wakhsháb, or river of Karátigín. No European is known ever to have seen this river, and doubt has lain not only on its true source (only recently dispelled), but on the exact position of its junction with the Panja.

In General Abramoff's recent notes on Karátigín, this river is stated, on native report, to rise among the western buttresses of Pamir, not far from the sources of the Panja. Some rumours collected by recent travellers seemed to bring it from the Karákúl itself, as we shall see hereafter. But M. Fedchenko has taken us by surprise, one of the results of his journey to the Alai steppe being the discovery that the Surkháb, under the synonymous Turki name of Kizil-sú, has its rise in that steppe, of the western portion of which it is the main if not sole drain.

In the upper portion of Karátigín, as we learn from the same authority, the Surkháb receives a tributary from the left called the *Múk*. Here again is the genuine traveller throwing light on the obscurities of past history. For in the history of Humáyún, under the year 1548, we find that emperor assigning to his brother Kamran the province of Khotlán or Kuláb, "as far as the frontier of *Múk* and Karátigín."[1]

The river Surkháb is stated to be in Karátigín very copious and rapid, running between precipitous banks, and owing to its depth and strength of current unfordable. At *Sar-i-pul*, nearly opposite *Garma*, the chief place of the principality, the depth is more than seven feet, and the bridge which gives its name to the place is fifty feet long. Numerous subsidiary streams enter the main valley, and along their deep glens are scattered many of the Karátigín villages. Even in the main valley, nearly throughout its course westward, the gorges are wild and narrow, sometimes admitting of only a dangerous passage along the river's bank for pedestrians in single file. Some distance west of Garma apparently the valley widens; as it turns south the mountains diverge, and eventually die into the plains of Kuláb.

The state of Karátigín is one of the least known regions of

---

[1] Erskine's "Baber and Humáyún," li. 360. It is not so easy to reconcile this Múk with the data given as to the *Munk* of Edrisi, a district of importance in Khotlán.

Asia; the darkness in which it lies to us is only surpassed by that of some portions of Tibet, and by the little state of Macha to the north of it on the head waters of the Zarafshán. I have, in a paper on Hwen Thsang's Oxus topography, conjecturally identified Karátigín with the *Holumo* (Garma ?) of that traveller,[1] and if the conjecture be well founded the name would be an early testimony to the Iranian speech of the population. The existing inhabitants are of the Persian-speaking race, called *Galchas*, of whom we know so little. They live secluded, without foreign trade or traffic through their territory, under a king or khan (who like so many of his neighbours claims descent from Alexander), and carry on agriculture to such extent as their rugged country and limited wants admit and require, with the breeding of cattle and horses, gold washing, salt mining, and a manufacture of excellent iron. Such rough estimate of the population as General Abramoff's information allowed him to make, amounts to one hundred thousand souls.

Kiepert's "Asia" identifies Karátigín with the country of the Parætacæ or Parætaceni of Alexander's historians (a suggestion which appears to be Burnes's), but the name in its present form is Turki; and unless it be a corruption of an ancient name, is probably a personal name transferred to a nationality, as in the case of *Chaghatai, Uzbek, Nogai,* and must have been that of some old Turk warrior, like the Alptegíns, Togrategíns, Sabaktegíns. Karátigín does not appear in the old Arabian geographies, and is I believe rarely mentioned in history. The name, however, does occur in the history of Taimúr, and several times in the memoirs of Baber.[2] From the latter we learn incidentally that a route between Hissar and Ferghana lay through it, probably the same that was travelled by Abdul Mejíd on his return from Kokan in 1861.[3] The government of Karátigín was bestowed by the emperor Humáyún on Mirza Askari, one of his rebellious brothers;[4] but this must have been a bitter joke, or at best a kind of promotion *in partibus infidelium*. The country is alleged to have been conquered in the early

---

[1] See "Jour. Roy. Asiat. Soc." for this year (1872).
[2] See pp. 36, 68, 73, 85.
[3] "Proc. R. G. Soc.," x. 148, *seqq*.
[4] Erskine's "Baber and Humáyún," ii. 360.

part of the present century by the king of Darwaz, who expelled the family of the old princes, and still held the country about 1834.[1] But it would seem from the recent Russian notice that the old dynasty recovered its possession. Another writer states that both Darwaz and Karátigín were subdued by Mahomed Ali Khán of Kokan (who died in 1841);[2] but probably this subjugation was only an incursion of the Alai Kirghiz from the Kokan territory, which Abramoff alludes to.

On issuing from Karátigín the river flows through *Kuláb*, a territory more or less coincident with the old provinces of Khotl and Wakhsh. Of those regions, which seem to have been so well-known to the Arab geographers of the ninth and tenth centuries, and then rife with trade and flourishing towns, our knowledge is now dim indeed. We look hopefully to the peaceful rivalry of General Abramoff and Major Montgomerie for early light. A good deal of the country would seem to be plain, and may still be populous far beyond our conceptions. The river is, or used to be, bridged somewhere below the Karátigín frontier; and mention of this bridge, known as the *Pul-i-sangín*, or "Stone Bridge," is already found in the tenth century,[3] and occurs often in the medieval wars of those regions, as in the history of Taimúr.

It has been the fashion in modern maps to represent the junction of the Surkháb with the Panja as occurring a few miles north of the confluence of the Kokcha, or river of Badakhshan, with the latter: a hypothesis founded on Wood's indication of an anonymous tributary in that position, apparently insignificant,

---

[1] "Jour. Asiat. Soc. Beng.," iii. 373.

[2] "Pandit Manphúl on Kohkand, Russia, and Bokhara," p. 3.

[3] "The river Wakhsháb rises in the land of the Turks, then flows through the land of Wakhsh, and in its course through the mountains is crossed by a bridge. No river of its magnitude is known, the channel of which is so restricted as that of the Wakhsháb here. This bridge forms the boundary between Khotl and Washjird" ("Istakhri," pp. 125, 126). In "Edrisi," as translated by Jaubert, this passage takes a different form; the river is represented as losing itself under a mountain, and running underground for some distance. This passage was, I imagine, known to the compiler of the anonymous "German Travels," who reproduces the feature in "Vochan." But there is a like story of the Oxus in an older writer than either—Polybius. He, however, places this subterranean plunge below Bactriana, on its entrance into the desert.—x. 48.

but which, in Walker's map, is entitled the Surkháb ("Redwater"). As Wood, in his ride from Kila' Chap to Yangkila' and Saiad, and back again, twice passed the mouth of this so-called Surkháb, so good an observer would scarcely have omitted to notice the confluence of a rival Oxus. No such river occurs in Macartney's map, which embodies a native Itinerary from Sharwán to Saiad and Kuláb; and there can, I think, be little doubt that the real confluence is where that map places it, viz. at least thirty miles above the Kokcha junction,[1] considerably to the north of Saiad, and beyond the utmost reach of Wood's ride, in the vicinity of a place called *Kurghán Tapah.*

19. The PANJA is the next in order, and the first in rank of the great contributaries. This river is formed a little way east of the fort of Panja in Wakhán, in nearly lat. 37° 2', long. 72° 44', and at a height of some ten thousand feet above the sea, by the union of two considerable streams descending from Pamir, viz. the river of the *Darah-i-Sarikol,*[2] and that of the *Darah-i-Mastoj,* or Sarhad Wakhan.

The former, and northerly, branch is that which Captain Wood traced to its source in a lake on Great Pamir, at a level of 15,600 feet above the sea. Doubts have been cast on the propriety of the name *Sir-i-kol,* which he ascribes to the lake, and, if Lake *Sir-i-kol* is to be absolutely rejected,[3] we may fairly follow some Continental geographers in adopting that of *Lake Victoria,* which Wood hesitated to bestow, until at least one of the indigenous names can meet with general acceptance. One of these, "the Lake of Great Pamir" (*Hauz-i-Pamir Kalán*), is too awkward, and another, "Lake Sikandari,"[4] is, as yet, too new to geography to be sufficiently authenticated. From the west end of the lake to Langar Kish, two or three miles above the Panja con-

[1] See "Caubul," ii. 411 (3rd edit.).
[2] Called by Faiz Bakhsh the *Sikandari* River, a name perhaps worthy of adoption, unless we call it Wood's Oxus.
[3] This should not be done overhastily. The name recurs more than once as applied to a high-lying lake, e.g., to one on the plateau of Shewa above Faizábád; and it may have in these cases an etymology referring to such a position.
[4] That used by Faiz Bakhsh.

fluence, Wood makes the length of the valley upwards of seventy miles. By measurement on Walker's map from his data it is about sixty-five. There are no villages above Langar Kish, and only one tributary is mentioned, the Zarzamín, which is apparently the same with the stream called in the higher part of its course the *Ab-i-Más*.

The southerly branch, joining at Panja, is called by Wood (p. 217) "the Stream of Sarhad," a name taken from the last inhabited settlements on its banks, which are termed *Sarhad Wakhát* ("the Wakhán Marches"). Wood's own impression was, that this contained the larger body of water. We have first acquired something like correct knowledge of its course from the *Mirza*. Like the sister stream it rises in a lake, but one of smaller dimensions, known as the "Lake of Little Pamir," or as *Barkat* (the Pool?) *of Yusin*.[1]

The valley is about one hundred miles in length from the lake to the confluence, and is therefore about thirty miles longer than the Darah-i-Sarikol.[2] The valley is in places very narrow, and for some miles above the last village there is barely a space of ten yards between the river and the cliffs. The Mirza's thermometrical observation made this lake about 13,300 feet above the sea, but the probability that it is substantially lower than Lake Victoria may be deduced from more solid facts. For, in addition to Captain Wood's own conclusion, from the temperature of the two streams, we observe that human habitation extends much farther up the Sarhad valley; the last village, Patúr, being forty-two miles from Panja. As far as this the valley is, for a high tract, well peopled, and not without agriculture, though the wealth of the people consists in their live stock, sheep, goats, kine, ponies, and *yaks*. Their houses, generally built contiguous, are of stone and mud, flat-roofed,

---

[1] This name seems to apply on the same principle as that of Sarikol is supposed to apply to Wood's lake; being derived from an adjoining state in the direction of which it lies.

[2] In the case of the latter, however, we have to add the considerable length of the lake, and that of a stream feeding it at the eastern end. This stream is mentioned by Faiz Bakhsh, and it may be gathered that its length is trifling. The difference in length of the two sources will thus probably be reduced to about fifteen miles.

and warmed by stoves. These are not described, but probably resemble the platform stoves of North China.

The district formed by the hamlets of the Sarhad Wakhán valley is also termed *Sárigh Chaupán*. This name, which is used by Faiz Bakhsh, appears in Baber's time, when the valley so called was held for many years (1503—1515) by Sultán Abubakr of Kashgar; and a little later (1529) we find his successor, Said Khan, marching to the conquest of Badakhshan through this same district of Sárigh Chaupán.[1]

This line is, in fact, the chief road across Pamir, Hwen Thsang's "Valley of Pomilo," by which he travelled from Wakhan to Kabandha or Sarikol; it is probably that by which Marco Polo travelled. And it is curious to find the Mirza reviving from his own impressions, though, perhaps, not without suggestion from the belief of his guides, the old story which Hwen Thsang relates of the double discharge of this Lake of Pamir. The fact itself is improbable, but it is evident from the Mirza's account that the watershed is very ill-defined.

The River Panja, formed by the union of these two rivers, flows to the S.W. for about sixty-six miles through the valley state of Wakhan. The floor of the valley varies from a few hundred yards to a mile in width, and has a mean elevation of about nine thousand feet above the sea. At the time of Wood's journey Wakhan was estimated to contain a population of no less than one thousand souls (exclusive, apparently, of Kirghiz nomads, who were just beginning to intrude), and he judged that it might be capable of supporting five thousand. The country was probably then in a very depressed state owing to Uzbek oppression, and we gather from Faiz Bakhsh that more villages exist now than did in Wood's time; but we have no specific data. The state is divided into four districts called *sads* (Hundreds ?), viz., *Istrákh, Khandút, Ispanj*,[2] and *Sárigh*

---

[1] See "Erskine," i. 339, 340, 510. Erskine has read *Sárigh* Júián.

[2] This is the *Panja* district. This prefix, *Is*, is found all through Wakhan and Badakhshan, e.g., Ispanj, Istrákh, Ishkashm, Ispingao, Ishkimish. And just as we find Panja here termed Ispanj, we find in some texts of Marco Polo *Casem*, or Kishm, termed *Scassem*, which looks like *Iskishm*. It is curious that we find this semi-mute detachable *s* in Tibetan names also, such as *s* Pin, *s* Piti, *s* Kardo.—See Cunningham's "Ladak," p. 34.

Chaupán with Pamir, and is under the rule of a Mír, feudatory of Badakhshan.

There are several passes from Wakhan into the upper part of the Chitral valley called Mastoj, of the chief of which mention has already been made.

The *Wakhis*, or people of Wakhan, are stated by Wood to be Tajiks, and with this Manphúl's information coincides, though Faiz Bakhsh calls them not only Hazárahs, but *Tartars*. They are of the Shíah faith. There can be no doubt that their name is identical with that of the great river on whose upper waters they dwell.[1] The name of Wakhan as a province occurs in very early Mahomedan writers, and it is probably represented by the *Oxiani* of the Greeks.

Beyond the western extremity of Wakhan the Panja makes a great elbow, turning northward. The feudatory province of Ishkashm occupies the elbow, and within this, on right bank of the Panja, near the Shighnan border, are the ruby mines, which for ages were so famous, now unproductive and abandoned. The Panja in running northward quits the field of our actual knowledge for a space of something like one hundred and seventy miles. We know that it traverses the valley states of *Shighnan* and *Roshan*, acknowledging the supremacy of Badakhshan, and then the independent principality of *Darwáz*, or, as it is often called, the *Darah Darwáz*.

Shighnan lies in great part, as it would appear, in a lateral valley called the *Shakh-darah*, probably a radical form of the same name. It is not impossible that we have in these names a trace of the ancient *Sacæ*, whom Ptolemy locates most distinctly in this mountain country; and if Major Leech's informant was right as to the application of the names *Shaghnan* and *Shighít* to districts of the Mastoj valley (or Upper Chitral), this would tend to corroborate the derivation. The people of Wakhan would then be a wedge of alien population driven into the middle of the *Sacæ*.[2]

---

[1] M. Khanikoff alludes to a Wakhi settlement in the Yarkand territory ("Ethnogr: de la Perse," p. 41), but there is, I apprehend, some misprint in his reference, and I cannot find the authority which he quotes.

[2] This may have something to do with the statement of Hwen Thsang,

All these Hill-states have different dialects or languages, known as *Wakhi, Shigni, Roshani*. And it is a curious fact that Wakhis, Shignis, and Roshanis all profess to be Shíahs in religion. Of neither Roshan, nor of the rugged and inaccessible Darwáz, do we know any particulars. Some evidence as to the identity of the latter with the valley of the *Comedæ* we have already referred to. The Panja is said to be bridged (no doubt with wood) in Darwáz.

20. We now come to the KOKCHA, the next of the important contributaries to the formation of the Amú, though of less considerable size than either of the preceding. The name (apparently from Turki *Kok*, "blue") is useful to geographers, and it occurs in Baber, but it seems to be by no means generally used in the country, where the stream is more commonly known as the river of Faizábád, or of Badakhshan. Indeed, among unsophisticated nations, with rivers as with mountain ranges, unless they be of the first class, famous over all a continent, like Indus or Oxus, proper names are apt to be a reflection from books, and are rare, as in our own country endless Esks and Avons indicate.

The Kokcha may be considered mature at the bridge called *Shashpúl* above the Faizábád defiles, and where its two main components, the river of *Vardoj* and the river of *Jerm*, unite.[1] The latter would seem to be the larger of the two; and indeed, according to Major Raverty, the Kafirs of the Hindu Kush look upon it as the true *Amú*, ascribing its origin to a lake on the northern skirts of their mountains.[2] The valleys of its upper streams form the districts of *Kurán, Anjuman*, and *Paryán*, subordinate to the province of Jerm. Kurán is mentioned as a

that the king of *Shangmi*, which appears to be Chitral, was of the race of *Sakiya* (iii. 207). It is worthy of notice that what has been regarded as a yak figured on the obelisk of Nimrúd, is described in the accompanying inscription as *Alap—Nahr—Sakiya*—"The Ox of the river Sakiya;" a title which may possibly characterize the Upper Oxus, rising among the hills of the Sakiyas, or *Sacæ*.—See Prof. Finzi, "Ricerche per lo Studio dell' Antichità Assira," p. 289.

[1] Wood regards the Jerm river as the Kokcha (p. 249), the Vardoj as a tributary. Faiz Bakhsh speaks of the Vardoj or Zebák river as the real "river of Badakhshan."

[2] "Jour. Asiat. Soc. Bengal," xxviii. 324.

principality in the seventh century by Hwen Thsang, and was of sufficient substance to send, in the following century, a mission on its own account to the court of China. In it lie the quarries or mines of lapis lazuli, visited by Captain Wood; as famous for many ages as the ruby mines of the Panja. The main valley of the Jerm river was formerly known as *Yamgán*, a name even now not obsolete. Its mineral riches lead the Badakhshis of the present day to derive the name from *Hama-Kán*, or "All-Mines." Jerm in this valley was the chief place of Badakhshan during Wood's visit, when Faizábád lay desolate. We are told by Pandit Manphúl that its old name was *Golán*, but the name of Jerm is found at least as far back as Taimúr's campaigns on the Kokcha.

The Vardoj river is mainly made up of three streams, which join near *Zebák*; one coming down from the small Lake of *Bazgír*, near the pass to Ishkashm; the two others descending from the Hindu Kush on the borders of Chitral, and the valleys of either affording passes into that country; the more easterly by the triple routes of *Kharteza*, *Agram*, and *Nuksán*, the more westerly by the *Doráh Kotal*, at the head of the high valley of *Sanglich*. Still further west a pass called the *Dozakh-darah*, literally the *Höllenthal*, leads into Kafiristan.

For some miles before its junction with the Jerm river the Vardoj flows through the plain of *Bahárak*, one of the richest and most peopled parts of Badakhshan, in which the former capital is said to have stood. It is there joined by the combined waters of the *Sarghalán* and the *Zardeo*, each of which gives a name to a district of the central province. To the north of this lies the high table-land of *Shewa*, affording the best pasture in the country, and by which a road leads to Kila' Kúm, the capital of Darwáz. On Shewá lies a considerable lake, bearing the recurring name of *Sarikol*. Apparently it discharges northwards into the Panja.

Between the Shashpúl bridge at the Jerm confluence, and the town of Faizábád, the valley contracts to a narrow gorge. Here probably applies the name of the *Tangi*, or Strait, of Badakhshan, mentioned by Benedict Goës, as well as in Oriental histories. Faizábád itself, which was utterly deserted in Wood's time, has now for a number of years (I know not how long) been reoccupied as the capital. In 1866 it still contained only about four hundred houses. The Mirza, in 1869, speaks of it as running about a mile along the right bank of the Kokcha, and as "nowhere more than half a mile in breadth," but such dimensions, if even approximately correct, must include a large amount of garden ground. The chief business carried on appears to be the slave trade, which has for years been a prominent scourge of all those Upper Oxus regions. Of the Badakhshan market Chitral is the chief source of supply, but all the Hill-states, Shaghnan, Wakhan, Darwáz, Sarikol, Kanjút, &c., appear to have been alternately actors and sufferers under the hateful system. Another trade, which it is a little surprising to find, is that in cast-iron utensils, which are fabricated here with skill. This art, utterly unknown in India, is practised throughout Turkestan, and is probably of Chinese origin.[1]

The town of Faizábád is unwalled, but the Mír has his residence within a square mud-fort at the north-west corner. The old citadel, called the *Zagharchi*, overlooks the town from the southern bank. A building called *Khirkat-i-Sharíf*, "the Holy Shirt," is looked on with reverence, having contained that relic of the prophet, which was carried away a century ago by the troops of Ahmed Shah of Kabul.

As we advance beyond Faizábád, the hills appear to keep pretty close to the river on the right bank. This is occupied by the district of *Yaftal*, hilly, but populous; and further on by the feudatory province of *Pasákú*, or *Shahr-i-Buzurg*. On the left bank we hear of plains, between the river and the hills, among which that of *Khimchan* (mentioned by Baber) is said to have been once the site of a great city. Above this is the plateau of Argu, now highly cultivated, and in the hands of the Mír and his nobles. The valley and Mírship of *Daraim* succeeds, said to be comparatively fertile and populous. This

---

[1] Chinese annals relate that as early as the first century B.C., the people of *Tawan*, or Ferghana, acquired the new art of casting iron utensils from Chinese deserters ("Julien," quoted by Lassen, ii. 615). It is probable that the Seric iron, mentioned by Pliny, was this material. It is well known that the Chinese tinkers have the art, totally unknown in Europe, of patching a cast-iron pot.

also I believe to represent one of the ancient states of Tokharistan, the *Himatala* (or *Hima-darah*) of Hwen Thsang, to whose king the traveller assigns a romantic enterprise in Kashmír.

The rivers of Daraim, Teshkan, Navi, and Mashhad, successively enter the Kokcha from the left. On a crag, near the confluence of the Teshkan river, once stood the fort of *Zafar*, the great stronghold of Badakhshan, and famous in the histories of Baber and Humáyún. The Mashhad river takes the name of a town on its banks, near the place where it is crossed by the road from Faizábád to Kunduz; and *that* is so called from certain early *martyrs* of Islám who are believed to have fallen there. A few miles above Mashhad, on the same river, stands *Kishm*, once a place of much note, and still the head of a feudatory province bearing the name. It is the *Casem* of Marco Polo, and is often mentioned in the histories of Taimúr and his house. The upper part of the valley forms the district of *Varsach*.

Only one more tributary of the Kokcha is indicated within the limits of Badakhshan, and that not very distinctly; that which drains the plain of *Kalaogán*, or Kila' Afghan. The fort so called is the frontier post, but the actual boundary between Badakhshan and Kunduz is the Hill Pass of *Lattaband*, some miles farther west, over a spur which here runs northward into the plain of the Oxus.

In the hills of Akbulák near this are mines of rock-salt, which supply the whole country, from Chitral westward to Kunduz, just as they did in Marco Polo's time. The salt formation is very extensive in this region, and is worked also in the hills of Kúláb and of Karátigín, both lying nearly in the same meridian with Akbulák.

Returning to the right bank of the Kokcha, we find that the valley begins to widen into alluvial plain about *Rusták*. This is the chief place of trade in Badakhshan, lying as it does at the exit of all the Hill countries, and at the intersection of roads from Kashgar, Chitral, and Faizábád, from Balkh and Khulm, and from Kúláb. The Kokcha is crossed by a wooden bridge as far down as *Karlogh*, some twenty miles below Rusták. This place, and the plain district round it, appears to take its name from a settlement of the Karlogh Turks, once so famous and numerous in Turkestan.

The Rusták Mírship extends to the mouth of the Kokcha, and beyond it, up the Oxus to *Yangkila'*.[1] A great part of this appears to be level and fine pasture. The central district of Rusták, immediately east of the confluence, is called *Chaáb* ("well-water"), from the fact that the inhabitants depend for their drinking-water on wells only, a circumstance quite exceptional in that region. This is one of the most productive plains in Badakhshan, and along with *Rágh*, the more hilly province which adjoins it on the north-east, gives birth to the finest class of men, both for *physique* and intelligence, in the country.[2]

In following the courses of the Panja and Kokcha, we have very superficially sketched the most important part of Badakhshan. The whole of the provinces recognised as forming that state and its dependencies, with their subdivisions where known are as follows:—

I. Central Province, which may be called *Badakhshan Proper*.
    A. Faizábád.   Districts—1. Faizábád.
                                    2. Yaftal.
                                    3. Argú.
                                    4. Shewá.
    B. Jerm.   Districts—1. Jerm.
                                    2. Khásh.
                                    3. Zardeo.
                                    4. Sarghalán.
                                    5. Vardoj.
                                    6. Kurán.
                                    7. Anjumán.
                                    8. Paryán.
II. Daraim.
III. Shahr-i-buzurg, or Pasaku (on right bank of Kokcha).
IV. Gumbaz (a small territory on left bank of Kokcha).
V. Farokhar (on the river of that name, running down to Tálikán).
VI. Kishm.   Districts—1. Kishm.
                                    2. Mashhad.
                                    3. Varsach.
                                    4. Teshkún.
                                    5. Karlogh.
VII. Rusták.   Districts—1. Rusták.
                                    2. Chaáb.
                                    3. Yangkila'.

---

[1] Or *Jankila* (of Wood).   [2] Manphúl.

VIII. Roshán.
IX. Shighnán.
X. Ishkashm.
XI. Wakhan.   Districts—1. Sad Istrákh.
 2. Sad Khandút.
 3. Sad Ispanj.
 4. Sad Sárigh Chaupán.
XII. Zebák, with the district of Sanglich.
XIII. Minján (or Mungán, a high district near the Hindu Kush).
XIV. Rágh.
XV. Daung. } These appear to lie in the unknown region between Faizábád
XVI. Asiába. }   and Roshán.

The central province is under the immediate government of the Mír or King of Badakhshan. The others are held either by relatives of his, or by hereditary chiefs, on a kind of feudal tenure. They acknowledge the Mír as paramount, and are bound to aid with military service in case of need, but he neither interferes with their rule, nor receives any substantial tribute from them. He again is now subject to the Amír of Kabul. No data whatever exist for an estimate of the population of Badakhshan, or the revenues of its rulers. We know but little of any part of it except the mere line of road travelled by Wood, and his native successors. And of some of the provinces which Pandit Manphúl speaks of as the most fertile and populous, our ignorance is as deep as it can well be.

Captain Wood unfortunately travelled in the depth of winter, and during nearly the whole time that he spent in Badakhshan the country was clad in snow. But the beauty of Badakhshan in more genial seasons is in great contrast to the bare and sterile regions which adjoin it;[1] it has often been celebrated by Eastern writers, and it sprang a vein of rare enthusiasm even in the usually staid and reticent Marco Polo. Baber contrasts the pine-clad heights, the soft and turfy hills, and the abundant springs of Badakhshan with the barren and rocky character of the highlands of Afghanistan. Burnes relates how both natives

[1] "Badakhshan is a dependence of Mawaralnahr, but not really a part of it any more than it is of Turkestan. It is a country *sui generis*, attached to the neighbouring regions only by vicinity of position, but presenting the most remarkable peculiarities in regard to animals, plants, and minerals."—"Masálak-al-Absúr" (a work of the fourteenth century), in "Notices et Extraits," xiii. 244.

and foreigners spoke with rapture of the vales of Badakhshan, its rivulets, romantic scenes and glens, its fruits, flowers, and nightingales. The brief notices of Manphúl, and Wood's few words on descending to the lower valley of the Kokcha, where the snow had disappeared, delightfully corroborate these charms (pp. 251, 252); whilst his contrast between the hills of Kabul and those of Kunduz (where he was in the Spring), is like a condensation of Baber's expressions (p. 268).

21. It remains to speak briefly of the Aksarai, as the last of the four great confluents that form the Ámú.

The stream of Bamian may be regarded as the principal source, fed by a variety of torrents which join from the Pass of Ak-robát and other gorges adjoining that famous site, the names of some of which appear to commemorate the traditions of its ancient population.[1] At the north-east end of the valley of Bamian the stream is joined by another of about equal bulk, descending through the wild Pimúrí gorge from the Pass of Hajjiyak; and on the volcanic rock which divides the streams, stand extensive ruins, whose name of *Zohák*, or, as it is sometimes more fully called, *Zohák-i-márán*[2] ("Zohák of the snakes"), connects it with the most ancient traditions of Persian history. The ruins, as Wood remarks in his too brief notice, do not bear an aspect of high antiquity. But, in fact, the site was probably occupied in comparatively modern times, by a city replacing Bamian, for in the days of Akbar it continued to give name to a district; and Abúlfazl mentions that the "Castle of Zohák" remained in good repair.[3]

From this the river turns nearly north, passing by the country of the Sheikh-'Alis, one of the most famous of the Hazara clans,[4] and about forty miles N.N.E. of Zohák, at a place called Char-dar (four gates) or *Chár-darya* (four rivers), it meets two

---

[1] Such as *Darah-i-Fauládi*, "the valley of cutlers;" *Darah-i-Ahangárán*, "of the blacksmiths;" *Darah-i-Surma*, "of antimony," or eye-paint.

[2] *Zohakmaran* in "Mem. of Humayun," p. 96; *Zuakumaran* in Leech's Reports.

[3] "Ritter," vii. 280.

[4] It is not clear to me whether the *Darah-Sheikh-Ali* is a part of the main valley, or a tributary valley from the right.

confluents of length at least equal to its own, the river of *Saighán* and the river of *Kámard*, both of which appear to rise in the vicinity of the *Band-i-Barbar*, where lie also the sources of the Balkh river, and both of which are crossed by the road from Bamian to Khulm.

From this point, if not earlier, the river would seem to take the name of *Surkháb*. It must continue to receive abundant supplies from the perpetual snows upon its right, but we do not know of any considerable confluent until the junction of the Andaráb river from the eastward, near *Doshi*, some eighty-five miles in direct line N.E. from Zohák. This tributary acting as a catch-water to the main ridge of Hindu Kush, to which it runs parallel for more than a degree of longitude, must bring in a large contribution to the Surkháb.

About *Ghori*, still a town of some note, the valley appears to open out considerably.[1] The river is or has been bridged at Thomri, half way between Ghori and Baghlán; a work ascribed to Aurangzib. It then receives from the right the Baghlán river coming down from Narin and the hills of Khost. Of the character of the country below Baghlán we have already spoken. The only remaining confluent of the Surkháb is that which joins immediately below Kunduz, called by Wood the river of *Khánábad*, but which seems also sometimes to bear the name of the chief of its contributaries, the *Bangi*. These contributaries are three, the river of *Farokhar* or of *Tálikán*, along whose valley runs the boundary between the Kunduz, or Balkh territory, and that of Badakhshan, the Bangi proper, and the *Shoráb*, a salt stream as its name implies, draining the western slopes of the mountains of Eshk-mushk (or Ish Kimish?). The Bangi is represented in Walker's map, and that in Wood's book, as a stream of very short course. But this is almost certainly erroneous, and the older representation of Macartney is in this respect preferable. There is indeed reason to suppose that its sources extend back nearly to the first spurs of Hindu Kush.[2]

---

[1] "Punjáb Report," App., p. cxlvii.

[2] According to the "Memoirs of Iumayun" (p. 89), that prince, *in the same day*, crosses one of the Panjshir passes (Túl or Khawák), and encamps on the banks of the Bangi. And there is some ground for connecting the name of the river with that of *Mungán*,

Burnes indeed speaks of Khánábad as "standing on a rivulet;"[1] but the river must deserve a higher title—he must allude to a branch or canal merely. The main channel is crossed by a stone bridge; but, as we learn from Wood, it was sixty yards wide, and there was another channel, besides a variety of canals.[2] Of the size and depth of the Surkháb, or Aksarai as it is there called, opposite Kunduz, either above or below the junction of the Bangi waters, I find no distinct estimate. Wood forded it much higher, near Baghlán, in the end of November. Burnes, in his narrative, does not mention how he crossed the river (in June) on his long ride from Khulm to Khánábad and back again: but he states, in a descriptive chapter, that neither of the rivers at Kunduz are fordable during the summer melting of the snows.[3]

22. As regards the Oxus itself, and the amount of its discharge, I know of no data later than Burnes's; these give us a good idea of the magnitude of the river at the time when he passed it. The general results that can be deduced from his observations at Khoja Sála—about one hundred and sixty miles below the junction of the Aksarai, and at Chárjúi, about two hundred miles still further down—are that the winter stream (*i.e.* the lowest) has a channel of about four hundred yards in width; that the discharge on the 17th June and 17th August, *i.e.* at a month's interval either way from the highest level, would be from sixty-five thousand to seventy-five thousand cubic feet per second;[4] but we have no means of judging what proportion the winter discharge would bear to this. The river

---

a territory high up on the mountains in the south of Badakhshan.—See a paper by the present writer on Hwen Thsang's Itinerary, in the "Jour. Roy. Asiat. Soc." for the present year (1872).—Probably, however, the river derives no supply from *perpetual* snow regions.

[1] Vol. ii., p. 192.

[2] The data given by Wood for the *secondary* channel, the main one being in great part blocked up at the time, give a discharge of about 1000 cubic feet per second for that portion of the water.

[3] Vol. iii., p. 175 (2nd ed.).

[4] A rough calculation from Burnes's data. This is barely equal to the *low-water* discharge of the Irawadi at the head of its Delta. Khanikoff ("Bokhara," p. 27) says that, according to Russian inquiry, the rise of the Oxus is from March till the end of May, whilst it falls from June to September.

above the Kokcha confluence appears to be annually frozen over, and sometimes again at Chárjúi, and even higher, whilst in the intervening portion the freezing is only partial. The river is well suited to navigation, and was largely navigated in ancient times (when in all probability it flowed into the Caspian), but now, in the portion with which we have to do, there is no navigation, and no boats except ferry boats. Fords cease at Hazrat Imám.

Like the great rivers in the plains of Upper India the Oxus has a secondary valley, marked by a bank, distant generally one mile and a half or two miles from the channel on either side; and this, though not often inundated, is the limit of moisture, verdure, and agriculture. Above this bank the levels of the primary valley have the sterile character already described.

Our information as to the absolute level of points on the river, or in its valley, is most scanty. Burnes states the level of Balkh at 1,800 feet (no doubt from an observation of boiling water). In Wood's book I find no observation of Kunduz; but Walker's map states it, I presume on his authority, at 900 feet. Dr. Lord, on the other hand, who stayed at Kunduz during Captain Wood's absence in Badakhshan, makes Kunduz not quite 500 feet above the sea; and from the leisure and care with which this deduction appears to have been made, it should probably be preferred.[1] It seems a little difficult to reconcile this with Burnes's estimate of Balkh, considering the relative position of the two places, but we have not sufficient knowledge to assert that they are inconsistent.[2]

[1] "The mean of three thermometers which had been carefully boiled and registered at the sea level."

[2] The distance from Kunduz to the Aral, measured along the Aksarai and Oxus, with a fifty-mile opening of the compasses on Kiepert's Asia, is about 800 miles. The level of the Aral is 33 feet. Kunduz, and, considering its swampy site, we may say the river abreast of Kunduz, is therefore only 467 feet above the Aral. Allowing for windings, this will give considerably less than six inches per mile for fall. Balkh, again, is believed to be about twenty-five to twenty-eight miles from the Oxus, near Termedh. This, by the rough calculation just made, should be about 450 feet above the sea, and therefore 1,350 feet below Balkh. Balkh stands "on a gentle slope which sinks towards the Oxus" (Burnes). If the height of Balkh be 1,800 feet, this slope will be about fifty feet per mile. It is possible.

The lengths of the four chief contributaries that we have described, measured with a fourteen mile opening of the compasses, on a map compiled to the best of my judgment, are as follows:

		Miles.
1. SURKHÁB OF KARÁTIGÍN from probable source to mouth of Aksarai, or Kunduz river	. . .	400
2. PANJA, from Barkat Yasín to the same point	. .	425
3. KOKCHA, from probable source of Jerm branch to same point	. . . .	225
4. SURKHÁB or AKSARAI, from source west of Bamian to same point	. . . .	220

And the whole length of the Oxus, from Barkat Yasín to the sea of Aral, will be with similar measurement close on 1,200 miles. The amount to be added to this for the full length of the stream can only be judged from apparent analogies, but I should estimate it at about 200 miles.

23. I will conclude this essay with an attempt to put into connected shape such facts as we possess on the topography and drainage of Pamir. It must be understood that the doubts are numerous and great, but the attempt is the result of much study, and may at least prove useful as a framework subject to gradual correction.

The length of Pamir from south to north, viz., from the northern base of the Darkot and Abigarm Passes above Yasin, to the Kizil Yart Pass north of Lake Karakúl, we may reckon provisionally to be about one hundred and eighty miles. The length from Kizil Yart Pass, if carried somewhat obliquely to the east of south, so as to take in the Pamir Tághdumbásh, south of Sarikol province, will approach, perhaps exceed, two hundred miles. But it is doubtful how far the last-mentioned plateau is in immediate relation with Pamir Proper.

The breadth of the plateau in the latitude of Lake Victoria, from the *Aktásh* of the Mirza on the eastward, to the termination of the plateau west of Lake Victoria, will be from ninety to one hundred miles.

In the latitude of Lake Karakúl it is probably a good deal

more. But we do not know whether the peaks seen by Messrs. Shaw and Hayward to the eastward of the 75° meridian, such as the *Tagalma*, stand on the plateau or on the spurs which run out from it towards the plains of Kashgar; and the longitude of Karakúl itself is at present uncertain within many miles.

We are informed by Pandit Manphúl[1] that Pamir is popularly divided into six portions, exclusive of the Pamir Tághdumbásh. These are, (1) Pamir Alichúr, (2) Pamir Khurd (or "Little"), (3) Pamir Kalán ("Great"), (4) Pamir Khargoshi ("of the Hare"), (5) Pamir Sares, (6) Pamir Rang-kúl.

The lakes, of which the names are given by the same authority, are (1) Karakúl, or Pamir Khargoshi, (2) Lake of Great Pamir, (3) Lake of Sares Pamir, or Ishal Kúl, (4) Lake of Pamir Khurd, (5) Rang-kúl, also in Pamir Khurd. But we hear also on various authorities of a *Túz-kúl*, a *Pulong-kúl*, a *Sassagh-kúl*, a *Yakh-kúl*, and a "Dysame Lake," on all which names we shall have something to say briefly; and I believe in the existence of a second *Rang-kúl*, to the north of Karakúl.

As regards the position of the lakes, and the different sections of Pamir: that of the *Lake of Great Pamir*, and of the Great Pamir itself, is ascertained, for we know the lake to be Wood's "Sarikol," or Lake Victoria,[2] discharging towards Panja.[3]

We know the *Lake of Pamir Khurd* to be that described by the Mirza under the name of *Barkat Yasin*.

Rang-kúl[4] is also stated to be in Pamir Khurd, and to be fed by the Aktásh stream running northward from Aktásh, a point on the steppe which seems to lie about forty miles between E. and N.E. of the upper end of Lake Victoria. Rang-kúl is said to be fifteen kos, say twenty to twenty-two miles, from Aktásh. These data,[5] when laid down, determine approximately the position of the tract called Pamir Khurd which

---

[1] App. to "Punjab Trade Report," p. cccxxxii. The information was derived apparently from Mahomed Amín.

[2] See "Punjab Report," *loc. cit.*
In the paper on M. Fedchenko's journey in "Petermann" (p. 161), the term *Little Pamir* is applied to the tract visited by Wood; but this is a mistake.

[4] The name is probably taken from that of the wild goat so called (*ante*, p. xlv).

[5] Derived from routes in "Punjab Trade Report," App. p. xvii., *j*, *k*, *o*, and from Faiz Bakhsh.

occupies therefore the S.W. part of the plateau. It is also thus intelligible how Wood, in ascending to Lake Victoria, should notice a track leading to Pamir Khurd as striking off *to the left* (p. 230), though the *Lake* of Pamir Khurd lay far on his right.

Lake of *Ishal Kúl.* Manphúl, though not quite explicit, seems to describe this as the source of the Shakh-darah river in Shighnan. We shall recur to this presently, but that supposition, as well as its position in the Chinese map of Pamir, indicates that it lies N.W. from Lake Victoria. Here, therefore, we place *Pamir Sares* on the west of the plateau, looking down towards Shighnan and Roshan. The name is probably *Yeshil* (Green).

Lake *Karakúl* is said by Manphúl to lie in *Pamir Khargoshi.* Abdul Mejid marks his third stage from Langar Wakhan (Langar Kish of Wood), as in Khargoshi, and Faiz Bakhsh notes passing Khargoshi in a similar position, *i.e.* north-west of Lake Victoria. And as Abdul Mejid made seven marches further in the steppe before reaching Lake Karakúl, this would seem to indicate that Pamir Khargoshi constitutes much the largest section of Pamir. The only data we have for the position of Karakúl are its existence at this point of Abdul Mejid's Itinerary, and the data of the Chinese map, and the Hydrography, which we shall quote further on. Both are very loose, but they are consistent so far as they go. I should approximately assume lat. 38° 40′, long. 73° to 73° 15′, as its middle point. Both Hayward's information and Shaw's ascribes very large dimensions to this lake, in fact a circuit of ten to fourteen marches. Abdul Mejid, however, gives it but four days.[1]

Pamir Alichúr I venture to locate on the eastern side of the table-land, north of Pamir Khurd, on the faith of the Chinese map, in which the name appears as *Ho-eul-tsu-eul*, and of a document which will presently be quoted.

Pamir Rang-kúl I conceive to lie to the extreme north, under the *Kizil Yart* range, beside the second and more northerly lake of that name. This is the *Riangkúl* of the Chinese map, and of many maps since Klaproth's. The existence of such a

[1] "Punjab Trade Rep.," App., p. clv.

lake in that position has been confirmed to me by the map which Colonel Lumsden drew from Mahomed Amín's information, as well as by the routes of the latter printed in the Punjab Report. And in taking down his statements a confusion, apparently arising from the existence of these two Rang-kúls, has led to an enormous error in one of his routes as there given.[1]

"*Sussugh Kol*" appears in the Itinerary of Abdul Mejid, as the next stage from Khargoshi, the fourth from Langar Kish. I had been inclined to identify it with *Ishal-kúl*. But Major Montgomerie suggests that it is really Wood's Lake. The size ascribed to *Sussugh Kol*, "one day's ride in circuit," would correspond fairly with the dimensions assigned to Lake Victoria by Wood. The name is, I imagine, *Sásik-kúl*, "the Fetid Lake," and it will be seen that Wood mentions this characteristic of the water of his lake (p. 237). On the whole, I am inclined to adopt my friend's suggestion, though the data are not sufficient absolutely to decide the question.

The *Yakh-kul* occurs on Abdul Mejid's march, one day short of Karakúl, and this is all we know about it. The name is presumably from *Yakh*, "ice."

Dysame Lake appears also in Abdul Mejid's Itinerary as the next stage from Karakúl. The name is altogether anomalous, and I strongly suspect that *Dysame* is a clerical error for "The Same!" Considering the size of Karakúl, nothing is more probable than that the travellers should have twice halted upon its shores.

Before attempting to identify the Túz-kúl and Pu-long-kúl, I will quote the authority which speaks of them.

This is the report of the Chinese general of the force which took possession of Kashgar, in 1759, and the date corresponds to 23rd November in that year. An extract from it is given in

---

[1] From *Aktásh*, very little above the latitude of Lake Victoria, a route runs north to the Alai and the Terek Pass. The first march is apparently to *Lake Rang-kúl*. But in detailing this route, Mahomed Amín, or his compiler, has leaped at once from this southern Rang-kúl to the Alai steppe, a distance of certainly more than one hundred miles, in one march! The fact being, I imagine, that the whole interval between the two Rang-kúls has been omitted.—See "Punjab Trade Report," App., pp. xxii. *k*, xxii. *o*.

a letter from the Jesuit Fathers da Rocha and Espina, dated from Kashgar three days later.[1] The report states that the Lieut.-General Fonte (Fu-te?) having learned that the Khojas had escaped towards Badakhshan, pursued them by forced marches of one hundred *lis* a day. He first overtook the fugitives near *Alchúr* (*Altchour* in the French), and engaged them there, but did not succeed in intercepting them. The general soon afterwards (2nd September, 1759) received intelligence that the enemy had taken up a position in the mountains covering Badakhshan. He learned from a *Púrút* or Kirghiz, thoroughly acquainted with the country, that the mountain in question was very lofty and precipitous. It lay between two lakes, one on the Kashgar side called *Pu-long Kol*, and one on the further side called *Isil-kol*. The Chinese general surprised the enemy here by a night attack, but the Khoja and his chief officers escaped towards Badakhshan.

In a notice of the same events from the Chinese Imperial geography, the second lake is called *Yeshil-kúl*.[2] It is of course the *Ishal-kúl*, or Lake of Pamir Sares.[3]

The *Pu-long-kúl* is most probably the *Rang-kúl* of Little Pamir; and the *Alchúr* of the Chinese general the *Pamir Alichur* of Mahomed Amín. Its position seems necessarily to be between the valley of Tash Kurghán, and the lakes above-mentioned; whilst an incidental notice by Faiz Bakhsh places it to the north of his route. On these hints I have assigned it a position in the map.

In the Chinese map, as well as in the geographical notice just referred to, we find the *Tús-kúl* or *Tússe-kúl*. It is represented in the map as the main source of the river flowing by Wakhan, Khandút and Istrákh, *i.e.* of the Panja. This seems to identify it with Lake Victoria. But the name appears to be

---

[1] "Lettres Édifiantes," rec. xxxi., p. 248.

[2] See "Magasin Asiatique," i., p. 93. The notice itself is founded on the *bouleversée* map alluded to at p. lxi. of this Essay, and makes the Oxus flow backwards into the lakes of Pamir.

[3] After the Chinese conquest a number of the Kashgaris, who had fled with the Khan Khoja to Badakhshan, settled down on Pamir in the vicinity of Lake Ishilkúl; but they eventually returned to their country.—" Punjab Trade Report," App., pp. cccxxxix-xl.

h

the Turkish *Túz-kúl*, or Salt Lake. Is Lake Victoria brackish? Wood, though noting that "the water emitted a slightly fetid smell, and was of a reddish tinge," does not mention having tasted it. There is an *Ab-i-Shor*, or Salt River, which appears to flow from the mountains on the southern shore of the lake into the other or Sarhad branch of the Panja, so there may be some foundation for such a name on the shores of Lake Victoria. But it is difficult to conceive that a lake with so copious an effluent as this has, in the northern branch of the Panja, should have salt waters.

The chief problem as to the hydrography of Pamir is the direction of discharge from Karakúl. The evidence is very contradictory.

Most of the testimony collected by recent travellers tends to throw it into the Oxus.

Thus Mr. Shaw was told by an old Kirghiz that it discharged westward into the Karátigín river. Lieut. Hayward heard the same from a Kirghiz chief at Kashgar, viz., that the sole outlet of the Karakúl was south and west through the hills of Karátigín.

Manphúl (on the authority of Mahomed Amín) says positively that the stream from Karakúl joins the Panja near Bartang on the borders of Darwáz, and is the largest of the five confluents that form the Oxus. He also tells us that the waters from Rang-Kúl (the southern lake so called) and Pamir Khurd unite and fall into the Karakúl.

Faiz Bakhsh says that the *Aktash* (*i.e.*, the stream flowing to Rang-kúl) unites with the waters of the Kanjúd-Darah (a very perplexing expression), and flows towards Karátigín, Kuláb, and Hissár, and so into the Oxus. He does not mention Karakúl.

Thus all these reports carry the drainage of Karakúl westward to the Oxus, though they disagree in minor points. The information furnished by M. Fedchenko seems to preclude the idea that the Karakúl drainage joins the Karátigín river.

The evidence on the other side is almost too vague to be worth quoting, except one statement, and that is so precise that I do not know how to reject it, till we have material for a conclusive judgment. This is contained in a Chinese work of authority, from which extracts were translated by M. Stanislas Julien in the "N. Annales des Voyages," for 1846. This says:

"The *Yamanyar*[1] issues from Mount *Guibuchak* (a part of the Tsungling), flows south-east for one hundred and eighty *li* (say sixty miles), receives the drainage of the *Aragu*[2] mountains, and then after sixty *li* it enters Lake Karakúl. It then flows eastward, passing south of *Chakharaller*,[3] and north of the mountain pass called *Kash-tashi-ling*. Then, after having flowed four hundred *li* (one hundred and thirty-three miles), it passes to the north of the military station of *Ilguchu*, and enters the Kashgar frontier. Farther to the eastward it forms the river of *Tailibuchuk*;[4] then flows eastward and divides into canals, watering the villages of *Kusen, Taskhon*, and *Khanairik*. Further east it arrives at the village of *Yopurkhu*, and stops short, not reaching the great river of Kashgar."

Mr. Shaw thinks the notion of the eastern issue from Karakúl may be explained by the fact that there is a smaller Karakúl on the eastern side of Pamir, at the foot of Tagalma Peak, draining into the Kashgar river. Faiz Bakhsh also notices this Karakúl, which, from his account, seems to lie between the Yambulak Pass (above Chichiklik) and Tagalma, and he describes it as draining into the river of Yanghisár. Nor is it possible to reconcile the precision of the Chinese account with this solution of the difficulty. I am sensible, however, that the Chinese precision may be factitious, and, after all, based on a map, and not on inquiry. But, in the face of statements so contradictory, I am unable to arrive at a positive conviction. Mr. Shaw, by a letter with which he has obliged me, seems to feel less confidence than he did in the western discharge of

---

[1] The Yamanyar is the river whose various branches flow past Yapchan, and between Yapchan and Kashgar, the Khanarik of Hayward's map—and see "Shaw," p. 460.

[2] A preceding passage of the same work shows that the *Aragu* mountains are those in which the sources of the Kashgar river lie. The real word is perhaps *Alai-koh*.

[3] This mountain of Chakharaller is prominent in the German baron's journey up the Yamanyar; but if Klaproth was the baron, this is easily understood.

[4] No doubt the *Telwachook* of Mr. Shaw, immediately north of Yapchan.

Karakúl. He believes that we shall find Pamir traversed from east to west by several hog-backed ridges, between which the drainage flows away. His great experience of the kindred regions renders it probable that he is a correct interpreter of native information. But the narrative of Abdul Mejíd does not suggest the existence of any transverse ridges of marked elevation till the Kizil Yart is reached. Nor do the divisions of Pamir, so far as we can make them out, appear to correspond with east and west natural demarcations.

It seems certain that the water from Pamir Khurd and the southern Rang-kúl reaches the Oxus, probably at Bartang, on the border of Roshan and Darwáz. And I am inclined, on the authority of the Chinese map, to suppose that the waters of Yeshil-kúl take a like course, and probably unite with the drainage just mentioned to form that large tributary of the Oxus which Manphúl alludes to.

I will notice only one more point in Pamir topography, that called *Aktásh.*

In three routes, viz., that of Mahomed Amín from Panja, *viâ* Sarhad Wakhán to the valley of Tash Kurghan;[1] that of Faiz Bakhsh, from Panja *viâ* Wood's Lake, to the same valley; and in the Mirza's route by Sarhad Wakhán, and the Little Pamir Lake to the same, we find a prominent point bearing the name of *Aktásh* ("white-stone"). And in both the first and the last it is noted that a road leads north to the Alai steppe from this point.

In spite of the last coincidence, I cannot satisfy myself that the Aktásh of Mahomed Amín and Faiz Baksh (undoubtedly the same) is identical with the Aktásh of the Mirza. The distances from Tash Kurghan are seriously discrepant; and if the places be identical, the Mirza has made some grievous mistake as to the hydrography. For his Aktásh is represented as on the river which flows down to Tash Kurghan, whilst that of the other two travellers is on a stream flowing north-west towards Darwáz.

On the whole, I have not ventured to identify them. But

---

[1] "Punjab Trade Report," App., p. xxii. *k*, and xxii. *o*.

the doubt is an important one for the adjustment of Pamir topography in the present state of our knowledge.

The late important journey of M. Fedchenko, when his details are published, will give us a *pied-à-terre* in the Alai steppe, and probably enable us to determine, with better approximation to truth, the position of the Kizil Yart Pass, with the northern termination of Pamir, and more loosely that of Karakúl.

PALERMO, *October* 10*th*, 1872.

NOTE.

AT p. xl. it is stated that there is no ground whatever for the belief that the Chinese were in military occupation of Badakhshan, and that the representation of such a state of things in the anonymous German travels (see p. lviii.) is a pure fiction.

Since this was printed I have found, in Wilford's paper on Caucasus (*Asiatic Researches*, vi. 457), a statement that the Chinese were then (last decade of 18th century) in possession of Badakhshan as far as Baghlan.

I do not think that this can mean anything beyond the fact that Badakhshan then acknowledged itself tributary to China (see p. xl.); but I have little doubt that this passage of Wilford's was the basis on which the representation of the apocryphal traveller was founded.

Wilford also states that Chitral was then tributary to China; a circumstance strongly corroborative of Mr. Shaw's identification of the modern Bolor of the Chinese with Chitral.

The knowledge shown by Wilford of the geography of that frontier is very remarkable, and far in advance of his time.

A PERSONAL NARRATIVE

OF A JOURNEY TO THE

SOURCE OF THE RIVER OXUS.

CHAPTER I.

Embarkation on the Indus.—Seaports of Sind.—A Dutch gun-brig.—Changes in the course of the Indus.—Present to the Amirs.—Pír Putta.—Site and Shrine.—T'hat'hah.—Manufactures.—Antiquity.—Falling banks.—Fishing on Kínjor Lake.—Sonda.—Aspect of the country.—Alligators.—Alligator feast.—Beluches.—Arabs.—A shooting match.—Jírk.—Arts in Sind.—Haïderábád Mausoléa.—Lakkat.—Shooting.—Hawking.—Archery.

THE depressed shore of Sind offers no remarkable object to the mariner's eye. The coast-line is submerged at spring-tides, when the delta of the Indus resembles a low champagne tract of verdure, with tufts of mangrove dotted along its seaward edge; and the approach to the embouchure of this far-famed stream has a dreary and unpromising aspect. Entering by the Hajámari mouth, we wound up its tortuous channel to Bander-Vikkar on Saturday the 17th of December, and there exchanged our sea-going boats for the Sindian *dúndi*, or river craft.

Sind has two ports, Vikkar and Karáchí. The former, situated on the river, is used only for the export of rice, the staple of Lower Sind; while in the latter, lying just without the delta, centres the foreign trade of the country. It is plain to all who are conversant with nautical affairs that Karáchí is the only safe seaport for the valley of the Indus. When the season is favourable the merchant may indeed send his goods direct to the mouth of the Indus; but everything here is subject to such constant change—the weather, the depth of water, the channels, and the very embouchure itself—that this voyage, even in February, is not without its hazards. As the danger is more in approaching the river than in quitting it, the exports may, in November, December, and January, be sent direct from its mouth: but all imports should go to Karáchí, which affords the only safe anchorage during the other nine months of the year.

After a short stay at Vikkar permission arrived from Haïderábád for the mission to ascend the Indus, when, threading the upward portion of the Hajámari, we entered upon the main stream at the village of Síyá'han.

In the neighbourhood of Vikkar is the imbedded hull of a Dutch brig-of-war, pierced for fourteen guns, affording proof, if any were wanting, of the ever-changing course of the Indus. It is vain in the delta of such a river to identify existing localities with descriptions handed down to us by the historians of Alexander the Great. The whole country from Kach'h to Karáchí is alluvial, and none of its spontaneous productions, the tamarisk tree for instance, exhibit the growth of a century. Higher up the course of the river, where its channels are more permanent, this tree attains to a large size, and this never being the case in the delta, our conclusion would appear legitimate, the soil at both places being the same.

Could the northern apex of the delta be as easily fixed as its triangular sides can be defined, we might then venture to speculate on the probability of Alexander having visited Kach'h or Gujerat. Burnes has, I think, shown that the mouth by which the Grecian fleet left the Indus was the modern Pítí. The "dangerous rock" of Nearchus completely identifies the spot; and as it is still in existence, without any other within a circle of many miles, we can wish for no stronger evidence. But I must own that, though both tradition and formation attest the Run of Kach'h as having in former years been an inland sea, I should, considering the short detention of the fleet at Pattala, be more inclined to look for the lake of Alexander's historian within the limits of the modern delta of the Indus than to appropriate the Run for its site. *Dunds*, or large sheets of stagnant water, formed by the annual rise of the river, still exist on the line of the Pinyárí. These abound in fish of a large size; and, though differing from marine species, the Greeks who state their identity may here be supposed, without impugning Arrian's veracity, to have come to this conclusion more from the large size of the fish in the lake than from a very minute examination of their varieties. Supposing then the Pinyárí to have been the eastern arm of the delta in the days of the Greeks, we should fix the site of Pattala where now stands the modern town of Jírk. But, as before observed, the absence of tangible localities involves us in a maze of doubt; and hence our deductions are oftener the result of fancy than sound inference.

The old Dutch-built vessel mentioned above affords negative evidence that the mouths of the Indus in her day were not more accessible than at present. She is built for shoal waters, as her sailing draft could never have much exceeded six feet. Her construction, like the "galliot," is round-sided, flat-floored, with little depth of hold—all qualities adapted to shallow seas. Her length is seventy-one feet and her width of beam twenty-five. The port-sills are now about two feet and a half above the ground, and the nearest stream (the Síyá'han) is distant 200 yards from the wreck. From 300 to 400 rounds of shot and shell, together with twenty musket-barrels and some pieces of brass and iron ordnance, were disinterred from her after-hold. The shot was of every calibre, from an ounce ball to a 12-pounder; and along with other rusty articles was forwarded to Haïderábád for the satisfaction of that court. The Amírs, we may well imagine, were better satisfied with this present than with a somewhat similar one since made them from Karáchí, when some 32-pound shot were lodged by H.M. ship "Wellesley" in the walls of its castle.

We have tolerable evidence that the Indus has never been more or less navigable than we now find it to be. Tavernier, nearly two centuries ago, said, "At present the commerce of T'hat'hah, which was formerly great, is much diminished, as the mouth of the river is always getting worse, and the sand, by increasing, scarcely gives room for a passage." Again, Captain Hamilton, who speaks very favourably of the Indus, marched, in the year 1699, with a caravan from Lari-bander to T'hat'hah, so that in his time there was a portage the same as at present;

and we are thus warranted in concluding that the navigable capabilities of the stream were then not greater than they now are. And lastly, Mr. Crow, a very accurate observer, who, at the close of last century, was the East India Company's agent at T'hat'hah, thus writes :—" The Indus, as a river, has few merits, except its periodical swell; its stream is foul and muddy, and so full of shoals and shifting sands, that flat boats only are safe, and scarcely any others used."

Every one who has written of Sind mentions the gross ignorance and timidity of her people; and last year at this place my introduction to them was marked by an occurrence somewhat confirmatory of this opinion. When the little steamer I then commanded entered the river, she was boarded by a deputation headed by the Nawab[1] of Vikkar. On their taking leave, some of the party would, contrary to advice, persist in crowding into the ship's punt. Pushing off from the vessel, the little boat heeled to one side, on which half a dozen frightened Sindis ran to the other; and the boat, as we all expected, turned keel-up, and swamped the deputation. Fortunately there was little current, and, the firm bank being at hand, no lives were lost.

The deltas of large rivers (the Nile excepted) are usually too monotonous to interest the eye. In the Indus, after passing the belt of mangrove that margins the sea-coast, and ramifies wherever the water is brackish, we meet with the tamarisk and reedy-grass,[2] varied occasionally with a solitary Parkinsonia,[3] which here, like the cocoa-nut palm on the coast of Africa, denotes the near neighbourhood of man.

When opposite to Pír Putta we rode over and visited this ziarat.[4] The hill upon which the buildings stand is of crescent shape, and from its northern brow you look down on a sheet of

---

[1] Governor.

[2] This gigantic grass attains the height of twelve and eighteen feet, and is often so dense on the banks of the river that it is difficult to force a path through it. It is most luxuriant between B'hkur and Mittun-Kote. The plant has a graceful stalk, often three-eighths of an inch in diameter, from the top of which droops a fringe resembling a feather. The Sindian name is Cáná. The stalk is jointed like the bamboo, but one-third of its whole length, measuring from the top, is continuous. This portion is called teli, and used in the construction of baskets, while of the other part a useful description of mat is fabricated, known by the name of kerī.

[3] Parkinsonia Aculea.

[4] Place of pilgrimage.

water in the stagnant Bagár, once a principal branch, but now a deserted bed, of the Indus. A ruin rises from the other horn of the crescent, while the space between contains the tombs of holy men. The elevated site of Pír Putta, and the beautiful white stucco with which its walls are covered, render it a remarkable object amid the dead flats of the delta; and it is discerned from the river long before you come abreast of the shrine. The saint who is here interred is said to have been contemporary with Saadi, the Persian poet, who flourished in the thirteenth century of our era. Pilgrims, while here, are supported by the chief of the district, who has stored up for their consumption large quantities of grain and ghí.[1] It is customary for strangers to contribute to this fund, and likewise to bestow some gift on the shrine. We gave alms to the poor, but were not permitted to take leave without being reminded that something was due to the tomb itself. Sind abounds in the remains of saints, and her morals are corrupted and her wealth dissipated by their depraved followers. This shrine is, next to that of Lal Shah-baz, at Sihwan, the most revered in the country.

The hills on which Pír Putta stands are of the limestone formation, with which a shelly deposit is largely incorporated. They rise about two miles south of the temple, take a northerly direction, dip under the bed of the Bagár, and reappear on the other side of the Mukalí hills, by which name they are known at T'hat'hah. Three and a half miles north-north-west of the town the range terminates; its general direction being about north-by-east, and south-by-west. The hills are tabular, but often disconnected, and their greatest elevation, I should think, under 100 feet. Their surface is barren of vegetation, if we except the milk-bush[2] and pelú[3] tree.

T'hat'hah is a place interesting to modern geographers, from its being the supposed site of the Grecian Pattala; but is better known in Hindustan by the fine productions of her looms. The town lies at the foot of the Mukalí hills, in the alluvial valley of the river, and three miles distant from its stream. The mounds of rubbish upon which the houses are piled slightly

[1] Clarified butter.   [2] A species of euphorbia.   [3] Salvadora Persica.

raise its site above the level of the valley. In the season of inundation its environs abound in swamps, and after heavy rain pools of stagnant water are numerous, both within the city and in its suburbs. Good dwellings are scarce; and, from the very perishable materials of which most of them are constructed, there is considerable trouble in keeping them in repair. A heavy shower of rain, by shedding their mud-plaster, disfigures the outside of a house that may yet be comfortable within, and gives an appearance of poverty where it may not really exist. Still, making a fair deduction for defective architecture, and the squalid habits of Sindís, the present state of T'hat'hah is the reverse of prosperous, while her inhabitants wear that blanched, sickly hue, the faithful index of an unhealthy clime. In the summer of 1836 I had ample reason to denounce this place as an unhealthy locality; an opinion which the sickness of our troops cantoned there during the year 1839 has unhappily verified.[1]

The manufacture for which this town has acquired some commercial celebrity in the East is the *lungí*, a rich fabrication of silk, cotton, and gold, variegated in pattern and of close texture. The raw silk in most estimation with the weaver is that from the Persian province of Ghilan.

On the hills behind T'hat'hah are the tombs of many a by-gone generation. The ground for a distance of four miles is one burial place. Many of the larger mausoleums, though falling to decay, are yet noble structures. The architecture cannot be referred to any of the legitimate orders, but there is a sombreness and solidity about it that well becomes the grave. Above the entrance door to one small neat enclosure, containing different-sized tombs, apparently those of the several members of one family, was inscribed in Arabic the single word *Allah* (God). Supposing them to have been struck by "the pestilence that walketh in darkness, or by the destruction that wasteth at noon-day,"[2] what word could better express the anguish of the lone survivor?

In the neighbourhood of T'hat'hah are the ruins of Kullan-Kote and Sami-Nuggur, places to which the natives ascribe a

---

[1] See a Report to Government, on the Inundation of the Indus, published at Bombay in 1837.　　　　[2] Psalm xci. 6.

high antiquity. The latter is a diminutive earthy mound three miles north-north-west of the town, built over with hovels; its elevation above the valley, and consequent security from inundation, having attracted inhabitants to it. Kullan-Kote, or "the Large Fort," is four miles from T'hat'hah, in a south-west direction. It is a fortified hill three-quarters of a mile in length by about seven hundred paces broad, and at one time was evidently surrounded by water, though the lake is now confined to its north and north-west angles. The outer wall in many parts is standing, but there are no vestiges within from which to conjecture what its internal arrangements may have been. The face of the hill overhanging the lake has a disturbed appearance. The rock is split into deep chasms, and huge blocks of conglomerate lie scattered below. A spot so suited to the Hindú ascetic has not escaped the wandering fakír: their habitations are, however, modern.[1]

From the advantageous site of T'hat'hah for commercial purposes, it is probable that a mart has existed in its neighbourhood from the earliest times. But as the apex of the delta is not a fixed point the site of this city must have varied as the river changed. As a place of traffic it would naturally be situate close to the stream, and exposed to its ravages; nor is it likely that the buildings of the ancient city were more substantial than those of the modern T'hat'hah, which, standing in the valley of the same wayward river, is still liable to similar calamities. Hence we have a series of names, Dewul, T'hat'hah, Brahminabad, Nuggur—T'hat'hah, and Sami-Nuggur, by which this commercial mart was known to successive dynasties, or perhaps bestowed on occasions when the river's encroachments rendered a change of site necessary. Deterred from the erection of any permanent stronghold in the plain, the inhabitants would naturally look to the neighbouring hills for refuge. The commanding situation of Kullan-Kote afforded them this, and

[1] In Kullan-Kote a quantity of wheat or barley was discovered in a state of charcoal. The incorruptibility of this combination of carbon is well known, and looking at the locality where the grain was found, it may have lain there for centuries, if not since the days of the Macedonian. We may perhaps infer from this discovery that Kullan-Kote has been destroyed by fire.

its name (*the large fort*) seems to imply its having been a place of refuge in times of danger. The love of building, restrained by natural causes in the valley, found full scope for its indulgence on the Mukalí ridge behind the town. Here, neither labour nor expense has been spared, but only for the absurd purpose of giving the dead better accommodation than the living.

Leaving T'hat'hah on the 10th of January, we looked in at Ratti, a little village on the opposite shore; where, in the opinion of one of its fair inhabitants at least, I had been an unwelcome visitor the preceding year. The circumstances were these:— the steamer had moored just below the village, when, at about seven o'clock in the evening, we were startled by a loud continuous noise, like the rush of falling water or the rolling of distant thunder. The up-heaving of the river and quick heavy roll of the vessel told us that part of the bank had given way. Before the water could regain its level another and another mass fell into the stream. We landed and surveyed the scene. Since sunset a great alteration had taken place in the bank of the river. One house had been ingulfed, and its inmates were now busy removing to a place of safety what had been saved from the wreck. Large fires were blazing on the verge of the bank, by help of which, the people were endeavouring to find where the next mass would part. Those whose houses stood nearest the stream were employed conveying their goods and chattels further back, aware that though the river's caprice might grant a respite for a day or two or more, yet its ravages would only be the more destructive when they were renewed: for when the current inclines to a new channel, the opposing bank must continue to be undermined until a shoal is formed, sufficient to give a new direction to the stream. The night was still and dark, save the dull sonorous sound of the plunging mass booming across the turbid waters, on which the beacon fires shed a leaden glare. The people are so accustomed to these visitations, that no screams were heard, nor was there a look of terror on any countenance: but one of the sufferers, the crabbed old lady to whom I have alluded, was uncharitable enough to attribute this disaster to the presence of the *firingis* (Europeans).

When the waters of the Indus are low, the noise caused by the tumbling in of its banks occurs so frequently as to become a characteristic of this river. During the silence of night the ear is assailed by what at first might be mistaken for the continued discharge of artillery; two, three, and even four reports are often heard within the minute, and even thirteen have been counted in that short space of time. In the angles of the reaches the occurrence is most frequent; but its effects being then mostly confined to worthless sand-banks, are attended with little detriment to the inhabitants.

On the 14th of the month we were abreast of Hiláyá, a village on the west bank of the stream, where hearing of a lake not far distant, we went to it. On the road we passed a small venerable looking square enclosure of plain freestone, which our guide informed us was the tomb of Jam Tamatchí, the father of Indus fishermen. It had its legend, which a Sindian gave us, pointing to an individual who, we were informed, was lineally descended from the Jam. Tradition is always worthy of a hearing; but if the Celtic bards of our own land are liable to the charge of having contributed to corrupt the sources of history, the fables current in Sind may be charged with the heavier offence of having directed its stream.

The method of fishing in Kínjor lake, though practised elsewhere in Sind, was new to me. Below that part of the water to be fished a line of nets supported on stakes runs right across the lake. At intervals along this barrier line short circular nets opening inwards are attached, like so many outworks of a fortification. These project considerably above the water, and are formed of double stakes, one perpendicular and level with the surface, the other long and slanting backwards. Between these hangs a bag-net, into which the fish falls when it tries to escape by leaping. The figure represents the position of the stakes.

When the nets are placed, a fleet of small boats assemble in the direction A at the head of the lake, and dispersing over its surface bear down on the barrier net. As the object of the fishermen is to frighten their prey, *tom-toms*,[1] *tambourins, triangles, cooking-pots,* and *shields,* are pressed into use for the occasion, and most discordant are the sounds that ensue. The fish driven before their pursuers, make for the opposite end of the lake at B, and encountering the principal net, are, in their endeavours to double it, piloted into a bastion. Here, their exit opposed on every side, and the noise increasing, they try to leap over what they cannot pass through; but however high they jump, it is only to drop into the trap prepared for them.

We halted next day near a village called Sonda. Hitherto the appearance of the country bordering the river had been monotonous and dreary. Here we had an agreeable change. From the head of the Hiláyá reach, on looking south, we could, for twelve miles, trace a noble stream full half a mile wide, and throughout the whole of that distance, as straight as an arrow in its course. The west bank for some distance to the south is lined by a low range of sandstone hills, between which and the river lies a belt of fine babool[2] trees. The opposite bank, though for a shorter distance, is clad with similar mimosa, and from among their dark foliage on both sides of the river little white turreted towers occasionally show themselves to the river voyager. The barometer gave 136 feet for the height of the ridge, in climbing which we roused, from under a prickly pear bush, a savage-looking hyena.

At this spot the Indus takes a sharp turn, and in the bend is a projecting rocky ledge, under cover of which, on its south side, alligators love to sun themselves. They are the *guryial* or long snouted variety, and are harmless, at least I never heard of their being otherwise. It is strange that at Karáchí, a place so close to the Indus, fakírs should possess the other species, none of which are met with in the river. Among the outlying hills that skirt the Hala mountains, about nine miles from that town is a hot spring, the temperature of which, where it wells from the earth, is 136° of Fahrenheit. The stream irrigates a small valley and supplies some swamps with water, in which the fakírs keep numbers of tame alligators. The pond where we saw the congregated herd at feeding time was about eighty yards long

---

[1] An Indian drum.   [2] Mimosa Arabica.

and perhaps half as many wide. It was shallow and studded with small grass-covered islets, the narrow channels between which would only admit of a single alligator passing through at a time. Two goats were slaughtered for that morning's repast, during which operation a dozen scaly monsters rose out of their slimy bed, crawled up the back of the tank, and eyed with evident satisfaction the feast preparing for them. All being ready, a little urchin, not nine years old, stepped without our circle, and calling *ow, ow, (come, come)* the whole tribe was in motion, and as soon as the amphibious animals had gained *terra firma*, the meat was distributed. Each anxious to secure a piece at his neighbour's expense, the scene that ensued was ludicrous enough, and not a little disgusting. A hind-quarter of a goat gave rise to a general engagement. One by one the combatants drew off till the prize remained in the grasp of two huge monsters. Their noses all but touching, each did his best to drag the bloody morsel from the jaws of his adversary: and a long struggle ensued, in which, by turning and tossing, twisting and writhing, they strove for the mastery. It was a drawn battle; for the leg was torn asunder, and each retained his mouthful, when, with heads erect, they sought the water, showing as they crawled along considerable tact in avoiding their less successful neighbours.[1]

---

[1] The wandering propensities of these animals, together with the disappearance of several children at Mugger Pir, have led to their removal from the lagoon mentioned in the narrative, and their confinement in a small enclosure surrounded by a high wall. In the centre is a deep pool supplied by a hot spring, and in this, a seething mass of filth, the hideous creatures wallow. The water in this pool is somewhat denser than oil, and in colour resembling pitch, whilst the effluvium given forth renders it impossible to remain long within its influence. On throwing the carcase of a goat into this den it was at once seized and dismembered. Here and there two animals, unable to sever a morsel by merely tugging, were to be observed the one holding fast whilst the other by a series of revolutions tore the bones or tough sinews asunder. A few moments sufficed to make an end of the goat, and quiet succeeded the splashing and plunging attendant upon the dining of a family of alligators. It was a horrid scene, and the imagination and pencil of a Doré alone could adequately convey a correct impression of the malignantly cruel and hateful appearance of those creatures. The collection is certainly unique, as I doubt the existence elsewhere of objects of veneration so strangely selected. Ere long Mugger Pir will be a thing of the past, for, owing to their pestiferous habitat, the alligators are rapidly dying off.

I should have mentioned before, that for escort duty the mission was provided with a small detachment of Arabs from the Rajcote residency. These men had not yet all joined, and at T'hat'hah twelve Beluches of the Jokíyah tribe were hired to accompany us through Sind. They entered our service with the greatest readiness, and proved by their subsequent conduct that they fully merited the confidence reposed in them.

Late events have unfortunately but too well established the insatiable appetite of the Beluche race for rapine. But let us not forget the wide distinction between the guilt of plundering an invading army's commissariat, and that of robbing the merchant or traveller. Both of these classes may with some confidence appeal to the honour of the tribes, and except being mulct in heavy duties have rarely suffered any loss, even among those natives who were the most active in harassing our troops. There is much to be said for these misguided people. Where clanship prevails, the chief and not his men is responsible for the actions of the tribe. The Khán of Kelat has since paid the penalty of his folly; yet, though disloyal to Shah Shuja, he gave his life to the cause he had espoused,—and who will venture to malign the motives of the man who set such a seal to his principles? During the late campaign across the Indus, it has been customary for some of the Indian journals to brand both Beluche and Afghan as cowards. The first are doubtless a vaunting race, but the storming of Kelat proved them good men and true. At Ghizni, though taken at a disadvantage, the resistance our troops encountered from an unprepared garrison shows of what the Afghans are composed. It is harsh to use such hard words against any nation, especially when we recollect there are pages in the early history of our own country, during the struggles between the English and Scotch for example, when the troops that fought bravely one day, acted like very cowards the next. A disorderly rabble, though composed of men individually brave, can offer no effectual resistance to disciplined battalions; but were the same men brigaded, officered and hedged about with cannon, they would soon become formidable soldiers.[1] We have proved this in India,

[1] The experience of later years has proved how correct was Captain Wood's estimate of the Afghan and Beluche character. Two well known

and Russia has done the same both with the Persian and the Turk. Far be it from me to palliate the many cruel murders of defenceless camp followers of which these men, both Afghan and Beluche, have been guilty. Yet man in his semi-barbarous state is so little given to reflection, and so much the child of impulse, that in judging of his actions where our own interests are at stake, we are apt to be swayed by prejudice and passion where reason only should decide. But to return to the Jokíyahs.

A question had arisen as to whether these mountaineers or the Arabs were the better marksmen, and it was agreed that an hour's practice should decide. A bottle was placed on a sand-bank, about seventy yards off, to hit which entitled the winner to a canister of gunpowder. Round followed round, and still the bottle stood unhurt; at length the Jumtí's mírbar [1] detected that the line of fire was direct on Mecca; and this discovery, while it opened the eyes of both parties to the cause of their former failures, had the additional effect of restoring their lost good humour. The bottle was shifted, and confidently this time did the marksmen kneel and take aim; but it was to no better purpose, not one of them could hit the mark, the alteration made having neither steadied the hand, nor improved the visual organs of either party.

A southerly gale springing up, our sails were soon opened before it, and by sunset of the 18th the fleet reached Haïderábád.

---

regiments of our Indian army are now formed almost exclusively of these men. Within the last sixteen years these corps have alternately served in three campaigns (Persia, India, and Abyssinia), and also done good service in China and Japan. So far from their deserving the stigma of cowardice, their fault, if such it be, has been an over anxiety to press forward; and we find in the War Office record of the Abyssinian expedition, a wing of the 1st Beluche Light Infantry noted as having made the most rapid march of any troops engaged. Men in a body well led are generally brave, but with the individuals composing these tribes courage is hereditary. As soldiers they are quick at learning their work, orderly and respectful, and though they are troublesome at times from an untameable mountain spirit, serious insubordination is rarely met with. Such material, well and sufficiently officered, provides a nucleus from which troops, worthy (when out of India) of reliance in every particular, are easily procurable; and having neither the ordinary caste prejudices of our Indian subjects, nor objection to travel, they would prove a most formidable enemy even should it ever be necessary to lead them against Europeans.

[1] Captain of state barge.

The preceding day had been passed at anchor, the heavy sand drift rendering it next to impossible for the crews either to track or sail the boats. Jírk was the only place of size which we passed, and in order to obtain some compass bearings I had occasion to visit it. The town is about midway between T'hat'hah and Haïderábád, close to the river, on the summit of a table-hill belonging to the sandstone ridge where the alligators bask. Its houses have stone wind-sails fronting the prevailing wind, by which means a stream of pure air is made to circulate through the several apartments when, out of doors, scarce a breath of wind seems stirring. This method of ventilation is very general in Sind, and none but those who have passed the greater portion of the twenty-four hours in a feverish state of existence, with the thermometer at 100° of Fahrenheit, can duly appreciate its use.

In a turner's shop in Jírk we saw a well-finished article turned off the lathe. It was only a drinking bowl, but the delicacy of touch with which the colours were laid on far exceeded my ideas of Sindian skill. Many of these people have naturally a turn for mechanics; witness the beautiful gun-barrels made all over the country, the much-admired products of the T'hat'hah loom, and a very handsome description of orange-shaped box, manufactured at Haïderábád; which last, when it finds its way into the British provinces, is placed upon the same side-table with the rarities of China and Japan. Timber being scarce in Sind, much ingenuity is often displayed in the patch-work of their boats, and individuals are to be met with who have successfully imitated the construction of musical boxes and other ingenious contrivances, and articles of fancy work.[1]

The mission remained a fortnight at Haïderábád; but as many descriptions of this court and capital are already before the public, I need not dwell upon the subject.

---

[1] The beautiful specimens of Sind lacquer ware and embroidery forwarded to the Kensington Museum, show the capability of the natives of that country to produce examples of those arts worthy in their way of comparison with similar productions from any part of the world. The Sind pottery is also greatly admired, and I am given to understand would find a ready market here, as considerable inquiry has been made regarding it, and the quantity sent has been quickly sold.

Before quitting the city we visited the tombs in its neighbourhood, and well were we repaid for the trouble. The hill on which the town stands is a mile and a half in length and seven hundred yards broad. Its direction is about north-by-east and south-by-west, whilst its height may be eighty feet. On the north end of this plateau are the tombs, and at its opposite extreme is the fort and town. The tombs of the deceased members of the reigning family are grouped a little apart from those of the preceding dynasty. Of the Talpurs, that of the reigning family Mír Kuram Ali is the only fine structure. Display characterized this chief in life, and a love of pomp seems to have gone down with him to the grave. It is a quadrangular building, with a turret rising from each corner, and a handsome central dome. But the mausoleum of Gholam Shah, of the Kalorá dynasty displayed by the Talpurs, is far superior to all the others. Its figure resembles that of Kuram Ali's, but without the corner turrets. The purest parian marble lines the inside of the building, which is highly ornamented with mosaic work and decorated with sentences from the Koran. The tombs of the Kalorás are neglected, but those of the reigning family are kept in tolerable repair.

The chief, Amír Nur Mohamed Khán, was evidently solicitous that his reception of the mission, and the sentiments he professed to entertain for the British government, should make a proper impression. Whilst guests at his capital we had been honourably entertained, and now that we were to resume our journey northwards, we were invited by him to accompany himself and his brother, Mír Nasír Khán, in a visit they were about to make to some Shikárgáhs (game preserves) at Lakkat, about forty miles north of Haïderábád, and which lay in our line of march.

The attachment of the Sind Amírs to field sports is well known. To gratify this passion, large tracts of land on the banks of the river are set apart for game-preserves, and kept in a state of nature. For so doing the Amírs have been censured, though I am inclined to think with too great severity. Were the population of Sind double its present number, there is ample land for their support without infringing on the ruler's prerogative. The exclusive privileges enjoyed by their Highnesses is not peculiar to Sind, but one that has prevailed in most countries in a similar state of society. The history of our own land more especially offers numerous examples of oppressive forest-laws. Hume tells us, that a king of England possessed sixty-eight forests, thirteen chases, and seven hundred and eighty-one parks. Further, that transgressors in these were, in Richard the First's reign, punished by mutilation and the loss of sight. No Sind Amír ever thus sported with the life of the subject.

Around Lakkat the country is covered with jungle, among which are the game-preserves. On reaching the village, the Amírs presented each of us with a suit of Lincoln green, after receiving which we were warned to be ready on the morrow. By sunrise next day we were on the hunting ground. The shikrágáhs are laid out in the form of triangles, and so connected that the game, on escaping from one enclosure takes refuge in another. Thus:—Entering No. 1, we took our station in a rustic booth at its apex, and patiently awaited the game's approach.

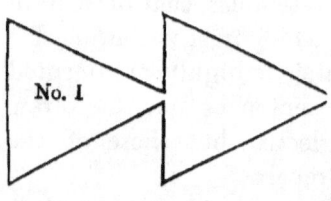

The shikárgáh was a thick forest of young trees, with plenty of underwood and tolerable herbage. In front of us was an open space of about ten yards square, and, for double this distance beyond, the forest was indented by narrow pathways radiating from the booth. A pack of dogs had been let in at the opposite end of the enclosure, and we had not sat long before we heard the noise of their approach. The jackal early took alarm; but seeming conscious it had only the dogs to fear, the cunning animal trotted leisurely across the cleared space into the next shikrágáh. Mír Nur Mohamed 'sat with a couple of guns before him, watching with a painful earnestness the jungle in front. At length in one of the lanes, a boar, a grizzly-looking patriarch, was detected showing his tushes. The Amír nodded and gave a gun to Captain Burnes; and had our gallant commander broken a bottle a hundred yards off, his skill as a marksman could not have been more highly complimented than for slaughtering this huge boar at arm's length. A few minutes more elapsed, when the underwood was seen to shake, and presently a deer broke cover. He came dashing down the green lanes at a gallant pace, but ere he could clear the break he was despatched by a ball from Nur Mohamed's rifle. It was an excellent shot. We beat up two preserves, but all the game they yielded was a couple of deer[1] and eight hogs.

We next attended their Highnesses on a hawking excursion; but the banks of the Indus were not here sufficiently open for this old English pastime. The Amírs nevertheless expatiated on the pleasure this sport afforded them, and enumerated the variety of birds in their possession, all which, they added, come from Afghanistan. Food was procured for the smaller of these falcons by a kind of archery that I never saw practised elsewhere. There is nothing particular about either the bow or the arrow, but in using the weapons the archer darted the arrow so as to strike the object with its side instead of its head. The larks, which he was shooting, were picked up stunned by the shock, but alive. Partridges are shot in the same manner.

At Lakkat I left my companions, and returned to Haïderábád, from which place my examination of the Indus commenced, the section of the river south of the capital having been accomplished the preceding year. From this time I only met the mission occasionally when it halted at the large marts on the Indus, for the purpose of procuring information on their trade and commerce.

[1] The kotapacha, or hog-deer.

CHAPTER II.

Halla.—Manufacture of earthenware.—Chunniah.—Ruins of Khodábád.—Altars of Alexander.—Otters.—Black partridge.—Castle at Sihwan.—River and crops.—Absence of trees.—Pulla-fish.—Fisheries.—Dur-myaní.—Wullí Mohamed Laghari.—Arrival of Dr. Lord.—Arore.—Mulala.—Importunity of Fakirs.—Anecdote.—B'hkur, Rorí, Sukur.—Sand storm.—Battle of Sukur.—A Mohamedan's beard.

SEPARATED from head-quarters, and by the nature of my employment restricted to the river, our intercourse with the Sindis was now mostly confined to river-lying tribes. The country indeed holds out no temptation to stray inland, and but few of its towns repay the visitant for the trouble he is at in getting to them. Halla and Khodábád we had been informed were exceptions; and on the 21st of February, being abreast of these places, I paid them a visit.

Halla is divided into the old and new town. The last division is much the larger of the two, and is the most considerable place between Haïderábád and Sihwan. Like the last mentioned town, it derives no small degree of importance from the shrine of a Mohamedan saint, that of Pír Mukdum Nu. The land around is highly impregnated with salt, and what little cultivation I noticed is confined to an old bed of the Indus, close to the smaller Halla. The bázár is partially roofed, but however effectual the covering may be as a defence against the sun, it does not keep out rain, for when we were here the ground beneath it was a perfect puddle. The bustle of its bázár showed that the place was thriving; and if agriculture does not flourish, the mechanical arts apparently do. Halla has been long noted for its excellent earthenware and Sindian caps. The latter being national, are worn by all classes, rich and poor, privileged and oppressed. The prosperity of the capmaker is evinced by numerous symbols of his craft in the shape of stout round-headed posts, which, standing out in the streets, fronting the shop-door, are more like kerb stones than signposts.

The manufacture of earthenware is confined to the new town. Here are two establishments, one employing six furnaces, and the other two. The clay is taken from the bed of the Indus, and the wheel upon which it is worked is evidently the potter's wheel of Scripture. The patterns are various, and such as are intended to contain rose-water, or slabs for the decoration of tombs, are tastefully executed, the latter especially being remarkable for warmth of tone and brilliancy of colour. The metallic oxides used are those of iron, copper, and lead.[1] In the composition of the finer articles, ground flints form a principal ingredient.

An earthy, soap-like substance that the natives term "*chunniah*" is obtained from lakes not far from Halla. Chunniah is largely eaten by the women of Sind.

The ruins of Khodábád are situated a little to the north-west of Halla, and cover two square miles of ground. It was a favourite residence of the Talpurs, and here many of their chiefs have been interred. Under one dome, and side by side, lie the founder of the dynasty, Futi Ali Khán, and his brother Mír Gholam Ali; while in an adjoining mausoleum are deposited the remains of Byram, Bejur, and Sobdar, chiefs of the same house, who suffered severely from the tyranny and vindictive spirit of the latter Kalórás. The mausoleum of Futi Ali is small yet neat, built entirely of red freestone, the only marble used being for the prayer-slab that fronts his grave. The other tombs are of a still simpler construction. The three chiefs lie on the same platform, and their graves are protected from the elements by a light canopy supported on pillars.

The tombs just mentioned are the only buildings in Khodábád which are in even tolerable preservation; of the dwellinghouses not one is entire. Little more than thirty years have

---

[1] Moordar Sung, the common litharge or protoxide of lead.

elapsed since this city rivalled Haïderábád in size and population. How perishable then must be the architecture of Sind! and, in a region such as this, how apt will the antiquary be to invest, in the ardour of his search, mounds of yesterday's formation with the sanctity of ages! In a mud basin undergoing continual change, such as the valley of the Indus south of the mountains, it is almost vain to look, after the lapse of so many centuries, for indications of the Grecian general's march. The Panjáb rivers are similarly circumstanced; it is therefore no matter for surprise that the altars erected by Alexander on the banks of the Hyphases have not been discovered. I do not think the account given by his historians favours the idea of their having been erected in the Alpine regions of the Panjáb. Alexander was evidently crossing the *plains* when the mutiny occurred that necessitated his return. In such a time of ferment the most easterly limit of his line of march would in all probability be the site of his altars, and the chances therefore are that they have long since been swept away by the changing streams of the Beas or the Sutledj.

On the evening of the 22nd of February, as the crew were securing our boat to the bank, they discovered a family of otters, which by their angry cries seemed to consider us intruders. Anxious to obtain one, an attack was forthwith planned, but though no precautions were omitted it was only partially successful. Two were made prisoners, and as many more escaped. The latter refused, however, to quit the neighbourhood, and throughout the night serenaded us with piercing shrieks, which were redoubled whenever the captives replied to their call. The two we had taken were full grown, but evidently the young of those which had escaped. The habitation of these interesting little animals had two entrances, which met before they reached their inner circular burrow, and were elevated four feet above the river, which in this month was at its lowest level. Two days after these otters had been taken I was awoke in the middle of the night by a noise proceeding from the fore-part of the vessel, and on inquiring the cause was told we were boarded by otters from the shore. When I got on deck the assailants were swimming alongside, giving utterance to a sharp peevish whine whilst those on board, after vainly struggling to get free of the bag that held them, grew calm, but still continued a low piteous moan. Whether the visitors were the parents of our captives, or strangers attracted to the boat by their calls, is matter of doubt. In either case the circumstance is remarkable, for since the 22nd we had moved ten miles onward, and crossed from the left to the right bank of the Indus.

When in the delta, the matins of the lark told us when day had dawned; but here the song of this early warbler is often interrupted by the partridge's call. In addition to the common grey partridge, Sind possesses another species of striking beauty. The head, breast, and belly of this bird are of a jetty black. A red ring encircles the neck. The back of the head is speckled white and black, while a large white spot is dotted under each eye. The wing-feathers are spotted yellow on a black ground. Those of the tail are short and downy, marked by delicate white and black bars towards their extremes. This is a heavier and altogether a nobler looking bird than the other. From the predominance of dark feathers in its plumage, it is usually called the black partridge.

On Friday, the 3rd of March, we passed Sihwan, famous in Sind for the shrine at Lal Shah-baz, and equally notorious for its beggars and courtesans. The castle is an object of interest to Europeans, from the bare possibility of its being one of those beleaguered by the Macedonians. Burnes speaks of it thus: "By far the most singular building at Sihwan, and perhaps on the Indus, is the ruined castle overlooking the town, which in all probability is as old as the age of the Greeks. It consists of a mound of earth sixty feet high, and surrounded from the very ground by a brick wall. The shape of the castle is oval, about 1200 feet long by 750 in diameter. The interior presents a heap of ruins, strewed with broken pieces of pottery and brick. The gateway is on the town side, and has been arched: a section through it proves the whole mound to be artificial." It is mournful to contrast Sihwan as we now see it with that city's once flourishing condition. The Ayen Akbari tells us that Sewistan, of which it was the capital, had forty thousand vessels upon the Indus; and, after making a due allowance for the bold assertions of Eastern authors, we learn from such a statement that it must once have been the centre of commerce and wealth. It is a singular coincidence, that the tonnage now upon this river is very nearly equal to what it was in the time of the Greeks. Two thousand vessels of all sorts, from the galley to the tender, are said to have composed the fleet of Alexander, and of these eight hundred are called by his historians vessels of war and transports. During the late military operations in these quarters, the vessels that would come under the latter designation were found to amount to about seven hundred, and if we include the small craft of the fishermen (the tenders of the Greek fleet) we might easily reach the larger number.

The method of building boats on the Indus is illustrative of another circumstance in Alexander's memorable expedition— that of transporting his vessels by land from the Indus to the Jalum (Hydaspes). In this country the sides and bottom of a boat are completed apart, and then brought together to form the vessel. The labour of carrying the largest boat may thus be much lightened, and is an operation of common occurrence in the present day on the banks of the Indus. The Macedonians had been in the habit of doing the same thing at the Isthmus of Corinth, and it thus becomes a question whether boat-building, as practised there, countenances the idea of Sindian naval architecture having had its origin in Greece.

Proceeding onwards, the bed of the river widened, and its immediate banks, when low, were either covered with pulse[1] or oil plants. These crops require no tending, and whether destroyed by the inundation or swept away by the stream, the farmer's loss is light. But valuable produce—such as sugar, indigo, cotton, and grain—requires greater circumspection; and fields of these are seldom seen exposed to such dangers, except when the waywardness of the river, by eating away the bank, has set at nought the most cautious calculations of the husbandman. When this unfortunately happens, as it often does, the bank for some distance above the fields may be observed fenced with tamarisk branches, which has sometimes the effect of preserving it from further waste; should, however, the body

---

[1] Phaseolus Mungo, or *Moong*, and the Phaseolus Aconitofolius, or *moth*.

of the stream have set in on the farmer's land, he must nerve his mind to witness the labour of a whole season lost in a single day.

These constantly recurring changes in the course of the Indus confuse the rights of property on its banks. We are told that geometry owes its origin to the inundations of the Nile destroying the landmarks in its valley. But the Sindians prefer superstition to science, and have resort to the following primitive mode of settling their differences:—Mír Nur Mohamed Khán we shall suppose to possess the east bank of the Indus, and his brother Mír Nasir Khán the west. On the inundation subsiding a new island rises in the stream, to which both parties lay claim. A boat is ordered, and a confidential servant on the part of each Amír, stepping on board, takes with him half a dozen empty earthen jars. The boat is now placed half a mile up-stream, beyond the island, from which position in mid-channel the twelve pots are committed to the guidance of the current. On whatever side the smaller number of these messengers pass by the island, the new-formed land is thereby decided to belong of right to the proprietors on that bank of the river.

This portion of Sind is populous and well cultivated. Numerous villages are seen from the river, and all of them embosomed in trees. Though the country produces no timber available for ship or house building, every village has its clump of evergreen, reared less for ornament than shade. Near Mitaní are a few gigantic peepul-trees,[1] which, standing singly in the fields, have a very agreeable effect. In a country like Sind, where there are no hedges, plantations, copses, or enclosures of any sort, to break the monotony of its level surface, it is good taste to encourage planting. The fakírs, who take a pleasure in gardening, are the great horticulturists of the country. I have known one of them to freight a boat at B'hkur to transport plants to Haïderábád, a distance of near two hundred and fifty miles. These people swarm in Sind, and are the pests of society, for their drain on the working man far more than counterbalances what little good they do; but the fakír here

[1] Figus religiosa.

mentioned deserved well of the community, at least in this instance.

The season for taking the pulla-fish had now commenced, and the animated appearance presented by the river's bank was indeed an agreeable change. Until lately the stream rolled silently onwards, whilst here and there the scattered huts of a few miserable fishermen, a boat occasionally dropping down with the current, or perhaps a herd of cattle swimming the river, were the only indications that the country was peopled. But at this time the Miánís, or villages, that remain unoccupied during one half of the year, become suddenly thronged by a busy and cheerful population. Here may be seen a crowd dragging to land a net of more than ordinary dimensions; while, clustered by the water's edge, stand expectant the children, the aged, and the infirm, all equally eager to learn its contents, and to shout their *Shahbash* should the "haul" exceed their expectation. Passing on, we observe the surface of the river to be dotted with little dark specks, which, on a nearer approach, are discovered to be fishermen supported by earthen jars, or upon dry reeds. Those mounted on the former frail but buoyant bark float much at their ease; not so the poor fellows who ride upon the latter. By degrees the reeds become sodden, and the fisherman's head is then just above water; but to counterbalance this inconvenience, his bark costs him no care, and at the commencement of every trip he launches forth upon a new one. The pulla-fish enters the Indus about the beginning of March, and quits it early in September: that is, they frequent it during the whole time the river is rising or full. In the latter end of May they are caught in the greatest quantity; the drag-net landing sometimes a hundred and fifty at a haul. As we ascend the river the fish is less plentiful. I have met with the pulla as high as Mittun-Kote; but there are no established fisheries north of B'hkur.

The river is portioned out into sections, where the right of fishing is strictly confined to their respective Miánís. The inhabitants of these villages are registered, and, besides giving every third fish to government, a tax in money is levied on the village. The amount was fixed by the Kalórás, and according as the communities have since their time prospered or declined, so is this assessment felt to be light or oppressive; the present government not having as yet made allowance for their altered numbers. The produce of the Miánís is sold by the fishermen on the spot to those who purchase this right of government: for in Sind the revenue is farmed to the highest bidder. The money obtained from these fisheries is part of the Dur-myaní, or general revenue of Sind.

I had heard so much of Wullí Mohamed Lagharí, whose memory is deservedly held dear by all classes in Sind, that when abreast of Lárkhánah I could not refrain from visiting the place of which he had been so long the governor. It is a rambling-built town, situated in a date-grove, on the banks of a fine canal. The necessaries of life are here exceedingly cheap, and water plentiful, whilst the luxuriant foliage of the mangoe-tree affords a cooling resort in warm weather to the inhabitants, who have thus reason for being attached to the spot, and have a Sind proverb—

"Hoard abroad, but squander in Lárkhánah."

It is really cheering to hear of such a character in Sindian annals as that ascribed to the Nawab. Peasant and noble alike applaud his virtues, and the rulers of the land did not refuse to profit by his counsel and advice. Many anecdotes of this chief are told by those who knew him, illustrative of his ready wit, his love of justice, and his deep knowledge of mankind. The following story shows his talents as a keen-sighted politician:— When Mohamed Azim Khán held power in Kabul, he despatched Mudut Khán with 20,000 horsemen to recover the arrears of tribute due by Sind. The Sirdar encamped near Shikárpúr, and sent forward an officer to demand the money. It was refused, and the Court of Haïderábád thought of nothing but repelling the Afghans by force of arms. Before proceeding to this last appeal, the Amírs sent to Lárkhánah for Wullí Mohamed Khán; and he, on being asked his opinion, counselled peace. On this he was saluted by the chiefs in durbar, by the opprobrious name of Wullí Ram, or the Hindú. Nothing daunted, the Nawab looked round, and inquired of the Amírs how high they estimated the life-blood of a Talpur? "Beyond price," was the reply. "Well then," said the sagacious Wullí Mohamed, "victory is in the hands of God; but should you try the fate of battle, whether vanquished or victorious, many of your relations, now present, will be missed at next durbar." This reasoning produced the desired effect; and Wullí Mohamed was forthwith deputed by their Highnesses to compromise matters with the Afghan Sirdar. The Nawab spoke in a different strain to Mudut Khán: "Are your people mad," said the wily chief, "to enter a country as enemies where there are seventy thousand Beluches, *Sahib-i-Shumshir* (excellent swordsmen), in arms to receive you. Try the issue if you will; but first listen to the advice of one partial to your countrymen. You are aware that the strength of Kabul is gone, and that the Vuzir has his hands fully occupied in keeping the tribes in check. You are in a country without a single friend; and if defeated, which it is certain you will be, you cannot expect to see Kabul again. To save your honour, I shall endeavour to persuade the Amírs to give you as road expenses (*nalbundi*) two lacs of rupees." Mudut Khán acceded to the arrangement, received a lac upon the spot, and bills on Kabul for the remainder.

On the 24th we reached Rorí, where, learning that Captain Burnes was expected on the morrow from Khyrpúr, on his way to Shikárpúr, we awaited his arrival. Next day he came in, bringing with him an agreeable addition to our party in the person of Dr. Lord, who had been appointed to the medical charge of the mission when it was first organized; but being at a distance from the Presidency when we left it for the Indus, he had only now been enabled to join us.

The ruins of Arore lie S. 26° E., three miles and a half from Rorí.[1] They occupy a rocky ledge, overlooking what appears to be a deserted arm of the Indus. From the existence of a substantial causeway connecting Arore with the Rorí side, it would seem that this bed, up to a very late date, was submerged by the waters of the inundation. The soil is of superior

---

[1] The ancient capital of upper Sind, also called Alor and Al-Ror. This city was famous in the early Mohamedan history.

quality; and when I visited the spot it was covered, south of the causeway, with crops remarkable for their healthy and luxuriant appearance. The causeway is 480 yards long, fifteen feet wide in the centre, and ten toward the ends. It has a central arch of fifteen feet span, besides five other small ones. The height of the former is ten feet. Arore is also known to the Sindís by the names of Kumun and Jatrí. While here, I heard of the ruins of a place called Mulala, on the east bank of the river, fifty miles to the north of Rorí.

Returning from Arore, we encountered a party of eighty-three fakírs on march for the shrine of Bhawul Huk at Multan. A heavy club graced the shoulder of each, and from it dangled behind a small lota or drinking-cup. They were a sturdy set, with little of the devotee in their looks. As they passed us I involuntarily gave them the road, while my thoughts reverted to an Irish gang on march to Donnybrook fair. The provoking importunity of these people is past belief. Sometimes they will surround your tent, and, what with their horns and stentorian lungs, almost drive you to desperation. While thus noisy and troublesome, their behaviour is often so truly ludicrous, that, though well inclined to be angry, you are constrained to laugh. The Amírs suffer equally with their subjects. I remember once to have seen a fakír make a most determined set on the charity of Mír Nur Mohamed Khán. The fellow would take no refusal; and on the Mír's sharply observing that "beggars on horseback could scarcely be in want," briskly replied, "that all he required was money to buy a saddle." His impudence did not avail him.

At Rorí a low bleak ridge, of limestone and flint formation, crosses the bed of the Indus. On the east bank the rock, crowned by the town of Rorí, rises abruptly from the river, and is washed by a current of four miles an hour at one season of the year, and of nearly double that velocity at another. On the west bank, where the town of Sukur stands, the ridge is depressed and is swept by a narrower and more tranquil stream. In the mid-channel are several islets; the tile-stained turrets on one near the east shore giving it more the appearance of a Chinese pagoda than a Mussulman's tomb. Two of these islands are famous in Sindian story: B'hkur for its strength, and Khadjá Khizr for sanctity. The banks of the river for some distance below B'hkur are fringed with the date-palm; and its appearance, always pleasing, is here heightened by the character of the neighbouring country. On the west bank stand the ruins of Sukur, with its tall minar towering gracefully above the dark date-groves. Red flinty hillocks form the background on both banks; while between them rolls a broad stream, adding beauty to the whole.

The Indus, throughout the whole of its navigable course, is occasionally swept by terrific blasts, which, while they last, prostrate everything before them. Fortunately, they give timely warning of their approach, and long before the gathering storm bursts, the careful tracker has moored his boat in security. At this place, on a subsequent occasion, I witnessed one of those short-lived sand-gales, which in strength and in sublimity of appearance I have never, either before or since, seen equalled. We were then on the Sukur side of the river. On looking across the water about four o'clock in the afternoon, gloomy clouds were seen coming along, their heavy masses evidently pregnant with the elements of a storm. Momentarily they deepened their dark hue, and as the waving masses moved and rose above the date-trees on the opposite shore, the grove almost appeared to be on fire, the boiling cauldron of clouds above representing smoke, while the lighter shades of the dense mass looked like flame. The grove was soon veiled in darkness, and an ominous silence hung over the Sukur bank, while the storm in giant strength stalked over the naked surface of the river, as yet unagitated by the smallest ripple. Presently the gust struck the bank where we stood with the blast of a hurricane, and for two minutes blew with a force which it was impossible to face. Cowering with others behind the pillars of a dilapidated house, though sheltered from the fury of the storm, we had yet ample employment to prevent suffocation from the torrents of sand it carried with it.

Sukur is the place where Shah Shujah, now King of Kabul, defeated the Sindian army in 1834. The expedition which the Shah then undertook for the recovery of his throne was, though thus far fortunate, eventually unsuccessful; and his Majesty, after a variety of hardships and adventures, again returned to his asylum in Lodiana. The slaughter at the battle of Sukur is said to have been considerable, and a still greater number of men are believed to have perished in the Indus than by the sword of the Shah's adventurers. One Sindian chief, high in rank and very corpulent, had taken the precaution of anchoring a boat in the stream, as a means of retreat in case of defeat. Exhausted and breathing hard he gained the boat, but no exertion of her crew could lift him on board. Time pressed, and life is precious. Absorbed with this one thought, he forgot both his dignity and the respect due to a Moslem's beard, and called out to his people, *"Rish bagír!"* (seize the beard)—an expression by which, as a sobriquet, he is still known in Sind.

CHAPTER III.

Shikárpúr.—A fair.—Shoes.—Sindí ignorance.—Bad roads.—Wheeled vehicles.—Predatory tribes.—Unsettled country.—Remarks.—Tiger-prints.—Buffaloes.—Swimming the Indus.—Horned cattle.—Herdsmen.—Plundered village.—Journey to Ahmedpúr.—Bullock-hackeries.—Nawab's Palace.—Guards.—Followers.—Warlike appearance.—Interview with Bhawul Khan.—Bhawulpúr.—A French adventurer.—Uch.—A drunken Afghan.—Arrival at Mittun-Kote.—Indus.—Accounts of the river by ancient and modern authors.

SHIKÁRPÚR did not equal my expectations. I knew of its extensive connexions in Central Asia, and had concluded that a place possessing so widely ramified an agency, and the residence of so many rich bankers, would, in proportion to its commercial importance, have surpassed in appearance the less favoured towns of Sind. But the only point in which it seemed to be superior was in the large and comfortable dwelling-houses of its wealthy Hindú merchants. The bázár is large, wider than usual, and, like that of most eastern towns, roofed over; but the covering was in a sad dilapidated state, while the shops were either ill supplied with goods, or their owners shunned display; it was however well frequented, and from its crowded thoroughfares I should conclude Shikárpúr a populous place.

While here, a Málã or fair was held in the dry bed of the Sind canal, to the banks of which I hurried, with a companion, to witness the festival. This rejoicing is held in honour of the periodical rise of the Indus, the blessings of which they partake of by means of this canal. Our way led through the principal bázár, but, except by a few elderly shopkeepers whom the love of gain still kept at their posts, it was deserted. Outside the city-gates numerous vehicles had taken their stand, which, for a mere trifle, were at the service of foot-passengers. They were in constant request, and many a happy group did we pass, comprised of all ages, sexes, and conditions. We had come out for amusement, but the annoying pressure of a dense crowd speedily made us sensible we were to pay for this pleasure. At length we got into the bed of the canal, and, having rode clear of the crowd, dismounted and secured our camels to the bushes on its banks. On foot we were soon lost among the multitude, with many of whom we had much friendly converse, and being in the native garb we enjoyed the scene without being ourselves objects of remark. Walking down the right bank of the canal, our attention was first drawn to a large peepul-tree, from beneath the spreading foliage of which issued the sounds of music and the song. This was a Hindú Nautch, and the singers were men. The audience were ranged in rows, encircling and pressing close upon, but never jostling, the performers. The females present outnumbered the men, but during the time we remained there was no unbecoming levity in the one sex, nor any quarrelling or drunkenness in the other. The rate of remuneration to the performers was left to the liberality of the audience, and here the cold prudence of the sect was as remarkable, though not so commendable, as their quiet and orderly demeanour.

Neither copper nor silver money were to be seen in the fair. Refreshments were paid for in cowrie-shells, of which there are ninety-six to a pice, the smallest copper coin in circulation.

Leaving the Nautch, we walked up to a party of four demure-looking men, who, in the society of their wives, were quietly enjoying a game at Chopper Kallú.[1] They civilly invited us to a seat on their mats. The game is played like chess, but, instead of sixty-four squares, the Shikárpúr board has ninety-six. Cowries were used as dice, and cone-shaped pieces of ivory for chessmen. We inquired of several such parties what the stakes were, but received for answer that they never played for money.

Observing a number of people entering a large building, we did the same, but, save some pretty faces and a hideous-looking member of the Hindú Pantheon, nothing was to be seen. It was the residence of a holy man, who, on such an occasion as

[1] Indian chess.

the present, would not fail to make the most of his credulous visitors.

As the evening drew on the crowd began to disperse, and from our station on the elevated banks of the canal we could see the ladies at parting shake hands with as much cordiality as is customary among Europeans. Many went down into the canal and bent their foreheads to its bottom, blessing the water-course for former gifts, and then for their anticipated continuance; others put a handful of its sand to their lips, then, scattering it in the air, made one or two circular motions with the body, and departed homewards. When men are seen on their knees muttering a manter, or spell, before a paint-besmeared idol in the gloomy recess of some dark and moist cell, it is natural for those blessed with a clearer light to regard with horror this profanation of the commandment, and to stigmatize those who so act as a nation of idolaters. But when we see individuals, in the gratitude of their hearts, prostrating themselves by the banks of a noble river, the agent and immediate cause of the soil's fertility, we are inclined to judge less harshly.

I had often before remarked that a native of Sind never travels without shoes or sandals on his feet; and to-day this was amply verified. In this respect he seems to think, with an Englishman, that if the head and feet be well protected, other parts of dress are of minor importance.

Zyndul Abdin Shah, eldest son of Mír Ismael Shah, the Haïderábád Vuzir, was at this time governor of Shikárpúr. As one instance of Sindí ignorance, out of many which could be enumerated, I may mention that the governor's brother asked us whether the Duryah or ocean had a periodical rise like the Indus, and if the water of the Ganges was salt or fresh.

On the 8th of April I left the party and returned to the river by a road that threatened us with many a fall before we got to the end of it. So rugged and rutty are the roads in Sind which lead from place to place, and more especially in the neighbourhood of towns, that exercise taken upon them, either mounted or on foot, approaches more to pain than pleasure. Communication between districts is kept up by roads on the edge of the desert, which, though somewhat similar, can be travelled over in wheeled carriages, and are less inconvenient than those in the alluvial valley. Carts are but sparingly used in Sind, though it is to be hoped they will ere long be more common; for although there will always be extensive tracts accessible only to the bullock and horse, still wheeled vehicles might be advantageously employed in all the drier and more elevated districts of the valley. The easiest way of journeying is upon the camel, though not at the snail's pace at which a caravan travels. The long-trot of a Sarí, or running-camel, is quite another thing.

From B'hkur to Mittun-Kote the western bank of the Indus is in the possession of lawless tribes, which occasionally make stealthy visits to those of more settled habits on the opposite side of the river. Their object is plunder only; but, though expert thieves, blood is sometimes shed. This insecurity of property was indicated at Lárkhánah by the new arrangement which is there first perceptible in the villages, the houses being either surrounded by a common wall, or a strong mud fort stands in the middle of the town, into which the inhabitants retire when danger threatens them. In Lower Sind, which is comparatively a quiet and well-ordered country, no such arrangement is observable in its villages. The predatory tribes are the Búrdí and Muzarí, both nominally subject to Khyrpúr, though Mír Rustum Khán, ruler of that country, takes no effective measures to put down so disgraceful a system of pillage. While the blood of his subjects is made to flow, and their property despoiled, Bhyram Khán, the Muzarí leader, is rewarded with lands, and at the time we passed up the river was an honoured guest at the court of Khyrpúr. The truth is, the territories of this state are split into so many independent principalities that no member of the family, even though possessing the power, feels himself authorized in employing it against these banditti. Were he to do so, he would be sure of making enemies, while, even though successful in putting down the robbers, he would gain no friends. The Amírs and their Sirdars are of the same Beluche origin as the guilty tribes, and this is another reason why the Khyrpúr chief regards the misdeeds of these men with so lenient an eye, and is so little disposed to test the fidelity of his own followers in a struggle where the ties of kindred and similarity of disposition unite, if not to sap allegiance, at least to render all offensive operations lukewarm and ineffectual.

These observations on the weakness of the Khyrpúr state are equally applicable to Haïderábád. Nothing but a strict adherence to the Chinese system of avoiding political relations with foreigners could have preserved peace in a country like Sind, so pregnant with the elements of discord. In pursuing this line of policy she has been favoured by her situation; for, with a dreary desert to the east, a high mountain-chain to the west, non-intercourse with the Panjáb states, and the river Indus closed, her position was virtually insular. It was her object to maintain it so. Neighbouring nations were ill informed of the real resources of Sind, and, as usual where uncertainty prevails ignorance is prone to magnify everything, while the Amírs took special care that the received opinion of their military prowess should not lack the support of a haughty, and in some instances an insolent, bearing. But this unsatisfactory state of affairs could not last long. It was unjust to India that a river designed for the good of many should be engrossed by a few, who turned its advantages to no good account. The British government therefore wisely determined on throwing open the navigation of the Indus. Once in treaty with an European power, it required no prophet to foretell that the crafty policy which had hitherto been the security of Sind could no longer avail it; for where power is portioned out, as in this country, among a number of independent chiefs, it is impossible but that difference of opinion will occur. Mír Mohamed Khán, who is now ostensibly the ruling Amír, is as a monarch virtually powerless; and should he be held responsible for the acts of his co-regal partners, misunderstandings will happen, distrust be engendered, and quarrels must ensue. Were our relations with Sind similar to those we have established with the protected Sikh states, there would be less distrust on the part of its Amírs, and more confidence on ours.

Wherever we landed between B'hkur and Mittun-Kote the print of tigers' feet was met with, and, what is singular, they were not once remarked below the former place. This was, perhaps, partly owing to the nature of the country, which here is poorly cultivated, while the banks of the river are fringed to a varying depth with a thick cover of reedy grass and tamarisk jungle.

Buffaloes in this portion of the river were likewise more numerous than lower down: they had completely seamed the jungle with their tracks. When green food fails them they crop the upper end of the reed or feathered grass, and large districts were observed which had thus suffered. Numbers of these huge tame brutes lay at the entrance to almost every creek, enjoying the luxury of mud and water, with only, perhaps, the tip of the nose or the curved end of a horn visible above the surface. In wild solitary tracks, where the tiger may be supposed occasionally to prowl, the tingle of a buffalo's bell is a sound at all times grateful to the traveller's ear.

The wealth of many families in Sind consists in their herds of horned cattle; and of their produce, hides and ghí, Karáchí exports a considerable quantity. The former are collected by a class of people called Memans, of the Mohamedan cast, who traverse the country solely for this purpose. The latter is brought up by Hindú merchants, and is, under the name of Karáchí ghí, much esteemed in India. The buffalo, the animal which furnishes the principal supply, is milked in the evening, and only once in the twenty-four hours. Although a large portion of the Sindian population leads a pastoral life, the country is essentially agricultural. Nowhere have I seen a greater scarcity of the natural grasses than in Sind, considering how the Indus bisects and fertilizes the soil. It is a diverting sight to witness a herd of buffaloes swim the river; all is noise and confusion, and considerable tact is necessary on the part of those who command the movement. A herdsman bestrides a bundle of dry grass, seizes a sturdy animal by the tail, and on this singular carriage takes the lead. The other buffaloes follow, while laggards, and any that may be vagrantly inclined, are driven up to the main body by the cudgelling of men in the rear. The herdsmen are armed with long light lances, for the defence of themselves and their charge.

On the 19th we passed the village of Allah Chatchur-ke-gote, the property of Nihal Khán, a Beluche of the tribe of Murry. It had been attacked and plundered by Muzarís, from the opposite or western bank, three days before our arrival. A villager lost his life, and two were wounded.

On reaching Mittun-Kote on the 29th I found a letter from Captain Burnes, directing me to join him at Ahmedpúr, in the country of Bhawul Khán. I started the same day; and slept that night at Khán-baila, a considerable town on the south bank of the Sutledj, eighteen miles from Mittun-Kote. The intermediate country had a rich soil, and its surface was often, as far as the eye could range, one continuous corn-field. It was harvest time; and crops of wheat and barley stood ready for the sickle, dressed in the rich livery of the season. Numerous labourers were in the field, all of whom spoke favourably of Bhawul Khán, or rather the *Khán*, as his subjects familiarly style him. The taxes are paid chiefly in kind, which is as agreeable to the ryot as it is favourable to their chief. Circumstanced as the countries bordering the Indus were until lately, money payments could only be made at a grievous loss to the grower; but now that he has an open market for his surplus produce, in addition to his own government, the case is altered, though it will take some years before the change will be appreciated, as in the end it assuredly will be. Were the rulers of this and the other countries bordering the river but capable of looking a little forward, they would be truly thankful to the British government for re-opening the Indus; since, by this just proceeding, their countries, and consequently themselves, must necessarily be benefited. If this enlightened act has not hitherto been attended with that measure of success which there was reason to anticipate, the fault is our own. A more clumsy treaty, even after it was patched up by I do not know how many amendments, than that which professed to open the river Indus, has seldom been framed. One would have thought that even in the hey-day of monopolies and municipal privileges, before Adam Smith had enlightened the world with more sound opinions on commerce, enactments to the following effect could hardly have been penned:—

That every laden boat, without reference to her size or description of cargo, (be it Kashmir shawls or grain,) shall, for permission to navigate between the sea and Lahore, pay a duty of 50*l*. Again, it was enacted that no description of military stores should be sent by the Indus. By the first of these sage regulations the river was shut against the merchant, and by the second prohibitory clause the British government was deprived of a tangible and immediate good—that of supplying the arsenals of the north-west provinces by the direct route of the Indus, instead of by the more circuitous line of the Ganges.

During the late military operations on this frontier, the above treaty was necessarily infringed; and we may now hope to see regulations for the trade and navigation of the river more politic and sound. The country is here inundated by the periodical swelling of the Indus. When the waters retire, the seed is thrown down, and the farmer has no further trouble till harvest calls him forth to husband his crops. The rice grown here is of superior quality; but the straw of the other grain is short, and the ear light.

For a short distance beyond Khán-baila, the country bore the same appearance of plenty as that which we passed through the day before. It soon, however, changed, assuming a dreary unproductive aspect—sometimes that of a woody hunting preserve, at others of a moist marshy land. This character continued up to Ahmedpúr, where I arrived about four o'clock in the afternoon of Sunday the 30th of April.

On the 2nd of May Captain Burnes had an audience of Bhawul Khán. Carriages for our conveyance to the palace were sent to the residence of Lieutenant Mackeson, agent for the Indus navigation, at whose house we were staying; but of these vehicles I cannot speak in terms of praise. They do not differ from the Rut or Hackery of Hindústan, save that they are drawn by mules, and not bullocks. When we reached the Khán's palace, five miles distant from Lieutenant Mackeson's house, what with bad roads, and want of springs to the carriages, all of us were severely punished. At first the jolting furnished matter for merriment, but before long the groans which, at every lurch, escaped my well-fleshed companion, told that with him at least it was no joking matter. In front of the palace were ranged the Nawab's disciplined troops—numbering about thirteen hundred men, clad in uniform, tolerably equipped, with banners waving, and music playing. They were drawn up in double lines, each two deep and facing inwards, forming an open column, down which the road led. The palace itself is a diminutive building of two stories, in a light agreeable style of architecture, more resembling an Italian villa than the residence of a warlike chief. At our visit the upper room was occupied by the select men of the tribe, while that below was crowded by others of inferior rank. Their appearance was most martial; nor have I ever seen any tribe which, in soldierly bearing, equalled these Daoudputras, as the Khán's own tribe is called. They are tall and bony men, with well formed, strongly marked features, and clear olive complexion, tanned somewhat by exposure to a desert sun. Their dark hair in flowing ringlets clustered behind the neck, or streamed over the face and dangled in front of the person. All wore large turbans, and were dressed in white, except about the waist, around which a lungí was gracefully folded. Every man had a large black shield, with no other ornament on its jetty surface than a few brass bosses. Ranged in single rows, each warrior chief, as he sat cross-legged upon the carpet with sword and matchlock at his knee, leant forward on his shield, and watched, with eyes fixed and mouth open, all that passed at the interview.

The room of audience was on the upper floor; and the skill of some native artist had been sorely tasked to ornament its walls and ceiling with paintings in various departments of his art;—flowers and landscapes, town and mountain scenery, the holy Mecca, and hunting feats of the Khán contributed to the collection.

On gaining the head of the staircase leading to this room, Bhawul Khán met us in person. The Nawab is about forty years of age, stout, and of a large frame, inclining to corpulency. He was plainly attired, but his manly look was improved by this simplicity of dress. After taking our seats, much conversation passed between the Khán and Captain Burnes. The commercial objects of the mission were fully explained by

Captain Burnes, and perfectly understood by his Highness, who on his part promised every assistance.

From Ahmedpúr we proceeded to Bhawulpúr, a town with which I felt more pleased than with any the mission had hitherto visited. The situation of Bhawulpúr is well known. Its streets are cleaner and wider than those of Haïderábád, the metropolis of Lower Sind, while its bázár, though not so large as that of Shikárpúr, offers a greater variety, and has a more prosperous look. Within the place are some fine gardens laid out in the Persian fashion. Though the largest town belonging to the Daoudputras, it is seldom honoured by the presence of the Khán.

Bhawulpúr enjoys a well merited reputation for the various silk articles which are here fabricated. The texture is generally formed of silk and cotton, and the cloth is justly admired for the beauty of its patterns, the lustre of its colours, and its enduring qualities. The trade in this staple article of their commerce was, at the time of our visit, remarkably brisk. We examined three establishments, having in all thirty looms, not one of which was without its web. Each weaver is restricted to a single pattern, to which from early youth he has been habituated. These men are comfortably housed in clean, well-aired apartments, and to judge of their condition by the appearance of their workshops, I should say that the Bhawulpúr weaver is, comparatively, in possession of superior comforts to this class of hand operatives in Great Britain. They work in large sheds open in front, with chunamed sides and flooring. The rooms are ranged in line, close to the back wall, in which is a large square aperture to give a free circulation. The open area in front is usually ornamented with one or more shade-yielding trees.

While here, we had an amusing visitor in the person of a Monsieur Argoo. He had quarrelled with Runjít Sing and his countryman in the Panjáb, and was proceeding to join Dost Mohamed Khán of Kabul. We were at dinner when the Frenchman arrived, but no sooner was an European announced, than Captain Burnes ran out to bring him in, and before many minutes had elapsed, Monsieur Argoo had taken wine with every one at table. The poor man's failing was soon apparent, for he proceeded to beat the tattoo with his elbows on the table, and as a tenor accompaniment, he made a knife vibrate between its under surface and his thumb. It was really done very cleverly, and the performance being highly applauded, the complaisant Frenchman knew not when to desist. Fatigue, sleep, and wine at length got the master, and we saw him safely to bed. Next morning at an early hour our guest was astir, roaming up and down the courtyard till he chanced to stumble on Dr. Lord, engaged in dissecting and stuffing birds. Watching him for some time, he exclaimed "*Quelle patience !*" and with a shrug of the shoulders passed into Captain Burnes's room. That officer was not yet dressed, on which Monsieur Argoo called out, "Why, Sare, the battle of Wagram was fought before this hour; and you still in dishabille! Vill you take vine vith me?" "No," replied Captain Burnes, "I never take wine before breakfast; but I shall order you some claret, as your countrymen, I am aware, like light wine in the morning." "Then, Sare," replied Argoo, "you insult me, you refuse to take vine vith me, and I demand de satisfaction." He ran out, and soon re-appeared, armed with a rapier, and asked Captain Burnes to send for his small sword, but the latter thought that, considering the shortness of their acquaintance, he had already sufficiently humoured this fiery little Frenchman, and Monsieur Argoo was politely requested to continue his journey, which he accordingly did that same evening.

This unfortunate gentleman had many good points in his character, but they were unknown to us at the time of his first visit. As a soldier and drill-officer, he was the first in the Panjáb; but his drunken habits, and violent temper, made him disliked by his brother officers. At Kabul, in October following, we fell in with him a second time, so that his journey from the Indus had occupied him fully five months. Whilst on the road, his dislike to Mussulmans had nearly cost him his life. It was only spared on his repeating the Kulmah or Mohamedan creed. Immediately on his arrival being known to us, Captain Burnes sent him a kind note, inquiring if he could be of any service to him; but the good-hearted Frenchman was so ashamed of his conduct at Bhawulpúr, and so oppressed by this unexpected return, that he could not be persuaded to visit us; and on his failing to obtain employment from Dost Mohamed Khán, he set out for Peshawar, without our having met him. We, however, learned that the day previous to his departure he had been employed in moulding leaden bullets, and that he had sworn to be revenged on the Mussulmans, for the ill-treatment on his former journey. The cause of Monsieur Argoo's failure in obtaining service, was his ignorance of the Persian language. Dost Mohamed Khán was partial to him, and though regretting his attachment to the bottle, offered him a regiment. Unfortunately for the Frenchman, the interpreter took advantage of his ignorance of the language, and in reply to a question on Argoo's qualifications for command, reported, as his answer, that if the Amír wanted a *drummer*, he could not suit himself better. The Frenchman required but little pressing to beat a *tattoo*, and the result was that he got his discharge that evening, and next day the interpreter (a brother adventurer) obtained the regiment.

Embarking in boats at Bhawulpúr, on the 12th of May, we dropped down the Sutledj to Uch, and as the boats here brought to on the night of the 14th, I embraced the opportunity to visit the town. Darkness, however, had cast her sable mantle around ere we reached its suburbs, but this *slight* circumstance we had not in our wisdom adverted to. Now, as the streets of an eastern town are neither illuminated by the magic gas jet, nor even the dull oil flame, we had no alternative but Sawney's, to gang back again. We had gone about half way to the boats, when a loud barking of dogs, and the voice of some one in trouble, made us quicken our steps towards the hamlet from which the noise proceeded. Here we found a drunken Afghan, who had lost his way, battling manfully, dirk in hand, with a pack of curs that had beset him. He had lost his sword, for as he swept the ground with it in front, dealing forth, as the bewildered man no doubt thought, destruction to his enemies, it had slipped from his grasp, and he now stood making, occasionally, a desperate thrust with his dirk, measuring at each pass his length along the ground. An Afghan chief had arrived from Dhera Ghazí Khán, and this worthy was of his suite. He had been to Uch, and there made too free with the wine cup, an excess which the company of a countryman and friend whom he accidentally met with, may palliate, if not excuse. The drunken man was proceeding to the river's bank to rejoin his master, who was there encamped; so extricating him from the canine foe, and gathering up his scattered weapons, we took him under our charge and saw him safe home.

Burnes, speaking of Uch, says, "The place is ancient, and highly celebrated in the surrounding countries, from the tombs of two saints of Bokhara and Bagdad. The Ghorian emperors expelled the Hindú Rajas of Uch, and consigned the surrounding lands to pious Mohamedans.

* * * * * * *

An inundation of the Acesines, some years back, swept away one half of the principal tomb, with a part of the town; and though the return of the river to its original bed is attributed to the miraculous interference of the deceased saint, the people have, as yet, failed to testify their gratitude by repairing his tomb."

On the 18th we descended the Chenab to Mittun-Kote, at the confluence of the Panjáb streams with the Indus, and here, before quitting that portion of the latter river voyaged by the Greeks, I may be permitted to offer a few remarks on the descriptions of the Indus given by Arrian and by authors of recent date. When the latter differ so widely from each other, the statements of the former should not be too keenly criticised. Burnes has been accused of *under*-estimating the size of the Indus; but with what degree of justice, the result of experimental steam-voyages will by this time have shown. It would, indeed, have been the safer side to err on, but he has done just the contrary, and drawn a too favourable picture of the capabilities of this river, both in his published work and practical notes. But if this may be said of the author whom we have named, what shall we say of those who declared the mouth of the Indus to be navigable to a line-of-battle ship, and to have a width of twelve miles? It is true that Colonel Pottinger spoke only from information obtained from the natives; but the results that sometimes ensue from the dissemination of loose statements, cannot be better instanced than by adducing the prospectus of a Steam Company for the navigation of the Indus, which was given to the public in 1834. This joint-stock scheme actually proposed stationing an old East Indiaman, as a depôt or receiving ship within the mouth of the river. Why, this class of vessels could not, if laden, even sight the coast of Sind, far less cross the bar of its shoal-streams. Thus much for modern authorities; let us now hear what the ancients say. Arrian states the Indus to have a medium width of forty stadia, and to measure fifteen where narrowest: that in its course, from the confluence of the Panjáb rivers to Pattala, it was one hundred, and lower towards the sea two hundred. These seemingly exaggerated statements have much perplexed the worthy Dean of Westminster, who, ignorant of localities, could not possibly be aware of the peculiarities of this stream. To me the measurements of the historian, though absurdly high, even taking the stadium at D'Anville's low estimate of fifty-one toises, contain all the evidence of a truthful narration. Let it be remembered, Nearchus commenced the voyage down the river in October, when the Indus is very low, and reached Pattala in July, when the periodical rise of the river is nearly at its height. The seasons would thus occasion great disparity in the accounts which have been transmitted to us of the river's estimated width. Indeed, Arrian expressly adds, "this is the breadth when it spreads its waters most." His measurements, therefore, embrace rather the belt of country inundated, than the *thread* or proper channel of the stream.

We now, at least, know what the Indus is *not*, and even this negative information may prevent much disappointment. The difficulties that arise, and the angry feelings engendered, through ignorance of matters which it is the province of physical geography to explain, need not, after the instances just quoted, be more than alluded to in this place. Proper vessels are now upon the Indus, and its capabilities for steam-navigation will be made the most of; but we cannot help reminding such of our Indian friends as are interested in the subject, that not only are the native craft of the river well suited to its peculiarities, but are also equally adapted to the commerce for which the Indus now is, or will shortly become, the highway. In conclusion, we may remark, that there is no known river in either hemisphere, discharging even half the quantity of water that the Indus does, which is not superior for navigable purposes to this far-famed stream. In this practical age the beauty of a river is measured by its utility; and although few people could sail without emotion upon the waters that once bore the bark of Alexander, there are numbers who would willingly give up all its classic associations, could they, by so doing, obtain for it the clear channel of an American stream.

CHAPTER IV.

Mittun-Kote.—Trial by ordeal.—Departure from Mittun-Kote.—Character of the country.—Kalórás.—Arrival at Dhera Ghazí Khán.—A trading mart.—Wrestling matches.—Alteration in the river.—Departure for Dhera Ismael Khán.—Aspect of the country.—Irrigating dams.—Earthquake of 1819.—Charitable feeling.—A water echo.—Takht-i-Suliman.

WHEN the Dheraját was a province of Kabul, Mittun-Kote belonged to the district of Dhera Ghazí Khán; but on the dismemberment of that kingdom it was seized by the Daoudputras, and Saduk Mohamed, father of the reigning Khán, gave it in fief on easy terms to Hafiz Mohamed Khoreishí, a holy man of the town. The son of this saint, Míha Khodá Buksh, was ejected on Mittun-Kote's being taken possession of by Runjít Sing, above eighteen years ago. The dispossessed Pír[1] has fixed himself at Chatcher, a village on the opposite bank of the river, fronting Mittun-Kote, that his eyes may be daily gladdened with the sight of the dome of a ziarat, which twenty-five years before he had built over the home of his childhood and the ashes of his father. The Seiks have been urgent in their request to Míha Khodá Buksh to resume his jaggir,[2] but in vain, the old man will not consort with kaffirs.[3] He has, however, strong hopes that Mittun-Kote may yet revert to Bhawul Khán, hopes strengthened, if not engendered, by the dome ever present before his eyes.

Whilst at Mittun-Kote, seeing a crowd one day congregated round a well, I walked to the spot and was witness to the following trial by an ordeal, which we may term that of "water

---

[1] A saint. In Mohamedan countries good men are often canonized before the grave has closed upon them.

[2] Jaggir, a tract of land given in fief.

[3] Unbelievers.

and the bow and arrow." The water in the well was eighteen feet deep, and in its centre stood an upright pole. Two criminals were to be tried for theft, one of whom was already in the well, clinging to the pole, with only his head above water. A little on one side, with his back to the criminal, stood an archer with bent bow and an arrow on the string. On a given signal the arrow was shot away, and the culprit descended below the surface of the water. No sooner had the arrow reached the ground, than a young man swift of foot left the bowman's side, and made towards it; on his reaching the spot where it fell, another runner, equally fleet, snatched up the arrow and set off for the well. As he neared us at a winning pace, all eyes looked over the parapet into the well, for the criminal's re-appearance. His friends breathed short, while hope and fear were depicted on every countenance. At last, the runner reached the goal, and the next moment the head of the suspected person emerged from the water. A loud shout proclaimed his innocence and the crowd's satisfaction.

The other criminal, an old man, now prepared to descend into the well, but before doing so a lock was shorn from his thin gray hairs, and fastened to the arrow as a charm to impede its flight. He was the reverse of confident, and his looks were certainly not in his favour. Prayers were offered, and many fingers pointed to the heavens, while voices exclaimed "*Allah will clear the innocent.*" The trial was gone through, and with the same happy result as before. These injured men were now placed upon the backs of two bystanders, and so mounted, were led through the crowd to receive its noisy congratulations. This over, their female relations came forward and contented themselves with imprinting a silent kiss upon the cheeks of the once-suspected men, who had thus established their innocence in the opinion of their countrymen, and the sound state of their lungs in ours.[1]

---

[1] The "Pariksha," or trial by ordeal, is an ancient Hindú ordinance, and in this instance the actors were probably Hindús, although the use of the word "Allah" would seem to imply participation in the ceremony by Mohamedans.

The rules for this peculiar custom are thus given in an interesting contribution to "Asiatic Researches," by Warren Hastings, Esq. The accused thus appeals to the God of Waters.

[" Preserve

CHARACTER OF THE COUNTRY.

By the 22nd of May, permission from Runjít Sing having arrived for the Mission to proceed to Attock by the Indus, the fleet on that day was again in motion, pursuing, with a favourable breeze, the voyage to Dhera Ghazí Khán, the next commercial mart where a halt was to be made.

Between Mittun-Kote and Dhera Ghazí Khán a low alluvial tract extends far inland on both sides of the river, which, though studded with farming hamlets, had no large villages; some were visible, situated above this alluvial bottom, but they were too distant for me to visit them. To the east the eye ranges over an uninviting level, but on the opposite bank are seen the Suliman mountains, which rising about Mittun-Kote, continue parallel to the Indus, till they disappear midway between the Upper Dhera Kalabagh, in the table-land south of Sufeid Koh.

This country is well watered, both from canals and the inundation, and as might be expected, the soil is rich and productive. The eastern bank is inhabited by Mussulmans, Hindús, and Seiks. The west solely by the first of these sects, who are mostly Beluche of the Gurchaní, Dízuk, Sagrí, Dushtí, Gopang, Koza, and Kalórá tribes. The Kalórás were the tribe which ruled in Sind prior to the Talpurs, and Abdul Nubbe was the last of the race who possessed authority in that country. His vindictive spirit and ferocious disposition forced, for self-preservation, the friendly and powerful tribe of Talpur into rebellion; and the result was the dethronement of the tyrant, his tribe's expulsion from Sind, and Futí Ali Khán's succession to the vacant musnud.

The Kalórás, now harmless wanderers, were indebted to the charity of a Kabul monarch for the means of subsistence. He gave them lands in the Dherajat, and this estate their descendants still retain, though somewhat curtailed of its fair proportions by their present masters. But the Kalórás have

---

"'Preserve me, O Varuna, by declaring the truth.' Thus invoking the God of Waters the accused shall plunge his head into the river or pool, and hold both thighs of a man who shall stand in it up to his navel.

"A swift runner shall then hasten to fetch an arrow, shot at the moment of his plunging; and if, while the runner is gone, the priest shall see the head of the accused under water, he must be discharged as innocent." — "Asiatic Researches," vol. i., p. 404.

no cause to revile the Seiks, when they contrast their own favoured condition with the other Mohamedans under Runjít's rule. The Maharajah has shown unusual forbearance towards this unfortunate community. No troops are quartered among them, and here the Mohamedan is even permitted to raise his voice in prayer. The Kalórás are held in much consideration, not only as having once been rulers, but also for the strictness of their religious observances ; and Runjít, with his usual discrimination, does not despise even the prejudices of an opposite creed, when, by a little hypocrisy, he can add to the stability of his own power.

On Tuesday, the 10th of May, we moored abreast of Dhera Ghazí Khán. This town stands on the alluvial bottom of the Indus, four miles inland, and upon the west bank of the stream. The country here for many miles round is inundated, and the town itself suffers when the river's periodical rise is unusually high. It is surrounded by date groves, from the produce of which the Seik government draw a considerable revenue. This town is admirably situated for traffic with the tribes among and beyond the mountains. At the foot of a pass, and on the bank of such a river, a trade, alike beneficial to the immense regions lying to the west, to India, and to Britain, might here be established. The day, we trust, is not distant, when an annual fair will be held at this place. What may be the ultimate result of this, it might be rash to predict, but that the measure would in no ordinary degree prove successful, the map itself seems to testify. It shows not only the immense regions to be drained of their raw produce, but also the millions of inhabitants who, unless we ourselves are to blame, will one day be supplied with British manufactures.

What is further favourable to Dhera Ghazí Khán becoming an emporium of trade is the festival of Sukkí Surwar, which is yearly held in the gorge of its mountain-pass. The rejoicings continue for five days, and bring together from districts far apart the saint's numerous followers. Many thousands of persons are thus congregated, and, while the fair lasts, the streets of Dhera Ghazí are thronged with merchants and devotees.

While here, we had an opportunity of observing how Mussulmans on the Indus spend their Sunday (our Friday) when dwelling in a town. In the suburbs a large concourse of people had assembled. They formed a hollow square, within which were the *palwans*, or combatants, the musicians, and a few Seik Sirdars. Seik soldiers paraded to keep order in the crowd, while their officers presided as umpires and distributed the rewards. The spectators were of both persuasions, Mussulmans and Hindú. The palwans were Mohamedans. I inquired of a decrepit and aged man the nature of these holiday recreations, when he replied with a sigh, "Ah Agha Jan,[1] in bygone times we had games and other sports. Under the Duranís the victor had a horse given to him, or he was crowned in the ring, amidst the shouts of his townsmen, with a Kashmír shawl, or had a golden-hilted sword presented to him; but these people" (added the sarcastic old man, as he cast a glance of contempt upon the Seiks within the ring) "give you a doputtah."[2]

The musicians struck up, and two young men came forward to wrestle. Striking the palm of the right hand against the folded left arm, they advanced to the centre of the ring, where, after smearing their hands and arms with sand, they stood on their defence. Eyeing each other with an eager and steady look, they paused for some time, measuring their adversary, each endeavouring to close with some advantage. At length they met, when, grasping each other's arms, their heads touching, the encounter for some time continued much after the manner of a ram-fight. Violent struggling followed, each trying to get his head under the breast of his opponent, which, when accomplished, the fall was sure. In this way one of the men was thrown, and while another match was arranging two children were led into the ring, and wonderful indeed were the gymnastic feats of these minor performers. They threw numerous somersaults, and hopped on one foot round the ring. Next, they swung their arms to and fro, jerking at the same time the body from an inclined to an upright position. Then, stretching themselves along the ground, face downwards, they rose to the full length of their arms, and kept repeating the movement,

---

[1] Anglicè, "your honour."   [2] A light scarf.

rising and lowering the chest, whilst only the hands and toes were permitted to touch the ground; thus the muscles of the body were brought into play, but more especially those of the chest and arms. The children were not more than five years old. This exercise however, though violent, was play to these little fellows, for they were not stimulated by rewards, but did it apparently to amuse themselves, none of the bystanders, except the Seiks within the circle, taking any notice of their play; and when called out of the ring to make room for another wrestling-match, they were as sprightly and fresh as when they entered it. Should they continue such feats, and reach manhood, they will be muscular men. The concourse which formed the ring itself was an interesting spectacle. Here was to be seen the half-civilised and gaily dressed Seik, who, *en déshabille*, draws a lilac scarf across his shoulders, over his anqarkha or white muslin shirt, and, instead of a turban, wraps round his head a small yellow band, the nation's favourite colour. With these effeminately attired but soldierly figures mingles the rude Beluche, whose shaggy locks, flowing robes, long matchlock, and huge shield, lend to his person a more independent, if not martial air. These rough-looking figures form a strong contrast to the handsome appearance of the Seiks, lounging about in their white flowing draperies, with their gay-looking gold-hilted swords, whilst here and there a naked savage in the character of a fakír, renders the *tout ensemble* truly Eastern, and the scratching inharmonious music contributes not a little to complete the effect.

Whilst at Dhera Ghazí Khán, a singular alteration took place in the appearance of the Indus, which may, perhaps, be worth recording. From the day of our arrival, the 30th of May, to the 6th of June, the river rose slowly at the average daily rate of an inch and a half. On the last of these days its width was 2,274 yards, its whole volume flowing on in one stream, and its surface unbroken by a shoal. On the following night the river fell eighteen inches, and next morning its bed was one confused mass of sand-banks, more resembling the wreck of some noble stream than the Indus in the month of June. On threading my way amongst the shoals, the principal channel was discovered on the eastern side of the bed, deep and rapid, but in width shrunken to 259 yards. Admitting the river to have been at its usual height on the 6th of the month, I am inclined to attribute its rapid subsidence, not to any deficiency in the river's ordinary sources of supply, but to the escape of a large body of water under the following circumstances. On our passage up the river we occasionally came to districts where the level of the stream was above that of the inland country, which was only preserved from inundation by somewhat higher land banking the river. When the Indus rises sufficiently to overflow this natural embankment, the rush of water that follows soon reduces the barrier's height. The low-lying district is flooded, and the quantity of water thus abstracted from the river alters, for a time, its appearance for the worse. Its equilibrium is, however, soon restored, and it resumes its beauty.

From Dhera Ghazí Khán, Lieutenant Leech and Dr. Lord crossed the desert to Multan, and rejoined the Mission at the Upper Dhera.

On the 7th of June we continued our progress to the northward, and at night experienced a violent thunder-storm. The wind throughout the day had been blowing from the north, but towards sunset dark clouds were seen to gather upon the summits of the Suliman mountains, and about nine o'clock at night the storm burst in severe gusts of wind, with heavy rain and lightning from the south-west. So vivid and fiery was the electric fluid, that it almost seemed to scorch us as it played above our heads, while its startling proximity involuntarily made us crouch to avoid the anticipated stroke.

We had not left Dhera Ghazí Khán many days when we remarked a visible change in the aspect of the country, and especially in the bed of the Indus. In fact, the valley and the bed of the river are here one and the same, since on both sides the stream is walled by banks thirty feet high, over which there is no evidence of its waters ever having risen. No canals pierce these barriers, and from this point the agriculture dependent on the Indus for irrigation is restricted to this sunken valley, which may be estimated at from five to ten miles wide. In this depressed bed the stream shifts its path, though it would seem but slowly, since, by Macartney's description of the Indus in 1809, it would appear that a lapse of nearly thirty years has produced no great alteration in this portion of its course. The river continues to run down the west side of the valley, and, according to the natives, is still, by the abrasion of its west bank, working its way in that direction. A broad fertile belt of rich alluvium is thus left to the right of the stream, and at some places under the west bank also. These grounds, unvisited by the river for so many years, have, by the annual decay of their rank vegetation, attained an elevation that exempts them (but that is all) from the general inundation of this low-lying district. They are, however, intersected by innumerable mazy off-shoots from the main stream, and in fact the whole of this low valley is liable to inundation. Here, therefore, are no towns or villages, but numerous hamlets and farm-steadings are spread over its moist surface, while the domed mosques of such towns as Dhera Dín Punah, Leia, and Rajun, stand upon its high bank overlooking the valley.

The foregoing description of the bed of the Indus requires to be modified with regard to some circumstances affecting its western shore. The Suliman chain on this bank is, between Dhera Ghazí and Dhera Ismael Khán, from thirty to sixty miles distant from the river, and by the drainage of these mountains has the west bank of the Indus in many places been destroyed, so that when the river is full a considerable tract of country is flooded through the openings thus formed. The streamlets from the range of mountains do not, as represented in the maps, join the Indus, their entire volume being ordinarily consumed in agriculture. Single-embanked dams, thirty miles in length, skirt the base of this chain, and receive their drainage, which is here the only means of irrigation,—water, except near the river, being too far from the surface to be obtained by wells. After long-continued rain these embankments sometimes give way, and then the pent-up water rushes down the plain and moves onward to the river with a wasting velocity and a wantonness of strength which at first nothing can oppose. The towns exposed to calamities from this cause are protected by a strong mud wall drawn around them.

The earthquake of June 1819, which devastated the British province of Kach'h, was felt far up the valley of the Indus, though the Sindís point to Maghribí, and the countries eastward, as the centre of its vibrations. The town of Dhera Dín Punah on the west bank of the river, which we passed on the 13th of June, suffered by that convulsion. The ground upon which the town stood sank from four to six feet, and, to increase the horrors of its already affrighted inhabitants, the streets were flooded for fourteen days, from newly-opened chasms in the Suliman chain.

Visiting one evening in this neighbourhood a village of Jat Mohamedans, I was pleased at witnessing an agreeable usage of the tribe. They were distributing among the poor the milk of a large herd of buffaloes. It is their custom to do so once a month in remembrance of Abdul Khadir, a Mohamedan saint. The pastoral tribe in Lower Sind do the same thing, and there Hindú and Mussulman alike share in this charity. How seldom does superstition wear so attractive a garb as it does in this instance, where, in doing honour to the memory of a good man, rival sects for a time forget their difference, and unite in befriending the poor!

As the river was now high, to avoid its strong current we sometimes for a distance threaded one of its many parallel branches. In one of these, eighty yards wide, its banks either level with the surface of the stream or just submerged, while the tall grass with which they were thickly clad was above the water, we were startled to hear our words repeated in a clear soft tone from among these rushes. This beautiful water-echo accompanied us to the end of the narrow channel.

As we advanced to the north, the Takht-i-Suliman, or the highest mountain in the chain became daily more conspicuous, and on the 21st of June, the day preceding that of our arrival at Dhera Ismael Khán, I ascertained its height by trigonometrical measurements to be 10,086 feet above the river, or in round numbers 11,000 feet above the sea.[1]

---

[1] In the geological manual of Henry T. de la Beche the line of perpetual snow in the parallel of 32° N. is fixed at 11,000, or about this mountain's height. The takht, however, lies in a somewhat lower latitude, 31° 38' N., and is only snow-covered in winter.

CHAPTER V.

Dhera Ismael Khán.—Old and new town.—Peasantry in the Dheraját.—Departure from Dhera Ismael Khán.—The wild palm.—Difficult tracking-ground. —Kaffir-Kote.—Country of the Esaw Kyl.—Khán Beg Khán.—Ahmed Khán, chief of the Esaw Kyl.—Interview with the chieftain.—Dislike to the Seiks. —Kurum river.—Pebbles in the bed of the Indus.—Arrival at Kalabagh.—The Indus during its swell.—Submerged island.—Unceremonious removals.— Pendant nests.—Mirage.—Bulrush-gatherers.

THE old town of Dhera Ismael Khán, with its wood of date-trees, was swept away by the Indus in 1829. It had been long threatened, for in 1809 it stood within a hundred yards of the stream, but its fate was not consummated until twenty years after its perilous site had been remarked by the Honourable Mr. Elphinstone.

The new town is well laid out. Its streets are straight and wide, though as yet houses in some of them are but thinly scattered. They are built of sun-dried brick, consist of a single story, and rise from a basement or platform about a foot in height. The bázár is roomy and well supplied. There was an airy clean appearance about this new town, that augured comfort and health to its inhabitants. I regret, however, to observe that the result of further observations in the Dherajat did not confirm the first of these suppositions. The country is abundant in both the necessaries and luxuries of life; and yet its peasantry are poorly clad, indifferently lodged, and, by their own account, worse fed. This remark is applicable to the west bank of the river, where the spirit of the people is embittered by Seik bondage; but it may be truly said that, from one cause or another, this is more or less the condition of the lower classes throughout the entire valley of the Indus: "The invasion of another conqueror, who would reduce the whole under any form of regular government, and open the communications again, would be a benefit to the country, instead of an injury or oppression; and if the Abdallís should in this instance tread in the steps of the Macedonians, one general despot who should govern the whole, and for his own interest protect it, would be better than a variety of petty tyrants, who desolate each other's territory without obtaining security for their own; or the predatory incursions of the barbarous tribes, who not only rob but annihilate the industry of the merchant and the cultivator." Let us substitute the word Britain for the Abdallís, and a mild government for Eastern despotism, and then we hope that the day anticipated by the worthy Dean has at length dawned.

Leaving Captain Burnes' party at Dhera Ismael Khán, I started for Kalabagh on the 2nd of July, with instructions to continue along the west bank of the Indus for the entire distance, should it be found practicable. Four days afterwards we came abreast of a mountain-chain, which in a northerly direction edged the stream for five-and-twenty miles. For the first two days we tracked along its base. A belt of good land lay between it and the river, of a varying width, but nowhere exceeding two thousand yards. It gradually lessened as we ascended the stream, until, on the afternoon of the 8th, we came upon the rock itself. This narrow fringe of cultivable land is shared by various Afghan families, whose means of existence are necessarily precarious, as the Indus is yearly reducing the size of their already contracted domains. This tract, where uncultivated, is covered with date-trees, not, however, that kind from which,

> "With fruit and ever-verdant branches crown'd,
> Judea chose her emblem; on whose leaves
> She first inscribed her oracles, and all
> The fortunes of her state,"—

but a species of dwarf wild palm that produces no fruit.

The difficulty of tracking now hourly augmented, until, on the afternoon of the 10th, a jutting portion of the mountain forced us to halt. Three hundred yards in advance there was firm footing, but in the intermediate space the mountain was scarped down to the river, which here, ten fathoms deep, rolled onward at the rate of seven miles an hour. The pelú-tree (Salvadora Persica) had taken root in crevices, at present hidden by the swollen river, and, though an impediment to trackers when the water is low, they were now extremely serviceable to our advance. From the sloping surface of the mountain the trees shot their strong boughs above water, about four yards outside the rock; and up this back channel a couple of boatmen, after several failures, made good their way, and then returned to us, floating down the river upon mussuks.[1] We thus succeeded in getting several warps (track-ropes) fastened above that portion of the mountain which retarded our ascent. The boat was now swung out into the stream, and we were proceeding to haul her ahead, when a change of current carried us forcibly away from the bank. To keep her from capsizing we were compelled to let go the different warps; and when we got beyond the shelter of the mountains it was found to be blowing a perfect gale, so that our only alternative was to scud before it, under a close-reefed sail, for the opposite bank. During the night the gale abated, and the wind changing to south, we recrossed the river, and landed on the west bank, about 100 yards above the scarped rock which had given us so much trouble.

At this place are the ruins of the castle of Kaffir-Kote, equally remarkable for its strange site and massive architecture. On the very summit of the mountain-chain several time-worn turrets of imposing appearance are seen, from which a dilapidated wall runs right down the face of the rock into the river. The natives of these parts assign to this castle an era long antecedent to the Hejira; and in this they are supported by its traditionary name. On comparing the numerous pigmy mud forts of modern times with the remains of this giant of antiquity, the result is not favourable to the exertions of the present day; or perhaps it would be more correct to infer that these countries, under the Hindú Rajahs, possessed greater power than they have done since the Mohamedan conquest. Slavery, too, would seem to have been prevalent in those days, for without such a supposition it is impossible to account for the remains of many

[1] An inflated skin of a sheep, bullock, or other animal.

similar structures in Afghanistan and the adjoining countries. Freemen would never have consented to the erection of such stupendous edifices, on sites so arbitrarily chosen, and so little calculated for the general good; and we may therefore conclude these to have been built by forced labour, and to have been so many mountain-eyries, of tyrant chiefs: or, if we view them in a more favourable light, the traces of wealth and knowledge that these relics of a younger world present, fill us with wonder at the mechanical skill required to raise such piles, or at the density of population, if physical strength alone were employed. But where now are those giants of the earth, those sons of Anakim's generation? Gone for ever: and whether we look to India's excavated caves, or to the banks of the Nile, in Egypt's mystic land, no clue has yet been discovered to guide inquiry through the dark ages that have followed the bright era of their origin. A moral catastrophe, antecedent to Alexander's invasion, seems to have blighted science and thrown backward the intellect of man. The round towers of Ireland, the pyramids of Egypt, the caves and other undeciphered Indian antiquities may be referred to this mysterious era; and an unrecorded irruption of savage hordes may perhaps have been the Lethean wave which swept over them.

Immediately after passing this ruin, we found ourselves in the country of the Esaw Kyl; and on clearing the mountains next day we reached Kundul, the frontier village of the tribe.

From Kundul we could discern the Salt range, which seemed to bound the valley of the Indus on the north. From this range, another swept in a semicircular curve to the south-west, till it almost joined those we had just left behind. The land thus shut in forms the country of the Esaw Kyl, and is a comparatively high-lying plain, resting one side upon the river, and enclosed on its three others by mountains.

We had not been long in the village when Khán Beg Khán, a person of consequence deputed by the chief of the tribe, paid us a visit. He came, he said, from his master Ahmed Khán, to welcome the English to his Kyl, and to furnish us with sursat, or daily rations. After due acknowledgments on our part, Khán Beg Khán took leave with an assurance that to-morrow he would send a strong party to drag the boat; a service which, having declined his other kind offers, I thought it politic to accept.

The morning brought us the promised trackers: but to drag the boat against a strong current under a constantly falling bank, thirty-three feet high, was more than we dared to try; so, spreading our canvas, we sought the eastern shore, along the low flats of which we tracked throughout the day, and at nightfall again crossed to the west side of the river. We made an excellent day's work, and, although it was dark, hit the bank at Shaikh-ke-Shair, a village at the confluence of the Kurum, a stream that here joins the Indus.

Late as was the hour of our arrival, the nephew of Ahmed Khán was at the river-side to receive us. What conversation we had was carried on, through an interpreter, in the Persian language, as Alum Khán knew only Pushtu, the vernacular of his country. The chief, he said, would visit us next day; a compliment I vainly endeavoured to shun, on the score of my poor accommodations being unfit for the reception of so great a personage. On taking leave, the young man pressed us to accept of a guard for the night, affirming with much *sang froid*, that, although such a precaution was unnecessary in the midst of his own peaceful tribe, still there were hill-men, against whom we should be on our guard.

Next day, before the sun had well risen, I was surprised by the chief's approach. An old bechoba[1] was hastily pitched, and into it, with due formality, Ahmed Khán was inducted. He opened the conversation by expressing deep regret that the difficulties of the navigation had prevented Captain Burnes from visiting the Esaw Kyl. He hoped, however, the day would yet come when he might prove to the Indian government the sincerity of his respect and esteem for our nation. "True," said the chief, "my country is but '*ticka zumen*,' a spot of earth, and the tribe, in strength, not what it once was; yet, such as we are, I and mine are at the service of your government." In vain did I assure him he was mistaken, and that the English nation sought not for territorial aggrandisement, but that

[1] A small tent supported by four corner sticks, without a centre pole.

in interesting itself in the tranquillity of nations bordering the Indus, its views were far more liberal and philanthropic. I then carefully explained to the chief the purely commercial character of Captain Burnes' mission. That its object was to determine the navigable capabilities of the Indus, that the boats of the merchant might be suited to its streams; to note what descriptions of raw produce, and to what amount the adjacent countries could exchange for articles of British manufacture, and to mark the taste and predilections of their inhabitants, that our merchants might adapt their investments to the wants of their customers. Ahmed Khán listened attentively, and asked many questions, where he did not clearly comprehend my meaning. When I had finished, he remarked with a quaint incredulous smile, "it might be so: but the Seik rule was a harsh one."

Conversation now took a more discursive range, and for an hour the chief sat asking innumerable questions about Europeans, their customs and inventions; but on no subject was he more inquisitive, than that of steam, and the various uses to which it is applied. He had heard that quicksilver was employed to generate it, and was surprised to learn that, for common purposes, water only was used.

The chieftain of the Esaw Kyl is about forty-five years of age, of a mild, placid countenance, and, though his figure is not handsome, there is something elevated and prepossessing in his demeanour. His escort consisted of twenty matchlock men. At parting, he again expressed great anxiety to meet Captain Burnes.

No people west of the Indus are more impatient under the yoke of Runjít Sing than the Esaw Kyl. A small Seik detachment, quartered in their country, was lately cut off to a man, and, to avenge this insult, an army was now on its march from Lahore. But Runjít, ever prudent, had secretly proposed an amicable arrangement to Ahmed Khán, who, sensible of his own weakness and the Maharajah's power, was prepared to accede to the terms offered, provided Runjít would not insist on stationing another Seik detachment among his tribe. Rather than submit to this, Ahmed Khán expressed his determination to take to the hills and try what modification in the Maharajah's sentiments a guerilla system of warfare would effect.

The water of the Kurum river is of a bright red colour. By this and other mountain streams the lands of the Esaw Kyl are irrigated. The Indus rolls past unheeded, as it here flows in too deep a bed to be turned to agricultural purposes.

Taking leave of the Esaw Kyl, whose hard fate I sincerely pitied, we kept tracking up the west bank, and at the village of Muddut Kyl, detected the first pebble in the river's channel. Three miles higher, at Chandina Ka-gote they were visible in its banks. Seven miles more brought us, on the 16th, to the town of Kalabagh, where Captain Burnes and his party had already arrived.

Having reached the mountains, I shall close this chapter with a few general remarks on that division of the Indus which lies between Mittun-Kote and Kalabagh, a portion of its course yet little known. The season it should be remembered, in which we voyaged, was that of the river's periodical rise, and the temperature of February does not differ more from that of July, than the shrunken stream of the one month from the full channel of the other. At some places, so diffused was the stream, that from a boat in its centre no land could be discovered, save the islands upon its surface, and the mountains on its western shore. From Dhera Ismael Khán to Kalabagh, the east bank was not once seen from the opposite side of the river, being either obscured by distance, or hidden by intervening islands, which, at this season, thickly speckle over its channel. Some are level with the water's edge, while others below it are only known by their sedgy covering. In other months, they are the resort of the inhabitants from both shores, many of whom, delighted with their fine pasturage, prolong their stay till dislodged by the rising river. Such laggards I have seen caught, and have enjoyed a hearty laugh at their unceremonious removal. When this is about to happen, the inmates are soon astir. The young men go in search of the cattle, whilst others speedily unroof the reed-built cot, and transport such part of its materials as may be useful in the erection of their new habitation, to a boat which they take care to have at hand. Between this vessel and the hamlet, parties may be seen hurrying to and fro, with bundles on their heads, their arms filled with children and earthen jars, and dragging rafters and other fragments of their houses after them. But in this month (July) the islands are abandoned, and as the boat swiftly glides amidst the mazy channels that intersect them, no village cheers the sight; no human voice is heard; the only sound is the plover's moaning call as it hovers above the falling bank, and dexterously seizes its prey while yet in the air, or skims it off the water. Here and there a boiling eddy rises to the surface, and even the wild swirl of its gushing, turbid current, is grateful to the ear amidst the profound stillness. A small grey speckled bird, that loves the water, nestles on these half-drowned islands, hanging its neatly constructed little nest to the top of a flexile grass stalk, and rears its young in security, when all is flooded beneath and around it. Lower down the river, about the vicinity of Mittun-Kote, the low sandy islands that disappear before the first wave of inundation, are, in the spring months, studded with the eggs of the plover. The bird's unfailing instinct thus beautifully exemplifies the truth of Solomon's words, that "for every thing there is a season, and a time for every purpose under the heavens."

As the eye wanders round, clumps of seeming trees edge the horizon. These may be plantations around villages on the high bank, or Talli trees in the river's bed, which the stream has respected for the last dozen years,—a long duration for all that blossoms here; or perhaps they are only bushes magnified by the atmosphere. The sun rises, the mirage is broken, and the last suspicion proves correct.

Out of sight of land, the voyager may for hours be floating amid a wilderness of green island fields, and when he supposes himself far from man, is sometimes startled at hearing a human voice from amid the expanse of rushes which surround him. It is the solitary bulrush-gatherer, who, with only his mussuk for support, braves all the dangers of the stream to procure the root of the bulrush for food for himself and his little ones. These people resort to such islands as are within a foot of being submerged, and, stationing themselves on the windward edge, seize hold of the rushes when detached by the action of the stream; nor does a plough turn up a furrow with greater precision than the current's surging waves slice down these ever-changing islands.

CHAPTER VI.

Town of Kalabagh.—High temperature.—River bathing.—Amphibious population.—Hindû Sunday's amusement.—Their general character.—Alum works.—Arrival of a Seik army.—Instructions.—Departure for Attock by the river.—The Duggah.—Swan river.—Dinghot.—Mukkud.—Author's mishap.—Town of Mukkud.—Influence of rain on the Indus.—Bundewan rivulet.—Mountain torrents.—Dead bodies.—Ascent of the river abandoned.—Success of the Seiks. —Departure for Attock by land.—Guide.—Sagrî Patans.—Seik bad faith.— Jats and Awans.—Arrival at Attock.

THE romantic site of Kalabagh in a gorge of the great salt range, through which the Indus rushes forth into the plain, was remarked and admired by Mr. Elphinstone's party in 1809. Its situation is certainly more picturesque than judicious. It is the hottest place between Attock and the sea, and it would require little trouble to prove it the most unhealthy. The water of the Indus is here reputed unwholesome, while an alum manufactory in the centre of the town keeps its inhabitants in an atmosphere as noxious as it is disagreeable. Many of the natives of the place suffer from a swelling resembling goître, which they attribute, and I should conceive justly, to the tainted air they are constantly inhaling. To a stranger the effluvia given out by the burning beds of alum is highly offensive.

The heat of this place must be excessive. Its inhabitants never think of passing a summer's day in-doors, but, quitting their houses, seat themselves under the umbrageous banian trees (Ficus religiosa), which here at intervals shade the river's banks. In these cool retreats, with the water actually surrounding their couches, the idle and the aged of the male population sleep or languish out the day; while their more thrifty partners divide their time about equally between the river and their spinning-wheels.

Bathing is here a great luxury, and much in fashion, especially with the women, who when so engaged expose their persons with an indifference which proves they can have but little delicacy, and still less sense of shame. But let us be just to the fair ones of Kalabagh. Scenes that to a stranger appear indelicate, are not so viewed by the husbands of these ladies, who themselves accustomed to frequent the river from infancy can see no impropriety in their better halves thus unceremoniously enjoying the luxury of its cool waters.

In truth the population of the banks of the Indus are almost amphibious. The boatmen of Lower Sind, for example, live, like the Chinese, in their boats. If a native of the Lower Indus has occasion to cross the stream, a pulla-jar wafts him to the opposite shore. At B'hkur the mussuk supersedes the pulla-jar, and from Mittun-Kote upwards every man living near the river has one. Kassids so mounted make surprising journeys, and the soldier with sword and matchlock secured across his shoulders thus avoids the fatigue of a long march. But the Hindú most enjoys the Indus, and delights to sport in its stream. The higher we advance up the river, the more manifest does his predilection for its waters become. At Attock the very boatmen are many of them Hindús—an employment quite foreign to Brahma's followers in the lower course of the Indus. The Sunday amusement of this class is to wanton in its waters. Confined to their shops throughout the week, with them the seventh day is one of relaxation and enjoyment. Early in the forenoon they repair to the river or canal, and there upon their mussuks float and talk till sunset. I have seen in one group a father and two children, the latter on dried elongated gourds, clinging to their parent, who bestrode a good-sized mussuk. Close to them came two grey-haired men apparently hugging each other, for they rode upon the same inflated skin, which, but for the closeness with which they embraced it, would have soon parted company. Next came sailing down an individual lying much at his ease, between the four legs of a huge buffalo's hide, while boys moved in all directions, mounted as they best could, some on gourds and some on skins.

The Hindús of these regions differ considerably from those

of Hindustan. They are less fettered by religious observances, unawed by Brahmins, less rigid in their diet, and altogether assimilate more to their Mohamedan neighbours. Conversion among them to the latter creed is not a rare occurrence, though in all cases which have come under my observation the motives were unworthy—love of money and ambition in the men, and affairs of the heart with the women. But the Hindús of the Indus have also their customs and superstitious rites. The bodies of the dead are burned, as with the rest of Brahma's followers; but children dying before they have teethed are thrown into the river. Many are the propitiatory offerings which are hourly committed to the Indus. A few reeds smeared with mud form a little raft, on which the devotee places as many lights as it will carry, strews it with rice or other grain, and having muttered some words of mystic import over this richly freighted fire-ship, the little bark is launched upon the stream. Often of a still evening have I watched the flickering lights of these votive offerings, as they were borne away by the current, and have been tempted to liken the river to Time, the Ocean to Eternity, man the frail, faintly illumined bark, and life its perilous and chequered voyage.

The alum manufactory employs three hundred labourers of different descriptions. The quantity of this article daily prepared is one hundred and twenty-two maunds, at an expense of one hundred and ten rupees. At the works its price is two rupees per maund, and on its removal the government levy a tax on every camel load, or eight maunds, of two rupees and a half.

A few days after our arrival at Kalabagh, the Seik army alluded to in the last chapter appeared on the east bank of the river, and there encamped. A party of Ghazí, or champions of Mohamedanism, had collected on the west bank to oppose their passage across the Indus, and as our little camp occupied the ground where the Seiks would probably land, a civil message was sent, requesting we would move elsewhere. This, however, proved mere gasconade, for the army crossed without encountering the slightest opposition, and not many days afterwards Ahmed Khán, by concession, made his peace with the Maharajah.

The boatmen of Kalabagh having reported the upward navigation to Attock impracticable at this season of the year, Captain Burnes was detained here some time by the difficulty of procuring bullocks to convey his party by land. As soon as he had obtained them he crossed to the Indian side of the river, and, under a Seik escort, left Kalabagh about the 22nd of July.

My instructions were to make the best of my way to Attock, by the river; or, failing in that, to hasten there by land, and thence descend the stream. I accordingly made choice of the strongest and fittest boat the place afforded, and commenced beating up for a crew to man her; but at first, neither the Malik's [1] threats nor high wages would induce the boatmen to volunteer. At length, thirty-seven men were obtained under an express stipulation that they were not to go higher than Mukkud, a town only twenty miles above Kalabagh, and on the 20th of July we commenced the ascent.

The boat [2] employed on this part of the Indus differs, though not materially, from the Sind Dundí. It is strongly built, and the extremities project more than with the Sind boat. The utility of the elongated bow and stern is very apparent in navigating the Indus where its banks are high and rocky; for when, for example, a strong current sweeps round a projecting point, the bow of the boat acts as a lever, and enables the trackers to swing her clear.

Masts and sails are not used here. In a channel so contracted, and with banks so high, the breeze is necessarily variable, whilst the wild swirl with which the wind comes over the stream, as it gushes down the lateral ravines, would endanger better boats than any which the Indus can boast.

On starting, the crew, in tracking the boat clear of the town, had an opportunity of trying their skill, and I was glad to find that there was a fair proportion of good hands among them. Towards sunset we reached the point where the Swan river flows into the Indus, and there we halted for the night. Just above the town of Kalabagh, the width of the Indus was 481 yards; nor during this day did the stream anywhere seem of a much less breadth. The trackers had no great difficulties to contend

---

[1] The governor. [2] The class of boat here alluded to is called duggah.

against, and I already began to augur favourably of the termination of the voyage.

Seven miles above Kalabagh we passed a rocky precipice, rising immediately from the river, the table summit of which is the site of Ding-Kot, a place of some celebrity in the early annals of Hindustan.

Next day we arrived at Mukkud; having thus made, without any extraordinary exertion, twenty miles from Kalabagh. Here the boatmen left us, although I made the most liberal offers to induce them to remain. From this to the 27th I was detained endeavouring to obtain a new crew. The Seik authorities of the place gave me every assistance; but they had even less influence with the boatmen than the Malik of Kalabagh.

The day of our arrival at Mukkud, believing that Captain Burnes might still be in the neighbourhood of Kalabagh, I felt anxious to communicate with him, that an order might be obtained from the commander of the Seik army, to their functionaries here, stimulating them to use every endeavour to complete my boat's crew. I accordingly wrote a letter; but as time was now doubly precious, I resolved to be the bearer of my own despatch, and to drop down with the current upon a mussuk, and come back by land the next morning. So after stripping, and tying a suit of clothes upon my head, I audaciously pushed off from the steep bank and launched into the stream; but scarcely had I advanced two yards, when, losing my balance, the buoyant skin jumped from under me, and I had to regain the bank as I best could.

A thousand times had I seen the mussuk used; and although I had never before tried it myself, I thought there could not be any great mystery in managing a contrivance so simple that children were permitted its use. I was, however, mistaken; knowledge is not intuitive, and, like all other *polite* arts, the skill to ride or swim steadily upon a mussuk is not to be acquired without some application. Inattention to the axiom on the present occasion, not only procured me a good ducking, but had nearly cost me my life. After my mishap, the man who was to have been my companion on the river proceeded with the despatch alone.

Mukkud is the principal town in the country of the Sagrí Patans; but though the tribe itself be yet free, their capital is in possession of the Seiks. The town is built at the apex of the angle formed by the junction of the Bundewan rivulet with the Indus, and so close to the steep banks of both, that the latter, whose periodical rise is here about fifty feet, now washes the lower story of some of the houses.

The bed of the Indus in the plain is so wide, that local rains produce no great change in the general appearance of the stream. The effect of heavy rain among the mountains is different; for, during the four days of my stay here, the river apparently from this cause alone rose nine feet.

Whilst at Mukkud, the Bundewan, a rivulet usually so small that it may be said to trickle rather than flow, was at times much swollen. One day in particular, it afforded me a good opportunity of observing the changeable character of mountain torrents. The rivulet had dwindled to its usual insignificancy, when a rain-cloud burst over the valley, and poured out a constant stream for ten minutes. The boys, aware of what was coming, repaired with their mussuks to a spot on the bank of the rivulet, a mile above its *embouchure*. About half an hour had elapsed when the roar of the coming torrent was heard, and presently the front wave of what was now a wild foaming river rolled past, which it no sooner had done than the assembled merry group plunged into its frothy stream, and as they sported like ducks upon its red surface, seemed equally delighted with the velocity and the foam.

The force of these torrents is indeed remarkable, and the *cutting* power of water can nowhere be better understood than by an examination of their dry beds. One in this neighbourhood, which I inspected, had a channel thirty-six feet wide, and perpendicular walls for its banks three and a half feet high. These banks were composed of pebbles and rounded stones, many of which were upwards of a hundred pounds in weight. The *débris* had closed their interstices, so that the whole had the look and almost the strength of a conglomerate formation. Had this channel been artificially hollowed the walls could not have been formed with more regularity.

Every day during our detention at Mukkud a corpse floated past the town; but those sickening scenes which often startle humanity on the banks of the Ganges are unknown here: life, I am inclined to think, is oftener lost in mountain torrents than in the main stream.

Our crew being at last completed, we left Mukkud on the 27th, and toiled against the stream till sunset. At day-break next morning we were again at the track-ropes; but the most unwearied exertions brought us in the evening no further than Tora Mala, a village distant but five miles from Mukkud. The ascent had now become extremely laborious; though not hazardous, as the obstructions we had to surmount were not in the river's channel, but arose from the wall-like nature of its banks. Quitting the boat here I landed and examined its channel as high as Sharkí, a village on its western shore. To this place I concluded the boat might possibly be dragged; but all hope of being able to advance higher was completely cut off by perpendicular banks several hundred feet high, which a little above Sharkí buttressed the river.

The method of tracking in this rocky section differs from that pursued further south only in the greater number of men employed, and the additional precautions used. A boat that ascends from Kalabagh to Attock in winter, when the river is low, must have a double crew; but during the summer, when the Indus is swollen, the voyage is altogether impracticable. Independent of other obstacles to the boat's upward progress, the great rapidity of the current is at this season an insurmountable impediment. From the wavy outlines of the precipitous banks, it is often necessary to cross from one side of the river to the other. In these cases it is more galling than I can well describe to find your boat, whilst you are crossing a stream two hundred yards wide, borne away by a sweeping current, and, despite the best efforts of her crew, landed below an impending cliff which can only be doubled by re-crossing and working up the bank you have just quitted. These unprofitable traverses kept me, as I have already stated, two days between Mukkud and Tora Mala.

In May of this year (1837), two months earlier in the season, the Seiks succeeded in getting five boats up the river: with fifty men to each boat they vanquished not only the physical obstructions, but, by the active friendship of Sultan Mohamed Khán, ruler of Kohat, were enabled also to overcome the difficulties resulting from the hostile disposition of the tribes along the banks. These boats were sent back about the 5th of this month; three reached Kalabagh, but the other two were wrecked on the way down.

These boats were requisite for the completion of the Attock boat-bridge, and as the Seiks of Peshawúr had been worsted in a conflict with the Afghans, Runjít Sing was extremely anxious to throw troops across the Indus for the protection of that rich, but to him unproductive, plain. Under these pressing circumstances, the boats in fifteen days were brought from Kalabagh to Attock. But what the Seiks had considered a hard task in May, with unlimited means at their command, would, I imagine, have been impossible even for them in the month of July.

There is no intercourse by the river between Attock and Kalabagh. The boats of the former place are restricted to the use of the ferry, and to the formation of bridges across the Indus when necessary; while those of the latter, besides the usual duties of the ferry, have to keep the alum works in fuel. In these wooding parties, two or more boats sail in company. When tracking is difficult, their crews banding together, first drag up one boat, and then return for another.

Convinced of the utter hopelessness of any further attempt to reach Attock by the river, I now proposed to fulfil the latter part of my instructions, and proceed there by land. The boat was accordingly dropped down the stream to Mukkud, and discharged. After some detention at this place, two ponies and a guide were procured, when, thanking the Seik authorities for the aid they had afforded me, Gholam Hussein and myself commenced our journey. As the Sagrí Patans are unfriendly to the Seiks, whose guests we were, it was necessary to make an easterly *détour* to avoid the lands of that tribe. Our road at starting led up the Bundewan's bed, where we were caught by a pelting shower of rain, and fated to stand longer than was pleasant, bridle in hand, soaked to the skin and crouching under cliffs in its time-worn sides. Around us was a picture of desolation. Hemmed in by hills, nothing could be seen but the rugged summit of walls of concentrating ravines, the aspect of which was arid and ferruginous. When the rain fell, a thousand cascades came streaming down their furrowed sides, and drove us from one nook to another, as the waters found an entrance. At length the weather cleared; we wrung our clothes dry, mounted, and arrived on the second day upon the banks of the Swan river.

Our guide was a Mohamedan, and heartily hated his Seik employers. He seldom spoke, but to anathematise the Kaffirs, and throughout the journey continued to call down curses on their race. I asked this man what he would do, were he to meet an unarmed Seik? "Murder him," was the laconic and savage reply.

East of the Indus, the Sagrí Patans are the only people who have not yet submitted to Runjít Sing's authority. The lands of this tribe stretch along both sides of the river, north and south of Mukkud. On the west bank, their country lies between the Kuttock and Bungí Kyl territories, while on the opposite bank, the Awans are found to the north and south of them. The tribe is both pastoral and agricultural, feeding large flocks of sheep and goats by the river's side, and cultivating the ground inland. The fleece of the Dümbí or large-tailed sheep, is beautifully white, and the wool was now selling at ten seers for a rupee. The Sagrí have no chieftain, but their place of resort and council is the valley of the Nirrah, on the east bank of the Indus, and close to Tora Mala. It is described as well stocked with fruit trees, with a fertile soil, and of sufficient extent to support 150 horsemen. Here some of their principal families reside. The Sagrí have a high reputation among their neighbours for bravery, and are accounted good swordsmen. They are of Afghan origin, and speak Pushtu. Many of them are in the habit of serving as mercenaries, both in Afghanistan and in India. This tribe could muster from 800 to 1000 foot soldiers, and about 200 horse.

When the Seiks in force overran their country, the Sagrí

Patans made no resistance, and the former having built a fort in the Nirrah valley, quietly took possession of the land: a tribute was then fixed, and the Seiks withdrew. The tribe, however, accuse Runjít Sing of acting towards them with duplicity and bad faith; and from the various circumstances which have come to my knowledge, I believe there is truth in the charge. Some time ago the governor of Mukkud sent to acquaint the Sagrí that he had received Runjít Sing's commands to levy a heavier tax than the one which had been fixed, and that in compliance with his master's instructions, he had now sent properly qualified persons to measure and re-assess their land. The Sagrí sent one of their body to remonstrate; but this deputy on the plea of sedition, was imprisoned in Mukkud, and for his ransom a fine of 700 rupees was demanded. The tribe retaliated by seizing a number of Seik ryots, and threatening to detain them until their clansman was released. The Seik governor replied, they were welcome to do so, on which the Sagrí paid the money, and on their deputy being released, the tribe with one consent rose in arms. The governor of Mukkud thinking, I presume, that he had not rightly interpreted his instructions, was now solicitous for an amicable accommodation. Trusting to the oath of this unprincipled functionary, the Patans sent seven of their number to arrange its preliminaries, and these men, strange to say, the infatuated governor likewise confined. No sooner was the fate of this deputation known in Nirrah, than the heads of families assembled, and after a short deliberation, the following message was sent into Mukkud: "Three times have the Seiks broken faith with us, and friendship henceforward between us can be no more. Our imprisoned brethren you may destroy, but to the Sagrí revenge is sweet." Between Mukkud and Nirrah, the Seiks had built a little fort called Nukka, to assist in keeping up the communication with their troops in the Sagrí country. The commander of this garrison seeing the tribe's preparations for war, applied for reinforcements, and accordingly, between fifty and sixty men were sent from Mukkud. The party never reached Nukka. The Patans had early intimation of what was contemplated, and assembling their strength, patiently waited in ambush for the approach of the detachment. The place selected was a narrow path-way, commanded by rocks overhead and at both ends. Every Seik soldier was massacred, and a few mercenary Afghans met a similar and more merited fate. After thus committing themselves, the tribe, until May, 1837, kept up an exterminating system of warfare, robbing upon the roads, plundering villages, devastating corn fields, filling up wells, and cutting off every small party they succeeded in way-laying. When pursued in force, they crossed to the west bank of the Indus, and harboured among the Kuttock and other friendly clans. The country east of the river, from the Swan on the South, to the Hurrú on the north, felt the effects of their depredations, and it was the diminution of the revenue from this region which brought the transactions we have briefly sketched to the knowledge of Runjít Sing. Orders forthwith arrived from Lahore to cease persecuting the Sagrí, to restore the prisoners to freedom, and to tax the tribe only to the amount they had formerly paid. These lenient measures on the part of the Maharajah are fast reclaiming this lawless, but justly incensed tribe; their lands are again becoming settled, and the deserted fields of Nirrah have resumed their beauty: men who have been deeply wronged are easily re-excited, and I feel certain that the sight of a Seik detachment in their country, unless its strength made it formidable, would again rouse the Sagrí to acts of violence.

On quitting the banks of the Swan river, we proceeded in a more northerly direction over a country where ruined hamlets and uncultivated fields bore ample evidence to late unsettled times. This was succeeded by a quiet district, where numerous smiling villages contrasted favourably with the desolate condition of those we had left behind. Its cultivators were Jats and Awans. The former are to be met with along the banks of the Indus, from its mouth to Attock, and also in the Panjáb. The latter are chiefly confined to the east bank of the river, and to that portion of it lying between Attock and Kalabagh. The Malik of the last-named town is chief of this tribe. The Awans are willing to take a daughter from the Jats, but will not give a female of their own to any of that tribe. The Afghans look upon both as one people, though the Awans profess to be descended from no less a personage than Hazrat Ali. Both tribes are followers of the Prophet, and their vocation is the cultivation of the soil.

Pressing on by forced marches, we forded the Hurrú river on the 3rd of August, and next day entered Attock.

CHAPTER VII.

Embarkation at Attock.—Berrí island.—An open plain.—Hurrú river.—Mountains.—Character of the navigation.—Niláb.—Ghori-Tarap whirlpool.—Dangerous eddies.—Great depth of the river.—A Kuttock outwitted.—Muncú.—Dangers off the Toe river and Soheilí rocks.—Dubber mountains.—Fearful eddies.—The Indus among mountains.—In the plain.—Characteristics of both.—Great velocity of the stream.—Dreadful when confined.—Upward navigation impracticable.—Villages on the river.

BY noon of the following day, I was prepared to descend the river from Attock to Kalabagh. Here there was no difficulty in procuring both boats and men; a large establishment of each being kept up by Runjít Sing for the construction of a boat-bridge, which he yearly throws across the Indus, which river between these two towns is called by the inhabitants on its banks the Attock. After breakfasting with Captain Burnes's party, which had arrived here early in the forenoon, I went down to the lower gate of the fortress where the boat lay. Before embarking, I measured the width of the stream here, and found it to be two hundred and eighty-six yards, but a little lower down where its channel is usually spanned by the bridge of boats, it is much more contracted.

At 11h. 55m. in the forenoon we cast off the painter,[1] pulled out into the stream, and as we passed the ferry, sounded and found the depth of water ten fathoms. Having gained the centre of the river, the boat was permitted to drop down with the current, and her crew instructed to keep her at all times as much as possible in its strength.

In a quarter of an hour from the time of departure we approached a spot where a bulging rock on the left hand split

[1] The rope by which a boat is secured.

the stream into two channels. The boat was steered to the right down the larger, which had a depth of twenty fathoms. The island thus formed is named Berrí by the boatmen. A short distance below this island the ruins of a place called Petore were descried among the mountains on the left bank; on breasting which we emerged from the Attock slate, by a range of which, thus far, the river had been margined.

The plain we now entered was very circumscribed, being only three miles in length, and bounded on both sides by hills at no great distance. The space between these had permitted the river to expand, and reduced its depth to four and a half fathoms. The banks were shelving and pebbly, and the course of the stream nearly due south. Several good-sized villages are situated hereabouts, whose inhabitants were now employed washing the sand of the river in search of gold. The Macedonians found no gold in India, and it is a singular fact that none of the eastern tributaries of the Indus yield it, though the parent stream does, and likewise every rivulet from the westward.[1]

Before reaching the end of the plain a range of black-looking mountains a-head was seen, apparently crossing the river's bed, and even when we were close upon them, no gorge or exit could be detected. The confluence of the Hurrú river, which here joins from the eastward, had just been passed, when our boat was forcibly carried by a violent current under the high impending cliffs of the left bank, and on sweeping round a corner we discovered, when we had time to look about us, that we were surrounded by mountains.

From Attock to the Hurrú, the Indus, though rapid among the slaty ridges, yet flows calmly on; but below this it assumes a very different character, which it retains to within a league of Sharkí, a village, it may be remembered, where I was discomfited in an attempt to reach Attock by water from Kalabagh. For the whole of this distance, huge boulders and long ridgy ledges occur in the channel of the river; over and among which the

---

[1] I have since learned that grains of the precious metal have been found in some of the Panjáb rivers, where they issue from the mountains. October, 1840.

mighty torrent tumbles and roars : its power is immense, and one is almost led to suppose that it would be sufficient to remove from the bed of the river many of the greatest obstructions. The course of the river is very crooked, and its bed being narrow, the immense volume of water pent within it rushing on with great velocity, has not space to sweep quietly round the corners, but is precipitated against the bank that faces the line of its direction, and is there heaped up several feet above the general level. At all such places we find a fall in the river, and immediately below it a dangerous eddy. The fall may have a height of four feet, measured on the bank which causes it, but it speedily lessens as it runs off towards the opposite side, where it sinks into the eddy.

Two miles below the Hurrú is Niláb, where the ruthless Tamerlane, when he marched on India, crossed the Indus. The town formerly stood on both sides of the river, though it has now dwindled into a miserable village on the eastern bank. The stream is here contracted, and twenty fathoms deep. The blue colour of its waters has given the name to this place. It possesses a ferry-boat, and from hence there is a road to Peshawúr.

The river from Niláb continues for eight miles to flow nearly due west, between blue limestone hills, that rise slantingly from its bed to a height of seven hundred feet. These hills are thickly studded with Fulah bushes, whose evergreen foliage upon the bare glassy sides of the blue rocks, looked exceedingly beautiful as we swiftly glided in silence along their base. This scene soon changed to one more stern, and more exciting. On nearing the end of the reach, a noise of angry water was heard, when the boatman informed me that we were approaching the whirlpool of Ghora-Tarap, the first danger that occurs on the river below Attock. The crew now went to prayers, then seizing the oars, they fixed their eyes upon the steersman, watching for his signal when they were to exert themselves. The danger here is caused by a series of those eddies which I have described as formed by the sharp angular turnings of the river, when compressed and cased in by high rocky banks, that admit of no lateral expansion. The steersman passed his boat down where the fall had a height of perhaps eighteen inches, caring little for this risk, but fearful of the attendant eddy. Though the fall was shot with startling rapidity, the boat when over seemed spell-bound to the spot, and hung for some time under the watery wall in spite of the most strenuous efforts of her crew. At last she moved, the men cheered, and out she darted into the fair channel. At Ghora-Tarap the depth was thirty-one fathoms, and the width of the stream, though I had not the means of measuring it, could not have exceeded two hundred and fifty feet.

At 3h. 20m. P.M. we reached a watch-tower of the Kuttocks overlooking the river. Here the high limestone hills, among which for the last seventeen miles the river had held its course, gave place to others of less altitude, which continued to bank this stream through the remainder of this day's voyage, which closed ten minutes before seven P.M. at Muncú, a village forty-two miles from Attock. From 5h. 20m. to 6h. 10m. the boat was delayed by a sand squall, so that we had averaged during the passage seven miles an hour.

Not far below the watch-tower a Kuttock hailed us from the right bank, and ordered us to land; taking aim at the same time by way of enforcing his command. We proceeded to obey, but intentionally plied the oars so sluggishly, that the current had borne us beyond the range of his matchlock, ere the Kuttock had discovered he had been outwitted. It was evident that he was terribly enraged, for we could see him leap from rock to rock with the agility of his own mountain goats; but if he had also possessed the antelope's speed, it would have availed him nothing among the craggy rocks that here buttress the river.

Next morning at 4h. 35m. the fastenings were let go, and out we swept upon the dark glassy surface of the river, still banked by the same hills as on the preceding day. It was necessary to be wary, for the deep channel was yet but faintly lit up by the grey dawn of morning, and scarcely had we cleared Muncú when the usual noise gave warning of rocks being near. These and a few others which succeeded to them were soon left behind, when we moved forward upon a comparatively clear stream, till at 6 A.M. we were abreast of the Toe river, and the Soheilí rocks lying off it. Having cleared this danger, we steered down along the right bank much incommoded by the turbulent water which, throughout the whole of this reach, is boisterous even where there is no apparent cause for such commotion.

At 10m. to 7 A.M. we passed through the Dubber mountains, a range that here extends on both sides of the river. The acute turnings among the steep bluffs caused by these mountains gave rise to numerous violent eddies, over which, had the boat's beam been less, she could not have safely ridden. In these we were often completely drenched by the surging waves, which flew up in jets when the boat came in contact with the whirling and angry current. We had passed but a few miles below these eddies, when Sharkí came in sight. The Dubber range may thus be styled the barrier gate of the Indus, for its southern bluffs are in sight from that village, and are the same which, as already related, deterred me from advancing higher up the stream. Hence to Kalabagh the river flows smoothly, or in a comparatively diffused stream free from rocks and other impediments. We reached that town a little after noon, having averaged from Muncú six and three quarter miles an hour.

What a contrast does the Indus in this part of its course present to the shoal and wide-spread river of the plain! Here it gushes down a valley varying from one hundred to four hundred yards wide, between precipitous banks from seventy to seven hundred feet high. Its character, however, is not that of a brawling stream, or a swollen mountain torrent, but as if conscious of its own magnitude and strength, the noble river pursues its course in silence, except where chafed by obstructions which itself has caused. The country, down the centre valley of which this ceaseless tide is rolled, may be described as a moderately elevated table-land, extending from Attock to the Great Salt range. The banks of the river throughout the whole of this distance are formed of hills that rise immediately from its waters, in bold bluffs or steep weather-worn slopes. At some places rising in mural precipices, at others rugged and broken, the blackened sides of the impending cliffs cast their dark shadows across the leaden surface of the narrow river, and tinge its waters still deeper with their gloom. Compressed by rocky banks several hundred feet high, the sullen stream, where not opposed, glides smoothly onwards, and but for the ever-changing form of the overhanging crags, and the varying outline of the banks, the boat would seem motionless, though borne on by a current of nine miles an hour, so stealthily does the river flow where its 'depth and velocity are the greatest. It is where the surface of the stream is ruffled and broken by opposing rocks, that the angry spirit of the river is roused and the turmoil is dreadful. The enormous body of water is crushed against the obstruction, and becomes white with spray and foam. If it be a rocky ledge in mid river, the water, after rising up its face, rolls off in huge waves that extend across both channels, forming dangerous eddies; and to keep clear from their whirling and tumultuous vortex requires both nerve and skill; whilst at the lower side of the ledge the river keeps dashing on, roaring among its jagged points and cresting them with foam.

From Niláb to within two miles of the Kuttock's watch-tower the river was quite a sluice. Black bluffs here encroached upon the stream, and produced fearful eddies. We must have passed down some of these narrows at the rate of nine miles an hour. In approaching them no noise is heard except a sort of gushing sound, till on turning a corner, the thunder of broken water falls upon the ear, its foam being just visible at the further end of a dark rocky vista. The boatmen kneel and commend themselves to their Maker; then seizing the oars with a firm grasp stand prepared to act. The noise becomes deafening, and the rocks are soon under the bows. To hesitate between the channels would be certain destruction: and here every one must admire the courage and firmness of Attock boatmen. Their nerve greatly lessens the hazard of this dangerous voyage, as does also the peculiar structure of their boats.

From the middle of May to September, the upward voyage may be pronounced impracticable. The downward voyage may be performed at all seasons of the year, although not without risk when the river is full.

The villages in this section of the Indus are perched on the verge of its banks, so that the inhabitants of many of them could at this season draw up water from their balconies. They stand on the bare rock, without a blade of vegetation near them. The heat of such houses may be imagined. They are generally forsaken in the middle of the day, at which time the inhabitants resort to the trees scattered up and down in the neighbourhood. A rough bed frame is placed under their shade, and on these the old folks dream away the day. The thrifty wife brings out her spinning-wheel, and parties so employed may be seen under every green tree.

CHAPTER VIII.

Escort.—Salt range.—A benevolent fakír.—Water-stored shed.—Pass of Shukur Durah.—Village.—Bungí Kyl.—Agha Maheide.—Start for Kohat.—Country improves.—Banks of the Toe river.—Frontier lines.—Superstitions.—Fine valleys.—Shadí Kyl.—Kohat.—Plain.—Town.—Fort.—Seik soldiers.—A love-sick youth.

THAT our old acquaintance the Malik of Kalabagh had more authority over his sepoys than over his boatmen, was evinced by the promptitude with which he furnished a party to escort us through the lands of the Bungí Kyl into the territories of Kohat, the route by which I was directed to join the mission at Peshawúr.

When prepared to start, I dismissed the Attock boatmen with a small present, giving them the option of accompanying us back to their homes by the way of Peshawúr and Kohat, or remaining with their boat until the navigation was open. They chose the latter alternative, and we parted. Kalabagh stands on the southern face of the salt range, just outside the gorge by which the Indus enters upon the plain. Behind the range is the Pass of Shukur Durah, up which our road lay. It was therefore necessary to boat the horses round the dividing mountain, in doing which, we had a good opportunity of observing its formation. The salt occurs here in compact glassy strata, dipping at an angle of 65°, but its large protruding blocks have no determinate form

Not far up the Pass is the residence of a fakír, who has devoted the best years of a long life to the charitable office of supplying water to travellers. In Shukur Durah the springs for twenty miles are either salt or fetid, and under a sultry summer sun this journey is always one of pain and fatigue; to the exhausted and thirsty traveller, no sight can therefore be more welcome than this good man's humble dwelling, nor any thought more cheering than the anticipation of the long array of earthen pots, brimful of the cool delicious element which he is sure to find within.

We met several parties coming down the ravine laden with dried grass for the Kalabagh market. These people called at the water-stored hut, and on leaving it, took the fakír's empty jars down to the brink of the river, where they left them to be brought back full by the first traveller returning from the town.

For two miles we proceeded up the Pass in a northerly direction, over a tolerable road, having the salt range to our left hand, and sandstone hills to the right. We then quitted the salt range, but continued to zigzag on through the sandstone, the defile becoming narrower as we advanced, whilst the road was so obstructed by large stones and rocky ledges, as greatly to impede the traveller whether mounted or on foot. This path continued to ascend without any improvement till we reached a cleft in the hills called Mussun, ten miles from Kalabagh, where some water trickles down the rock, but so fetid that it would be considered undrinkable were it not that no better is to be had. Here we passed the night.

Next day, the 9th of August, a march of thirteen miles brought us to the village of Shukur Durah at the head of the Pass. On quitting Mussun, the defile opens, the mountains become rounded, and small patches of cultivation are seen to skirt their base.

The country we had just passed through is inhabited by the Bungí Kyl, a tribe of Afghan origin, whose thieving propensities and vagabond life are notorious among their more correct and wealthy neighbours. They occupy both banks of the Indus for some distance north of Kalabagh, and are almost equally numerous with the Sagrí Patans, but are neither so industrious nor respectable. Their flocks are small, and there are but few of them; while their limited extent of cultivated land is scattered here and there in patches undeserving the name of fields. The country is wild in aspect, and its soil unkind; and to rear the coarsest grain requires patient labour and a continuance of favourable weather. Should abundant showers not fall, the barren sandy soil is scorched by the July sun and deadened to vegetation; then it is that famine drives the poor starving wretches forth to prey upon their more favourably located neighbours. This predatory tribe live chiefly upon the west side of the river; but its opposite bank is the principal scene of their depredations. If hotly pursued, they will at all times rather abandon their stolen booty than risk their lives in its defence. Murder with them is a rare crime.

The Bungí Kyl are nominally subject to the Malik of Kalabagh, whom they assist in all his contests with the neighbouring chiefs; but they are not bound to serve abroad. In their disputes among themselves, the malik's award is final; and when a fine is levied, the judge, after taking a moiety to himself, distributes the remainder among the principal men of the tribe.

Should an individual who has been plundered by the Bungí Kyl have the hardihood to follow the thieves into their lone haunts amid the wild recesses of this savage region, he will, if poor and a stranger, recover the greater part of his lost property; but should he chance to be a person of consequence, he will fare still better, for the whole will be restored, and he himself feasted.

To rob from one another is accounted dishonourable among them, and the same feeling keeps them from disturbing the peace of their friends the Sagrí. Grain left in the field is generally as safe as when stored in the court-yard. Sometimes, however, their inherent vice breaks out, and the more honest tribesmen suffer. On such occasions, which they profess to look upon as lamentable instances of national degeneracy, the heads of families are assembled, and the thief is compelled to restore the property, and is mulct in a fine sufficient to feast his judges. To this entertainment all parties sit down, the thief amongst the rest, silent and moody at the unfortunate discovery, the others talkative and jovial, and luxuriating at his expense. But these honourable and justice-loving vagabonds have no such clear perception of the distinction between "meum et tuum" when the goods of a stranger come within their grasp.

Hospitality, the most prominent virtue of a rude people, is

not better observed by the noble clan of Duraní than by the thieving Bungí Kyl. A stranger when he has broken bread with one of the tribe may afterwards feel perfectly secure, and at his ease among them.

At the village of Shukur Durah we were met by Agha Maheide, a Persian gentleman, deputed by Sultan Mohamed Khán to escort Captain Burnes up the west bank of the river should he have preferred journeying on that side. Agha Maheide came well attended, which enabled us to part with our Kalabagh escort sooner than we otherwise could have done.

On the 10th we set out together for Kohat. The first halt we called, was at the fine large village of Kurrilsum, three miles before entering which we crossed the Lun rivulet. The name of this petty stream implies salt, an appellation it well deserves, for its waters were brackish; all the horses, however, and many of our party drank of it.

The country both to the east and west was rugged and mountainous, but that portion over which we journeyed gradually improved, until the soft features of its grassy valleys presented a pleasing contrast to the broken and pointed summit, the savage cliffs and the grim iron visage of the sandstone district between Kalabagh and Shukur Durah.

Next day a pleasant ride over a fine country with an agreeable chatty old man for a companion, for such we found Agha Maheide, made me regret that the march was not a longer one. Twelve miles from Kurrilsum brought us to the small river Toe, on the green banks of which, shaded by trees and cooled by its crystal stream, we lounged through the heat of a sultry day. This clear brook has its source from springs in the Tiri country, but its principal supply is from snow, which in that elevated region lingers at the bottom of the deep ravines till summer is nearly spent. To this river the lands of the Bungush owe their fertility, and well do the inhabitants deserve their good fortune. Nowhere had I seen land cultivated with such praiseworthy care. Nearly all the water of this little stream is made to flow in many meandering channels, scattering its blessings everywhere. From our encampment on the Toe, four villages were to be seen within a distance of two miles, all watered by this river.

Four miles south of the Toe the lands of the Kuttocks end, and those of the Bungush commence. The former are termed, in allusion to their sterility, *khushk* or *dry*, while the latter are called *aube* or *wet*. The Kuttocks depend on rain for their crops, but the Bungush irrigate their fields from the Toe and other perennial brooks.

The place of our encampment was a ziarat called Turkumul, round the burial-ground of which the whole country seemed to have piled their grain. On the march we had passed two other villages, where I remarked what appeared to be a similar provident care for the sustenance of the departed in the land of spirits. In one place of sepulture, the usual household utensils were stored, and I verily thought with the same pious and kindly feeling that makes the relatives of a North American Indian bury him astride his war horse, or in his canoe paddle in hand. But such was not the case. Here the dead sentinelled the chattels of the living. In troublesome times, when a man is fain to quit his native village until the return of order, he prefers trusting his valuables to the sacred guardianship of such a place, rather than to his weak and failing brother. I inquired of Agha Maheide if such was really the case, and whether thieves would not be induced to violate the repository from the certainty of being able to do so with impunity. The old man put the forefingers of his right hand to his lips, and looked at me, exclaiming, " God forbid ! bad as men are, they are not yet so utterly profligate." Religious feeling thus accomplishes what the government is unable to do: it ensures the safety of property: nor can, perhaps, a stronger instance be shown of the firm hold which superstition has over the human mind. Here we find it overcoming the worst passions, and the most confirmed habits of depraved men, much in the same manner as in the dark, solemn oak groves of the Druid, the impious were deterred from touching aught beneath the consecrated shade.

In the evening we moved forward to the village of Doda, the country continuing beautiful. We had mountains to the east and west, while the intervening plain was ribbed by parallel ridges connecting them together. The long narrow valleys, rich and sheltered, lying between these lateral chains, looked the very abodes of peace and comfort. In one of these valleys which we crossed during this day's march, a village called Shadí Kyl was built on the slope of its northern ridge. Before the doors of the houses a small clear brook glided by in a shallow bed, bordered with grass and with a row of mulberry trees. From the bank of this rivulet the fields spread out, clothing the region with one sheet of green. This valley and some others like it, were, however, but the exceptions, for since the Seiks seized Kohat its ruler has been compelled to levy a tribute on his people, which they, though perhaps able, are not willing to bear. Many have, in consequence of this, abandoned their homes, while the lands of others are suffered to lie fallow. We saw several deserted villages, and in one fine large valley there was not a single spot that evidenced the presence of a husbandman.

On the following day we marched for Kohat. When within four miles of the town we were met by the Lieutenant-governor Kheirulah Khán, a grand-nephew of Sultan Mohamed Khán. He came gaily attended, and a rabble crowd accompanied him, among which, with banners flying, music playing, horses careering, and spearsmen exhibiting, we entered the fortress under a salute of thirteen guns.

The geological formation of the country between Kalabagh and Kohat is sandstone and limestone. The latter did not appear till we had passed the village of Shukur Durah, when it was visible in the first ridge we crossed, and continued on to Kohat. Its presence not only brought fertility to the soil, but good water to the surface: whilst all the streams among the sandstone are more or less brackish. The height of these ridges varied from five hundred to one thousand feet. At some places the sandstone rose out of the ridge in mural precipices, while the slopes were strewed with slabs and fragments of limestone, looking as if the sandstone had been protruded through the rock. On the summit of these walls a piece of iron slag was found, which would seem to refer their disruption to igneous agency. Through these ridges the Indus has cut its channel, and it is where this occurs that its stream is so boisterous. At Hassan Abdal and Fatteh Jungh, on the Indian side of the river, not only have we the blue limestone formation, but springs both of naphtha and water similar to those of Kohat.

From my apartment in the fort, the eye embraced at a glance the whole plain of Kohat. It is a very fine extent of country, in diameter about seven miles, and susceptible of the highest cultivation. Its numerous enclosures, irrigated by the Toe, have more the appearance of an assemblage of gardens than fields. Of gardens, however, there are but few, as the Seik soldiers, on capturing the place, felled its fruit trees for fire-wood!

The town of Kohat is a paltry-looking place, containing a population of about 2000 souls. It has some copious springs, which supply the town with water, and are besides used to irrigate the land. Here is a Mohamedan ziarat, and a Hindú Dharmsala. The former named Hadjí Bhader, has a pretty little mosque attached to it, in the court of which a fountain supplies water for the ablution of the faithful. The running streams in the neighbourhood of the town are margined by the willow-tree, and a few others of larger growth indigenous to India are scattered along their banks. Kohat, although deprived of its gardens, is still a delightful residence; and to the Afridi and other wild tribes, inhabiting the savage mountains to the north and west, its willow-banked streams and luxuriant plain must indeed make it appear an elysium.

On the top of a scarped rock commanding the town, the Seiks have erected a triangular fort, the apex of which faces east; and although not a very *sublime* military work, is sufficiently strong to resist such troops as are likely to attack it. Its length is two hundred yards, and its greatest width fifty. It mounts two brass three-pounders. Within the walls there is a well; but as its waters are brackish, the garrison is supplied from the town.

One morning, during my sojourn at Kohat, two Seik soldiers entered the durbar, and in a bullying strain enquired of Kheirulah Khán how long he intended putting them off with evasive answers, instead of paying them the tribute-money, to receive which they had been deputed. This was the revenue of a small mountainous district called Tiri, which is managed by Sultan Mohamed Khán for Runjít Sing. It yields about a thousand rupees per annum. More than twenty Mussulmans hung their heads in silence while the audacious soldiers all but insulted their governor. Kheirulah Khán had recourse to entreaty to soothe these violent men. It was evident that he felt their taunts keenly. How keenly, those only can judge who know the angry feelings that exist between the two creeds. For a Mohamedan governor to be thus rebuked in his own durbar, and that too before a guest, by a couple of unarmed Seik soldiers, was an insult which I could not have imagined one of the faithful would so tamely have endured. I could not, however, but admire the patient and cool tact of Kheirulah, who, while his blood must have been boiling in his veins as he listened to the cutting language of the fellows, was yet careful neither by word nor deed to commit his master.

While here, a handsome youth one day entered the Bechoba and threw his turban at my feet. He was in love, he said, but his passion was not requited. Hearing of a firingí passing through the country, he had come many miles to solicit a charm by which the heart of his lady-love might be softened. He was greatly disappointed when I declared to him that I had no such treasures to dispose of, and although I took some pains to explain the absurdity and worthlessness of the tasseems or charms by which the fakír dupes the simple, he left the tent melancholy and incredulous.

CHAPTER IX.

An Excursion in the Kuttock country.—Misfortunes at starting.—Sulphur mines and Naphtha springs.—Reflections.—A warm bivouac.—A Kuttock chief.—Gumut village.—Religious and social character of Mohamedans.—Prayers for rain.—Murdered travellers.—A horse exorcised.—Return to Kohat.—Notice of the Kuttocks.—Bungnsh.—Kheirulah Khán's durbar.—Quit Kohat.—Reach Peshawúr.—Agha Maheide.—Kabul river.—Visit Attock.—Return to Peshawúr.—Town.—A Seik review.—Quit Peshawúr.—Jamrud.—Murdered grass-cutters.

I WAS unwilling to quit Kohat without visiting its sulphur mines and naphtha springs. On communicating my desire to Kheirulah Khán, a guide named Gholam Khader, was ordered to be in readiness, and at an early hour on the morning of Monday the 14th, we started for the Kuttock village of Sheikh, in the neighbourhood of which lay the objects of our visit. The road led in an easterly direction along the southern base of the Afridi or Khyber chain, a broad belt of high mountains which here separate the two plains of Peshawúr Kohat. Towards evening we reached the Kuttock village, somewhat jaded by the heat and a march of thirty-six miles.

A servant was to have accompanied us with refreshments; but unfortunately, at starting, in the darkness of the morning, we got entangled among the cultivated land of Kohat; and when relieved from this provoking dilemma by the growing light of day, neither he nor the sumpter-mule were visible. The villagers, however, on our route, brought us fire, wood, and water, and as the tea-pot was always to be found in my own saddle bags, we managed matters pretty well.

Three miles north by east of Sheikh is the opening in the mountains in which both the sulphur mines and naphtha springs are situated. On entering this ravine, the springs, five in number, were discovered at its bottom, small in size, and not very productive. They may yield, perhaps, five gallons a day. The colour of the naphtha is dark green, its smell highly sulphurous, and its temperature that of the atmosphere. This ravine had evidently been rent asunder, as the projecting points of one side were faced by corresponding indentations on the other. Its whole length is not more than three hundred yards. The formation is limestone, large masses of which, scorched but not calcined, are strewed around. Salt water impregnated with sulphur oozes down the bottom of the ravine.

After reaching the upper end of the naphtha ravine, you turn to the north, and ascending for four hundred yards, arrive at the sulphur mines. The limestone is here much calcined, and the sulphur is found either incorporated with or encrusting the stone. Where this deposit occurs, the hills seem to have been once coated over with slabs of a reddish-brown colour, which, burst by some pressure from within, now strew the surface with their fragments. When the strata are exposed to atmospheric influence, the stone is of a blueish colour, and so friable, that pieces may be picked out of them by the hand.

The sulphur is obtained by putting a quantity of the ore into an earthen vessel, upon the top of which three other vessels are luted one above another. The two central pots have apertures at top and bottom; the upper one is closed at the top. A fire is applied to the lower vessel and continued for twenty-four hours; at the expiration of which time, the earth will have parted with its sulphur, and the pure mineral be found adhering to the upper and intermediate vessels.

This sulphurous district extends twelve miles from Sheikh, in a south-east direction. It is but nine miles from Khushalghur, a village on the west bank of the Indus, from which the downward navigation is at all times open. When we recollect the inexhaustible supplies of salt that are found near that river, that veins of good coal have been discovered, and that the neighbouring districts of Bunnu and Tak are rich in iron and other ores, we cannot but pause to admire the wisdom of a kind Providence in storing these natural treasures in a situation so favourable for the supply of a wide circle of population. From these magazines the valley of the Indus and the Panjáb can by an easy water communication be supplied; and when progressing civilization shall have unlocked these elements of natural wealth, a great change, political and moral, may be expected.

On our return from the mountains, instead of proceeding direct to the Kuttock village, we spread our saddle-cloths under a fulah bush in the bottom of a shallow ravine, and there awaited the hour of noon, as I was anxious to get a mid-day observation. Whilst here, we were visited by Hussein Khán, the Kuttock chief, who expressed great surprise that on so sultry a day any man should prefer the oppressive heat of the jungle to the cool shade of the village. I got rid of the chief by promising to call at his house in the evening; but I soon found that he had good reason for his surprise.

This was one of the most trying days I ever remember to have spent. The bush was too small to screen us effectually, and the wind came down the ravine heated as from an oven. To remain in the ravine until the evening, as I had intended, was impossible. Our mouths became parched, and the skin peeled from our lips. We could bear it no longer; and at 3 o'clock in the afternoon we saddled our horses, and made our escape into the village.

After passing an hour with Hussein Khán, who, I could see, smiled at the promptitude of our visit, we again mounted, and putting our horses into a brisk trot, we reached Gumut, twenty miles west of Sheikh, at 8 o'clock in the evening. The moon was shining brightly as we entered this village, which I perceived was large, and composed of three detached clusters of buildings, each of which was a little village of itself. A large mud-built fort in the centre protected the whole. The cattle had been driven in, the milking hour was past, and all the inhabitants were enjoying themselves; the grown-up people, seated upon charpoys outside their doors, were chatting together, while the children were sporting about in the open space in front of the houses, and the thoughtless happy laugh of the young men and maidens caught our ear. We inquired for the Malik. He soon appeared, and led us to the mosque, the usual sheltering place of the way-faring stranger. It was already occupied, so we took up a position in the open air in its front. The boys now took our horses by the bridles and led them about till cool, whilst others procured us charpoys, water, firewood, and fire. The Hakim brought us a large bowl of milk, and a vessel to boil our tea water. He communed with the guide for some time, and seeing we were in need of rest, very considerately withdrew. It was late ere I could get to sleep, and even to that hour parties of women continued sauntering about, apparently enjoying a quiet walk and friendly converse, after the labours of the sultry day. Though we reached Gumut very much fatigued, no sooner had we dismounted before the mosque than the guide, and another horseman who had joined our party, went a little apart, unbound their kammer-bands, spread them out, knelt and said prayers. The Koran, though it teaches much that is wrong, contains also a large proportion of good. Often since that time have I observed that the Mohamedans, both old and young, however worn out by fatigue, or suffering from hunger and thirst, have postponed all thought of self-indulgence to their duty to their God.

It is not with them the mere force of habit; it is the strong impression on their minds that the duty of prayer is so important, that no circumstances can excuse its omission.

Among Mohamedans there is much kindly feeling. Their religion knits them as it were into a general fraternity, in which every member, rich or poor, is, though a stranger, always affectionately received. Much of this charitable disposition is no doubt to be traced to those causes which make the inhabitants of thinly peopled districts so generally hospitable. More, however, is attributable to the precepts of the Koran. Nor are the followers of Mohamet exclusive in their benevolence, for all strangers share their charities; and though the Christian be not met with the open arms that welcome a brother Mussulman, he is courteously received, and treated with kindness and respect. A Mohamedan looks upon Christians in the light of benighted and misguided men; but yet people of "*the Book*," who, though not heirs to the high destinies of Mohamed's followers, are nevertheless, from the sacred character of Isau (Jesus), entitled to the commiseration of the faithful.

We learned from the Malik of Gumut, that the Mullah had that day been praying for rain; and that on the morrow all the villagers, headed by their aged priest, would again in the open air, and in the face of heaven, supplicate their Maker for that nourishment to their ground, without which the fields of the Kuttock may be tilled, but can never be reaped. On similar occasions the Hindú makes prayers and offerings to his favourite idol, and seeks by the frivolous mummery of unmeaning ceremonies to obtain the object of his wishes. How infinitely more beautiful and pure is the Mussulman's humble and pious acknowledgment, that in Jehovah's hands rest the destinies of all flesh.

At an early hour on the following morning (Wednesday, 16th,) we were in the saddle and on the road to Kohat. Before emerging from the rough hills and broken gullies that bound the plain of Kohat to the south, we passed several graves by the road-side. A heap of stones thrown carelessly together marks the spot where the rahgeer or traveller lies. In former years many Afghans resorted to Hindustan, where they took service in the independent states, and after a stay of some years returned to their native land, carrying with them their scanty but honourable savings. These poor fellows were, it seems, often cut off by cool-blooded miscreants while upon their homeward road. These cairns are, therefore, melancholy memorials, each of which is connected with a tale of violence and blood.[1]

As we neared Kohat, our horses were completely knocked up. That of Gholam Khader Khán had been flagging for some time, and he now beat the poor beast so unmercifully about the head, that I felt compelled to interfere. On my lecturing him on the cruelty and impropriety of such conduct, he assured me

---

[1] In the present day we find many Afghans in the ranks of our Indian Army, who have enlisted in order to lay by a few rupees wherewith to return to their homes. Unfortunately, however, as with their fathers, so it is with them, and the cherished hope of years still too often results in disaster and death. Enquiry by the writer regarding such men who had left his regiment has often met with the reply, "On the way to his country he was murdered."

that the horse was a *haramzada* (a rascal), that a kote or spirit had taken possession of the beast, and that the plan he adopted was the only one calculated to expel the demon. The magic process proved, however, somewhat too successful, as the poor animal died the next day.

This little excursion gave me an opportunity of mingling somewhat among the Kuttocks, and of gleaning a good deal of information regarding them.

The tribe is now broken into two parts, known as the Kuttocks of Akora on the Kabul river, and the Kuttocks of Tirí in the province of Kohat. Hussein Khán, whom I met at the sulphur mines, is the head of the Tirí division, and one of his cousins governs the other. Both are, however, subject to Runjít Sing, and are under the immediate rule of Sultan Mohamed Khán, his viceroy. They are much exasperated against the Seiks, and no less partial to Dost Mohamed Khán of Kabul. Hussein Khán showed me a letter from the Kabul chief, detailing his defeat of the Seiks at Jamrud. He told me how much he regretted Sultan Mohamed Khán's engagements with the Maharajah, and added that it was entirely owing to the former's influence with the tribes that the Kalabagh boats had been permitted to ascend the river to Attock. The Kuttocks can bring into the field about 1000 fighting men, all foot soldiers. The lands are the property of the cultivators, who pay a nominal duty to their chief. For example, the village of Gumut pays yearly eighty rupees, but the revenue of Hussein Khán is principally derived from a tax on merchandise and the sale of salt. It is estimated at 30,000 rupees; but I greatly doubt its reaching to that amount. The Kuttock lands are too arid for pasture, and the flocks owned by the tribe are therefore few.

The lands of the Bungush, of which Kohat is the capital, are very fertile. They are said to yield a revenue of 80,000 rupees. The governor of the district keeps a small force in pay for its defence, amounting to 100 horse, and about double that number of infantry. Kohat has been given by the Seiks as a jagger to Sultan Mohamed Khán, who has confided the government of it to his nephew, as I have already mentioned.

Next day, having completed the necessary observations for fixing the position of Kohat, I went to durbar and got my rukhsut, or permission to quit the place. Kheirulah Khán, the governor, was seated in his Kutchery, or justice hall, hearing and answering the complaints of his people. The room was filled by respectably attired Mussulmans, each of whom in turn stated his grievance. I was surprised at their freedom of speech, and their bold, manly, nay, almost boisterous manner, so different from the slavish cringing of a Sindí to his Amír, or the supple accommodating tone of an Hindú before his chief.

Two individuals who had been in disgrace were this day again admitted into favour. A piece of cloth as a nazar or present, was wrapped round the head of each, in token that their past offences were forgotten. The poor men seemed to feel the graciousness of the act, and as they left the hall amidst the whispered gratulations of their countrymen, were unable to restrain their emotion.

At six o'clock in the evening of the next day we commenced our night journey, escorted by Agha Maheide, and long before the morning dawned had emerged from the defiles of the dividing mountains upon the plain of Peshawúr. As soon as the increasing light enabled me to pick out my way across the plain, I left the staid old gentleman to pursue his more leisurely pace; and giving my horse the bridle, set off for the town, where I arrived in time for an excellent breakfast with Captain Burnes, rendered doubly agreeable by the cordial welcome which he gave me.

In closing these brief memoranda of my journeyings in Kohat, I should indeed be ungrateful were I to omit making honourable mention of my cicerone, Agha Maheide Khán. Old, nay, almost decrepit, as he was, his exertions to afford me every comfort and accommodation possible were unintermitting. There was a cheerful kindness in his manner which could not but excite my gratitude; although I well knew that his conduct was dictated by his respect for the government I served, and not for myself individually. I parted from the good old man with feelings of respect and friendship.

The day succeeding that of my arrival at Peshawúr I started

for the Kabul river, with the intention of descending it to Attock, where I wished to take another set of chronometric observations to determine its longitude. This river bounds the plain of Peshawúr on the north, and though there called the Lundi, the stream, from its source to the Indus, is better known by the appellation of the "Kabul."

On the 21st I reached Attock, much pleased with the scenery on the banks of the Kabul river. The following day was devoted to taking the necessary observations, and on the succeeding one I rejoined the mission at Peshawúr.

This town has suffered much at the hands of the Seiks. In fact everything, both in Peshawúr itself and the surrounding plain, bears the stamp of violence and oppression. In whatever direction the eye is turned, it rests upon uncultivated fields and half tenanted villages. No sooner do you pass Akora on the road to Peshawúr, than signs of the ravages of war may be discerned. The groves of large tamarisk trees which used to shelter the traveller, have been levelled, and small forts erected in their place. The fine caravansary of thirty-two cells a side, where the foreign merchant stored his goods, and the wayfarer found an asylum, has been converted into a residence for the commander of the garrison, and the adjoining mosque has been pulled down, because it was a bone of contention between the subjugated Mussulmans and their haughty oppressors. To soothe the irritated feelings of both creeds, Monsieur Avitabile, the governor of Peshawúr, has built a mosque for the one, and a temple for the other, within the walls of the square. Where the Bala Hissar, or palace of the Afghans, stood, the Seiks have built a substantial fort, in the erection of which they recklessly destroyed a large portion of the Bagh-i-shah, or King's garden, and disfigured the rest.

While we were at Peshawúr the Seik forces were reviewed. There were upon the field three brigades of infantry, numbering 8,000 men, besides 12,000 irregular cavalry. On reaching the parade-ground, we rode down the infantry line; and though I am no soldier, I could not help admiring its *matériel*. The men were tall, slim fellows, well set up, with a fine soldierly bearing. They were neatly dressed in well-cut uniforms, and

H

all their accoutrements clean, and in the best order. Their bright gun-barrels, however, I could not approve. After this inspection, we took our seats in a small lodge erected for the occasion, when the brigades manœuvred singly in its front. They were first marched past the lodge in review order. This over, they were formed into line, and exercised with blank cartridge, firing from flank to centre alternate volleys, by whole companies. They were next ordered to prepare to receive cavalry. A square with a gun at each corner was immediately formed by each brigade, when a file firing opened, which was much better sustained by one of the three than by the other two.

As the cavalry were not expected to perform any evolutions, they merely rode past in front of the lodge. The chiefs at the heads of their respective contingents were all clad in chain or plate armour, and had their helmets ornamented by heron feathers. The troops wore so great a diversity of colours, that a Seik chieftain present, as he looked down upon these moving masses, likened them to a flower garden. Side by side were to be seen the grim steel-clad warrior on his henna-dyed charger, and the gaily attired lancer upon his gorgeously caparisoned steed, waving his small pointed banner. Onward they moved, cheering as they went, and shouting the national battle cry, "Wah gurují ka fatteh!"—may the Guru be victorious!

On the 28th of August the mission moved forward to Jamrud, a Seik fortress at the west end of the Peshawúr plain, commanding the entrance to the Khyber Pass. A few days were spent here negotiating with the Khyberies for the passage of this defile, during which these people showed their deep-rooted hatred of the Seiks, by cruelly murdering two defenceless grass-cutters, and making off with a herd of camels. Instant chase was given, and the camels were recovered, but the same hills that enabled the animals to be recaptured favoured the escape of the ruffians. The bodies of the murdered men were brought into camp, one with the throat fearfully cut, the other a headless trunk.

CHAPTER X.

Wah gurují ka fatteh.—Wussulam Alaikum.—Grinth.—Koran.—Rival nations and creeds.—Enter Khyber.—Seik scalps.—Ali Masjíd.—A character.—A mountain torrent.—"Topes."—Presents to the Khyberies.—Height of mountains.—Sufeid Koh.—Pine forests.—Supply of ice.—Province of Naujbnchar.—Surkh Rúd or Red river.—Range and Pass of Karkatcha.—Enter Kabul.—Mohamed Akbar Khán.—Amír Dost Mohamed Khán.

On the 2nd of September we took a friendly leave of the Seiks, and very soon after we had bade them "Wah gurují ka fatteh," or constant victory, we heard the well-known salutation "Wussulam alaikum," or peace be with you, of their adversaries the Khyber Maliks, welcoming us to the country of the Afghans. We had been under the protection of the former people ever since our first meeting with them at Mittun-Kote, and their conduct towards us had been, with few and unimportant exceptions, invariably kind. It was gratifying to perceive that in spite of their opposite creeds and hostile feelings, the presence of a British agent was equally acceptable to both parties, Hindú and Mohamedan; and though the poverty of the Afghan would not permit him to be more than hospitable, yet his sobered, trustworthy deportment was infinitely more pleasing to us than the ostentation and arrogance of the Seik. The relative situation in which these two nations are now placed may have a considerable effect on their behaviour to others, but for my own part, I could not help thinking that I saw truth in the gravity of the one, and much of varnished artifice in the polite and studied attentions of the other.

Nor was the change we had just made, in other respects, less calculated to arrest attention. To the emanations of Baba Nanak had succeeded the revelations of Mohamed. The Grinth or holy book of the former had given place to the Koran of the latter, and on the precepts of this book were based the laws of the land we had entered, its moral code and social system, its government and its commerce.

To the Christian there was much in this change to excite a painful interest, whilst seeing around him one gross superstition taking the place of another, and he is led to pray, in the pure spirit of his own benevolent creed, for the accomplishment of David's prophecy;—"When all kings shall fall down before the Lord; all nations shall serve him."[1]

Dost Mohamed had ordered Agha Ján, the governor of Jelalabad, to meet the mission at Khyber, and escort it with all honours to Kabul. But Agha Ján was not forthcoming, and the Maliks of the Pass seemed inclined to detain us until his arrival. On this, Captain Burnes told them that he wanted no other escort than the Khyberies, and no better security for his baggage than the presence of themselves. Without more ado, we threw ourselves on the honour of this thieving community, and although the act might be a rash one, we had no reason to repent it.

A short distance from the entrance of the Pass several Seik scalps were seen in the middle of the road, partly covered with earth; trophies of the field of Jamrud, where some months before our arrival the Afghans had routed a considerable body of Seik troops, and slain their leader Harri Singh.

We wound up the Pass to the fort of Ali Masjíd, and were there received by its commandant, an ill-conditioned, dissipated-looking Englishman; slipshod, turbaned, and robed in a sort of Afghan dishabille—having more the look of a dissipated priest than a military man. His abode was a cave in the mountain, from which he and his hungry followers levied black-mail on the passing Kafilas. The Seik fortress of Jamrud was at this time dependent for water on the stream that runs through Khyber, and the chief occupation of the young Lieut.-Colonel, for so he styled himself, was to stop the supply, and again to permit it to flow on being bribed to do so.

Lieut.-Colonel Rattray received us at the head of his *column;*

[1] Psalm lxii.

which, drawn up for the occasion, had something approaching to a military look; but no sooner did the commandant attempt a manœuvre, than a most ludicrous scene ensued. In utter hopelessness of restoring his scattered legion to order, he disbanded it forthwith, and then the *Lieut.-Colonel* commenced whacking his men with a cudgel; but he was soon overwhelmed by numbers, and compelled to desist. In the evening he came into the tent to inquire, with all military formalities, what were the orders for to-morrow's march; when he took occasion to point out to Captain Burnes an error in his Narrative, assuring him that although forty bottles of wine might formerly have been procured in Kabul for a rupee, nothing like that number could be now obtained. Before retiring, he requested, with a degree of quiet impudence, which was really meritorious, a loan of 50*l.* to defray the expenses of the march, for which he gravely tendered an order on his regimental pay-officer in Kabul. Failing in this attempt, he hit upon the expedient of quartering his men upon the mission; and to accomplish this, issued a *General Order*, which, as a specimen of bombast, was quite a curiosity. A captain's guard was ordered to one place, a subaltern's to another, until the whole of the lean crew was disposed of. No sooner had these cormorants taken up their stations than they piled arms, and asked for food. The result was, that the *Soorsat* (provisions) Dost Mohamed had intended for the mission was made over to these hungry soldiers.

When Mr. Rattray became acquainted with our different pursuits, he made the round of the camp and waited on us individually, proffering, *for a consideration,* to put us each in possession of the information he had amassed during a long sojourn in these countries. To Dr. Lord he promised an account of the rivers in Karakorum, and the site of all the valuable ores between the Indus and Kabul. To Lieut. Leach, the military resources of kingdoms and states, from Lahore to Mushid, from Sind to Kashmir. To me, a map of half the continent of Asia, in which should be delineated every river and mountain chain, every town and route. He borrowed from Captain Burnes the volumes of his travels and those of Forster and Elphinstone, and from these sources and his own fertile imagination, he would, had we encouraged him, have furnished us with a full and particular account of countries he had never seen, and tribes, the very names of which he had not before heard. Some time after this, when we were in Kabul, this man became a convert to Mohamedanism, much against the wish of Dost Mohamed Khán, who thought him a disgrace to any creed, and expressed in strong terms the contempt he felt for men who could change their religion to improve their fortune. The Khyber commandant was altogether a singular character; void of all principle, but clever and well informed. His autobiography, written at the request of Captain Burnes, affords another proof how often the real events of life exceed in interest the wildest conception of fiction.

As the fort of Ali Masjid is perched high up the mountain, we encamped in the bottom of the pass, which from its mouth to that station, is a steep, walled, but not rugged mountain ravine. For some distance beyond the fort, it assumes more the character of a deep defile; its north side being a mural precipice, rising many hundred feet in height, while the opposite side, on which the fort hangs, falls back as it rises, but is nevertheless steep. In the afternoon the gathering clouds betokened rain, and we were engaged removing the baggage from the dry bed of the torrent, when it began to fall. The Khyberies rendered us efficient aid: but for which, much property would have been lost. So quickly did the waters come down, and the little rill swelled so rapidly into an impassable stream, that our party was divided, some having sought shelter upon the right, and others on the left bank. The rain continued, and innumerable cataracts came pouring over the mural cliffs, which in contrast with the blackened rocks, looked like streaks of silver. The roaring torrent now filled the bottom of the ravine, while we, unhoused and drenched to the skin, sat terribly out of humour among horses and baggage, watching its fierce struggles among the opposing rocks, and wondering when the tumult would be over. The rain cloud was at last emptied, and an hour afterwards the little brook meandered as quietly down the ravine as it had done before the storm.

A day's halt was necessary to dry our wet tents, and to repair damages; after which we passed safely through the Khyber mountains, and debouched upon the Kabul river at Dhaka. The pass on this side of Ali Masjíd is wider than the portion already described, and has more the character of a valley than a ravine.

In our last march one of those "topes," or mounds of masonry, which are so numerous in Afghanistan, was seen occupying the summit of a small hill on the north side of the valley. The solid structures which have so long defied "time," and which the apathy of the natives left undisturbed, have at last fallen before the enlightened curiosity of Europeans; and as the entire deposit of many, consisting of coins and relics, are already in the East India Company's Museum, and other cabinets of the learned, we hope soon to hear that modern research has, by deciphering their inscriptions, dispelled all doubt of the purpose for which these singular piles were originally erected.

Before we left Dhaka, the Maliks of Khyber were assembled to receive from Captain Burnes the reward of their praiseworthy forbearance towards us whilst we were among the mountains. The presents made them were of very trifling value, but derived a higher worth from the kind, yet impressive, and dignified manner in which they were bestowed. The Khyberies left the camp in high glee, promising that our kasids, or letter-carriers, should be made "free of the pass;" a declaration which, all things considered, has been tolerably well kept.

From Dhaka we journeyed along the fertile valley of the river to Umber Khana, where a branch road leads to Jelalabad. It is usual for merchants going to Kabul to take this route as being the safest; but escorted as we were by Agha Ján (who by this time had joined us), we had no occasion to make so useless a détour. Leaving, therefore, the Jelalabad road to the right, we held on nearly due west over the rough broken ground that skirts the range of Spenghur, or Sufeid Koh (snow-clad chain). Beyond the Kabul river towered the giant Himalaya, while close to us, on our left hand, rose the range already mentioned, clad in a mantle as pure as its more elevated neighbour. The result of some trigonometrical observations at the village of Synú, when combined with our barometrical measurements, gave 14,000 feet for the height of Sufeid Koh above the level of the sea, and 20,248 for that of the highest part of the Himalaya in the meridian of 70° 50' east.

The hoary head of one mountain has given its name to an entire range; for though it be known throughout its whole extent as Sufeid Koh, or the white mountains, yet the only portion of it which reaches the line of perpetual congelation lies between the meridians of Synú and Gandamuk. Its outline is broken and irregular. The chain is formed by a succession of parallel ridges that rise like steps into the region of eternal snow. The two nearest ridges are covered with pine forests, in which are trees of a large size. The timber is of the best quality, and is brought in large quantities to Kabul, where the frame of every house is made from the fir tree. I do not remember to have before seen so highly resinous a wood. In one species of tree which resembled the Scotch fir, the pitch actually oozed out and dropped from its cones.

Among the many advantages that will unquestionably accrue to western India from the opening of the river Indus, the European inhabitants in the Bombay presidency will not consider as one of the least important, the prospect of a constant supply of ice. This article is sold in Jelalabad, a town situated under Sufeid Koh, and on the bank of the Kabul river. From Jelalabad to Akora on the same stream, there is a raft navigation, and from the latter place to the sea, there is no impediment to river boats. The ice should be embarked at Jelalabad between the 1st and 5th of September, so as to be carried down the stream by the latest freshes of the swell, by which arrangement the sea-going vessel (which should be waiting in the river) will catch the last breathings of the monsoon in her voyage to the presidency. The time which the combined river and sea voyage would occupy may be thus stated:—

From Jelalabad to Akora	3 days
„ Akora to Kalabagh	1½ „
„ Kalabagh to Mittun-Kote	5½ „
„ Mittun-Kote to the sea	9 „
River voyage	19 „ [1]
Time for transfer of cargo	3 „
Sea voyage	8 „
Total	30 days.

[1] The author has himself made this voyage in less time than is here stated. Upon the Indus the boats do not move at night.

In carrying out the details, there will at first be some difficulty, but none that a very small outlay will not overcome. The fir-wood of the raft, and the boat herself, would bring a handsome profit in Sind; and surely ice and fresh English-looking apples, pears, plums, and cherries, the far-famed, seedless pomegranates, besides all descriptions of dried fruits, would render the traffic profitable.

Though the general appearance of the country lying under Sufeid Koh is remarkably barren, there are, nevertheless, among the inequalities of its stony, sand-coloured surface, many sweet valleys, which, like islands in the desert, appear only the more beautiful from the sterility that surrounds them. The name of this province is Nanjhnehar, derived from a Pushtú word signifying nine rivers, the supposed number of rivulets that intersect the district.[1] It has a length of fifty-nine miles, and a mean width of about fifteen. It is bordered on the north by the fertile plain of Jelalabad, while to the south it gradually slopes upward towards the snowy chain, among the roots of which its higher valleys insinuate themselves. The tribes of Nanjhnehar are, it is said, addicted to robbery, and their fort-like dwellings are certainly not the best signs of a settled country; yet on our route we saw the inhabitants industriously and, as it appeared, contentedly occupied in the cultivation of their fields. Though quiet and respectful in their demeanour, there was a dash of the mountaineer in their mien; but men so singularly situated, that they can look to the hills above them and proclaim them to be Yaghistan or rebel land, while a rich plain studded with villages skirts the lower edge of their own bleak domain, must be expected to exhibit traits of character and temperament peculiar to themselves. From Khyber to Kabul there is no waste land; every spot capable of cultivation has been turned over by the plough or the spade; and so great is the command of water, that even the acclivities of the hills which enclose the small circular valleys are successfully

---

[1] The popular etymology quoted by Captain Wood is, as often happens, a fanciful one to suit the modern form of the word, which is corrupted from the ancient Indian *Nagarahára*. Sultan Baber mentions that the name *Nangenhár*, as he calls it, was written Nekerhár (*rather Nagarhár*) in many histories.

cultivated. It is here no uncommon thing to see a stream of water conducted along the face of a hill forty feet above the fields below; and when rivulets are wanting a running stream is procured from kharaizes or tunnel-wells.[1] In these secluded valleys orchard, garden, and field are beautifully blended together. They abound in mulberry, pomegranate, and other fruit trees, while the banks of the small streams that meander through them are edged with a fine sward enamelled with wild flowers and fragrant with aromatic herbs. These delightful spots seem little fitted for the abode of the robber and assassin. A love of country and of home must be engendered by them; and after having seen the Afghans in their snug valleys, I am not surprised at their disinclination for travel: stern necessity, however, often drives them abroad. In Afghanistan, as in all other Asiatic nations cursed with an unstable government, the population of the several districts is perpetually varying; in some it has diminished, in others increased; whilst the census of the entire nation must show a progressive augmentation. The lands that yield a ready return, that is, the well-watered valleys, are already occupied; but in those districts where water has sometimes to be brought from a distance of four or five miles, at very great expense, it requires considerable capital to attempt the cultivation of waste lands. If the hills will feed sheep, the surplus population become pastoral; but if, as is the case with Nanjhnehar, they present a naked surface, many of the dwellers among them will, it is feared, as their numbers increase, be compelled by actual want to resort to a life of violence and rapine; and although we must blame, we cannot but pity them.

The road continued full of ascents and descents over larger tracts of barren surface, interspersed with small fertile valleys, till we reached the Surkh Rûd or Red river. The bed of this stream is here narrowed by two ridges of blue slate, that rise like walls on each side of its deep cut channel. In 1606 a fine

---

[1] Shafts are sunk about every fifty yards, and connected by a gallery under ground, along which the stream is conducted. Water in this way is often brought from a distance of miles. To construct a kharaiz considerable knowledge of levelling is indispensable.

arch was thrown across by Ali Mardan Khán: it still remains, after a lapse of two centuries, in good preservation, a monument of his public spirit.[1]

I have already mentioned that Nanjhnehar has the Jelalabad plain to the north, and Sufeid Koh to the south, but I omitted to say that its east and west extremes are bounded respectively by the hills of Khyber and Karkatcha. After crossing the Red river we neared the latter ridge, over which there are four different roads. That of Lattabund, the most southerly, had been traversed by Capt. Burnes in 1832. The others were now to be examined, and that of Karkatcha, the highest and most northerly, was allotted to me. Parting with my companions, I turned off to the left, and having passed through the vale of Hisarak, noted for its seedless pomegranate, entered the bed of a stream tributary to the Surkh Rûd river. Up this we wound our path to near the summit of Karkatcha. On entering among the mountains, the bed of the stream contracted to a narrow defile not more than ten feet in width, the sides of which were naked, craggy, and precipitous, while its bottom was encumbered by the trunks of huge fir trees, and here and there crossed by ledges of rock. On nearing the ridge of the pass, we quitted the defile and kept to the right, along the face of mountains which here assume a more open character. On the top of the pass are the ruins of two windmills, said to have been erected by Mahmud of Ghizni, and on a clear space a little below them some slight traces of buildings, together with remnants of brick and pottery, mark the place where a town had been situated. The Pass of Karkatcha has an elevation of nearly 8000 feet; and from it we looked down upon the various mountain and hilly chains that intersect the country about Kabul. The hills forming this pass have both their east and west faces covered with almond trees: there is also plenty of the uzulzus or wild indigo, and numerous wild flowers and fragrant plants. The mountains are of blue slate; and though they have soil upon them to their summit, they have no grassy covering. The

---

[1] The canal from the Jumna which is carried through the Paniput and Delhi districts to the city of Delhi, owes its origin to the same noble, and his name is still popularly attached to it.

black wolf (Gurgh-i-Siah), the fox, and the leopard are met with here, and these, with many other animals, are said to be numerous upon the adjacent mountains of Sufeid Koh.

At Bhut-khak I rejoined the mission, which entered Kabul on the 20th, escorted by Mohamed Akbar Khán, the favourite son of Amír Dost Mohamed Khán. He brought out a large cavalcade with him; but though scarcely twenty-one years of age, he was the largest man in the cortége. He conducted us at once into the Bala Hissar, and introduced us to his father. Dost Mohamed Khán is about forty-five years of age, and looks worn out and aged before his time. His frame is large and bony, and all his features strongly marked. There is a sternness in the general expression of his features, which is increased by his flowing, jet-black beard, but his countenance is lighted up by eyes of peculiar brilliancy and intelligence: when he fixes them upon those by whom he is addressed, they actually seem to flash with approbation or dissent. From the ease with which he ran over the names of places visited by Captain Burnes in 1832-3, it is evident that his memory must be a good one; and the various subjects on which he spoke, the good sense of his remarks, and the readiness of his replies, proved that his conversational talents were of no mean order. When any one of us addressed him, he sat with his eyes riveted upon the speaker, and his whole soul appeared absorbed by the subject; when he himself spoke, though he did not resort to Persian gesture, nor assume the solemnity of a Hindú rajah, there was that in his manner and tone of voice which enforced attention.

Our welcome had been cordial; and as we left the apartment I could not help contrasting the audience we had just quitted with the scene in a Haïderábád durbar on a like occasion, and the bearing of the blunt, homely Afghan with that of the vapouring Beluche. Dost Mohamed's reception of the mission was less warmly expressed than that of the Sind Amírs, but the ruler of Kabul felt what the others only feigned. He deemed himself honoured by the arrival of a British mission at his capital; while on the contrary the potentates of Sind, when they grant an interview to a British agent, affect to think that the condescension is on their part; they consider only the servant who is sent to them; but the more intelligent Afghans view in the servant the government which he represents.[1]

[1] The reader will at once see how little of new matter has been introduced in the foregoing chapters, and the pages of history which chronicle the wondrous changes time has worked in the East within the last thirty-four years, best show how hopeless, and at the same time profitless, a task it would be fully to comment upon them in such a work as the present. The character and habits of the people of Sind, the Panjáb, and Afghanistan indeed are little changed, though, in the two former, British rule is now better understood and appreciated. The physical geography of the countries of course remains unaltered, and the description given in these pages of the Indus, &c. &c., is as true to nature as if it had been printed yesterday; whilst opinions which the author may have occasionally hazarded as to the probabilities of the future have rarely been proved erroneous by the experience of later years.

CHAPTER XI.

Map of Afghanistan.—Province of Koh Daman.—Kabul race-course.—Shukur Durah.—A noble prospect.—Beauty of the scenery.—Gardens of Danow and Istalaf.—Baber's description of Istalaf.—Great abundance of fruit.—Plain of Bogram.—Coins.—Turkish settlers.—Roig Rawan, or the moving sand.—Ziarats.—Dost Mohamed Khán's belief.

ONE of the objects which Captain Burnes had greatly at heart was to obtain materials for the construction of an entirely new map of Afghanistan, in which actual survey should supersede hearsay information. In prosecution of this design, we had not been long in Kabul before he obtained its ruler's permission to visit the Koh Daman; and I shall venture to give a brief description of this fair province, although it will somewhat interrupt the narrative of my travels.

The valley of Koh Daman lies north of Kabul, from which it is separated by a low creeping ridge, not far from the town. At the upper extremity of this valley rises the snowy peaks of Hindú Kosh, while those of Pagman overlook it on the west. To the east it is bordered by a lower range, which decreases in height as it goes south, until it sinks into the low ridge crossing the bottom of the valley. So enclosed, the Koh Daman has a length of thirty-one miles and a medium width of seven. The western side of the valley is much higher than the eastern, along which the drainage of the opposite mountain flows. From the base of the Pagman much *débris*, splintered rocky fragments, and heavy boulders, are strewed over the plain, having been loosened by the winter's frost from the granite peaks above. The sides of these mountains are split by numerous ravines, down which come tumbling rills of the purest water. The slopes of their rugged channels are thickly planted with the mulberry, and every moderately level spot is clad with fruit trees or the vine. The mountains at the head of the valley throw out three streams, which are named Ghorbund, Parwan, and Panchshir. The latter issues from the north-east corner of Koh Daman, and the Ghorbund from its north-west. The Parwan, which flows between the other two, unites about four miles below the hills with the river of Ghorbund, which, thus augmented, joins the Panchshir at Ali Burj on the north-east end of the Begram plain, in latitude 34° 59′ 46″ north. A few miles east of this junction the Bari-ke-ab falls in from the south, and the drainage of the valley thus collected into one channel flows through an opening in the eastern hills to join the Kabul river, of which it is the northern fork. That portion of the Koh Daman watered by the northern streams is a basin lying full forty feet below the level of the south part of the valley. The latter is a stony and comparatively infertile tract, whose principal produce is fruit, for which both soil and climate are well suited. The former yields grain, cotton, tobacco, artificial grasses, and vegetables, but scarce any fruit besides the mulberry, of which, however, there are innumerable plantations.

Koh Daman is a favourite country residence of the wealthy inhabitants of Kabul, and is almost as thickly studded with castles as with gardens. They are strongly built, and are, in fact, mimic representations of the old baronial residences in our own land. Life and property are here very insecure; and I really believe it would be difficult to find any two neighbouring castles, the owners of which are not either covert enemies or at open feud with each other. This, and the exactions of Dost Mohamed Khán, have forced a number of families across the Hindú Kosh, where I afterwards met many natives of this valley whose hearts still yearned for the pleasant home of their youth.

On the 14th of October we set out upon our excursion. In the environs of Kabul the roads lead by the side of brooks, and are usually edged by willow trees. Many passages both in the Old and New Testament have been made familiar to our minds by an attention to the customs still prevalent in Eastern countries; and the circumstances under which we here find the willow illustrates Isaiah xliv. 4—"And they shall spring up as among the grass, as willows by the water courses."

Half an hour's walk from the Balar Hissar brought us upon the Kabul race-course, a fine, straight, broad road, nearly three miles long. It is belted on both sides by vegetable gardens, beyond which lie those of fruit. Nowhere have I seen better cauliflower and cabbage than were now growing here. Quitting the race-course, the road led over cultivated fields to the base of the low ridge that separates Kabul from the Koh Daman. About ten o'clock in the forenoon we stood upon its crest, and after enjoying the beautiful prospect that was spread around us, descended its northern slope, and arrived a little before noon at Shukur Durah. This is a delightful village; and whilst rambling over its gardens, climbing its grassy slopes, or lounging under the fine foliage of its stately walnut trees, I felt that Koh Daman deserved all the praise which the Kabulies bestow upon it. We scrambled some distance up the barren side of the Pagman ridge, and from our elevated position had a noble view of the whole mountain-girt valley. In the plain were green fields and corn lands, while every ravine that gave passage for a rill from the mountains streaked their sterile surface with foliage of a mingled hue. The castles of the nobles might be seen peering through the trees—at one moment gleaming in the sunshine, and the next darkened by the passing cloud. The leaves had not begun to fall, but, like old age, autumn has its heralds; and amidst the healthy foliage of many a tree signs of the "sear and withered leaf" were not wanting.

From Shukur Durah we continued along the base of Pagman to Danow and Istalaf. The orchards at both these places had more of a wintry look than those we saw at Shukur Durah. The season, however, had been backward throughout the valley. The grapes in some of the gardens were still unripe, though the other fruits had long been gathered in. The hedges in this neighbourhood bore the common haw and a description of cranberry; beneath them shot out the burr-thistle and the stinging-nettle, while the "wee modest daisy" spotted every bank where the ear detected the gurgling sound of water.

These sweet districts, full of clustering hamlets, here and there stretching up the side of a barren and forbidding mountain-chain, though rich and fertile in themselves, derive much adventitious beauty from their peculiar situation. In the plain they would be but "green fields and fruitful vineyards," but here they are gems of fertility set off by the desolation that surrounds them. The thermometer at sunrise indicated a temperature of 43°; nor did it at any subsequent hour of the day range higher than 68° in the shade. This to an Indian is a bracing temperature; and buttoning close my surtout, I was uncertain whether most to admire the scenery of the valley or its invigorating climate.

A stranger cannot be long in Kabul without hearing of Istalaf. Its gardens are famous throughout Afghanistan, and were so in the days of the Emperor Baber.[1]

Those, however, who have been accustomed to trace perfection in the regular arrangements of our botanical gardens might feel dissatisfied with the rugged charms of Istalaf. Though its gardens are not laid out with square and line, to me the varying outline of the ground they occupy gave them a charm which all the skill of Repton himself could never have equalled on the plain.

As we approached Istalaf by a road leading over the wavy ground about the base of Pagman, we saw nothing of the town or its suburbs till we gained the south bank of the hollow in which they lie; the whole then burst on view with panoramic effect. Seating ourselves upon the grass, we contemplated at leisure the lovely scene. A row of white bark chenar trees (the plane trees of Baber) edged one side of the ravine, and bending their aged boughs over the chasm, occasionally shed a withered leaf that might be seen circling into the depths below. On the

[1] In his pleasingly written commentaries, he thus speaks of the place:—"Few quarters possess a district that can rival Istalaf. A large river runs through it, and on either side of it are gardens, green, gay, and beautiful. Its water is so cold that there is no need of icing it. In this district is a garden, called Bagh-e-Kilan (or the Great Garden), which Ulugh Beg Mirza seized upon. I paid the price of the garden to the proprietors, and received from them a grant of it. On the outside of the garden are large and beautiful-spreading plane-trees, under the shade of which there are agreeable spots finely sheltered."—*Memoirs of Baber*, p. 107.

opposite bank stands the town, piled house upon house, stretching up the shoulder of the mountain that overlooks the valley. The sunny slopes around were now tawny with the vine, and the broad ravine for a mile and a half along its course was one mass of chequered foliage. A considerable stream holds its way in the bottom of this valley, which, chafed and torn by a rocky bed, produces a noise which, when heard beyond the ravine, sounds like a long-continued moan.

The greater portion of the fruit brought by the traders into Upper India is from the Koh Daman. Here are grown grapes of a dozen different kinds, apricots of six sorts, mulberries of as many, besides endless varieties of apples, pears, peaches, walnuts, almonds, quinces, cherries, and plums. Though the vintage this year was late, the grapes were very plentiful. The only two descriptions that will bear exportation are the Huseini and Saibi, and these could be bought at the gardens for twopence a-pound, while others, too luscious for export, were selling at very little more than a halfpenny.

In the bottom of the valley nearly east of Istalaf is the plain of Begram, the locality where such numbers of old coins have lately been disinterred. It contains about twenty-four square miles, and, except some slight ridges, the rubbish apparently of dilapidated buildings, it is a perfectly dead level, on which rain stagnates as it falls. Though many thousands of coins have been collected, the hoard is by no means exhausted. During the few hours of our stay, some children sent out in search of them, returned with thirty-five copper pieces. When gleaning the surface is attended with such a result, what splendid success may be expected to crown the systematic and assiduous researches of Mr. Masson, the British Agent at Kabul!

Baber, when he conquered Afghanistan, located a number of his countrymen in Koh Daman, the descendants of whom are now among the most prosperous in the valley. When addressing each other, they still speak the Turkish language, though Persian is the medium of communication with their neighbours. On the road to Begram we passed several of their castles.

At the upper end of Koh Daman, on its eastern side, the face of the hills, at one particular spot, is covered with fine sand, called Reig-Rawan, or the moving sand. To this the natives of the valley ascribe the utterance of strange unearthly sounds, and by their marvellous relations induced us to visit the spot. The moving sand rests upon a base of 100 yards wide, and stretches up the face of the rock for 250 yards, with an acclivity of about 45°. At 3 P.M. the temperature of the sand on the surface was 103°, while at the depth of ten inches it was only 75°. Looking down from the top of this sandy, inclined plane, it is seen to lie in a hollow of the rock fronting west-south-west. The formation of the adjoining rocks are limestone, and a loose, conglomerate sandstone. The first is both fractured and calcined, and the same appearance is observed at other places along the side of the valley; but is always local: that bordering the moving sand is strictly so. From Reig-Rawan there is no other sand deposit visible, though further south, and on the east side of the valley, there are one or two smaller stripes, but which are not asserted to be vocal. The west side of Koh Daman is composed of granite, and the prevailing wind is from the north, but no sand is likely to come from either of these directions. From the known propensity of the ignorant to exaggerate every thing connected with supposed supernatural agency, we did not come to the place very confident believers in the current tales of Reig-Rawan. However, we did as we were directed, and sent six men to the top of the sandy stripe, while we took up a position in the most favourable place to hear any noise that might be emitted. The party above came trampling down, and continued their march to the foot of the inclined plane; but without eliciting the slightest sound. This was repeated again and again, but only once with any success. The sound then heard was like that of a distant drum, mellowed by softer music. The secret of Reig-Rawan is, I should imagine, that of the whispering gallery. The slightest indentation in the sand is immediately filled up by the fall of the particles above. Moving waves are thus produced by the heavy tramp of a descending party; and the rustle of the dry sand is condensed and reverberated by the circular conformation of the rocks around.

Not far from the moving sand is an artificial cave of small dimensions, within which reposes the body of a holy man who came thus far from Arabia in search of a resting-place. Fastening his steed to a tree hard by, he descended into the earth, from which, like the spectre of Loch Awe, he has never again appeared to mortal eye. In this valley there are many such places of pilgrimage, with similar legends attached to them; and I may here mention Dost Mohamed Khán's opinion of them. When we returned to Kabul from this excursion, he inquired, amongst other things, what we thought of the ziarats in Koh Daman, and added, although the Mulvi[1] was present, that for his part he was no believer in such absurd vanities; and that those who were, differed little from Kaffirs.

From Reig-Rawan we visited the mouth of the Panchshir valley. A short distance within its gorge, it contracts so as not to leave a foot-path between the stream and its steep, black sides. But before quitting the mountains, the water expands to a width of eighty-seven feet, with a depth of twelve. Here it is crossed by a wooden bridge, and from the centre of this rickety fabric the best view is obtained. Looking upwards, a snaky line of intermingled white and green water is seen leaping and twisting among the huge stones that pave its narrow bed. Presently it enters the basin over which the bridge stands, where the quiet, unruffled surface of the stream pleasingly contrasts with the turmoil above. The current here is hardly perceptible, and so beautifully transparent is the stream, that the stones at the bottom can be counted. The water glides slowly onward till it reaches the lower lip of the basin, when it pours down with a headlong fury, tumbling and foaming as violently as ever, until it is lost sight of in the extensive mulberry plantations of Gulbar, a straggling village on the banks of the Panchshir, just without the valley.

While employed mapping the Koh Daman, I was unexpectedly recalled by Captain Burnes to Kabul, for the purpose of accompanying Dr. Lord, whom he was about to send into Turkistan.

[1] The principal Mullah.

CHAPTER XII.

An Uzbek Ambassador arrives in Kabul.—Object of his Mission.—His success.—Mirzá Buddi.—The Passes of Hindú Kosh.— Make choice of Parwan.—Start for Turkistan.—Afghan Elchi.—A mistake of the Kafila Bashi.—Deserted by the Afghan Elchi.—Bad roads.—Dangers among the Mountains.—Enter the Parwan valley.—Encamp at the foot of the Pass.— Guides.—Ascend the Pass.—Its dangers.—Forced to return.—Death of the Afghan Elchi.—Hindustanies among the Snow.—Return to Kabul.

TOWARDS the end of October an officer on the part of Murad Ali Beg of Kunduz arrived in Kabul with presents for its ruler. A dozen good horses obtained him an honourable reception, and enlisted the warmest sympathy of Dost Mohamed Khán in the object of his mission. Mohamed Beg, the brother of the Uzbek chief, had long been a martyr to ophthalmia in its severest form. Shrines had been invoked, and charms essayed, but all in vain, and the faculty in Turkistan had pronounced the case to be hopeless, at the very time when the news of a British mission being at Kabul reached Kunduz. At this welcome intelligence, the flagging spirits of the patient revived, and Mirzá Buddi, the physician and confidant of Murad Ali Beg, was deputed to bring, if it were possible, the Firingi hakim or English doctor over the Hindú Kosh.

Mohamed Beg is described as having been in his younger days a hard-hearted and deliberately cruel man, the ready tool of his tyrant brother. But age and infirmities had now softened his disposition; and whether the chief felt pleased or otherwise at the change, he showed himself grateful for former services by the interest which he took in his brother's recovery.

Captain Burnes was greatly pleased at this opportunity of securing for his government, on such easy terms, the friendship of

Murad Ali Beg, with whom he was already personally acquainted, and determined at once to send the medical aid requested. Accordingly on my return from Koh Daman, I found the Uzbek ambassador in high good-humour at the successful termination of his mission. Dr. Lord was at this time absent on a geological tour, and Captain Burnes only waited his arrival to despatch us both to the court of Kunduz. Mirzá Buddi, under whose guidance we were to travel, was an honest, warm-hearted, old man, of about sixty. His bland and winning manner contrasted singularly with his large figure and harsh Tartar features. Dr. Lord and myself became greatly attached to him; nor was any visitor so welcome to our little bechoba as the mild, friendly, and simple-minded Uzbek, the leading feature of whose mind appeared to be an anxiety to do good to all around him.

It was necessary to decide by what pass we should cross the Hindú Kosh. There are four; and the caravans make their selection according to the season of the year and the more or less peaceable state of the country which borders them. The most direct lead through the plain of Koh Daman, where, diverging as they enter among the mountains at its head, they wind up the course of the streams described in the last chapter, and from which the several passes take their names of Ghorbund, Parwan, and Panchshir.[1] The fourth road makes a considerable détour to the westward, and crosses the chain by the Pass of Hajikak. It remains open longer than any of the others; besides which advantage, the road by Bamian, although circuitous, rewards a stranger with a sight of its colossal idols, caves, and other records of the existence of a race of men unknown either to history or tradition. But this route had been travelled by several of our countrymen; and, therefore, although the season was late, we resolved to make trial of the Parwan Pass.

To protect our Indian servants from the sleety blasts of the snowy chain, each of them was provided with a posteen, or coat of sheep's skin, having the woolly side next the person; and on the 3rd of November, all the necessary arrangements being

---

[1] These constitute rather four *groups* of passes than four passes: the actual number of the latter being much greater than four.

completed, Doctor Lord and I started for Turkistan, escorted by Mirzá Buddi, and accompanied by an Elchi or ambassador from Dost Mohamed Khán to Murad Ali Beg of Kunduz.

Though only a fortnight had elapsed since I quitted Koh Daman, the frosty mornings had made sad havoc among the foliage of its groves. The wintry wind now rustled through the dry leaves, and everything looked bleak and desolate.

On the 5th we reached Charekar, the largest town in Koh Daman, and situated at the mouth of the Ghorbund valley. The Kafila Bashi, or leader of the caravan, forgetting that we had selected another route, brought us here by mistake. We were, however, told that a good cross-road connected the two valleys, and that by it we should reach the river of Parwan on the morrow.

While here the Afghan Elchi thought proper to separate his party from ours, and without imparting to us his intention, continued his route up the Ghorbund valley. The fact was that the Elchi had left Kabul without money, or at least pretended he had done so, and wished us to advance him a sum for his travelling expenses. This being peremptorily refused, the Elchi felt so annoyed that he revenged himself by deserting us.

Next morning we clambered up the shoulder of the mountain forming the eastern side of the Ghorbund valley, and kept across the hills for Parwan. The whole of this day and the next was spent in painful travel, toiling up steep acclivities and descending their opposite slopes. The hills took the conformation of horse-shoe crescents, detached from each other for some distance below their summits, but connected at the base. The *good* cross-road promised us by the Kafila Bashi was nowhere to be found; and we experienced the usual fate of those who follow short cuts, and were soon bewildered among the mazes of the mountains. The man who had got us into this dilemma was, however, to be pitied. Not a yabu or baggage pony cast its load or lost its footing, but its irritated driver consigned to all manner of punishments, not only the Kafila Bashi himself, but his whole race, especially his father; and all this in language by no means complimentary nor characteristic of Persian politeness.

Late in the evening we arrived, very weary and somewhat disheartened, at the bottom of a deep dell, along which was scattered a village named Sambala. Its male inhabitants, armed to the teeth, as is customary with these mountaineers, kept hovering about the encampment, wistfully eyeing the baggage, but restrained from any act of violence by the knowledge that we were guests of both Kabul and Kunduz. Nothing but this kept the savage crew from considering our property a lawful prize—a waif brought by dame Fortune to their very doors. We were early astir next morning, and anxious to quit what was rightly considered a dangerous neighbourhood. My companion would not leave the camp till he had seen everything off the ground, while I rode ahead to reconnoitre. None of the villagers were stirring; and our long Kafila moved slowly forward, winding along the sides of the mountain till we reached a shallow ravine, on the opposite bank of which stood a tower commanding the ascent on that side. On approaching the foot of the tower, we saw that it was full of armed men; and others quickly made their appearance from all quarters. We were soon surrounded. By this time many of the baggage ponies had descended into the ravine, and those which had not were in equal peril from robbers in the rear. Three men came out of the tower, with whom a parley was held; and we were given to understand that we must pay certain taxes before the Kafila would be permitted to pass. On our arrival at their village the preceding evening, the Kafila Bashi had given their chief what was customary; but he, seeing so much baggage so ill protected, deemed it expedient to revise his scale of charges, and now asked for more. Matters were on the point of being amicably adjusted, when fear seized upon the kirakush or mule-drivers, and in the tumult that ensued a hare-brained Persian levelled his musket at a mountaineer. The party with whom we were conferring immediately fled into the tower, and in an instant matchlocks were seen in every direction pointing into the ravine. We were completely in their power. It was a trying moment; for had the Persian drawn his trigger, we should have been massacred. He had, however, but time to point his musket when it was wrenched from his hand by one of his companions, who was fortunately cooler-headed than himself; on perceiving which, an old woman stepped forward to the edge of the ravine and stayed the hand of her highly-offended countrymen. A war of words now ensued among the incensed and disappointed band, in which the shrill piercing voice of the woman rose high above the rest. Her garments hung in tatters, and her manner and gesticulations were fierce and wild. One moment pointing with her half-bared arm towards our party in the ravine, the next fiercely turning upon the men, she appeared to be loading them with reproaches. One of the party, and one only, she deigned to intreat and caress, and we discovered that this favoured individual was her son. At length her eloquence was successful, and we were permitted to move on.

A few of these vagabonds continued to dodge the caravan throughout the day; they molested us, however, but little, their depredations being limited to snatching a turban from the head of an unsuspecting mule-driver. Presuming that our road into Turkistan was to be by a usual Kafila route, we had not stinted ourselves in baggage and servants, and our party, though large and encumbered, was for the same reason comparatively unarmed; the weapons it could muster being only two crazy matchlocks, the imprudent Persian's musket, and our own pistols and fowling-pieces. We were, besides, entangled among the folds of the mountains and uncertain of the road. It was therefore with no small pleasure that we emerged, a short time after sunset, into the Parwan valley, at the village of I-angheran.

Next day we reached the head of the valley, and though the hour was yet early, pitched our tent at the foot of the pass, that we might have an entire day to cross its ridge. The place is called Sir-i-lung,[1] an appellation which is also given to the inhabitants of the valley who dwell in a few straggling hamlets.

---

[1] Sir-i-lung, or as given by other writers Sauleh-aulang and Sal-aulang. The name is applied to one of the two passes which cross from Parwan, and this must have been the pass first attempted by Dr. Lord and Lieut. Wood for the village of Ahangaran (or blacksmith's village) mentioned in the preceding paragraph, appears in Major Leech's itinerary of the Pass of Sal-aulang.

The chief of the tribe soon presented himself, and we arranged with him to procure us guides for the morrow.

The ground where we had encamped was covered to the depth of a foot with snow, and our eyes suffered severely from the dazzling reflection of the sun's rays. The Indian servants, who had never seen snow before, surprised at the warmth thus produced, tauntingly observed that blankets and woolly coats were useless in such weather. The stories they had heard of the severe cold in England could not, they said, be true, for here there was snow all around, and yet the cold did not equal that of the winter months in Hindustan.

The morning of the 9th broke in clouds and gloom. More snow had fallen in the night, and this, combined with the lowering weather, made us hesitate to start. The guides, however, now presented themselves, with huge boots and straw trussings on their legs, a short skin jacket belted close to their body, and also the usual posteen, the latter being tied behind their saddles ready for use. They all rode mares of a small size, but remarkable for strength and endurance. Both men and horse looked as if, under any circumstances, they would doggedly do their duty. Dr. Lord was very desirous of proceeding, and felt annoyed at the delay which had already been caused by the mistake of Hyat, our Kafila Bashi. The appearance of these men decided us, and in a short time the Kafila was again on the road.

Dense white clouds, which looked like hills of snow, were rolling along the mountains' summit from the north-west, in which direction lay the pass. The breeze rose as the day advanced, and came sweeping along the hollow up which we marched, driving before it a sleety drift more like ice than snow. When about half way up the ascent, Dr. Lord, Mirzá Buddi, and myself, sought the shelter of a friendly cliff, and there awaited the arrival of the Kafila, which had fallen some distance in the rear. Joined by Norrudji Ferdonji[1] and Kassinath our Munshi, we again set forth; but it was only to struggle

---

[1] A talented Parsi lad, who accompanied Sir Alexander Burnes throughout his late Kabul mission, and whose laudable curiosity to see strange lands prompted him to volunteer for the present journey into Turkistan.

unsuccessfully against the storm. The wind had lulled, but the snow on the hill was too deep for our horses. The guides now took the lead by turns, and for a considerable distance their hardy little ponies made a track, in which our larger but less active horses managed to follow. At length even the ponies of the guides gave in, and the snow again falling heavily, their riders were at fault, and we lost the road. It was now judged prudent to retrace our steps whilst return was still possible; and this decision, under the blessing of a kind Providence, saved us from the fate of the poor recusant Elchi, who, with four of his attendants, perished in this day's snow-storm in the Pass of Ghorbund, several miles to the westward of Parwan.

This rough march had nearly proved fatal to our Indian followers. Their terrors and complainings now were a perfect contrast to their elated feelings of the day before. All of them had slunk to the rear except Norrudji and Kassinath, who were cheered on by Mirzá Buddi and ourselves. They, too, at last gave in, and with tears in their eyes entreated us to return. All the poor fellows sat on their horses more like logs of wood than living men, and were dismounted by every stumble the animals made. Whenever the Indians found themselves sprawling in the snow they became perfectly helpless, and often did the kind-hearted Uzbek dismount and extricate them from their perplexity. Some of them, afraid of being left behind on our return, invoked the aid of the Sir-i-lungi to help them down the mountains, promising them money for so doing. That vagabond fraternity, seeing the children they had to do with, readily assented, but did not fail to make the most of so good an opportunity, and pilfered the poor fellows most unmercifully.

We now gave up all hopes of being able to enter Turkistan by any of the eastern passes at so advanced a season of the year, and next day saw us marching back on Kabul, where we arrived on the 13th, with the intention of taking the route by Bamian.

From the foot of the pass to the village of I-angheran the Parwan valley is a narrow, rocky defile, with either high bluffs for its sides, or mountains rising with steep acclivities; but after passing that village assumes a softer character, the mulberry-tree rising in terraces up its scantily earth-clad sides. The valley is here very tortuous, and at every turn a portion of the mountain projects into the stream. Upon these outlying shoulders there are always patches of level ground, upon which are erected the castellated buildings of the Sir-i-lungi.

A violent wind throughout the cold season blows in the lower half of the valley. The trees fronting the gorge in Koh Daman take the direction of this prevailing wind and slant to the south. Where the cultivated soil is so very limited, the question naturally arises, how so many inhabitants are fed. The mulberry-tree is what the date is among the Arabs, and a flour made from its unripe fruit is the principal support of these Kohistanees or hillmen throughout the year. Thus even the biting north wind is beneficial; for were the mulberry to ripen on the tree, it would not be so well adapted for a staple article of food.

CHAPTER XIII.

Start by Bamian for Turkistan.—A hen-pecked husband.—River Helmand.—Immigrant Hazaras.—Tribes.—Allegiance.—Hucksters.—Hazara females.—Depraved hospitality.—Hazara family.—Anecdote.—Pass of Hajikak.—Fuel.—Pass of Kalu.—Pimuri defile.—Ruins of Zohawk.—Akrobat.—Ungracious reception.—A ringing stone.—Sykan.—Assafœtida.—Slave tribute.—Kamrud.—Reflections.—Mirzá Buddi's tenantry.—Mazar ziarat of Hazrat Ali.—Arrival in Kunduz.

OUR experience of the eastern passes taught us the importance of not tarrying long in Kabul. We allowed ourselves, therefore, only one day for repose and for reducing our baggage to light marching order; and having got rid of the useless Hindustani servants, now as anxious to remain behind as they were formerly solicitous to go with us, at an early hour on the 15th of November, we set out by the Bamian route for Kunduz, and that night slept at Rustam Kyl, a village twenty-five miles west of Kabul, and the second stage on the Turkistan road. Proceeding onwards, we wound up the valley to Sir-chesme, one of the sources of the Kabul river. We had now entered the country of the Hazara, many of whom passed us on the road, wending their way to Kabul in search of employment.

On mustering our party at Rustam Kyl, it was found that sundry travellers had attached themselves to the Kafila for greater security on the road. Among these was an unfortunate Mussulman, whose story clearly proved that, despite all Mohamed's enactments in support of the husband's authority, the wife in Mohamedan countries sometimes rules the roast. This votary of Hymen had, if he spoke the truth, been in reality sacrificed at the altar, for ever since he entered the connubial state, his spouse had rendered his life miserable; and to make matters worse, his children as they grew up sided with their mother. On the day we left Kabul he had been soundly drubbed by the fair lady, and in a fit of despair joined our Kafila, resolved on a separation, and to place the twelve thousand feet barrier of the Hindú Kosh, between himself and his Xantippe. How frequently these matrimonial disagreements may occur in Kabul, I know not, but it is very seldom indeed that a Mohamedan parent has to complain of disobedient children. Among both Afghans and Uzbeks, such conduct is of very rare occurrence.

Quitting Sir-cheshme, we crossed the Pass of Hunai and the Plain of Urt. This latter, though undulating and hilly, is an elevated table-land of about six miles broad, dividing the water of Kabul from those of Herat and Kandahar. Along the north face of this table-land runs the Helmand, which rises at a place called Fazindaz, in the neighbouring mountains of Pagman. Where we crossed the stream it was twelve yards wide and less than a foot in depth. The current was brisk, and in the morning the stream was laden with young ice. The Ab-i-Siah, or black water, is a feeder of the Helmand, and up its valley we journeyed to Gulgatui, a hamlet on the southern side of Hajikak. In the summer season the upper waters of the Helmand are a favourite resort with the pastoral tribes of eastern Afghanistan.

Every day we encountered parties of half famished Hazara, abandoning their inclement mountains for the less rigorous winter of the plains. Some of the groups presented sad objects of compassion; their torn garments ill protecting them from the cold. To see the aged of both sexes, ill clothed and scantily fed, toiling on through the snow, and exposed to all the asperities of the season, might almost induce one to tax Providence as partial in the distribution of its gifts. But to the honour of these poor people, though hard pressed by misfortune, and lacking even the common necessaries of life, they viewed their lot with another eye and in a better spirit. Though not cheerful, they were resigned, and if the destitute condition of his children did sometimes cloud a father's brow, could it be wondered at, for can any trial of a parent's fortitude be more severe than to hear his offspring call upon him in vain for bread? The early fall of snow this year, had, they told us, destroyed the crops, and as they had been unable to pay the usual tribute to the Amír of Kabul, Dost Mohamed, their sheep had been seized. Without the means of passing the long dreary winter now closing in upon them, they were compelled to emigrate to the plains where the wealthy would employ them in keeping the roofs of their houses free from snow, clearing the foot paths, bringing firewood, and in the other drudgery of the household. This is a misfortune that often overtakes the Hazara, and yet so improvident are they, that they never think of providing against it. The Hazara and Eimaks occupy the whole of the mountain belt, extending from Kabul to Herat. The former live on the eastern part of the belt, but do not extend in that direction beyond the Ghorbund valley. They are quite a Tartar race, and even more marked with the disagreeable features of that nomade people, than the Uzbeks in the valley of the Oxus. They strongly resemble the Kirghiz of Pamir. Among individuals of the same nation, the mere differences of locality produce a strong effect on the physiognomy. A low-lying plain smooths and tames down the characteristic features, which, in mountainous regions, are seen in their full sharpness and strength. The following is a list of the Hazara tribes:—

No. 1.		No. 2.	
Names.	No. of Families.	Names.	No. of Families.
Da Murda	2,000	Da Murda	
Durbi Ali	1,000	Dal Timur	
Ism Tunur	1,000	Deh Kundí	
Dia Zingi	5,500	Durghan	
Dowlat Pai	2,000	Jakuri	
Marak	1,000	Naur	
Kuptscom	3,600	Badaws	
Yarkhana	500	Syud Dan	
Zhalek	200	Tazak	
Tejuk	100	Sugh Pah	
Die Murza	300		
Deh Zingi	5,000		
Sheikh Ali	3,000		
Tatar	1,000		
Jurghai Burjeghai	1,000		
Diah Pollah	2,000		

The first of these lists contains the eastern tribes, and the other those of the west. The number of families is roughly stated, but will in some degree show the comparative strength of the eastern tribes, and their relative importance among themselves. Estimating the ten western tribes, the strength of which I had not the means of ascertaining, at 10,000 families, we shall obtain for the aggregate of the Hazara nation, inhabiting the Paropamisian chain, a population of about 156,000 souls.

Of these tribes the most powerful are the Deh Kundí, Dia Zingi, Deh Zingi, and Sheikh Ali. Sometimes they are subject to Kunduz and at other times to Kabul. They now own allegiance to the former, and annually send Murad Ali Beg a tribute in slaves. In paying this inhuman tax, the custom is for a certain number of houses to join together, and when the value of a slave is collected, he is furnished by them. In years of great scarcity, such as that in which we visited this people, it is not unusual for a Hazara family voluntarily to dispose of one or more children. It is a sacrifice to which they are compelled by necessity. But generally they speak with detestation of the practice of man-stealing, and never mention the Uzbeks, who enslave them, but in terms of loathing and hatred.

Hucksters from Kabul visit the Hazara country, and are enabled advantageously to barter white and coloured coarse cotton cloths, Peshawúr lungis, and the poor fabrics of Koh Daman, for carpets, felts, and ghí. A very durable, brown-coloured chogha or pelisse, much worn in Afghanistan, is also obtained of the Hazara. They have fine sheep of the Dhumba or large-tailed species, and a small but hardy breed of horse, well adapted to their mountains. The country abounds in lead and sulphur.

The Hazara females go unveiled. They are much softer featured than the men, and have a healthy florid complexion. Their figure is delicate, and would appear but ill fitted to brave so severe a climate. All out-door work is, however, performed by the men. The women are by no means shy of strangers; but, I believe, that what in a Mussulman country appears a want of modesty is only a freedom of manner resulting from the liberty in which both sexes are reared, and not any laxity of morals. The Afghans brand the race as immoral, and all agree that the tribe of Jakuri is notorious for a singularly depraved species of hospitality, which compels the host to transfer his wife to the embrace of his guest. The Hazara are Shiahs—heretics—in the eyes of Suni Mohamedans; and those orthodox detractors assert that such a creed is a cloak for every crime.

We passed the night at Gulgatui, under the roof of an Hazara family. The house was of stone, low, flat-roofed, and contained a considerable number of apartments, in one of which the females slept, and in another the men of the family and ourselves. The fire-place in the kitchen or sitting-room was merely a hole scooped in the earthen floor, while the smoke found a vent through two apertures in the roof. On the top of the house was piled, in bundles, the winter's store of fuel. On the whole, an Hazara house, with a cheerful fire on its hearth, is a snug berth enough, could custom but reconcile one to its smoky atmosphere. The head of the family was a hale, hearty old man, who had been married thirty years, the last twenty of which he had lived in this house. The whole stock on his farm consisted of two cows, as many calves, and a few sheep. For the little spot of ground which he occupied, he paid to the ruler of Kabul a portion of the village tax of sixty rupees. He told us that in this bleak region the men, for seven months out of the twelve, have little other employment than to bring fuel from the hills. We retired early to rest; and when they imagined us to be sleeping, the whole family cautiously entered the room in which we were lying, and which adjoined the kitchen, lit the candle, and minutely examined such articles as had been left upon the table. A plated candlestick, in particular, astonished them; and after handling it over and over, a young woman, casting a furtive glance at Doctor Lord and myself, deposited the treasure in a corner of the room. Having finished their survey, a large basin of water was brought in, from the half-frozen stream before the door. This and a few mouthfuls of coarse barley bread formed the frugal supper of the family. The fire was now extinguished, and all retired to rest. Next morning, when we were prepared to start, the fair thief inquired if we missed nothing; and we, wishing to discover the motive that led her to secrete the candlestick, pretended a total ignorance of the scene we had witnessed the preceding night. The secreted treasure was now produced; but whether the laughing culprit had hidden it for better security, or merely to frighten us with the loss of so costly an article, we could not well determine. To these simple-minded people it must have appeared of immense value. At all events it was evident that no dishonest motive had prompted the conduct of the Hazara maiden: and we left the house well pleased with our reception.

On the morning of the 19th we commenced the ascent of Hajikak, which we accomplished with great ease, and encamped in the afternoon at the village of Kalu, in a narrow valley bearing the same name. Hajikak is geographically remarkable as dividing the waters of the Afghan country from those of Turkistan. South of this pass the streams join the river Helmand, and those on its northern side the Oxus. It has just been remarked that the chief employment of the Hazara through the long winter is to collect fuel. This fuel consists of a description of furze commonly called buta, and sometimes "Kollah Hazaras," or the Hazara's cap. It grows luxuriantly on the highest mountain, and there is considerable risk in getting it into the valleys. Towards evening the gatherer collects the produce of his day's work on a convenient point of the range overlooking his home. The large bundle is then launched, when it slides down the mountain's side in a zigzag line between the jutting crags, and sending up a volume of dust like that caused by the brisk passage of a troop of cavalry along a dusty road. The sides of the mountain are in this neighbourhood furrowed by the tracks of the buta collectors.

We had followed the direct Kafila route thus far, but it now became necessary to make a small circuit to avoid the Pass of Kalu, which was covered with snow to a depth that prevented our attempting its ascent. Continuing, therefore, our route along a valley, having the range of Hajikak to our right and that of Kalu to our left, we made a considerable détour and doubled the latter range; thence we were conducted to Bamian by the precipitous defile of Pimuri and the volcanic valley of Zohawk.

The Pimuri defile is of a peculiarly wild character. The mountains that wall this narrow ravine have evidently been rent asunder by some tremendous subterranean convulsion. Their bases nearly join, and their sides rise almost perpendicularly. Beetling crags threaten the traveller from above, whilst immediately below his insecure pathway, a brawling stream cascades through the length of the chasm. At one place the stream is bridged over for a distance of 200 paces by a portion of the mountain that has fallen across the ravine.

The ruins of Zohawk occupy the corner of a volcanic wall, which separates a valley so named from that of Bamian. They are scattered over a considerable extent of surface, but there is nothing grand or imposing in their appearance. The light style of the architecture would lead one to fix the era of Zohawk's erection in an age less remote than is generally assigned to it by popular tradition. Geographically the site of these ruins is remarkable, as being the junction of the two streams which form the south-west fork of the Kunduz river. On quitting Bamian we crossed the Pass of Akrobat, and arrived at a small valley on its north side. Our reception at this place, where we first entered the dominions of Murad Ali Beg, was not very cordial; for the governor of this elevated[1] and ungenial district, on hearing of our approach, quitted his fort and left Mirzá Buddi to look elsewhere for supplies. Before reaching this valley we saw on the way-side a very remarkable stone, known by the name of Juring-juringi. It is a cube of eight feet and of a green colour. When struck by any hard substance it rings like bell metal. To Akrobat succeeded the valley of Sykan, inhabited by Tajiks, being the first of that race we had seen north of Hindú Kosh. The Hazara are now no longer met with in distinct societies, but are incorporated with the Tajiks, whose protection they purchase by an outward compliance with the orthodox religion. Sykan stands in a fruitful vale; its mountains also yield large quantities of assafœtida, and the district where it grows is as regularly apportioned out to individuals as the corn-fields in the plain, and the property in it as carefully guarded. The produce of

---

[1] Akrobat is 10,200 feet above the sea.

this plant is usually brought up by the chiefs, and sold at a monopolizing price to Kafilas in their transit through the country.

At Sykan we met a man of the Deh Kundí tribe, bringing part of the yearly slave tribute to Kunduz. The able-bodied slaves were chained together; the aged, who were too infirm to walk, rode on donkeys, and behind them were bound children, whose extreme youth rendered them happily unconscious of the home they had left and the liberty they had lost. They all of them were squalid and dirty, and the ragged pieces of clothing that hung from their shoulders were but a poor substitute for covering. One haggard old woman, on whose lineaments Time had traced many a wrinkle, presented an appearance scarcely human; she was a humiliating sight.

From Sykan we descended by the Pass of "Dundan Shikun," or the "Tooth-breaker," into the valley of Kamrud, and remained during the night with a Tajik chief named Rahmutulah Khan, the same drunken old man who so piteously bewailed his empty flagon to Captain Burnes's party in 1832. Kamrud supplies a large body of water to the Kunduz river. Under its fort this stream had a width of twenty-four feet, a mean depth of two, and an average current of four miles and a half an hour. Its source is at the head of the valley, where it issues from an aperture in the rock. Here is the Ziarat of Khaji Abdullah, much resorted to in the hot months, but now rendered inaccessible by ice and snow. Summer and winter, the volume of water of this mineral spring is unaltered in bulk. It now had a temperature of 48°, that of the air being 34°. The fort of Kamrud is 5,600 feet above the sea.

In very mountainous regions, the occasional violence of the streams is adverse to the employment of water as a moving power; still, throughout the Paropamasian chain, both east and west of the Indus, corn mills driven by water are very frequently met with. The mountaineer, taking advantage of his situation, erects that simplest of machines, the water wheel, and is enabled to grind his corn with ease and at little cost, an operation which, when performed by manual labour, is the severest tax on the cultivator of the ground. In many localities this water power could be vastly increased, and streams, portions of which are now only employed to turn a few corn-mills, might be made subservient to the production of those articles of clothing, which, at present, after they have half circumnavigated the globe, are purchased by the inhabitants of the very regions where the raw material is produced. For such a purpose, few places are more favourable than the valley of Kamrud; but radical must be the changes wrought in the habits of these people before the man-seller will betake himself to so honest an employment, and the blood feuds of centuries be quenched. Still such blessings may one day attend the march of civilization; some powerful chief, fixing himself on one or the other side of the snowy chain, may have strength to control these turbulent sons of the mountain, and give a direction to their energies more favourable to civilization. Glens that now only echo the matchlock's report, may then as closely resemble Switzerland in the moral character of their peasantry, as they do in their scenery and local advantages. As we continued our journey by the road familiar to all travellers into Turkistan, I need not particularize its stages; they have already been frequently described. On the 28th we reached Khurm, the estate of Mirzá Buddi. His son and some of his tenantry came a few miles to meet him, and welcome him back; and no one who witnessed his warm reception could have suspected that under this show of affection rankled the deepest animosity; yet such was the case, for shortly after we quitted the country, poor Mirzá Buddi was barbarously murdered in his own house.

In the Khurm valley we overtook another slave party from the Hazara country. The owners, to the astonishment of our party, were men of Kabul. They appeared greatly mortified at being seen by us, hung down their heads, and wished, but in vain, to escape notice. The Khirakushes recognised them as inhabitants of Chardeh, a plain in the vicinity of Kabul, and at once charged them with carrying on a traffic, as degrading to an Afghan as it is accounted honourable in an Uzbek. They were asked how they could face their clansmen after such disreputable conduct. In extenuation of their conduct, they stated, that after trading to a considerable extent with the Hazara, and waiting twelve months for a settlement of their claims, they had been unable to obtain payment. The correctness of the demand was readily acknowledged, and slaves, valued at its full amount, offered in lieu of all claims. At first they refused this mode of payment, but were at length induced to comply. Unable after such a description of compromise to return direct to their own country, they were now proceeding to the Uzbek mart of the Khurm, or Tash Kurghan, there to realize by sale the proceeds of this discreditable barter.

Nothing surprises one so much, nor is more difficult to be accounted for on rational principles, than the marked shades of difference which often, as in this case, are exhibited in the moral character of neighbouring nations. Here we have two races of men, professing the same belief, whose habits in many respects are alike, and whose location and pastoral pursuits offer many points in common, yet differing in almost every feeling that marks the man, and which in their combined influence constitute the peculiar genius of a people. Of the freedom enjoyed by the Afghans, the Uzbeks know nothing. The liberty of the slave they capture is not more at their disposal than their own life is in the hands of their chief or Beg. To love of country, a feeling dominant in the breast of an Afghan, and which glows with more or less intensity in the soul of every other people from the Zahara to the Esquimaux, the Uzbek is almost a stranger. The custom of man-stealing appears to have smothered every better feeling, and the practice of trafficking in human beings extends even into their domestic arrangements; for their wives are as much articles of property as their slaves, and are bought and sold with the same callous indifference. Again, among the Uzbeks, though the tribes are numerous and distinct, we do not detect that attachment between individuals of the same clan, or that devotion to its common head which has ever been the bond of union in all countries where this primitive arrangement of society prevails. When the Kattaghan, indeed, mentions his tribe, it is with a conscious feeling of superiority, but Murad

Beg, the ruler of Kunduz, is a Kattaghan, and the pride of the Kattaghan is founded on their belonging to the tribe of their chieftain, and not on their own ancestral lineage. I never knew an Uzbek of any of the other tribes boast of his descent. The truth is, that among this people, as with other semi-barbarous nations, the most honoured tribe is always the one headed by the strongest chieftain; for he who can make himself dreaded, is sure to be respected.

A little below the village of Khurm, we struck off to the right for Kunduz, and despatched Kassinath to Khurm, together with those supernumeraries of the party who had attached themselves to our Kafila for protection on the road. Most of these were pilgrims on their way to the shrine of Hazrat Ali of Mazar. The sanctuary stands about twelve miles from the old city of Balkh, and twice that distance west of the modern town of Tash Kurghan. It is famous on both sides of the snowy chain, for its sanctity, and for the miracles performed by its patron Hazrat Shah. Once in the year a fair is held, during which the blind, infirm, halt, and maimed of many a distant region crowd to Mazar, and encamping round its shrine, watch day and night for the saint's interposition in their behalf. Of this numerous band, some few are restored to health probably by the change of air and scene; a considerable number die on the spot, and the larger proportion return as they came, bewailing their want of faith, and their sins, but never questioning the potency of Hazrat Shah. From Tash Kurghan to Mazar the road is much infested by highwaymen, but while this holy fair lasts, robbery is unknown, although at other seasons it is unsafe to pass between these places without an escort.[1]

The plain between the streams that water Kunduz and

[1] This mosque is held in great veneration by Mussulmans in general, but especially by the Shiah sect, who declare that it contains the sepulchre of Ali the son-in-law of Mohamed. It was built by one of the princes of Timour's family, and within it is the pretended tomb of *Shah Murdan*, or "The King of Men," by which title Ali is generally known in Khorassan. According to Ferrier's "Caravan Journey," to which work I am indebted for the above information, this shrine is resorted to from all parts of Central Asia, and possesses immense revenues. The actual tomb of Ali is at Nejef near Bagdad.

Khurm, has a wavy surface, and, though unsuited to agriculture, affords excellent pasturage. The only village on the road is that of Hazrat Baba Kamur, where we halted for a night. On the eastern side the plain is supported by a ridge of hills sloping down from the mountains to the south. We crossed it by the Pass of Archa (so called from the fir trees that cover its crest), from the top of which we had a noble view of the snowy mountains to the east, the outliers of Hindú Kosh. Next day we forded the river of Kunduz, and continuing to journey along its right bank, through the swampy district of Baghlan and Aliabad, reached the capital of Murad Beg on Monday the 4th of December.

CHAPTER XIV.

Murad Beg in Durbar.—Kunduz.—Character of the chief.—Uzbeks.—Tribes of Tartary.—Tajiks.—Uzbek intolerance.—Influence of the Mullahs.—Predestination.—Meals.—Salutations.—Horses.—Dogs.—Uzbek ladies.—Cemeteries.—Mohamed Beg's case.—Consultations.—Obtain leave to trace the Oxus.

THE day following that of our arrival at Kunduz, we were invited by Mirzá Buddi to accompany him to Durbar. Our reception was most gracious. After exchanging the usual compliments of an eastern court, Murad Beg expressed himself highly gratified with our visit to Kunduz; and turning to his Mirza or secretary, directed him to read Captain Burnes's letter aloud. When the Mirza had concluded, Murad Beg exclaimed, " Khoob Khoob," *good good*. A piece of Russian loaf sugar was then placed before us, and the few presents we had brought were produced. A spying glass and some bottles of essential oils, with other restoratives, particularly pleased him. Each bottle was separately examined, and he requested Dr. Lord to communicate through the native medical assistant, a knowledge of their contents to his secretary. This was done; and in the chief's presence the bottles were labelled. The apartment in which we were received measured about thirty feet by fifteen, with a portion of its floor elevated more than a foot, and well carpeted. The Begs were seated in rows on one side of the room, and below them on the less elevated part of the floor stood grouped the Mír's personal attendants and household slaves. Opposite the Begs, his legs carelessly stretched on a coloured felt, and leaning back on a large silken pillow, was Murad Ali Beg. The head of the room was reserved for us. The number of Begs present was large, and all of them old men. This is not to be reconciled with the known insalubrity of Kunduz. We may presume, however, that having such mature advisers prudence guides the councils of the chief. But if, as an Algerine once hinted to a British Admiral, the wisdom of a people is to be estimated by the length of their beards, but little of Solomon's mental superiority is inherited by the Uzbeks.

Kunduz, though the capital of Murad Beg, is one of the most wretched in his dominions. Five or six hundred mud hovels contain its fixed population, while dotted amongst these, and scattered at random over the suburbs, are straw-built sheds intermixed with the Uzbek tent or Kirgah. Gardens and corn fields alternate in its suburbs and extend even into the town. Nothing, in short, can be imagined less resembling a metropolis. Overlooking the east end of the town is the fortress. This is merely a mound, of an oblong figure and considerable extent, strengthened by a mud wall, and a dry ditch. The wall is in a dilapidated state on all sides but the south, on which is the principal entrance by the bázár gate. On the north-east end of the fortress is the citadel, the winter residence of Murad Beg. It is an irregular structure of kiln-dried brick, surrounded by a moat. It has many loop-holes for matchlocks; there are also guns within it, but none are mounted on the walls. The dry ditch which surrounds it, though now laid out in gardens, can be filled should occasion require it. Inside the fortress the inhabitants are either Uzbeks, or Hindús connected with Atmah the Dewan Begi, or steward of the chief. The appearance of Kunduz accords with the habits of an Uzbek; and by its meanness, poverty, and filth, may be estimated the moral worth of its inhabitants.

Murad Beg, the head of this Uzbek state, is one of those prominent political characters that unsettled times, and a disorganized state of society, produce. Such were Mohamed Ali in Egypt and the late Runjít Sing in Hindustan—men whose fortunes were based on mental superiority; and though Murad Beg cannot be ranked with either of these remarkable men, the Uzbek will not suffer by comparison with them, when we take into account the rudeness of the material on which he had to work. Little craft enters into the character of his chieftain, but to his splendid talents he unites what does not always accompany them, strong common sense. His forces, composed entirely of cavalry, are well adapted to predatory warfare, for which neither infantry nor guns are essential. The horses though small, have great power, and will endure much fatigue for ten successive days; carrying grain for themselves and their rider. The habits of his subjects are equally well fitted to this mode of life; and the absolute authority which he has over them, places their services at all times at his disposal. There is not a man in his dominions, let him possess what authority he may, but must yield it up at the nod of the Mir. His own tribe are devotedly attached to him, and seldom mention his name without exclaiming, "*May God add to his riches.*" He is not equally popular with the Tajik mountain states, which he has subdued; but among these all spirit of resistance is so completely crushed, that while Murad Beg lives, there is no chance of their attaining freedom unless aided by a foreign power. Still these people, though indignant at the Mír's arbitrary rule, do not deny his great abilities, and especially his talent of quickly penetrating into the counsels of other men.

But with all his high qualifications Murad Beg is but at the head of an organised banditti, a nation of plunderers, whom, however, none of the neighbouring powers can exterminate.

Able as he is to bring together in a surprisingly short space of time, a body of 15,000 horsemen, inured to predatory warfare, and to those stealthy attacks for which Turkiman and Uzbek are equally celebrated, he feels himself perfectly secure from the assault of any of the chieftains by whom he is surrounded, nor, indeed, were they to league together could they successfully oppose him. The only people who, though occasionally chastised, have hitherto escaped subjection, are the tribes on the north bank of the river Oxus. Murad Beg, aware that his description of force was ill-calculated to retain conquest when made, razed every hill fort as they fell into his hands, but reserved the Uzbek strongholds in the plain. These, Tash Kurghan excepted, are held by members of his family, or by men whose interest is identified with his own. The conquered experienced more favourable treatment than was to have been expected at the hands of the Uzbeks, in whose character clemency is no ingredient. If the chief himself be not wantonly cruel, his conduct is often needlessly severe; but of this more hereafter. Not the least remarkable trait in the character of this man is the contrast afforded by his well ordered domestic government, and the uninterrupted course of rapine which forms the occupation of himself and his subjects, whose "chuppaws," or plundering expeditions embrace the whole of the upper waters of the Oxus, from the frontier of China on the east, to the river that runs through Balkh, "the mother of cities," on the west. His government is rigidly despotic, but seldom is absolute power less misused. The rights and property of his subjects are respected, merchants are safe, and trade is encouraged. Punishment for crime, whether against individuals or the state, is most summary; for theft and highway robbery, if the highway be *in their own country*, for that makes a wonderful difference, the only award is death. An offender, when detected, never escapes punishment, and sentence is no sooner pronounced than executed. This prompt procedure is little in accordance with the beautiful maxim of English Jurisprudence, that it is better many who are guilty should escape than that one innocent man should suffer; yet the certainty of punishment has lessened the commission of crime. Countries in former times closed to the traveller, may now, with Murad Beg's protection, be as safely traversed as British India.

The Uzbeks are a tribe of Tartar, or rather Scythian origin, which, in a comparatively modern era, crossed the Jaxartes and fixed themselves in Transoxiana. The descendants of the ruthless Jangez Khán then occupied that country, but were soon forcibly dispossessed. Their chief, the renowned Baber, after vainly endeavouring to stem the torrent of invasion, yielded to its strength, and led his forces into Hindustan, where he established the Mogul empire called after Mogul Khán, the founder of his line. Those of the disinherited nation who neither submitted to the Uzbek nor accompanied their chief, retired across the river Oxus; and in the Turkimans of that locality I think we may recognize their descendants. In the early part of the sixth century, the Turks of the Altaian chain first emerged into notice. In a few years after their first appearance, among their other conquests, was that of Nephthalites, or white Huns of Soghdiana—that is, Samarkand and Bokhara, the countries from which the Uzbeks expelled the Turkimans. The beauty of the latter race has long been celebrated by Persian poets; and as the name of Turkiman is otherwise obscure, we may perhaps be justified in supposing them the mixed progeny of Huns and Turks. The Turkimans boast of having founded the Ottoman Empire, and, moreover, point to the mountains of Imaus as the original seat of their ancestors; and tradition goes far to establish the consanguinity of the Osmanlee and the Turk of the Oxus. Though the languages of the various hordes that now roam over Central Asia are different, there is reason to believe that the Huns of antiquity are the prototypes of them all, whether designated Kalmucks or Kirghiz, Uzbek or Turkiman. Most of their names have had a personal origin, such as Tartar, Noghai, Uzbek, and Moghul. The first, corrupted to Tartary, has now become a generic term for the Scythia of the Roman historians, though I do not remember to have heard it used by the Uzbeks of Kunduz. From this custom much ambiguity has resulted. It is, however, foreign to my purpose to descant more at large on the wandering hordes that now occupy these wilds; yet so interesting is all connected with these shepherd tribes, which more than once have overrun Europe and Asia, that I could not omit giving the subject a passing notice.

The Uzbeks of Kunduz have genuine Tartar features, though the physiognomy of their chiefs is becoming softened by intermarriage with the Tajik, a Caucasian race whom I believe to be the indigenous inhabitants of Persia, and perhaps of Transoxiana also, and who are now found widely scattered on both sides of the Paropamasian chain. A Tajik is not permitted to marry the daughter of an Uzbek; but this unjust distinction is the only social difference that now exists between them. The Uzbeks are Suni Mohamedans, and consider an intolerant persecution of the other sect as the best evidence of the sincerity of their own faith and of their attachment to the Prophet. They are much fettered by their priests, or Ishán Kajahs, to whom they yield implicit obedience in all things, temporal and spiritual. Whatever may be thought of the effect produced by this influential class on Mohamedan society generally, I do not hesitate to say, that among the Uzbeks it is the reverse of good. These mullahs, or priests, are the most notorious slave dealers in the land, and encourage the odious traffic among their disciples, by readily purchasing of them whatever victims of the Shiah creed they may entrap. The good of the soul is assigned as ample extenuation, and religion here, as but too often has been the case elsewhere, becomes a cloak to crime instead of a guide to virtue.

It is rare to find an Uzbek of Kunduz who can read and write; so that the Tajiks, who are less illiterate, and the Hindús also, frequently rise to consequence among them.

They are as firm believers in predestination as the Turks. I remember that, having on one occasion deplored the untimely end of a chief whom Murad Beg had put to death, an Uzbek in company called out "*his time had come—spare your pity;* for 'Be nusseeb'—*nothing happens that is not ordained.*" The Uzbek never utters a sentence which has the slightest reference to the future, however certain the events spoken of may be, without the prefatory words "Nusseeb bashud," or, *if we have luck*; and were the subject of his discourse the probability of the sun's rising the next morning, it is ten to one that he would introduce this saving clause. With the Afghan it is the same; and were we to judge of their piety by their frequent repetition of the supplicatory words "Inshallah," or *please God*, it would be difficult to rate it too high.

All ranks in Kunduz eat twice a day — at "Chasht," or about nine o'clock in the forenoon, and at "Nimaz Akhúr," or twilight; pillaw and soup, with good leavened wheaten bread, constitute the repast; mutton is the flesh in general use. That of the horse, though eaten, is not often exposed in their markets; it is too expensive for the generality of the people. On the banks of the Oxus the pheasant is very plentiful, and is a delicacy greatly esteemed by the inhabitants. A meal is never concluded without tea; it is also drunk at all hours of the day; but this beverage, says the Uzbek, "goes for nothing." Yet tea in this country is not the meagre unsubstantial fare it is with us; it is termed "*Keimuk chah*," or cream tea; and the cream is so rich and clotty as to give one the idea of its having been mixed with oil. Fat is sometimes added, and salt is the uniform substitute for sugar. The tea is made in a large iron pot, from which it is baled out with a wooden ladle, and handed round to the company by the host in small china bowls. After a few trials Keimuk chah has rather an agreeable flavour.

When an Uzbek on horseback meets a chief or other superior, he forthwith dismounts and makes his salam. One foot, however, remains in the stirrup, and so rapid are his movements, that he has regained the saddle and set off at a canter almost before you are conscious of his having touched the ground.

The Kunduz breed of horse is very inferior to that of the Turkiman, or even to that which their countrymen rear about Shehr Sabz and the environs of Bokhara. The animal to suit Murad Beg and his subjects, must be small and hardy, adapted to the hilly country as well as to the plain. Speed is a secondary consideration; endurance everything. Their fore and hind quarters are remarkably large. One year from the day on which a colt is foaled, it is mounted and ridden by a light weight for a considerable distance at full speed, after which for two years it is not again saddled, and at three years old it is regularly broken in. Shoes are used only upon the fore feet, and in shape are a perfect circle. Like the rest of their race, the Uzbeks are extremely fond of horses and racing. Many idioms in their colloquial language have reference to them. For instance, if you inquire how far any particular place is distant, you are answered "ek doweedah" (a gallop); or if you ask what time any operation will require, the answer is still the same—"while you may gallop so many miles."

The dog in Turkistan, although not elevated to so important a rank as the horse, is still as useful and as highly esteemed as in more civilised communities; and here we have an example of those caprices and contrarieties which everywhere distinguish man. To ask an Uzbek to sell his wife would be no affront, but to ask him to sell his dog would be an unpardonable insult, "Suggee ferosh," or *dog-seller*, being about the most offensive epithet that one Uzbek can apply to another. In speaking of the Uzbek ladies, I must not omit recording that they are admirable housewives; so that though they lack beauty they have a more enduring claim on the affection of their lords. Like others of their sex, they strive to dress well, and as is too frequently the case with our own fairer country women, they disfigure their natural beauty by vain attempts to improve it. The sleeves of an English gown look as if they were intended to conceal a couple of small barrels instead of two slight and delicately proportioned arms; and in Turkistan the fashion leads to equal absurdities. Like the mantilla of Spain, the gown of the Uzbek lady envelopes the head, as with a hood, and from about the ears are suspended the sleeves, long narrow slips of cloth that sweep the ground, and which, dangling to and fro as the portly beauty rolls along, bring to mind the stories told by Ptolemy and the elder historians, of a long-eared race of men. The gallants of Kunduz love to show themselves off clad in scarlet or some equally bright and glaring colour, while the ladies, on the contrary, wear dark clothes, or dress in pure white, with only a showy silk handkerchief bound round the head or held in the hand.

Those who like myself have resided in a country village, and trod the green sodded churchyard every Sunday, cannot but feel displeased at the little attention which the Uzbeks pay to their cemeteries. While all around is grassy, the burial-ground remains naked and unattended to. Situated without the suburbs, the heaps of red and brown earth, like mounds carelessly raked together, are painful to the eye, as indicating a spirit callous to the obligations of friendship, parental affection, or conjugal love. Still more revolting is it, when obliged to thread our way amongst these cities of the dead, to observe on many of the graves signs that the jackal has been burrowing there. South of Hindú Kosh more attention is bestowed upon the burial grounds. Slabs with appropriate inscriptions are common among the wealthy; and the great, both in India and

Afghanistan, have mausoleums erected to their honour with the splendour of which nothing in Europe can vie.

The very first visit to the patient, Mohamed Beg, enabled Dr. Lord to decide on his unfortunate case. The sight of one eye had gone for ever, and the visual ray of the other was fast waning. So elated, however, were the hopes which the poor man had conceived of the Firingí's superior knowledge, that the task which now devolved on Dr. Lord of undeceiving him, as to his power to work miracles and restore the blind to sight, was one of great delicacy and of some hazard. Mohamed Beg was told that all which the utmost skill could achieve would be exerted to preserve the remaining eye, but that cures were in the hand of God, and he must trust to Providence for a favourable result. Predestination here favoured the doctor's moral lessons, of which he was not sparing, and Mohamed Beg from this date was more of a Mullah than an Uzbek chief. We had now been a week in Kunduz, and as there was every probability of our being compelled to remain the winter, the question arose how we could most profitably employ this sojourn in Turkistan. The great object of my thought by day and dreams by night had for some time past been the discovery of the source of the river Oxus, and, thanks to my fellow traveller's tact and Mirzá Buddi's good-will, Murad Beg on the 10th of December conceded his permission to me to trace the Jihun, an appellation by which this river is better known among the Uzbeks.

CHAPTER XV.

Start on an exploratory expedition.—Fellow travellers.—Gholam Hussein, Abdul Ghuní Yesawal.—Servants.—Marco Polo.—Kunduz Plain.—Phenomena.—Khana-a-bad.—Hospitable students.—Snug quarters.—Reflections.—Badakhshies.—Colleges of Khana-a-bad.—The town.—Journey to Talikhan.—Character of the road.—Nature of the mountains.—Koh Umber.—Eagles and crows.—An embarrassed interview.—Reach Talikhan.

Monday the 11th of December was fortunately a market day in Kunduz; so that the articles required for our expedition were at once obtained; and lest Murad Beg might recall the permission he had given, we started that same evening for Badakhshan and the Oxus. We adopted the costume of the country, as a measure calculated to smooth our intercourse with a strange people, and we had little baggage to excite cupidity or suspicion. Coarse clothes to barter for food with the inhabitants of the mountains, was our stock in trade; and my chronometers and other instruments the only articles of value which I took with me. Dr. Lord accompanied us for the first few miles, and parted from us with cordial wishes for the success of our expedition.

The most important of my fellow travellers was Gholam Hussein, Munshi, cook, and "*servant of all work*," in whom were more sterling good qualities than I at one time believed it possible to find in the breast of a Hindustaní. More intimate acquaintance with Eastern countries has considerably modified my unfavourable opinion of their inhabitants, and taught me to dissent from those wholesale terms of abuse which Europeans too often lavish on the native population. It will generally be found that our opinions of a people rise as our acquaintance with them increases. Vice in every community is sufficiently prominent to be seen without being sought after; but the wise and good shun notoriety, and it is only when we probe society deep that they are discovered. Gholam Hussein was a native of Jaysulmir, but had been from a lad in the army of Sind, where, after a faithful servitude of sixteen years, he had attained the rank of Jemidar, and a salary of twenty rupees a month. While the Seiks continued to threaten Sind, this pittance was regularly disbursed; but no sooner did the Indian Government come forward and avert the impending invasion, than the Amírs, relieved from their personal fears, displayed their accustomed avarice; and orders went forth to reduce the pay of all "Pardési," or *foreign troops*. At this juncture the mission entered the Indus; when Gholam Hussein, with whom I had become acquainted during my previous sojourn in Sind, left the service of the Amírs and entered mine. Of a swarthy complexion, and diminutive height, his frame was thick set, strong, and active. On horseback the rotundity of his figure and his consequential air obtained for him, from my witty and mirthful companion Dr. Lord, the sobriquet of Joss. Luckily the meaning of the word is, to this day, unknown to the Munshi. A disclosure must have been attended with unpleasant consequences, since few followers of the Prophet could be more strictly orthodox than this honest little fellow; and the slightest hint of a resemblance between himself and a Chinese idol, would have been a deadly affront. Gholam Hussein's failing was a naturally irascible temper, but this fault he admirably subdued, and never suffered it to appear save where the ebullition was productive of good to his master. He possessed a fund of anecdote, and was, besides, tolerably skilled in Eastern lore.

Another of our small party was Abdul Ghuní Yesawal, a Tajik by descent, but at heart a genuine Uzbek. He had been educated for a Mullah, but had long ago renounced the cloister for the field, and was now, as the affix "Yesawal" implies, an officer of Murad Beg's household. He was a jocund, good-hearted soul, though, perhaps, a little too susceptible of the tender passion. After a day's march, when a glowing fire and the enlivening cup of tea had mellowed his rugged nature, I have listened to him expatiating on what he termed the three best friends of man, and what, next to life, should be most cared for. These were the Koran, a horse, and a sword. The first he would uncase from its numerous clumsy leather coverings, kiss the volume, and holding it out to the Munshi, swear by *Khoda* there was no book like it. A good horse, he would sagely remark, was a *great blessing*, it was invaluable; for what did it not do?—it procured a man his livelihood, and obtained for him his wives. That, in fact, without the horse, it would be impossible to *steal*, and then the Kattaghan's occupation and glory would be no more. His sword was a very poor one, but that mattered nothing: His imagination could revel in the superb weapons possessed by the Mír; while to prove the keen edge of his own, he would step beyond the threshold, and with superabundant flourishes hack away at the willows, the almond bushes, or whatever trees stood near. Had his affections been always as platonic as in these three instances, he would have saved himself a world of disquiet, as the sequel will show. There was a gravity in the man's appearance which contrasted strongly with his absurdities of conduct, and added point to the good-humoured jests in which he freely indulged. This man's home was at Talikhan, and he was deputed by the Kunduz chief to accompany us thither, and through the remainder of our journey. Ibrahim a Sindí, and Mahomed Cassim from Hindustan, carried the chronometers. Three Kabul men had the charge of the yabus, and two other Afghans that of the horses.

Before proceeding further, I must call the reader's attention to the travels of Marco Polo, the distinguished Venetian, who, towards the close of the thirteenth century, startled and delighted Europe with a description of civilized communities, then perfectly unknown. For a very long series of years this interesting work did not meet with the attention it deserved. The learned suspected it to be a fictitious narrative, or at best a mere compilation from hearsay authorities. Some, however, there were, and these men of profound and original minds, who amid the ignorance and bigotry which characterized the middle ages, perceived the real importance of the work.

Among such stood pre-eminent, Christopher Columbus. Though the writings of the Venetian tended to mislead that great man on many points, there is little doubt but that they were principally instrumental in stimulating him to attempt reaching India by sailing in a direction due west. Columbus failed in this object, but added a New World to the geography of our globe. In latter times the genuineness of the Travels has never been seriously impugned, though the exaggerated statements of their credulous author continue fit subjects for pleasantry. The perusal of Marsden's "English translation of Marco Polo," a work illustrated by copious and most erudite notes, first impressed me with a conviction of the authenticity of the narrative; and this has been strengthened by my subsequent travels through countries described by the Venetian. In this neighbourhood we first came upon his track; but I shall reserve my observations on the old traveller and his work for another occasion, since they would lead me into dissertations ill suited to this narrative.[1]

The day was far advanced when we left Kunduz. The afternoon had been cloudy; but as the sun went down, the moon, near her full, served to show the path. As night advanced the sky cleared, and we could then trace the shadowy outline of the mountains that look upon Kunduz; and we congratulated ourselves that on the morrow we should be above the gloomy atmosphere of the fens, and enjoy, what, at this season, is a rare occurrence in these plains—a pure sunshiny day.

The open plain we were now crossing is encircled on all sides by mountains, except on the north, where the river Oxus flows; and is intersected by the rivers of Kunduz and Khana-a-bad, both tributaries of the Oxus. The country strongly resembles the delta of the Indus, but is more moist and unfavourable to human life. The jungle grass is here taller and more dense. We saw but one village, though the number of rice mills at work and the continued barking of dogs proved that the region must be populous.

[1] The Life and Travels of Marco Polo, by Colonel Yule, C.B. (1871), has supplied a most valuable addition to geographical lore; and to it I am indebted for some interesting comparisons between the text and the Venetian's description of the same localities.

As we neared the river of Khana-a-bad the ground gradually rose and became drier; but before reaching the stream we had to cross four canals and as many rivulets, and from the velocity with which the water flowed in these, I infer that the upper portions of this plain might be easily drained.

During the whole of this march a veil of mist kept flitting before us. It vanished as we approached; but no sooner did one gauze-like screen disappear, than in succession another and another was discovered. The vapour cloud was seen against the clear azure sky, struggling to gain the higher regions. But not a breath of wind shook the long grass jungle, and the marsh miasma, if such it were, rose but to a certain height and there became stationary, floating above the spot where it had risen. At nine in the evening we forded the river, and immediately afterwards arrived in Khana-a-bad, the summer residence of Murad Beg. The stream abreast of the town runs in two channels. That on the west bank, though only three feet deep, was so rapid as nearly to unhorse me. With some difficulty, however, I escaped; but the Munshi was less fortunate, and got a complete ducking. Its width did not exceed fifteen yards, but its velocity was fully five miles an hour. The other branch had a width of sixty yards, and ran immediately under the walls of Khana-a-bad. It now discharged but little water, for though the principal course of the river, the stream had lately been led into another channel, while the bridge across it was under repair.

It was late when we entered the village, and to the hospitality of some of the students in its Madrasa, or colleges, we were indebted for shelter and for firing. Our horses were soon stabled in a corner of the court-yard, and, having seen that their provender bags were not empty, we entered as snug a berth as the most fastidious traveller could desire. A march of seventeen miles through a thick grass jungle often knee deep in water, performed in a keen winter's evening, had prepared us to welcome rest and shelter wherever found; and as we stretched ourselves upon the comfortable warm felts, and sipped our tea, I felt a glow at my heart which cannot be described. A calmness of spirit, a willingness to be satisfied and pleased with everything around me, and a desire that others should be as happy as myself. How often must every worn-out traveller have experienced this; and why is it that we should no sooner be restored to our wonted vigour than this placid temper leaves us, and we suffer ourselves to be ruffled and disturbed by every trivial occurrence?

Our kind entertainers were from Badakhshan, and the present state of that country became the subject of conversation. As the young men recounted what it had suffered under the iron rule of Murad Beg, they all but shed tears. There are here two institutions dignified with the name of colleges for the education of youth. One owes its existence to the governor of this district, and the other to the Kunduz chief. The latter, which is by far the largest, contains forty apartments. They are very poorly endowed; but should the reader smile at the following details, let him recollect that we are speaking of an Uzbek tribe on the outskirts of even Tartar civilisation.

The annual revenues of the two establishments are as follows:—

MIR'S COLLEGE.		GOVERNOR'S COLLEGE.	
Cash	144 rupees	Cash	150 rupees
Wheat	30 sacks	Wheat	50 sacks
Rice	10 ditto	Rice	20 ditto
Mash (pulse)	2 ditto.	Mash (pulse)	5 ditto.

The students pay no fees, but support themselves by labour. Divinity and law are the only branches of learning strictly taught; and these, with a sprinkling of the Persian poets, constitute the entire system of scholastic acquirements. The Koran and its commentators are the source from which he draws his ethics, and a work entitled the *Babool Kismut* his law.

Khana-a-bad stands upon the east bank of the river of that name. The stream is crossed by a stone bridge, now undergoing repair. Behind the town rises Koh Umber, an isolated mountain remarkable as dividing the plains of Kunduz and Talikhan. Khana-a-bad contains a large, ill constructed fort, and 600 mud-built houses; but the two colleges and the governor's residence are the only buildings entitled to even a passing notice. A large portion of its inhabitants are Badakhshies. The town is governed by Musa Yesawal, a household slave of Murad Beg, deservedly high in favour with his master. He was then just returned from the western frontier, whither he had been with a considerable body of troops to protect it from Bokharian aggression. The climate of Khana-a-bad is superior to that of Kunduz.

After a good night's rest we awoke completely refreshed; and cordially thanking the poor, but kind-hearted students for their hospitality, were soon on the road to Talikhan.

There was a fresh, cold breeze, but the thermometer indicated a temperature of 42°. Had we not been provided with the means of measuring it, I should, from the degree of moisture in the atmosphere, have supposed it to be at least 10° lower. A cloudy morning ushered in a gloomy day. Clouds floated low about the mountain sides, and the course of the river far onwards could be traced by the heavy masses of fog that hung over its surface. These, put in motion by an easterly wind, came rolling down the valley like circling clouds of smoke from the muzzle of some enormous gun. For the first ten miles we followed the banks of the Khana-a-bad river, upon an excellent road, although slippery from the effects of yesterday's rain. This brought us to the spot where the waters of the Bungi join the Khana-a-bad, which is here called the Talikhan, and which we forded just above the point of junction. Then leaving the Bungi river to the right, we proceeded for a further distance of four miles, through low rounded hills, which on both sides met the river, and among which the road assumed a worse character, though at no part of it is a horseman obliged to dismount. The boundary line of Kunduz and Talikhan is in this rugged part of the road, a fact of which the traveller is apprised by a custom-house on the road-side. In this neighbourhood the hills rise about two hundred feet above the river. All of them are grassy, and the slopes of some are under cultivation. Koh Umber towers full 2,500 feet above the surrounding level, and a large portion of its bulk was now encased in snow. This mountain is central to the districts of Talikhan, Kunduz, and Hazrat Imam; and its pasturage is common to the flocks of the three plains. We were told that it had not always stood where we saw it, but had been placed there by a holy man, who transported it from Hindustan; as a proof of which, our informant assured us that upon the mountain's side might be gathered every herb indigenous to India. Koh Umber, as seen from these plains, forms a grand and remarkable object: it therefore is not to be wondered at, that an ignorant and superstitious people should borrow from the marvellous to account for its somewhat peculiar position.

Above the hills numerous eagles were seen soaring, and large flocks of the white-backed or hooded crow. During summer the latter frequent the hilly country, but when winter sets in, they come down into the plain. Emerging from the hills, we drew up for some time at the entrance of the Talikhan plain, and I went a little distance from the party to get the bearings of a remote range of hills, which here first came into view.

On returning, I found Abdul Ghuní in earnest conversation with a stranger on horseback, behind whom was sitting a very handsome female slave, and it was evident from his manner that the Mullah was waxing wroth. He seemed anxious to detain the horseman, who, on his part, insisted upon proceeding. On my nearing the disputants, the stranger rudely gave his horse the whip, and struck off at a brisk pace along the Khana-a-bad road.

Abdul Ghuní gazed on the receding couple for some time in silence; then turning to me and sighing most piteously, he said, "Alas, alas, my lord! when I left my house in Talikhan, the very last order I gave was, that she whom you have just seen should not be sold. My other slaves were all for sale: but this one! this favourite one! I had thoughts of taking to wife!" and here the sighs began again. It appeared that in the Mullah's absence at Kunduz, a Khurm slave-dealer had visited Talikhan, and made a tempting offer for the favourite. The sum was large, and Abdul Ghuní's brother at once concluded a bargain. Unspeakable, therefore, was the Mullah's astonishment and grief, when she, the object of his tenderest affections, whom he had pictured to himself as already at the door to welcome his return, was thus unexpectedly encountered, seated behind a burly stranger, on her way to the Bokhara market. He raved and swore that the transfer was illegal, and that the dealer should give her back. He would be revenged, he would appeal to the Mír. But the thought of the twenty-six golden tillas (about 17*l*. sterling), for which the fair lady had been sold, by degrees calmed his grief, and in a resigned, but melancholy tone, he exclaimed, "She is too cheap, too cheap: the villain will get forty tillas for her in Khurm."

As a drizzling rain had set in, we crossed the plain, a distance of about ten miles, at a canter: and by three o'clock in the afternoon, when it began to pour in earnest, we had reached Talikhan, and were comfortably lodged in our conductor's Mehman Khana, or house for the reception of guests.

CHAPTER XVI.

Ataluk Khán—A descendant of Alexander the Great.—Talikhan sparrows.—Kirghis slaves.—Market days.—Mohamed Cassim Khojah.—Pass of Latta-band.—Mountain scenery.—Superstitions.—Kila Afghan.—Wolves.—Earthquake.—Karabolak.—Meshid valley.—Legend.—Agurdurah.—Nahwi.—Taishkhan.—Junasdurah.—Wild hogs.—Vale of Duraim.—Plain of Argu.—Reishkhan.—Khojah of Kashgar.—Chittah.—Aspect of country from Latta-band to Chittah.—Absence of inhabitants.—Dreary appearance.—Fyzabad.—Reflections.—Glen of Kash.—Arrival in Jerm.

THE 13th December was passed in Talikhan, awaiting the return of a messenger from Kunduz. As the weather was ill suited to travelling, we had no reason to regret this detention; more especially as we were admitted to an interview with the governor, and had a visit from a still more interesting individual; from no less a personage, indeed, if his own account were true, than a lineal descendant of Alexander the Great.

Ataluk, the son of Murad Beg, bears a close resemblance in personal appearance to his father, and his subjects add in character likewise. He is entrusted with the government of Talikhan, which, after Hazrat Imam, is next in importance to Kunduz. The Prince occupies a larger and better fort than his father, and is surrounded by at least equal state. He appears to be a sensible young man, but has the selfish and repulsive look common to his countrymen.

Mohamed Shah, our other visitor, was portly and well favoured; but there was nothing in the lines of his good humoured countenance that bore out his bold assertion, that the blood of Sekander Zool-Kurnein ran in his veins. Fifteen years ago, his father, the reigning prince of Badakhshan, was defeated by the Kunduz chief and banished his country, on which, Mohamed Shah and his two younger brothers were placed here by Murad Beg, under the surveillance of his son.

Though poor and unfortunate, the family is much respected by their countrymen, among whom, Mohamed, the head of the house, is still honoured with the title of Shah, or king.[1]

Talikhan is not so large a place as Khana-a-bad. I should not suppose it contained more than from three to four hundred houses, which, like those of the latter place, are merely hovels. Its inhabitants are chiefly from Badakhshan. The town stands about three hundred yards from the river, and is a most disagreeable place in rainy weather—the streets being then scarcely traversable. Here, as at Kunduz, the sparrow builds its nest in the most exposed situation; but no one thinks of injuring the confiding bird, and in this respect, the habits of Uzbek children are superior to those of Britain. These birds here associate in larger families than I remember to have seen elsewhere.

Among the slaves of Abdul Ghuni, who was still disconsolate for the loss of his favourite, were two Kirghis from Pamir. Although their features were Chinese, their complexions were fair, and even rosy. One, a good-looking young woman, had a child at her breast, and cried bitterly when detailing the circumstances attending her capture. The other was more advanced in years, and did not seem to feel the loss of liberty so acutely.

The following day a market was held in Talikhan. In all the principal towns of Murad Beg's dominions, it is customary to hold them twice a week. Though we left Talikhan at an early hour, the thronged state of the roads leading into it, soon apprised us that the day was no ordinary one. Troops of horsemen were hurrying into market, many riding double. Gaudily painted cradles, toys, bird-cages, skins of animals, and white and striped cotton cloth, were the articles forming the stock in trade of most of the dealers. All whom we met were blithe and jocund; and but for the difference of dress, and the large

---

[1] As will be seen later the chief of Wakhan also claimed the same lineage, and several other chiefs do likewise. The legend of the Alexandrian descent of the princes of Badakhshan is mentioned by Baber and other Eastern authors.

Pundit Manphûl states that the present Mírs of Badakhshan do not claim connection with the old princes of the country. Their dynasty is one comparatively recent.

proportion of those who rode, I could have fancied them my own countrymen hastening to some merry fair in old England. We counted the horsemen on our line of march, and found there were two hundred and ninety. At least twice that number rode donkeys, and there might be a hundred individuals on foot. Admitting the three other approaches to the town to have been equally crowded, the influx from the neighbouring districts into Talikhan on market days, will be nearly four thousand souls. The circle of country supplied by this town, may be considered as having a diameter of eighteen miles.

On our route, and at the distance of a few miles from Talikhan, resides Mohamed Cassim Khojah, the Sayíd who treated Moorecroft, the traveller, so well. I made a point of calling on the good man; and had prepared myself to meet a decrepit old chieftain, but was agreeably disappointed. The Sayíd has either but little passed the meridian of life, or the corroding cares of this world have not made their usual impression on his face or figure. I thanked him in the name of our countrymen for the protection he had afforded the traveller. When he heard that the fame of this good act had reached Firingistan he was silent, but his eye spoke joy. Such instances of benevolence are not of every day occurrence; and when we remember where it took place, and that the favoured party was of our own creed and nation, it surely is the duty of those in power, to send the Sayíd some written acknowledgment, if only to show that the British can appreciate virtue.[1]

Bidding farewell to this worthy man, we struck off to the left, and were soon at the base of a mountain ridge, beyond which lay Badakhshan. The road through this barrier is by the Pass of Latta-band; and by noon we reached its entrance. For an hour we kept winding through a defile called Au-durah; and towards its summit, where the ascent became more abrupt, we first met the snow. The road, however, continued good, and at about 3.30 P.M. we gained the crest of the pass. From this spot the prospect was glorious. In every quarter snow-clad peaks shot up into the clear sky. Looking towards Kunduz, Koh Umber, with its hoary summit and regular outline, stood

[1] This has since been done by Sir Alexander Burnes.

pre-eminent in the plain. To the east, where our road lay, the horizon was bounded by the high snowy range of Khoja Mohamed, which, crossing the country in a north-east and south-west direction, divides Badakhshan, and is the eastern barrier of Darwaz and Shagnan. Between us and this range, and seemingly at our feet, the Kokcha, or river of Badakhshan, rolled its green waters through the rugged valley of Duranah; while to the north could just be discerned the blue hills of mountainous Karatagin. The summit of Latta-band is wide and level: we travelled along the top of the pass for an hour and a half, before we commenced the descent on its eastern side. Here we picked up the carcase of a black eagle; a noble bird, which had been recently shot, and from which the claws, beak, and wings had been cut off. The two first of these, tied round the necks of children, are thought to keep off the evil eye.

At the foot of Latta-band, on the Badakhshan side of the mountain, is Ak-bolak (or white springs), a thriving village, the property of Mohamed Cassim Khojah. We left it on the right hand about sunset, and pushing along the plains, soon reached our halting place in Kila Afghan. The length of this day's march was thirty miles, and we were little more than nine hours upon the road. We had left Talikhan with a slight hoar-frost in the morning, but here snow covered the ground, and the thermometer had fallen to twenty-eight degrees. Everything spoke a difference in the level of the two places, and by observation, I found Kila Afghan to be nearly a thousand feet more elevated than Talikhan. Mohamed, the governor, came to the door of his castle, and bade us welcome in the Mír's name. A large fire was soon kindled in the open air; seated round which, we received and returned the salutations of his people. After some time spent in this friendly manner, we retired within doors, and amid a more select company quaffed

"The cup that cheers, but not inebriates."

As the night wore on, we began to feel uneasy at the prolonged absence of my attendant Mohamed Cassim. He had fallen behind the party about sunset, and had not yet come up. The governor, who dreaded wolves, sent out several men to look for him. These animals are here both numerous and daring; as a proof of which, our host mentioned what had occurred to himself some years ago. He had been to Kunduz on some urgent business for the Mír; and on his return reached the Kotul or Pass of Latta-band about midnight. The pass was cleared without accident, but on proceeding through Ak-bolak, the wolves gathered on his track, and but for the timely assistance of the villagers, would have eaten both horse and rider. So daring and close were their assaults, that they had already torn away with their teeth the saddle-cloth, and his own mantle. Some of the wolves repeatedly went ahead of the horse, and by scratching with their hind feet threw up snow so as to frighten the animal, and bewilder its rider. Had three minutes more elapsed before succour reached him, his doom would have been fixed. It was now near midnight; but before going to rest I walked out into the open air, expecting the arrival of the missing man, or the return of those sent out in search of him. A halo full thirty-five degrees in diameter encircled the moon, though otherwise the sky was beautifully clear. It was, however, bitterly cold, and there being no signs of the party's return, at length we all sought our felt couches, and were soon asleep.

Kila Afghan is famous for its springs, of which there are said to be 450 in the neighbourhood. Its fort, with every house in the village, was thrown down by the earthquake of 1832, and by that fearful calamity many lives were lost. Next morning we were agreeably surprised at Mohamed Cassim's return. After losing our track he had the good sense to make at once for Ak-bolak, which village was in sight when he parted from us. In consequence of the detention occasioned by this man's absence, the sun was high in the heavens before we left Kila Afghan, but by making a forced march we reached Taishkhan, distant twenty-six miles, before dark.

Here, in 1823, the Badakhshies, under Miryar Beg Khán, made their last stand for independence against the power of Kunduz. The forces of the latter, consisting of 10,000 horsemen, were led on by Murad Beg in person. The opposing army was less numerous by 1000 men, and partly composed of foot soldiers. After skirmishing with various success, the Uzbeks made a general charge, and put the Badakhshies to flight, killing and wounding 300 of them, with a very trifling loss to themselves. The conquered army fell back on Fyzabad; but though the troops of Murad Beg were flushed with success he was unable at this time to follow up his victory, and Badakhshan, for two years longer, retained her waning independence.

Quitting the plain of Karabolak we crossed a rough waste, four miles wide, and entered the narrow and pretty vale of Meshid, through which meandered the largest stream we had yet forded in Badakhshan.[1] This valley is reported to have been extremely populous in former times, and the Badakhshies assert that of hardware artificers alone it once contained 10,000 workmen. The kings of Badakhshan passed the winter season at Meshid, and the summer at Fyzabad; and there is a legend current here that in former days the valley was sadly infested by scorpions: to avoid them a certain king, named Suliman, had a residence built on the summit of the mountain which now bears his name. His meals were prepared in the valley, and transported to the Takht, or throne, by a line of men, placed side by side, who passed them on rapidly from one to another. His timid majesty, however, at length met his death from the insect he had been at such pains to avoid, and which, concealed amongst a bunch of grapes, found access to his person, in spite of all his precautions. These traditions are at least evidence of the populousness of these countries in olden times. The valley does not now contain a hundred families.

From the valley of Meshid we ascended a steep hill, called Agur-durah, on the further side of which runs the small stream of Nahwi. From this to our halting-place at Taishkhan, a distance of nine miles, the road led over a hilly country. In most places the ground was covered with snow: but the steep

---

[1] This is the Varsach river, on which stands the town of Kishm, as well as Meshid. The latter (place of martyrdom) takes its name from some early martyrs of Islam who are supposed to have fallen there, and are buried at Gumbaz on the banks of the Kokcha north of this (Pundit Manphûl).

sides of the valleys showed us that the whole of this wavy district was pastoral. Taishkhan is governed by Mirza Muksud, a relation of the deposed Badakhshan family. It is a secluded valley, little more than a musket-shot across, and is washed by a fine stream, along the margin of which are some large and aged mulberry trees.

No sooner had the day dawned than we saddled, and commenced the ascent of Junasdurah, a huge mountain-ridge that rises immediately beyond the Taishkhan valley. On gaining its summit we found, by the boiling-point of water, that we had reached an elevation of 6,600 feet. Steep, however, as this pass is, Murad Beg, with his accustomed dogged perseverance, dragged a heavy piece of ordnance over it; and in more than one place we came upon the traces of its wheels. From the crest of the ridge we had a view of some fine mountain groups, and I took the bearings of Khoja-Mohamed, Argu, Takht-i-Suliman, and Astanah, the most remarkable among their peaks. Descending the eastern side of Junasdurah our march was rendered less fatiguing by following hog-tracks in the snow. So numerous are these animals that they had trodden down the snow as if a large flock of sheep had been driven over it. At the foot of the pass lay Duraim,[1] a valley scarce a bow-shot across, but watered, as all the valleys in Badakhshan are, by a beautiful stream of the purest water, and bordered, wherever there is soil, by a soft velvet turf. To Duraim succeeded the plain of Argu; but, though once the happy home of 6,000 families, its surface was now desolate, and neither man nor beast was visible. Beyond this plain is the wavy district of Reishkhan, a name associated in the mind of a Badakhshi with all the misfortune of his country. About a century back, Khan Khojah, a Mohamedan ruler of Kashghar and Yarkand, eminent for his sanctity, having been driven from his dominions by the Chinese, took shelter in Badakhshan, bringing with him 40,000 followers. He was wealthy, which circumstance, added to the beauty of his harem, excited the

---

[1] Duraim, or Darah-i-aim, is one of the best districts of Badakhshan according to Pundit Manphúl. It constitutes one of the fifteen feudatory provinces which acknowledge the supremacy of the Mír of Badakhshan.

cupidity of Sultan Shah, who, at the time of the khoja's arrival ruled in Badakhshan. This coming to the knowledge of the ex-ruler of Kashghar he, with his people, fleddown the valley towards Kunduz; but were overtaken by Sultan Shah, at Reishkhan. The khoja's adherents were defeated, and he himself made prisoner. He sued for life, but in vain; on which the holy man cursed Badakhshan, and prayed that it might be three times depopulated—that not even a dog might be left in it alive. Already has the country been twice bereft of its inhabitants; first by Kohan Beg of Kunduz, about forty years back, and again by Murad Beg, in 1829.

Descending Reishkhan we entered the valley of the Kokcha, and, traversing an open plain, reached a small hamlet, named Chittah, where we halted for the night.

Since crossing the Pass of Latta-band we had travelled along the left or south bank of the Badakhshan river, over a succession of steep ridge-like hills and deep narrow glens, occasioned by numerous lateral shoots which the chain of mountains to the south throws out towards the Kokcha. In this ridge the most conspicuous peaks are Kishm and Takht-i-Suliman; but these, though lofty, were now lost in the superior chain which diagonally divides Badakhshan, and at the foot of which we had arrived. This range is pierced by the river Kokcha, and at the gorge of its valley, on the right bank of the stream, opposite to our encampment, were the ruins of Fyzabad, the former capital of Badakhshan.

Since quitting Talikhan we had been journeying through a depopulated country. The dreary appearance of winter was not enlivened by the sight of man or beast, for not a single wayfarer did we meet on the road, and, except the partridge, which was very plentiful, and the hog-tracks before mentioned, there were no indications of animal life. It was certainly no season for travelling; but scanty indeed must the inhabitants of that country be, in which a journey of eighty miles can be performed without meeting a human being, except in hamlets thirty miles apart.

Of Fyzabad, once so celebrated throughout the East, scarcely a vestige is left save the withered trees which once ornamented its gardens.[1] Its fort, the dilapidated walls of which are still standing, occupied a rock on the left bank of the river, commanding the entrance of the upper valley, which is here 400 yards wide. Behind the site of the town the mountains rise in successive ridges to a height of at least 2000 feet. Before it flows the Kokcha, in a rocky trench-like bed sufficiently deep to preclude all fear of inundation. Looking up the mountain-valley, the ruined and uncultivated gardens are seen to fringe the streams for a distance of two miles above the town; while in an opposite direction the Kokcha winds through a grassy plain, which, sweeping out from the base of Khoja Mohamed, is encircled by swelling hills alike fitted for agricultural or pastoral purposes. The town could not have been substantially built or its ruins would be more prominent. Although but a few years have elapsed since its walls were levelled, its site can only be recognised by the appearances I have described. Murad Beg must have had evil councillors when he destroyed Fyzabad, and forcibly removed its inhabitants to Kunduz, a place only fit to be the residence of aquatic birds. He has lost both in men and revenue by the measure. It was impossible to behold the desolation of so fair a scene, without commiserating the unfortunate exiles and execrating their tyrant, or without shuddering to think, that one man, as ill-advised as cruel, should have the power to work so much mischief and to make so many of his species miserable! But, alas, the history of every age presents us with a catalogue of similar atrocities, nor will they cease until education and pure religion are diffused over the entire world. From Fyzabad to Jerm, the modern capital of Badakhshan, towards which we now directed our steps, there are two roads; one along the banks of the river, the other somewhat more to the south by the Pass of Kasur, and the high-lying glen of Kash. The latter, though the most toilsome, is the shorter of the two, and as we were not encumbered by baggage, I resolved to take it. After getting a meridian observation of the sun, we set out up the valley

---

[1] It is pleasing to find from the narrative of the Mirza referred to hereafter that Fyzabad has, since the time of Captain Wood's visit, to a great extent regained its former importance

which, though it rapidly narrowed, continued to present traces of terrace cultivation. Five miles beyond Chittah we crossed the rivulet of Ishpingow, and shortly after passed Karacka, a hamlet embowered in fruit trees. Beyond it are the ruins of Mobaruk and Childokhturan, connected with which are legends too gross for notice. Here we left the Kokcha, and turning to the south, commenced the ascent of the mountain of Kussur. The road wound along its face, and being rough and slippery, from the combined effects of frost and snow, the summit was not gained without considerable labour. Midway we encountered a flock of 1,400 goats and sheep coming down the pass, and had to stand with our backs to the rock till they had filed by. Towards evening we gained Kasur, a small village situated at the entrance of the glen, at an elevation of 6,600 feet, and thirteen miles distant from Fyzabad. The latter place is 3,500 feet above the sea. When we left it the ground was free from snow, but in Kasur it was full a foot in depth.

Next morning, the 18th of December, we set out for Jerm, with the thermometer at 7° of Fahrenheit. The breeze was fresh and pierced us to the very bone. Several springs occur in this glen, all of which had a temperature of 53°. On arriving at the bottom of the Kasur mountain, we turned off to the left and held our way down the course of a brawling torrent which led us into the valley of the Kokcha, close to Jerm. On arriving at that town, our first applications for food and shelter were unsuccessful, but, after repeated disappointments, we at length prevailed upon an honest Tajik to receive us as his guests, and had soon wherewithal to appease our keen appetites, sharpened by cold and a twenty-four hours' fast. The town of Jerm, although the largest place in Badakhshan, is little more than an extensive cluster of scattered hamlets, containing at the very utmost 1500 people. The fort is substantially built, and is the most important of any we saw in Murad Beg's dominions. Both it and the town are situated on the left bank of the Kokcha river.

CHAPTER XVII.

Interview with the governor of Jerm.—Start for the Lapis-lazuli mines.—A crazy guide.—Partridge hunting.—An unwelcome reception.—The Kokcha river.—An iron mine.—Shrine of Shah Nasr.—Firgamu.—Preparations for visiting the mines.—A description of the mines.—A village sacked by Kaffirs.—Anecdote of Abdul Ghuní.—Re-enter Jerm.

I LOST no time in delivering to Mirza Suliman Khán, the governor of Jerm, my credentials from the Khunduz Mír, apprising him at the same time of my desire to trace the Amu or Oxus to its source, and also to visit the ruby mines and those of lapis-lazuli. He readily promised me every assistance, but said that it was now too late in the season to perform the first two journeys, and that a month ago a Kafila had been compelled to return to Badakhshan, after having reached Wakhan; but that the road to the mines of ladjword (lapis-lazuli) was still open, and if I decided on an excursion thither, he would be happy to furnish me with a guide. I consented, although with regret, to this arrangement, and as it was quite uncertain how long the road might remain open, I resolved to visit the mines forthwith, and accordingly we set forward the next day. The valley of the Kokcha, in the neighbourhood of Jerm, is about a mile wide; but not far above the town it contracts, and the mountains having suffered from earthquakes, the road is rugged and the land uncultivated. Passing on we had to climb an irregular mass of earth of great extent, that completely blocked up the road on the left bank of the stream, and which had evidently slipped down from the mountain above. On the summit of this slip stands the village of Firgamu, around which the uneven surface of the ground is laid out in fields. It would therefore appear that the catastrophe which brought this immense mass into the valley is not of very recent occurrence. Beyond this the bed of the Kokcha becomes so narrow, that a man without risk can leap across its stream, which runs about seventy feet below the surface of the valley, pent in by rocky walls. After passing the Khustuk rivulet, which joins the Kokcha by a cascade of twenty feet drop, we reached the village of Senna.

We had got but little way from Jerm, when it was discovered that our guide was ill-qualified for his task, and was, or affected to be, crazy. To every question he replied by a quotation from Hafiz, the purport of which was, that a man in love was the laugh and sport of his acquaintance. Had it not been for the venerable looks of the reciter, I should have been inclined to think that he himself had left his first love behind him in Jerm. He was escorted back, and in his stead Mirza Suliman sent us a much more competent guide. I may here remark that on our return to Jerm the governor's mirza, in the course of conversation, gravely asked me whether I had not conjured the spirit of the poetical guide into a jackass, for, added he, the man is now discovered to be a fool for the first time in his life, and it is known in the bázár that you left this place with only four donkeys and have brought back five. Murad Beg's letter had introduced me to his representative in Badakhshan as a Munujam, a term in Turkistan equivalent to astronomer or alchemist; so that the secretary, although from politeness he acquiesced in all that was said to expose the absurdity of this and similar stories, evidently had his doubts on the subject, and I dare say retains them to this day.

On the road we saw a party of sportsmen hunting partridges, which is here a very common diversion with both Uzbek and Tajik. The irregularities of the valley appeared to me to be unfavourable to the amusement, but this evidently gave to these fearless riders a keener appetite for the sport.

Abdul Ghuní had escorted the crazy guide back to Jerm, and in his absence our reception by the natives was less cordial than usual. After many refusals we at last took possession of an untenanted building standing apart from the rest, and consisting of a small room about ten feet square. The floor was damp and muddy, but a little dry straw remedied these evils, and heartily glad we were to get screened from the piercing cold without. We had not been long here when some of the villagers entered, and taking a corner to themselves, quietly said their prayers, and then departed without asking us any questions. It was clear that we had got possession of a mosque, the most appropriate shelter for strangers where there is no Mehman Khana. As soon as it became generally known that a Yesawal was of our party, the male part of the inhabitants deserted their homes, but were induced to return by the assurance that the officer they dreaded would only tax their hospitality in a very moderate degree. We were now conducted into the best house in the village, and had set before us *Ashbakola*, or pea-soup, thickened with wheaten flour, and flavoured with kroot, a kind of cheese, making altogether a most excellent dish in cold weather.

On starting in the morning it became necessary to retrace our steps for some distance, as we had to cross the Kokcha, and the best ford lay below Senna. Hitherto we had been following the left bank of the river, but the mountains now pressed so close upon the stream that further progress on horseback on that side became impracticable. The width of the river was here forty-three yards, with a depth of two feet and a half, and a medium velocity of four miles and a half per hour. The temperature of the air was 33°, that of the water 36°. The bed of the stream was about sixty feet below the surface of the valley, and the section of its banks thus exposed showed thick masses of conglomerate resting on thin horizontal strata of sandstone. In the early part of the forenoon the sky was cloudy, and the thermometer down at 23°; but as the day advanced the sun shone out, and by noon we were suffering from heat. Numerous parties from the head of the valley passed us on the road, carrying to Jerm their yearly tribute in kind.

Continuing our journey up the right bank of the Kokcha, we crossed various mountain-rivulets, and saw others which flowed into the river on the opposite side. The Ziarat of Shah Nasr was the first inhabited place we came to on this day's march, and here we spread our felts for the night.

A little below the Mazar the mountains are highly ferruginous, and, at one particular spot, a small hill, almost wholly composed of iron-ore, protrudes through the surface of the valley in the very path of the traveller. As the formation actually crosses the road, its existence must have been known for a very long period; and yet so tedious are the processes here resorted to for obtaining and smelting the ore, that the progress hitherto made has been slow in the extreme. The surface of the hill bears evidence indeed of having been battered in every direction with sledge-hammers, and at one place it is pierced by a shaft, six feet wide, to the depth of eight feet. It must not, however, be imagined that the inhabitants of these parts are ignorant of the value of the ore; on the contrary, the Badakhshies smelt iron more successfully than any people in the East,[1] and with the articles they make carry on a profitable trade with Eastern Turkistan and the tribes on their southern frontier; but they possess neither sufficient capital nor skill to work their mines advantageously, and the unsettled state of the government keeps back everything like mining enterprise. The deficiency of wood for fuel is another disadvantage.

Shah Nasr Khusrau, whose remains are here interred, came originally from Mecca, and died in the year of the Hidjrut 393.

We heard, for the first time, in this Astanah, that the earth is supported on the shoulders of four holy men, of whom it need not be added that the saint of Badakhshan, the before-mentioned Shah Nasr Khusrau, is one. His companions are—Sultan Yar Khoda Ahmed, of Afraziab; Sheikh Fureed Shukkur Gunge, of Hindustan; and Imaum Ali Mooza Raza, of Khoristan.

Shah Nasr is the patron saint of the Kohistan, and much revered by the inhabitants of the Upper Oxus. For the support of this Ziarat a tract of land was assigned at the time the buildings were erected; and in return for an indulgence which has been confirmed by the subsequent rulers of Badakhshan, the Mazar is bound to furnish the wayfaring man with food, water, and a night's lodging. Its inmates complained that wheat will not grow upon their land, though it does on that of

---

[1] The art of iron-casting possessed by the people of Badakhshan is also practised at Bokhara. It was probably received from China in the first instance.

their neighbours. The grain, they said, springs up and forms an ear, as in other fields, but no wheat is in it, and the straw alone will not repay them the labour of cutting it down. There must be something in the soil inimical to the growth of this grain; but the inhabitants of the Ziarat have found a better reason, alleging that the saint in compassion to human frailty has kept wheaten bread from them, that their passions might be easier kept under, and their tendency to sin be the less. The white dome of this Mazar is visible a considerable distance down the valley. Leaving a trifle at the shrine in return for the hospitality we had experienced, we went on to Firgamu, a village eight miles farther up the valley, and on the opposite or left bank of the Kokcha. We were now approaching the haunts of the Kaffirs, a nation of unbelievers occupying the most inaccessible portion of the Hindú Kosh. Fearful tales were related of their hatred of Mohamedans. Our last halting-place had often suffered from their vengeance. In one of their night attacks, which was yet but too well remembered by the inhabitants of the Mazar, the Kaffirs, surrounding a neighbouring flour-mill, cruelly butchered eight of its inmates.

Towards sunset it blew strong; a gloomy mist darkened the heavens and canopied the narrow valley: the wind, veering from point to point, swept in violent gusts, threatening some fine old walnut-trees under which we were lodged. This was the shortest day of the year, and, as we listened to the warring elements without, my thoughts reverted to Scotland and the social gaieties of her winter.

Firgamu stands at the head of the fertile portion of the Kokcha's valley, which, south of this, takes the name of Koran.[1] Beyond Firgamu the mountains rise immediately from the bed of the river; and there the scanty population live in glens opening on the Kokcha, but none in the main valley itself. Our hardy yabus, though accustomed to rough roads, were here useless; and exchanging them for those of the country, we left them at the village to await our return. As the greater portion

---

[1] This name has long been given to the upper valley of the Kokcha. It occurs in the book of the Chinese pilgrim Hwen Thsang, in the seventh century, as the name of one of the small states into which the Oxus regions were then divided. It is also mentioned by some of the old Arab geographers. It is still a recognized subdivision of the province of Jerm.

of the distance from Firgamu to the ladjword mines had to be performed on foot, we bartered our Uzbek boots for leather buskins *(kumaches)*, and, with a willow staff to assist us in climbing, set out upon our expedition.

A party of countrymen had been sent forward to mend the road, to lay temporary bridges over chasms in the path, and to find a new track where the old one had been defaced by the earthquake of 1832. The time allowed them was, however, too short for the performance of these several duties; yet, though they had not effected much as pioneers, they did us good service elsewhere. After a long and toilsome march we reached the foot of the ladjword mountains, but were too exhausted to visit the mines that night. One of the party, Hussein, an Afghan, had fallen on the road, and was too severely bruised to come on; but, with this exception, despite of the poet's warning, we arrived unhurt.[1] Where the deposit of lapis-lazuli occurs, the valley of the Kokcha is about 200 yards wide. On both sides the mountains are high and naked. The entrance to the mines is in the face of the mountain, on the right bank of the stream, and about 1,500 feet above its level. The formation is of black and white limestone, unstratified, though plentifully veined with lines, thus:—
The summit of the mountains is rugged, and their sides destitute of soil or vegetation. The path by which the mines are approached is steep and dangerous, the effect of neglect rather than of natural difficulties. The mountains have been tried for the lapis-lazuli at various places; but the following is a section of the principal and latest worked mine:—

The verse runs thus

"If you wish not to go to destruction,
Avoid the narrow valley of Koran."

The shaft by which you descend to the gallery is about ten feet square, and is not so perpendicular as to prevent your walking down. The gallery is eighty paces long, with a gentle descent; but it terminates abruptly in a hole twenty feet in diameter and as many deep. The width and height of the gallery, though irregular, may be estimated at about twelve feet; but at some places where the roof has fallen in its section is so contracted that the visitor is forced to advance upon his hands and knees. Accidents would appear to have been frequent, and one place in the mine is named after some unhappy sufferers who were crushed by the falling roof. No precaution has been taken to support by means of pillars the top of the mine, which, formed of detached rocks wedged together, requires only a little more lateral expansion to drop into the cavity. Any further operations can only be carried on at the most imminent risk to the miners. The temperature at the further end of the mine was 36° of Fahrenheit, while in the open air at its entrance it was 29°.

The method of extracting the lapis-lazuli is sufficiently simple. Under the spot to be quarried a fire is kindled, and its flame, fed by dry furze, is made to flicker over the surface. When the rock has become sufficiently soft, or, to use the workmen's expression, *nurim*, it is beaten with hammers, and flake after flake knocked off until the stone of which they are in search is discovered. Deep grooves are then picked out round the lapis-lazuli, into which crow-bars are inserted, and the stone and part of its matrix are detached.

The workmen enumerate three descriptions of ladjword. These are the Neeli, or indigo colour; the Asmani, or light blue; and the Suvsi, or green. Their relative value is in the order in which I have mentioned them. The richest colours are found in the darkest rock, and the nearer the river the greater is said to be the purity of the stone. The search for ladjword is only prosecuted during winter, probably because, labour in the mine being compulsory, the inhabitants are less injured by giving it in a season of comparative idleness than when the fields require their attention. Perhaps, also, during the cold of winter the rock may be more susceptible to the action of heat, and thus be more easily reduced, than when its temperature is higher. Within the last four years Murad Beg has ceased to work both the lapis-lazuli and ruby mines; and the reason assigned for his altered policy is the small success which has hitherto attended the operations.[1] The mines, the produce of which was exported to Bokhara and China, have been known from a very early period, and the ballast ruby of Badakhshan has furnished the poets of Persia with many a simile. I need scarcely add that the beautiful blue called ultramarine is obtained from the lapis-lazuli. After carefully inspecting the mines we set out in the evening on our return to Jerm, and put up that night at Robat, a deserted village seven miles down the valley. It stands at the mouth of a little stream on the right bank of the Kokcha, by the valley of which the Kaffirs usually make their inroads into Badakhshan. Some time back the inhabitants of the village were attacked by these fierce people, and, contrary to their usual custom, the slaughter was indiscriminate; all perished, women as well as men. Since then there have been no permanent settlers in the valley above Firgamu. As we moved among the lone hamlets it was some satisfaction to know that the passes between us and these barbarians were now blocked up with snow. Still they are as daring as cruel, and the bare possibility of a night attack from them did not tend to make our slumbers the more tranquil. There is a more than churchyard solitude about a region such as this, which has been rendered waste and desolate by the hand of the murderer and the robber, and every record scattered around of its former peaceful state comes with a crushing weight upon the heart.

The next morning ushered in Christmas-day; and at an early hour we continued our march down the valley. The journey,

---

[1] Pundit Manphúl, a Hindu gentleman who was some years ago representative of the Panjáb government in Badakhshan, mentions that the produce of these mines is now of a very inferior quality, and in quantity about thirty-six *poods* annually. The best quality sells at Bokhara at about thirty or sixty tillas (twelve or twenty-four pounds) the pood. Colonel Yule, in his "Marco Polo," truly remarks that it is ominous when a British agent, writing of Badakhshan products, finds it natural to express weights in Russian *poods*.

as before, was for the most part performed on foot. Abdul Ghuní, though a good horseman, was no pedestrian. He had never, he assured us, walked so far since he was a lad. Every two or three hundred yards he would sit down to rest, and give utterance to his grief in lamentations so prolonged and vehement as to be irresistibly ludicrous. It was Ramazan too; and hunger added to his other sufferings. It is true that, as a traveller, he might have eaten without infringing the Prophet's laws, but it was more meritorious to fast. Added to this, Abdul Ghuní, who prided himself upon being a good Mussulman, had up to this day kept the fast month most rigidly; and it was provoking, he said, to sin when only three days more remained to complete it. Eat, however, he did, and voraciously too; and quieted his conscience by vowing, as he concluded his repast, that he would expiate his offence by manumitting a slave on his return to Talikhan; a vow the performance of which I greatly doubt.

On the 26th we saddled at daybreak, and rode into Jerm, a distance of thirty miles. The latter part of the journey was performed in a heavy snow-fall: but whatever the danger in such weather from other causes, there is comparatively little risk of losing your road in a mountain valley, where the hills around you constantly point out the path.

Considerable fatigue and some danger had attended this journey; and had the only result been the examination of the lapis-lazuli mines, I should have thought the price paid for that gratification had been too dear: but I had also seen a country interesting in many respects, and very little known to Europeans; and on the whole, therefore, I returned well contented with the excursion.

CHAPTER XVIII.

Badakhshies surprised by winter.—Their dwellings.—Advantages and disadvantages.—Expenses of housekeeping.—Domestic utensils.—Light from reeds.—Dress of the Badakhshies.—Their character.—Winter's employment.—Starved partridges.—Ahmed Shah.—Chinese.—A Jew traveller.—Novel punishment for theft.—An Alchemist outwitted.—A partridge hunt on the banks of the Kokcha.—Earthquakes.—Kaffirs.—Dinner-party.—Marriage customs.—The independent Mirza.—The intrepid ironmonger.—A faithful dog.—Register of the weather.

From the 26th of December to the 30th of January we were detained in Jerm by the inclemency of the season. The snow took the good people of Badakhshan completely by surprise. Not expecting so hard nor so early a winter, they had made no adequate provision for their live stock; and no sooner did the snow cover the ground than there was a cry for fodder and fire-wood. We took up our abode with Hussein, our former host, who, though at first suspicious of his guests, became ere long our warm friend and almost constant companion. It is customary in these countries for relations to live in the same hamlet, often to the number of six or eight families. An outer wall surrounds this little knot of friends, within which each family has its separate dwelling-house, stable, and cattle-shed; and a number of such hamlets form a kishlak, or village. In Hussein's homestead were four houses, one of which had been vacant ever since its former inmates perished in the earthquake of 1832. This was now our abode. The style of building does not differ throughout the country, and our quarters at Jerm may be taken as a fair specimen of them all. The site is the slope of a hill, and a rivulet is usually not many paces from the door. Its course is here and there impeded by large, whitened boulders, glassy-smooth from the constant action of running water; while its banks are shaded by a few gnarled walnut-trees, and the lawn adjoining planted in regular lines with the mulberry. Down in the bottom of the valley, where the rivulet falls into the larger stream, lie the scanty corn-lands of the little community. The mountains rise immediately behind the village, and their distant summits retain their snowy covering throughout the greater portion of the year. An enclosure is formed by running a dry-stone wall round a space proportioned to the size and wealth of the family. The space thus enclosed is divided into compartments, the best of which form the dwelling-houses, whilst the others hold the stock. These latter compartments are usually sunk two feet under ground, while the floors of the rooms for the family are elevated a foot or more above it: flat roofs extend over the whole. In the dwelling-house the smoke escapes by a hole in the middle of the roof, to which is fitted a wooden frame, to stop up the aperture when snow is falling. The rafters are lathed above, and then covered with a thick coat of mud. If the room be large its roof is supported by four stout pillars, forming a square, in the middle of the apartment, within which the floor is considerably lower than in the other parts, and the benches thus formed are either strewed with straw or carpeted with felts, and form the seats and bed-places of the family. The walls of the house are of considerable thickness: they are smoothly plastered inside with mud, and have a similar though rougher coating without. Where the slope of the hill is considerable the enclosing wall is omitted, and the upper row of houses are then entered over the roofs of the lower. Niches are left in the sides of the wall, and in these are placed many of the household utensils. The custom of relations grouping together has its advantages, but they are not unmixed. Many of the sorrows of the poor are thus alleviated by the kindness of friends: the closeness of their intercourse adds to their mutual sympathy; and when death occurs, the consolation which the afflicted survivors receive from those near around them is great indeed. But to the newly-married couple the benefits derived from this arrangement are frequently very dearly purchased; and the temper of the poor bride, it is to be feared, is often permanently *damaged* by the trials she has to undergo at the hands of a cross-grained mother-in-law. Thus it often happens that the bitterest enemies are inmates of the same house. Were I to venture an opinion on so *very delicate* a subject, it would be in favour of a separate establishment for all newly-married people; but in these barren Alpine lands it is poverty which renders it necessary thus to congregate together. Small as is the population in many of the valleys or narrow mountain glens, it is yet too great for the limited extent of their corn-lands. In Badakhshan, as elsewhere, marriage is a new era in life; and when both parties have health and strength, they would do wisely not to stay and increase the number of mouths where food is already scarce, but remove at once to those districts depopulated by the tyranny of Murad Beg, where means of support can be more easily obtained. The woman would readily give her consent to such a procedure, but pride or indolence, or the love of home, would make the husband adverse to it.

The domestic arrangements of these people are as simple as with other mountaineers. Whilst we were at Jerm a neighbour of Hussein's was married. This gave us an opportunity of learning at what outlay the peasantry of this secluded region can commence housekeeping. I will state the articles separately. The first and largest item is—

	Tangas.	Rupees.
The purchase of a wife	0	25
Bedding	0	6
Antimony for the lady's eyes	3	
An iron boiler	0	2
A wooden bowl and spoons	3	
Flour-sieve	2	
Drinking bowl	1	
Table-cloth	2	
Dresser	2	
Knife for cutting beans	3	
Wooden ladle	1	
Frying pan	6	
A wooden pitcher	2	
Stone lamp	4	
Iron girdle for baking	2	
Culinary and other utensils	31 or	1½
Carried forward		34½

	Tangas.	Rupees.
Brought forward		34½
Lutta, or head covering	10	
Kurta, or shirt	40	
Pajamah, or trousers	20	
Kufsh, or shoes	20	
Wife's wardrobe	90 or	4½
Lallah, or turban	6	
Takuu	2	
Chukmun, or cloak	40	
Chamboor, or shoes	10	
Jurab, or stockings	6	
Kummer for the waist	40	
Pajamah	10	
Karid, or long sword	40	
Tufungh, or matchlock	200	
Matchlock furniture	22	
Husband's wardrobe and equipment	376 or	18¾

57¾, or 5*l*. 14*s*. sterling.

The vessels for holding water are made from the fir-tree, and those for containing flour from the red willow; the latter are circular and hooped. Earthenware is scarce, though in some families very pretty china bowls are to be met with. The bread is baked upon a stone girdle: the lamp is of the same material, and its shape is nearly that of a shoe. The bullet-mould is also of stone. Besides the lamp a very convenient light is obtained from a reed called "*luz*," about an inch in circumference. It is pasted round with bruised hempseed, and bunches, thus prepared, are to be found in every house, suspended generally from the rafters overhead. When it is wished to extinguish the burning reed, a circle of the bark is peeled off, and the flame, when it reaches that spot, expires of itself. Throughout Badakhshan I remarked a great disinclination to extinguish a light by blowing upon it with the breath.

The hill-men always go armed, but the inhabitants of the open valleys very rarely do so. Nevertheless there is not a house in Badakhshan without its quota of rusty old matchlocks. In dress the people differ little from the Uzbeks. They wear the same peaked skull-cap, and when a turban is superadded, its colour is generally white.

At the season of our visit every man wore thick coloured worsted stockings, and warm woollen cloaks, or chukmuns. On the cold days three of these cloaks were not an uncommon allowance. The shoes in use resembled half boots, made from goats' skin, and mostly of home manufacture. Instead of the heavy kammerband, or shawl, round the waist, the Badakhshi ties a handkerchief, and no native of the country ever thinks of setting out on a journey without a staff in his hand.

In former times Badakhshan was noted for the social qualities of its inhabitants, and we could still discern indications of this generous spirit, but few have now the means of being hospitable; and poverty under a task-master has produced a selfishness that exists not among Tajiks who are free. Among those communities which were styled Yaghi, or rebellious, we always experienced a more hearty welcome than from their kinsmen in the lower valleys, who, though richer, were galled and irritated by their Uzbek oppressors. Where independence is wanting, it is seldom that man retains his generous feelings.

The stranger who now enters a Badakhshi village is not welcomed as he formerly was; now every one strives to get rid of the intruder by turning him over to his next neighbour. According to old custom, there is a Mehman Khana in each village, and the head man or Aksikhail (Elder) is responsible for the comfort of the guest, who, if he be connected with the government, will not have to complain of any want of attention; but the poor man will only be provided with a lodging, and, for a meal, he must look to the really charitable.

This season in Badakhshan is one of inactivity. Most of the inhabitants are husbandmen, ignorant of those handicrafts which, among the peasantry in other countries, give occupation for the winter's day. While snow covers the ground, they busy themselves about their court-yards, digging and re-digging little channels to carry off the drainage; now and then throwing in a wisp of straw to their cattle, or shovelling the newly fallen snow from the flat roofs of their houses. Thus idling away their time, they cheat themselves into the belief that they are busy, though the only really active members of the homestead are their thrifty wives, who may be seen bruising *zoghur* (oil-seeds) for their lamps, attending to the cattle in the cow-houses, or superintending their culinary operations. Should there chance to be a loom on the premises, it gives animation to the entire scene, for besides the one who weaves at it, two or three others are at work preparing wool or cotton for the next web. The women are fair, tolerably good-looking, and do not veil themselves as is customary in most Mohamedan countries. Females of the wealthier families, however, do. They are modest, of pleasing manners, and are good housewives; though they speak of themselves as inferior in these respects to Uzbek ladies. Towards the end of our stay at Jerm, we were considered more in the light of old acquaintances than guests. Visitors of both sexes would occasionally drop in upon Hussein, and seldom failed to exchange friendly words with us. Seated in snug quarters, by a glowing charcoal fire, we heard the news, or, as they expressed it, the *gup* of the day. It is singular that throughout the whole of our sojourn in this region I was never suspected of being other than a Mussulman, though hundreds knew me to be a Firingí, a term which, by-the-bye, merely conveys to them the idea of superior intellect. It was the same with their chiefs; and even a holy man of Jerm, a native of Hindustan, who ought to have known better, contributed to the delusion. This saint, however, I was reluctantly compelled to undeceive on an occasion which I shall have to mention hereafter. Of course I did not contradict the current opinion to which I owed much of my easy intercourse with this unthinking and not very observant people.

On the last day of the year a partial thaw occurred, sufficient to clear the housetops of snow, and more closely to compress that which now everywhere covered the ground to the depth of a foot, or more. The starving partridges, attracted by the dark roofs of the houses, entered the village in coveys in search of food. They were so exhausted, that when once they alighted, they could not, until they had rested some time, rise again on the wing, and every time they attempted to do so, their flight grew shorter and shorter. The whole strength of Jerm was on the alert, man and beast, so that if the poor birds escaped the hands of men, the dogs were certain to have them. The slaughter was great, and for many days afterwards partridges smoked on the table-cloth of every Jerm family. We lived on these birds during the greater part of our stay here. This partridge is the common bird of Afghanistan; its back and wings are brown, the sides black-barred, the feet and bill red, and the pinions short.

On New-year's day, 1838, we visited Ahmed Shah, the Pír, or head Mullah of Jerm, who had emigrated from Hindustan when the British mission of 1809 was at Peshawúr. He had travelled much, and made a long abode in Eastern Turkistan, which country he entered by the road of Wakhan, and left by that of Kokan. The difficulties of the first of these routes he described as great, arising chiefly from the height of Pamir, the severity of its climate, and the almost total absence of inhabitants. Of that by Kokan he spoke more favourably. The Pír was a large, stout, cheerful old man, who looked much younger than he reported himself to be.

He told us that throughout his travels he had supported himself, as all his class do, by begging; and truly, to judge by the merry looks of the fraternity, the trade must be a prosperous one.

He was in Yarkand when the lamented Moorcroft's messenger arrived there to request permission for his master to visit that city; on which occasion, a mandarin of Ahmed Shah's acquaintance told him that the Chinese had determined not to admit Mr. Moorcroft, for, added the noblemen, we are persuaded were a Firingí to enter the country some dreadful evil would befall us.

Of the jealousy which characterises the Chinese, their fear, and distrust of foreigners; the wakeful vigilance with which their frontiers are guarded, and the efficacy of their restrictive measures, he had many anecdotes to tell; while, like every other native of these countries with whom I conversed on the subject, he praised their probity and good faith. Yarkand is not included within the limits of China Proper, but is nevertheless subject to the emperor, and a neutral ground, where neighbouring nations are privileged to meet the subjects of the celestial empire for purposes of traffic.[1] No one except its governor is permitted to enter China, and he visits the frontier town of Eela once a year. At the time Yarkand and Kashkar were wrested by the Chinese from the Mohamedan family who had previously held them, their inhabitants traded with Eela. The occasion of their subsequent exclusion, and the advance of the commercial entrepôt to Yarkand, was, according to my informant, as follows. A foreign merchant informed the magistrates of Eela that he had lost his *Koorgeen*, or saddle-bags. The man was required minutely to describe them, and to make oath to their contents. He swore to the value of one hundred silver yambos, and was then dismissed after being told to come back on a given day, when, if the saddle-bags were not recovered, the State would make good his loss. On the appointed day the merchant presented himself, when, to his great chagrin, the Koorgeen was produced. It had not been opened, and much to the crafty man's annoyance, this was now done by the authorities; when, instead of the sum he had sworn to, the articles it contained were found not to exceed a few yambos in value. A circumstantial detail of the whole affair was transmitted to Pekin, and the emperor decided it to be for the benefit of his exchequer, and the moral good of his subjects, that the admission into the country of barbarous and unprincipled foreigners should forthwith be prohibited. This may, or it may not have been the case; but from the story, we learn the high estimation in which the Chinese character is held among those most intimate with them.

All our visitors spoke in high terms of Yarkand, and appeared

---

[1] In 1863 the Chinese were expelled from Eastern Turkistan by a rising of Kuchari mercenaries in their employ. Aided by Moslems from all quarters the rebels soon gained the upper hand, and with the proselytism of some and the murder of many of her people, the power of China in these little known regions became a thing of the past. In 1865 the prowess of the present ruler of Eastern Turkistan, known as the Atalik Ghazee, compelled his immediate neighbours to recognise his sovereignty; and though his career has presented all the characteristics of intrigue and murder which are inseparable from the foundation of an Eastern dynasty, still, from the experience of his intrepid visitor, Mr. Shaw, he appears to be a ruler under whom trade is likely to flourish, and who, to a certain extent, encourages intercourse with foreigners.

delighted with its climate, and inhabitants. They expatiated on the peculiarities of the Chinese, and the contrast which they exhibit when compared with other nations. Many accounts of their customs and habits, which I received when at Jerm, were afterwards confirmed by a travelling Jew, who had tried, but failed, to accomplish a journey through their territories. This man was a Russian by birth, and had been for many years a traveller in the countries bordering the Caspian and the lake of Aral. Hearing that records of the missing tribes were to be obtained in Kashmir, or Tibet, he was journeying thither when my Munshi, Gholam Hussein, fell in with him at Balkh. This man's original plan was, to penetrate by the route of Kokan, Kashkar, and Yarkand; but, though skilled in the various languages of Central Asia, and conforming to the dress and habits of its people, the cunning of his nation was no match for the honest zeal with which the public functionaries of Kashkar executed the orders of their emperor. Suspicion attached to his character; and after proceeding as far as that town he was forced to retrace his steps. A large guard, he said, was stationed in a tower above the city gate, from which all caravans could be seen, while yet distant. Before they are permitted to enter the city, each individual is strictly examined; their personal appearance is noted down in writing, and if any are suspected an artist is at hand to take their likenesses. Interpreters for every current dialect are also present. To each of the persons subjected to this vexatious investigation the Chinese make a present of a few tangas.[1]

The Jew traveller mentioned a singular, and, I should infer, an efficient punishment for the crime of theft, inflicted in the Chinese cities through which he had passed. The criminal is not incarcerated, but made to walk the street with a clog attached to his feet, or a wooden collar suspended about his neck, of a size, and for a time, proportional to the offence.[2]

---

[1] A small copper coin.

[2] When garrisoned with the second Belooch regiment in China, in 1863, an amusing, though in a sense tragic, incident came under my notice, in connection with this peculiar and effective punishment. A coolie, caught red-handed stealing from the men, was sentenced to a month's wearing of the cangue, and exposure at the barrack gates under the eye of a sentry. Feeling his position intolerable, or

I remember to have seen the same kind of punishment successfully resorted to on board ship. The delinquent, a Portuguese, had been so repeatedly convicted of theft, and so repeatedly punished, that at length the cat-o'-nine-tails fell powerless on his back, but what bodily pain failed to accomplish a sense of shame did. A black board was strapped to his back and upon it was written, in large white letters, the word "*Ladrone*," or thief. This pressed like an incubus upon the man, and effected a complete cure.

On the 5th of January we were agreeably surprised in our Jerm retreat by a visit from an Afghan, whom we had known in Peshawúr. The reader should be told that in August, 1837, Captain Burnes employed a Hadji of Peshawúr to travel into Chitral for the purpose, amongst other things, of ascertaining the truth of certain information he had received as to the existence in that country of idols, and inscriptions to which the natives ascribed a very remote antiquity. Our visitor was the Hadji's travelling companion, and his story was a sad one. As far as Chitral, every thing appears to have gone well; but there they unfortunately associated themselves with a pírzada, or Mohamedan of a religious character, and to this friendship they attributed all their mishaps. On the road to Badakhshan sickness overtook the party, and on reaching Khyrabad, a village not far from Jerm, were hospitably entertained by the Pír of the place. Unfortunately the poor Hadji was of a temperament more ardent than scrupulous, and, in his anxiety to get well, told his credulous host that he possessed the secret of making gold, and that if the Pír would cure him, he, in return, would impart to him the invaluable process. The host did his best; appointed a female slave to watch over the invalid, and, in fine, by his skilful treatment, succeeded in closing seven of the eight ulcers that had broken out on the Hadji's legs. When

---

perhaps life itself to be so from cold and want, the poor wretch, watching his opportunity, made for the town moat, which at high water flowed within a few paces of the barrack gates, and thinking to end a miserable existence plunged in; but not to drown, for the wooden collar, acting as a buoy, supported the head above water, and down the stream floated the would-be suicide amid the jeers of the lookers on, until at last he was rescued after being sufficiently punished by a good ducking.

the cure was thus all but completed, the Pír pressed the patient to fulfil his contract. The Hadji's falsehood was now apparent, and at the recommendation of their *pious* and considerate fellow travellers, the Peshawúr pírzada, both the Hadji and our visitant were imprisoned by the disappointed saint. Daily was the unfortunate man branded with a red-hot iron, for the Pír still believed that the philosopher's stone was in his possession, and that a proper degree of heat would bring it out. At length the Hadji's health gave way under this rough treatment, and death seemed about to relieve him from further suffering. His host fearing that his own character might suffer under such a contingency, released the prisoner from irons and discontinued his system of torture. But both the Hadji and his companion were still under surveillance. Without loss of time we extricated the poor men and sent the Hadji down to Kunduz, where, by the skill and kind attention of Dr. Lord, he speedily recovered the use of his limbs, and was at length restored safe and sound to his employer.

About this time I accompanied Mirza Suliman on a hunting excursion along the banks of the Kokcha. Partridges were the game. The whole landscape was one sheet of dazzling whiteness. In the sun's rays the silvery pearls of the snowflakes shone like grains of mica in the sand, with a brilliancy that pained the eye. The sky, which for the last ten days had been obscured, was now clear through its whole extent, save where a few small misty clouds streaked the pure azure. The weather was cold, but we were warmly clad, and a brisk canter through heavy snow on such a day gives a new impulse to the spirits, a new value to existence. I came to the ground prepared to enjoy the sport; nor was I disappointed. Parties of foot and horsemen lined the banks of the river, each accompanied by a number of dogs. The men on foot and the dogs occupied the rough and broken ground bordering the Kokcha, while the horsemen stood aloof and ran down the birds which the beaters and dogs disturbed. The partridges seldom took to either the mountains or the plain, but crossed and recrossed the river, to the great annoyance of the sportsmen. We bagged nearly 500 birds.

The next day and the following we were startled by repeated

shocks of an earthquake. The sensation was that of a sudden wrench rather than a tremulous motion. The first shock took place at five minutes past four o'clock in the afternoon of the 7th, and was repeated with more violence towards midnight on the 8th. On both occasions the inhabitants left their houses, and, rendered cautious by the awful calamity which befell them in January, 1832, would not re-enter them until many hours had elapsed after the shocks were felt. That visitation had been indeed awful.

In the very hamlet where we lodged, of the twenty-five persons it contained, twelve perished. In each of the four houses there was death, and in one of them not a single individual escaped. So general was the havoc which the earthquake caused, that on the following day the governor, as a means of estimating the total loss of life, caused an exact census of three large hamlets to be taken, and the result was, that out of 310 souls, 156 were missing. In the neighbouring valley of Sir Gholam, out of a population of 155 persons, only 72 were saved; nor were the shocks of this earthquake confined to the valley of the Kokcha, the vibrations extended through every lateral defile. The very mountains were shaken, and numerous landslips and torn strata remain the evidences of a convulsion, which reached from Lahore to Badakhshan, though its point of greatest intensity was the upper valley of the Oxus. In Wardodj, a portion of the mountain fell into the valley, and dammed up its stream for eight days, at the expiration of which time it found an outlet over the embankment. The stream has now cut down a channel to its former bed. The whole of the Wardodj valley has suffered at different times by earthquakes. At one spot, a part of the mountain half a mile in length had slipped down, leaving a large gap in the chain of hills. Upon this landslip grows the dwarf fir-tree, which, though unknown to the valley, is found upon the mountains from which the mass had fallen.

Of all our Jerm acquaintances none was more welcome to our fireside than one of those singular people, the Siah-posh or black-vested Kaffirs. He was an uncommonly handsome man of about 25 years of age, with an open forehead, blue eyes, and bushy arched eyebrows, his hair and whiskers black, and his figure well set and active. He would sometimes bring us a present of a few partridges, and returning the Mohamedan salutation with which we greeted him, take his seat at the fire without further ceremony. Cross-legged he could not sit, for in this respect the Kaffirs differ from all eastern nations, and like Europeans prefer a chair or anything raised to a seat upon the ground. He gave us an animated account of his countrymen, and pressed us to visit them when the passes opened. As an inducement to do so, he promised us plenty of honey and oceans of wine. His sister was married to Mirza Suliman; but though thus connected with Mohamedans, he bore them the most deadly ill-will, and even in their presence would recount the numbers that had fallen by the bow or spear of his countrymen. "The Mussulmans," he said, "were responsible for the blood thus spilt, for since they hunted down the Kaffirs to make them slaves, the latter had retaliated; for the loss of liberty was worse than the loss of life." The governor of Badakhshan had done much to assuage the fierce passions on both sides, and since his appointment truces of various length have existed between his people and the Kaffirs, during which the latter have been supplied with salt, in exchange for their honey and wax. A good understanding existed between him and some of the strongest chiefs in the Kaffir country, which was further cemented by the marriage I have mentioned. But in such a government as that of Kunduz, upheld solely by rapine, the lenient system of the Badakhshan governor was not likely to meet encouragement from Murad Beg. Mirza Suliman was told that he must make a yearly descent upon the Kaffirs or resign his government. Like an honourable man, he chose the latter alternative, and was succeeded, before we left the country, by some one more likely to act up to the instructions of the Mír.

The Mussulmans unwittingly give high praise to this people when they acknowledge, as they readily will, that one Kaffir slave is worth two of any other nation. They add that they resemble Europeans in being possessed of great intelligence, and from all that I have seen or heard of them, I conceive that they offer a fairer field for missionary exertion than is to be found anywhere else on the continent of Asia. They pride themselves on being, to use their own words, brothers of the Firingí; and this opinion, of itself, may hereafter smooth the road for the zealous pioneers of the gospel. Unlike the Hindus and Mohamedans, they have no creed purporting to be a revelation; but, as far as I could discover, simply believe in the supremacy of a deity, and that men who have been good and hospitable on earth will be rewarded in heaven. At present there are many and perhaps insuperable difficulties to their conversion to Christianity; but let us hope that the military operations now carrying on to the west of the Indus may in due time be instrumental in guiding the yet unsophisticated mind of the Kaffir to a knowledge of the true God.

Whether their claim of brotherhood to Europeans be founded on tradition, or be a mere assumption of their own, I have not the means of ascertaining. For my own part, I believe them to be of the same race as the natives of Badakhshan, that is Tajiks, and that on the invasion of the Mohamedans they fled into the fastnesses of the mountains, whilst the rest of their countrymen, submitting to the invader, were converted, and so retained their lands in the plain.

On the 27th we dined with the principal merchant of the place. There were nearly a dozen guests present besides Abdal Ghaní, Gholam Hussein, and myself. The first course consisted of pillaw, mutton, and partridge; for the second, we had tea without sugar, but rich in fat, and, according to Uzbek custom, the leaves were handed round for dessert. Thanks were offered up both before and after the meal: the host himself remained standing, attending to the wants of his guests. From this man, who had often been in Yarkand, I obtained good information of the upper course of the Oxus, and he likewise mentioned the fact of coal being used for fuel in the Chinese city of Eela.

We were not the only feasting party in the village. It is customary in Badakhshan for a bride not to enter the house of her parents during the first year of her married life. On the anniversary of her wedding day she visits her mother with much formality, and receives a present proportioned to her parent's means: a cow is the gift usually bestowed. This ceremony over, a feast to her female friends is given under her husband's roof, at which none of the men are permitted to be present. One of these marriage feasts took place on this day.

Of all our visitors Mirza Sala was the most regular. He had always something to communicate: either how affairs were going on at Kunduz, or what the tribes in our neighbourhood were doing. He was, as his title implies, a secretary or writer; but, poor man, like the rest of his countrymen, he had had his vicissitudes. I liked his independence of character, and the frankness with which he expressed his sentiments. One day when speaking of the changes that had taken place in this country, he exclaimed with genuine energy, "Since Badakhshan has lost her independence, many of her chiefs have gone to Kunduz, and are there sharing with the Uzbeks the fruits of the land. I know this, but for myself, my coarse cloak and my homely pea-soup have more attractions than the brocade dress and rich pillaw of the Uzbek, if to possess the latter, I must desert my native country and bow at the feet of a conqueror. No; they would be no pleasures to me."

In looking back to the days spent in Jerm, I must not omit making honourable mention of a worthy ironmonger, our next door neighbour. He was the sole iron manufacturer in the country; and the community being in a great degree dependent on him for that indispensable branch of manufacture, Ismael was truly a man of no small importance. The Russian pots, he said, were not to be compared with those he made, which always brought a higher price in the market. Nevertheless, in spite of our honest friend's assertion, I must remark, that the foreign ones are here in very general use, and that amongst the wandering Kirghiz of Pamir they are universal—there is not a Kirgah without one. One of Ismael's trading speculations was remarkable, inasmuch as it showed the natives of this region to be possessed of considerable energy and perseverance. With forty iron pots he loaded five yabus, and made his way into Chitral. Here he readily disposed of them, and after investing part of the proceeds in honey, started for the Chinese frontier. In crossing the Cuner river a mule was carried down by the stream, and to add to Ismael's ill-luck it was the one which carried his surplus cash. The animal was recovered, but its load had disappeared. On reaching Pamir he lost a mule by the cold of that elevated region. Still, nothing daunted, he pressed on for Yarkand, where he safely arrived and sold his Chitral investment to such advantage that he cleared fourteen times the value of his original venture—the forty cast-iron pots. Fascinated by the pleasures of the place, he stayed there three years, and finally left Yarkand a poorer man than he entered it.

The ore he uses comes from the mines of Arganjika, in the neighbourhood of the village of Khyrabad. In smelting it he employs charcoal for fuel, and limestone as a flux.

Having enumerated those persons to whom we were most indebted for friendly attentions at Jerm, I feel bound to make mention of a canine friend whom I procured here, and who was called Jermy in honour of his birthplace. In our subsequent wanderings he proved, like all his species, serviceable and faithful, and woe betide the stranger who, regardless of his warning bark, ventured after nightfall within the circle of our pack-saddles. When the day of parting came I tendered a small present to our kind host for the trouble we had occasioned his family; but Hussein, fearful it might be in return for the dog he had given me, refused to accept it until assured it was not so; for in this respect Uzbek and Tajik are alike prejudiced, and dread, above every other opprobrious stigma, the epithet of dog-seller.

The following is a register of the weather during the month of our detention in Jerm:—

JANUARY, 1838.

THERMOMETER.

Day.	Date.	Sunrise.	Noon.	Sunset.
Monday	1	31° snowy	48° clear	° clear
Tuesday	2	23 clear	36 do.	29 do.
Wednesday	3	32 snowy	41 snowy	35 do.
Thursday	4	25 clear	46 clear	...
Friday	5	32 sleet	35 sleet	28 snow
Saturday	6	14 clear	26 clear	24 misty
Sunday	7	18 do.	...	...
Monday	8	23 snowy	29 snowy	19 clear

JANUARY, 1838.

THERMOMETER,—continued.

Day.	Date.	Sunrise.	Noon.	Sunset.
Tuesday	9	10 clear	26 clear	18 clear
Wednesday	10	18 ...	...	...
Thursday	11	...	...	...
Friday	12	...	...	...
Saturday	13	...	...	...
Sunday	14	...	...	...
Monday	15	...	...	...
Tuesday	16	18 clear	40 clear	29 clear
Wednesday	17	25 snowy	39 do.	20 do.
Thursday	18	18 ...	39 ...	...
Friday	19	16 ...	39 ...	...
Saturday	20	26 cloudy	39 ...	...
Sunday	21	...	...	...
Monday	22	26 ...	39 ...	...
Tuesday	23	...	...	...
Wednesday	24	24 cloudy	39 cloudy	31 cloudy
Thursday	25	20 clear	40 ...	31 do.
Friday	26	28 cloudy	41 ...	32 do.
Saturday	27	26 do.	42 clear	34 snowy
Sunday	28	26 clear	40 ...	32 ...
Monday	29	24 do.	41 cloudy	33 cloudy
Tuesday	30	...	42 do.	36 snowy
Mean		23	38	28½

Maximum 48
Minimum 10

CHAPTER XIX.

Inhabitants of Badakhshan.—Tajiks.—Kaffirs.—Mullahs.—Good-breeding of the lower classes.—Grave deportment of Mohamedan children.—Arrival of Messengers from Shagnan.—Obtain permission to visit the Ruby Mines.—Religious discussion.—Slave-dealing.—Reflections.—Start for the Ruby Mines.—Execution of Criminals.—Kokcha River.—Khyrabad.—Kosh Darow.—Keen air.—Yowl.—Thieving Donkeys.—A suspicious death.—Robat.—Zé-bak.—Preparations from milk.—Pass of Ish-kashm.—Plains of Ish-kashm.—A way-worn traveller.—Misfortunes of a tribute-levying party.—Fail to reach the Ruby Mines.—Some account of them.

I HAVE ventured an opinion that Badakhshan was originally peopled from Balkh, and I am led to this belief from its inhabitants being Tajiks and the language Persian: there is, however, neither record nor tradition in the country to support this conjecture. That its ruby mines brought Badakhshan into notice at an early period we may well believe; but of its condition prior to the Uzbek irruption, in the commencement of the sixteenth century, nothing authentic is known. That event planted a Mohamedan dynasty in Hindustan, during the palmy days of which the fate of Balkh and Badakhshan seems to have been one and the same; nor did the decline of that splendid empire sever this union, since on the rise of the Durani monarchy both of these dependencies lapsed to Kabul. This connexion is proved by a document still in the possession of a family in Munjan, a small village on the crest of a pass leading from Kabul into Badakhshan. This writing shows that the inhabitants of the country hold their lands on condition of giving shelter and food to the king's messengers.

If the remote and inaccessible character of Badakhshan paralysed the edicts of the Delhi emperors, and caused its dependency to be more nominal than real, we may readily infer that under the disjointed rule of the Duranis its subjection has been still more nominal. Accordingly we find that when the country was lately attacked by the Kunduz chief the circumstance passed unheeded in Kabul; and Badakhshan, till overrun by Murad Beg, has never known the real miseries of a conquered country.

None of the three great Tartar invaders, Jangez Khán, Tamerlane, or Shebani Khán, seem to have penetrated so high up the valley of the Oxus, though some of the followers of Baber, when expelled from the rich plains of Soghdiana by the Uzbeks, sought shelter here; and their descendants, not having intermarried with the Badakhshies, are still to be recognised both by name and physiognomy. My principal reason, however, for assigning a Persian descent to the inhabitants of Badakhshan is their creed. Prior to the Uzbek invasion their religion, like that of Balkh, seems to have been Shiahism. There is no absolute proof of this, but it appears a fair inference when the following facts are considered. The last Tartar invaders were Suni Mohamedans, all of whom conceive themselves bound to wage interminable war with the other sect, for the purpose of converting them to the orthodox belief; and of this privilege it is well known they have never ceased to avail themselves. What has been the result?—Shiahism, extirpated in the open country, has sought and found refuge in the most inaccessible depths of the neighbouring mountains, in cold and hungry glens, that can only be entered during the summer months. Accordingly we find that in the open valley of the Kokcha the inhabitants are Sunis, though every Tajik hill-state around it is of the opposite creed. Nor can the people of the valleys have been long of their present belief, since Murad Beg, in his *chapows* or forays has more than once accused certain districts of an inclination to lapse into heretical opinions, and as a preventive, marched off all the inhabitants to the slave-market of Bokhara.

The Tajiks are a numerous people, diffused over an extensive range of country both north and south of Hindú Kosh. They are a handsome race of the Caucasian stock; wherever found they in general speak the Persian language; and though some may now be met with beyond the limits of that once extensive empire, it is only under circumstances which tend to show that their destinies have ever been more blended with that monarchy than with any other. Yet the Tajik himself points to Arabia and to the country around Bagdad as the primeval seats of his ancestors; and as this belief is general it at least merits attention. Their name, they say, is derived from *Tadj*, an ornament for the head, and was bestowed on their forefathers, who stand accused of stealing this symbol of royalty from Mohamed's head; but they are too numerous to be the descendants of the Arab warriors who during the first century of the Hijra overran so large a portion of Asia. The actual descendants of these first disseminators of Mohamedanism are still numerous in these countries, but they bear no proportion to the Tajik part of the population.

The word Tajik has been said to mean the descendant of an Arab born in a foreign country; but surely if this definition of the word were correct we should find Tajiks in Africa as well as in Asia. To many countries in the former continent the Arab bequeathed his language with his creed; and if the word Tajik had this original signification, it is not easy to conceive how it should have been bestowed on their descendants in one country and withheld from them in another.

I take the inhabitants of Kafferistan and the other mountain regions whose solitudes have scarcely yet been invaded, to be of the same race as the Tajik, and the latter to be the indigenous inhabitants of the open country wherever they are now found. The mountain districts to which I here allude have peculiar dialects of their own; but there is a strong resemblance between their inhabitants and the Tajik of the open country, and those points in which they do differ are the result of physical causes, evidently not of blood. These societies are Kafferistan, Chitral, Wakhan, Shagnan, and Roshan, and the most probable way of accounting for their peculiar dialects is by supposing them forced into their present fastnesses at a very early era, antecedent to, or at least coeval with, the first spread of Islamism. Of these several states the Kaffirs alone have successfully held out against the progress of that religion. Possessing a country strongly fortified by nature, they continue to wage an interminable war with every true believer, and have repaid on the faithful with a tenfold vengeance the injuries their forefathers suffered when idol temples were razed to make room for the mosque.

The Tajiks make good companions, particularly the Mullahs, who have far more liberality of sentiment than their untravelled disciples. They were always pleased to be visited by us, and used to say we were no Uzbeks, but like themselves in features and complexion. Though their own temperament is grave, they delight in a lively associate. Keep talking to them, and no European, with such an audience, can ever want subjects of conversation—and you are sure of their good-will: look solemn and you make enemies. Nothing is more common at the close of a spirited conversation than for them to exclaim, "He is a good companion; he speaks well." On our quitting a party the Mullah would sometimes run a dozen yards after us, bellowing out, "We are friends, are we not? What need I say more?"

Nowhere is the difference between European and Mohamedan society more strongly marked than in the lower walks of life. The broad line that separates the rich and poor in civilised society is as yet but faintly drawn in central Asia. Here unreserved intercourse with their superiors has polished the manners of the lower classes; and instead of this familiarity breeding contempt, it begets self-respect in the dependant. A kasid, or messenger, for example, will come into a public department, deliver his letters in full durbar, and demean himself throughout the interview with so much composure and self-possession, that an European can hardly believe that his grade in society is so low. After he has delivered his letters he takes a seat among the crowd, and answers calmly and without hesitation, all the questions which may be addressed to him, or communicates the verbal instructions with which he has been entrusted by his employer, and which are often of more importance than the letters themselves. Indeed all the inferior classes possess an innate self-respect, and a natural gravity of deportment, which differs as far from the suppleness of a Hindustani as from the awkward rusticity of an English clown. Of this public manner of transacting business north of Hindú Kosh, I have seen repeated instances. When Murad Beg receives a letter he deliberately unfolds it, calling out all the while for a mirza, or mullah, to decipher its contents. This official, after scanning it over to himself, reads it aloud in a high sonorous voice; then slowly folding it up, hands it back to the Mír, who tucks it under the folds of his turban.

Even children in Mohamedan countries have an unusual degree of gravity in their deportment. The boy who can but lisp his "*Peace be with you*," has imbibed this portion of the national character. In passing through a village these little men will place their hands upon their breast, and give the usual greeting. Frequently have I seen the children of chiefs approach their father's durbar, and stopping short at the threshold of the door, utter the shout of "Salam Ali-kum," so as to draw all eyes upon them; but nothing daunted, they marched boldly into the room, and sliding down upon their knees, folded their arms and took their seat upon the musnud, with all the gravity of grown-up persons. This precocity of manner is owing to their early introduction into the society of men; and though it does away with much that characterises youth with us, I doubt whether the system be not better than our own. On the 30th of January some natives of Shagnan arrived with letters from the chief to Mirza Suliman. From these men we learned that they had travelled upon the Oxus, which was frozen from Darwaz upwards. This was glorious news to us, who had been lingering in Jerm, hoping rather than expecting that such an occurrence would enable us to visit the ruby mines, which are situated in the valley of that river, and close to Shagnan. It was the only chance I had of reaching these mines; for when there has been a deep fall of snow, the only communication between Badakhshan and Shagnan is by the Oxus, and it is not every year that the route on the ice is practicable.

We lost no time in putting our plans into execution, and that day I waited on the governor, and got his permission to set out. Having embraced our numerous acquaintances, it only remained to take leave of the Pír, whose benediction, it was believed, would facilitate our enterprise.

Ahmed Shah had summoned together some of the persons of most consequence in Jerm to bid us a last farewell. On crossing the threshold of his door it unfortunately happened that Gholam Hussein's rosary was in my hand. This the quick-sighted man immediately perceived, and notified to the assemblage as an unerring proof of my orthodox belief, and that in fact I really was, what he had always suspected me to be—a good Mussulman. Now, though well inclined to favour such an opinion among the commonalty, I could no longer, when so directly alluded to, continue the deception. I at once told them that I was a Christian; nor could I avoid briefly stating to them what was the groundwork of that faith. This brought on what I had uniformly wished to avoid—a religious discussion, in the course of which I was told by Hazrat Ishan, the holy man, that the ascension of our Saviour took place 392 years antecedent to the commencement of our era, and that we ought to call our current year not 1838 but 2230. One of the company said that he had seen the Angeel, or New Testament, in the But Khana, or idol-temples of the Russians, for so he called the Greek churches from the number of pictures they contain; and that the volume was so large that it would take a yabu to carry it. "Now," added he, "as all that is needful for man to know is contained in the Koran, from which, as everybody knows, both the Old and New Testaments were compiled, how much there must be in the Christian Bible that is useless." This observation of the merchant had great weight with the audience. In short, I was getting worsted in the argument, when it struck me to produce the book which our friend the traveller had seen in what he considered such bad company in Russia. With the Pír's permission it was sent for. It was the small Oxford edition, containing both the Old and New Testaments, elegantly bound, the present of a valued friend. The effect it produced was singular. All present kissed the sacred volume, admired the rich gilding of its leaves, and were surprised, I might even say awed, by the clearness and beauty of its type. The merchant was silent, but as several of the persons who were present had evidently warmed towards me, I took an opportunity of turning the conversation to another subject, and one in which Ahmed Shah was deeply interested—that of *slave-dealing*. I exerted myself to point out, in the most impressive terms I could use, the deep guilt of this degrading traffic, and how contrary it was to every principle of humanity and justice. I was listened to with attention: but I greatly fear that whatever impression I made was only transitory. Ahmed Shah, to whom all the others looked up as their example and guide, was the largest dealer in slaves of any one in the town. He had now thirty on hand, and has received from Chitral as many as a hundred in a single investment. It was not to be hoped that a few words from a stranger, and an unbeliever, would turn him from his established course of trade.

It is difficult to imagine any train of reasoning which can reconcile the conscience of a rational being to the atrocities of the slave-trade. The ready excuse among Mohamedans, that the captives are converted to Islamism, though it may have its weight with the crowd, is too shallow to deceive men whose minds are comparatively enlightened. They well know that the conversion is never real; that the poor wretches who assume Mohamedanism do so only to render their bondage less severe. For my own part I can perceive one and only one mode, by which the traffic in human beings may be done away with. It is in the general diffusion of knowledge. The time will come, though it may be still far distant, when the printing press shall perform as great wonders through the whole of Asia as it has done, and is still doing, in Europe. Then, and not till then, will man know what is his duty towards his fellow men. That slavery can continue to exist in any nation where instruction, moral and religious, is generally diffused, I hold to be impossible. Let all those who are anxious for the abolition of slavery, and the conversion of the heathen nations, exert themselves to diffuse education among them. Assuredly this is the broad foundation on which missionary exertions should be based. It is true that education alone will not make Christians; but we are firmly convinced that, under Providence, it is the best means to accomplish that end. But education, as we find to be the case in our own country, must commence at a very early age to be really beneficial.[1]

[1] In the report of the great trigonometrical survey of India for 1869 and 1870, it is stated that between Kabul and the Oxus slavery is as rife as ever,

On the last day of the month we set out on our journey, and crossed over to the right bank of the Kokcha, by a good wooden bridge in the vicinity of the fortress. From the centre of this bridge condemned criminals, bound hand and foot, are thrown into the dark pool beneath. No executions took place whilst we were resident in Jerm, but not many days prior to our arrival an unfortunate man perished in this barbarous manner. He had been heard to utter sentiments injurious to Murad Beg; and those in power, more anxious to show their zeal than to fill their office honestly and humanely, took advantage of a few unguarded words, and deprived the poor man of his life.

Continuing down the valley, which gradually widened as we advanced, and along the right bank of the Kokcha, we reached, after a ride of nine miles, the river of Wardodj. From this spot the Kokcha turns sharp round to the westward, after receiving tribute from the Sir Gholam and Wardodj valleys, both of which open to the eastward. Beyond this, and under a range of lofty mountains to the north, lay the little village of Khyrabad, the scene of the alchemist Hadji's sufferings. In the same range are the iron mines of Arganjika, the source of wealth to our Jerm acquaintance, the ironmonger. Here the Kokcha's valley is not more than three miles wide, nor does it exceed that width at any point south of Fyzabad.

After halting a short time, and viewing the wintry aspect of the snow-covered mountains around us, we turned our horses' heads in the direction of the Wardodj valley, and commenced our journey up the left bank of its stream. This valley soon narrowed, so that no belt of level land margined the river; but where patches did occur, they were cultivated. Shortly after entering Wardodj we passed the ruins of a Kaffir fortress. Evidences of earthquakes were frequent, especially of the one of 1832. On the following day a market was to be held in

---

extending through Hazara, Badakhshan, Wakhan, Sirikul, &c. A strong man likely to stand work well, is, in upper Badakhshan, considered of the same value as one of the large dogs of the country, or of a horse, about 80 rupees. The value of a slave girl is considerably more, according to her looks; men, however, are almost always exchanged for dogs. In lower Badakhshan and more distant places, payment is made in coin.

Jerm, and numerous parties passed us, bound for that place. There being but one market town in Badakhshan the peasantry come from a considerable distance to attend it, and are thus obliged to start a day or two before that on which it is held. Many of these people wore coverings of horse-hair before their eyes, to shield them from the ill effects of the snow. Some had them of network, and made after the fashion of our spectacles. About four o'clock in the afternoon we dismounted at Kosh Darow, a poor village, five miles and a half from the entrance of the valley. On starting from Jerm it was necessary to hire a man to lead my new acquisition, *Jermy;* for though we were great friends whilst under his old master's roof, neither coaxing nor threats would induce the dog to follow us one step beyond the threshold. We applied to several of the poorer inhabitants, but without success; and the man who at length volunteered his services was much better off than many of those who refused the employment. I have frequently observed that the poor of these countries are little inclined to make themselves useful, or to do an obliging act; nay, that men, in the last stage of destitution, prefer to sit idle rather than perform a trifling service that would bring them a reward.

On the 1st day of February we breakfasted much at our leisure, and the day was well advanced before we commenced our journey, for we found that in this cold bleak valley, whose sides rose from 2,000 to 2,500 feet above us, and which was only looked into by the sun at mid-day, the keen air of the morning was too much for our Indian servant, the only one remaining with us, for his companion, Mohamed Kassim, had been nipped by the cold, in our trip to the Ladjword mines, and, on our return to Jerm, had been sent back to Kunduz.

We passed in the course of the day, three scantily-peopled villages, and put up at a fourth, named Yowl. The character of the valley remained unchanged, except that here we remarked indications of cultivation on ledges of level ground, several hundred feet up the face of the mountains. The wind that blows down this deep defile is called "Bad-i-Wakhan," or wind of Wakhan, noted throughout all Badakhshan for its severity. It is indeed piercing. It continues during six months of the year, from the end of autumn to the middle of spring, freshening as the weather clears, but lulling when the clouds gather. When it dies away you are told, "the wind has gone to sleep." These people, like the Uzbeks, deal largely in figurative expressions. With the Uzbek, everything is computed by the galloping of his horse; and here, if you inquire the distance between two neighbouring places, you will be answered, "While soup is preparing you may go the distance," drinking soup being as every-day an affair with the one people as riding is with the other. Yowl is but 6,600 feet above the sea, yet beans will not grow here, and its few mulberry-trees look sickly. The walnut, however, flourishes, and the few varieties of stone-fruit, which are cultivated, succeed well. Wheat is the common grain.

Here, as elsewhere, the donkey is used for every purpose of drudgery. Almost every one of them you meet upon the road is maimed: one has his tail docked; another wants his ears, or has both of them slit; while a third combines in his mutilated person not only these blemishes, but has lost an eye, and is perhaps lame of a leg. All such animals are "*bad characters*," and these punishments have been inflicted for crimes committed. When a young animal first visits a neighbour's field, a good drubbing intimates to him its owner's displeasure. Should the ass again trespass, a slit ear quickens his exit. As he grows older he becomes more wary; but few attain to old age without carrying about them signs of their youthful indiscretions. If the ill deeds of their owners had been recorded by a similar process, the mutilation would probably have been much more extensive.

Next morning, when in the act of mounting our horses, the wail of a female drew our attention to the house adjoining that in which we had slept. I walked over its roof, and, looking down through the square hole in the centre, perceived that the room was filled with women weeping for the dead. Gholam Hussein made his way into the house, and, to our grief and surprise, there lay the corpse of a fellow-traveller Mohamed Amín, a young man who had accompanied us from Jerm. The nails were much discoloured, and I at once suspected foul play.

The poor fellow was the native of a hamlet among the mountains, at a short distance from Yowl, and had long been attached to a girl who lived at the latter place. Her parents were averse to the marriage; and Mohamed, thinking that his poverty was the ground of their objection, left the mountains for the plain, and was now returning, after a four years' absence, with his hoarded gains. He had served during this time with Ataluk Beg, of Talikhan. Prior to our reaching Yowl, he told us his story, and solicited Abdal Ghaní Yesawal to procure him an interview with his betrothed. The poor fellow wished to stay the night at her village, but could not venture to do so, unless publicly invited by the Mír's Yesawal. Abdal Ghaní promised to befriend him. On reaching Yowl, Mohamed came up to our party, and, in the presence of the villagers, requested the Yesawal's permission to go on, adding that his own home was close at hand; and after so long an absence he could not think of sleeping anywhere else. Abdal Ghaní, in an authoritative tone, overruled his objection, invited him to sup with our party, and added that to-morrow he might go to his home. Mohamed, with feigned reluctance, consented. The melancholy sequel has been told. The grief of the poor girl was excessive, and her parents attributed his death to poison, and roundly denounced Mirza Suliman as the guilty person. They asserted that he was known to have long borne ill-will towards the deceased. That the guilt rested with Mirza Suliman seemed improbable, as eight and forty hours had elapsed since the young man had left Jerm. It was, however, clearly ascertained that he had drunk of the governor's tea before quitting his presence. Others traced his death to the curdled milk of which we had all liberally partaken the previous morning. Everything tended to strengthen my conviction that the poor fellow had been intentionally poisoned; but regard for our own safety restrained me from expressing that opinion.

We had not proceeded far when an aged female was seen coming down the valley. She proved to be a near relation of the deceased. Having heard of her kinsman's arrival at Yowl, she was now hastening to greet him. The poor woman's grief excited the sympathy of every one.

During the march a lead-coloured mist streaked the mountains, about a thousand feet above their base. Eagles were seen sailing over our heads; but when highest they were still below the summits of the mountains, which, in this part of the valley, reach a height of nearly 4,000 feet. The wind blew so strong, that we were forced at some places to dismount. No snow lies long on the ground. All that falls is soon whirled into the stream. Great havoc has been made by earthquakes. The appearance of one landslip in particular was singular. Though it continued to bear the dwarf trees of its native mountain, yet its surface was dotted over with small cone-like swellings, which would seem to have been caused by convulsions subsequent to that which brought it down. A ride of six and twenty miles brought us to Robat, a hamlet of seven families, where we halted for the night. Its elevation is 8,100 feet above the sea, and the valley had here assumed a very bleak appearance. The red willow and white poplar appear to be the only trees which can stand against the blast of the *Bad-i-Wakhan;* and even in sheltered situations there were but few fruit-bearing trees.

The frontier of Badakhshan seemed to recede as we advanced. Since the day of leaving Kunduz, the invariable reply to Abdal Ghaní's grumblings about the quality of his food has been " What do you expect to get when you reach the frontier ? " In these poor districts Jerm is the capital; and in Jerm it is Kunduz.

The next stage was to Zé-bak, and a cold march we had to get there. The wind fortunately had changed, or we could not have accomplished this stage. As it was, the thermometer had sunk to the 6th degree above zero ; and the effect of a violent wind at this temperature in regions so elevated, has only to be felt once, to be ever afterwards dreaded. At the fifth mile from Robat, the mountains on both sides fall back, and leave a level plain, varying in width from one to two miles. Three miles farther on, is a hamlet called Gow-khanah, situated in the middle of the plain, and fronting two openings in the eastern range of mountains, one of which leads to Chitral, and the other in Kafferistan.[1] The former is only two days' journey from this

[1] There are two roads towards Chitral from Gow-khanah and Zé-bak; one leading through the district of Sanglich and crossing the chain of

hamlet. At Gow-khanah we tarried for some hours to warm ourselves, and made a luxurious meal on newly baked bannocks, warm butter, and kurut. This latter dish I have already commended. Its flavour somewhat resembles cheese, and it is thus prepared: when the milk is taken from the cow it is curdled; and in this state is termed *Joghrat*. This is churned, and the buttermilk, which is called *Doagh*, after being well boiled is poured into a bag of not very close texture. The whey drains off, and the clotted residue is the kurut. If it be of peculiarly good quality, no butter is extracted from the milk. Kurut is a most indispensable article in the food of these poor people. It enters into all their culinary preparations. Their soup, whether of beans or wheaten flour, is flavoured with it; and we owed to it the relish of many a meal, which would otherwise have been very poor. An alderman himself, provided he had been as cold, fatigued, and hungry as we were, must have honoured it with his approbation.

Resuming our march, we crossed the plain to the mountains on the right hand, and rode through a tangled forest of red willow-trees at their base, till we came opposite Zé-bak. At one point in this range, there is evidence of extensive volcanic action. Large deposits of sulphur are also in the neighbourhood, but they were then buried deep in snow. It was late in the evening when we reached Zé-bak, which is distant fourteen miles from Robat, and is next to Jerm, the largest place in Badakhshan. It contains about fifty houses. Its site is under the western range of mountains, and is slightly elevated. The houses here, instead of standing apart in hamlets, as is customary, adjoin each other, giving to Zé-bak almost the appearance of an English village.

It continued to snow throughout the night, and when we resumed our journey the next morning, the 4th of February, it was still falling heavily. The plain, which was overgrown with

---

Hindú Kosh by the pass called *Dorah*, nearly south of Zé-bak; the other runs to the south-east, and affords three distinct passes over the mountains. The route by one of these, the Nuksan Pass, has been recently traversed and surveyed by one of Major Montgomerie's emissaries. The road into Kaffiristan also leads by Sanglich, and thence by a pass called the *Dozakh Dara*, or valley of hell.—(Faiz Baksh.)

willow, was in many places marshy; and it was no easy matter to prick our way onwards through the thickly grown trees, burdened as they were with snow, nor did we reach the head of the valley, a distance of ten miles, without sundry mishaps. We then crossed the southern range of mountains on our right hand, and debouched on the plain of Ish-kashm. The pass is 10,900 feet above the sea; and its crest divides the valleys of the Oxus and Kokcha. Here the eastern fork of the latter river has its rise, while on the Ish-kashm slope, the drainage falls at once into the Oxus; which can be seen from the crest of the pass, but was hidden from our eyes by the snowy mantle which covered the landscape. The Ish-kashm plain has a width of about five miles. Behind it rise, though not abruptly, the towering mountains of Chitral, while in front flows the Oxus, along the southern face of a range of hills, less high but more mural in their aspect.

Not far from Zé-bak we encountered a way-worn traveller, with the skin of a horse wrapped round his body, forcing his way through the willow bushes. He was one of a party of Badakhshies, servants of Mirza Suliman, who had taken advantage of the Oxus being frozen, to visit Darwaz, whither they had been directed to carry presents from their master. On their return the river had burst its icy fetters, and could no longer be trusted. The steep mountain banks offered no safer road, and the party went back to Darwaz, where they would be obliged to remain till the summer sun opens the passes into Badakhshan. The individual whom we met, was, however, determined to persevere; and he succeeded, though at the expense of his horse, which he had been obliged to sacrifice to save himself.

Hardly had this singularly clad traveller passed us, when we fell in with a number of Ish-kashm horsemen, the chief of whom, when informed of our destination, reined in his horse, and told us that he and his companions were just returned from the ruby mines. He had been sent by Murad Beg to collect the annual tribute at Gharan, a place consisting of a fort and a few hamlets in the vicinity of the mines. On coming upon the Oxus at Ish-kashm, they found the river no longer frozen and the road down its banks being impracticable to horsemen they dismounted at that village, and performed the remainder of the journey on foot. The tribute was received in kind as usual, and they set out on their return. More snow had, however, fallen in the interim, the road was obliterated, and what was still worse, avalanches repeatedly rushed down from the mountains into the river below. The party was separated into three divisions. One went forward to track out the road; a second carried the tribute and took care of the live-stock, while he himself with the third brought up the rear. Four days before we met him, and whilst at the distance of six miles from Ish-kashm, as they were proceeding in this order he saw, on casually looking upwards, what appeared to him a sheet of mist rolling down the mountain-side. He was not long left in uncertainty as to its real nature: down came the avalanche with the roar of thunder, carrying with it into the Oxus, the whole of the centre division. Nothing more was seen of them or their charge; every man, every animal, was in an instant overwhelmed and destroyed. The other land parties reached Ish-kashm in safety, but several of the men had been severely frost-bitten. One poor fellow who rode beside the chief, had lost an arm.

At Ish-kashm we crossed the Oxus, here thirty-five yards wide, upon the ice, or rather upon bridges of frozen snow; and upon these we attempted to continue our route down the river, but we had not proceeded far before the slender covering we trod upon, gave us warning of its instability. The river when lowest had been firmly ice-bound; but being already on the increase, it had burst its winter fetters, and though it might still be crossed, it was upon irregular masses of snow and ice heaped together, and not upon solid ice. The mountains in which the mines are situated were in sight, but however much I regretted turning back when the object of my journey was so nearly attained, there was no alternative. To proceed by the river was impossible; and had I been inclined to attempt the road along its banks, which I certainly did not think myself justified in doing, the melancholy fate of the Mír's party had so dispirited the men of Ish-kashm, that no offers of remuneration, however large, would have induced them to volunteer their services as guides.

The ruby mines are within twenty miles of Ish-kashm, in a district called Gharan, which word signifies caves or mines, and on the right bank of the river Oxus. They face the stream, and their entrance is said to be 1,200 feet above its level. The formation of the mountain is either red sandstone or limestone largely impregnated with magnesia. The mines are easily worked, the operation being more like digging a hole in sand, than quarrying rocks. Above Ish-kashm the water of the Oxus is beautifully transparent, but after issuing from the mountains below Darwaz, it is of a dirty red colour. The galleries are described as being numerous, and running directly in from the river. The labourers are greatly incommoded by water filtering into the mine from above, and by the smoke from their lamps, for which there is no exit. Wherever a seam or whitish blotch is discovered, the miners set to work; and when a ruby is found it is always encased in a round nodule of considerable size. The mines have not been worked since Badakhshan fell into the hands of the Kunduz chief, who, irritated, it is supposed, at the small profit they yielded, marched the inhabitants of the district, then numbering about five hundred families, to Kunduz, and disposed of them in the slave market. The inhabitants of Gharan were Rafizies, or Shiah Mohamedans, and so are the few families which still remain there.[1]

[1] According to Pundit Manphúl these mines are still unworked. At his request one of them was opened in 1866, but without much result. Marco Polo mentions the royal monopoly in their working, which has continued until the present day.

CHAPTER XX.

Fall out with Abdal Ghaní.—Make up the quarrel.—A mounted Kirghiz matron.—Her steed.—The Yak, or kash-gow.—Ishtrakh.—Shah Turai of Kundut.—A Kirghiz encampment.—Kila Panj.—Mineral spring.—Issar.—Streams from Mastuch and Pamir.—Vestiges of the ancient Fire-worshippers.—The Wakhan chief.—Difficulties.—A Kirghiz escort.—Some account of that people.—The Kazaks.

DISAPPOINTED in one object of my journey, I turned with increased ardour to the other; and despite the remonstrances and croakings of Abdal Ghaní, resolved to trace the Oxus to its source. The ease with which we had crossed the Pass of Ishkashm, seemed to presage success; and the winter was now sufficiently advanced to enable us to determine with some degree of confidence whether it would be mild or severe. Appearances spoke favourably; and we resumed our upward march along the left bank of the river. The Yesawal, thinking to shake my resolution, refused to be of the party, left the house where we lodged, and took up his quarters in another. High words had before passed between us; and he chose this opportunity of showing his resentment. Our misunderstanding arose out of my anxiety to prevent as much as possible the system of extortion which he practised in every wretched hamlet on our route. He never entered a place without proclaiming his dignity, and demanding something in the Mír's name, threatening those who refused, and making large promises to others who were more compliant. I had often before remonstrated with him on this subject, and had even promised to indemnify him for any loss he might sustain by abandoning a line of conduct that could not fail to compromise our good name. For a time he appeared to accede to my request, but his self-denial was not proof against the temptation of a pair of worsted stockings, or a woollen cloak; things which the poor families who were his victims, could ill afford to part with. The secret system of plunder which he henceforward adopted, was even more detestable than the open one which he abandoned. I again remonstrated with him, but to no better purpose. It was, he said, the custom of the country, and with such I had better not interfere; that he knew his duty, and that I should find I could not do without him. Abdal Ghaní spoke the truth: for no sooner was it known that we had quarrelled, than food grew scarce, and guides were not to be had. Without the Yesawal's consent, no man would take a letter which I had written to Mirza Suliman, detailing our difficulties, and soliciting that instructions might be given to the chief of Ish-kashm, to send a trustworthy person with us into Wakhan, to the chief of which district I was accredited by Murad Beg. Seeing how completely we were in this man's power, I deemed it prudent to compromise the matter, and we left Ish-kashm as good friends as ever; and likely to continue so, since beyond that town, the authority of Murad Beg is little reverenced; and I soon found that the Yesawal no longer dared even to hint at the perquisites due to his office.

Proceeding up the valley of the Oxus, with the mountains of Shakh Durah on our left hand, and those of Chitral on our right, both rising to a vast height, and bearing far below their summits the snow of ages, we arrived early in the afternoon at the hamlet of Ishtrakh, having before passed Kila Khoja and Pullu, the first inhabited places since we entered Wakhan. We reached the village in the middle of a heavy snow-fall; and its houses built amongst fractured pieces of the neighbouring mountains, must have been passed unnoticed, but for a Yak, or Kash-gow, as the animal is here called, standing before a door with its bridle in the hand of a Kirghiz boy. There was something so novel in its appearance, that I could not resist the impulse of mounting so strange a steed; but in doing so I met with stout resistance from the little fellow who had it in charge. In the midst of our dispute the boy's mother made her appearance, and very kindly permitted me to try the animal's paces. It stood about three feet and a half high, was very hairy and powerful. Its belly reached within six inches of the ground, which was swept by its bushy tail. The long hair streamed down from its dewlap and fore legs, giving it, but for the horns, the appearance of a huge Newfoundland dog. It bore a light saddle with horn stirrups; and a cord let through the cartilage of the nose, served for a bridle. The good Kirghiz matron was not a less interesting object than her steed. She was diminutive in stature, but active and strong, and wore some half-dozen petticoats under a showy blue striped gown, the whole sitting close to her person, and held there, not by ribbons, but by a stout leather belt about the waist. Her rosy cheeks and Chinese countenance, were seen from under a high white starched tiára, while broad bands of the same colour protected the ears, mouth, and chin. Worsted gloves covered her hands, and the feet were equally well taken care of. She chid her son for not permitting me to mount the kash-gow; and I quite won the good woman's heart by praising the lad's spirit, and hanging a string of beads about his neck. Strutting up to her steed with the air of an Amazon, she emptied the flour she had obtained at the village, into her koorgeens, took the bridle out of her son's hand, and vaulted astride into the saddle. The sight appeared to be new, not only to us, but to the inhabitants of Wakhan; for the villagers had thronged round to see her depart. They inquired if she would not take the boy up behind her? " Oh no," was her answer, "he can walk." As the mother and son left us, a droll-looking calf leisurely trod after its dam; and when the party disappeared amid the falling snow-flakes, the rugged, half-clad Wakhanis exclaimed, as if taken by surprise, " None but a Kirghiz boy could thrive under such rough treatment."

The yak is to the inhabitants of Tibet and Pamir what the reindeer is to the Laplander in northern Europe. Where a man can walk a kash-gow may be ridden. Like the elephant, he possesses a wonderful knowledge of what will bear his weight. If travellers are at fault, one of these animals is driven before them, and it is said that he avoids the hidden depths and chasms with admirable sagacity. His footing is sure. Should a fall of snow close a mountain pass to man and horse, a score of yaks driven ahead answer the purpose of pioneers, and make, as my informant expresses it, "*a king's highway.*" In this case, however, the snow must have recently fallen; for when once its surface is frozen and its depth considerable, no animal can force its way through it. Other cattle require the provident care of man to subsist them through the winter. The most hardy sheep would fare but badly without its human protection, but the kash-gow is left entirely to himself. He frequents the mountain slopes and their level summits. Wherever the mercury does not rise above zero, is a climate for the yak. If the snow on the elevated flats lie too deep for him to crop the herbage, he rolls himself down the slopes and eats his way up again. When arrived at the top, he performs a second summerset, and completes his meal as he displaces another groove of snow in his second ascent. The heat of summer sends the animal to what is termed the old ice, that is to the regions of eternal snow; the calf being retained below as a pledge for the mother's returning, in which she never fails. In the summer, the women, like the pastoral inhabitants of the Alps, encamp in the higher valleys, which are interspersed among the snowy mountains, and devote their whole time to the dairy. The men remain on the plain, and attend to the agricultural part of the establishment, but occasionally visit the upper stations; and all speak in rapture of these summer wanderings. The kash-gows are gregarious, and set the wolves, which here abound, at defiance. Their hair is clipped once a year in the spring. The tail is the well-known Chowry of Hindustan; but in this country, its strong, wiry, and pliant hair is made into ropes, which, for strength, do not yield to those manufactured from hemp. The hair of the body is woven into mats, and also into a strong fabric which makes excellent riding trousers. The milk of the yak is richer than that of the common cow, though the quantity it yields be less. The kurut made from it is considered to be first rate, even superior to the produce of the Kohistan of Kabul, which has great celebrity in Afghanistan. The Kirghiz never extract the butter.

The first yaks we saw were grazing among the snow on the

very summit of the rugged pass of Ish-kashm, and at the village of this name, I procured one for Dr. Lord, and despatched it to Kunduz in charge of two trusty men. But so cold a climate do these singular animals require, that though winter still reigned in the Kunduz plain, the heat was too great, and the yak died within a march or two of the town. In fact it began to droop as soon as it had passed Jerm. Some years back, an Afghan nobleman succeeded in bringing two or three of these animals to Kabul, but even the temperature of that city, though situated 6,000 feet above sea-level, is not sufficiently cold to suit their constitution. They declined as the snow left the ground, and died early in the spring.[1]

At Ishtrakh, a rivulet from the Chitral mountain falls into the Oxus, by following up the course of which, a man on foot in the summer months may reach the seat of Shah Kittore, ruler of Chitral, on the third day. We now learned that the valley of the Oxus, for some distance upwards, was uninhabited, and the wind was too strong and keen for us to attempt to bivouac on its unsheltered surface unless compelled by necessity. So we set off at midnight, and reached Kundut, the residence of Shah Turai, after a cold ride of forty miles, and having been thirteen hours in the saddle. This monarch of fifteen families gave us a warmer reception than the poverty of his capital had

---

[1] The yak may be seen in a domesticated state in London, Paris, Antwerp, and other places. When a sufficient stock of them is maintained (which, for want of space, has not been the case in Regent's Park), these animals appear to thrive in Western Europe. All the yaks now in Europe are of Chinese origin. It is a question, however, whether the wild yak is the true pristine stock of the domestic races. Mr. Blyth, one of the best authorities on the subject, is inclined to think not. He notices a remarkable difference between the horns of all the wild yak heads he has examined, and those of the tame yak and domestic humped cattle generally; in the latter the horns do not project forward beyond the plane of the visage, whereas in the wild yak they do so project very considerably, as in European humpless cattle, and also in the fossil *B. urus*. Mr. Blyth remarks: "Whenever in domestic humped cattle the horn projects forward beyond the plane of visage, it does so abnormally, and curling downwards. I never saw an instance to the contrary among the myriads of humped cattle I observed in India. The horns are constantly even with the plane of visage in the bisons of Europe and America, the buffalo, domestic humped cattle, and the domestic yak. They project *forward* only in the typical *B. taurus* and the wild yak." It would appear that the true wild yak, with these projecting horns, has not been brought to Europe.

prepared us to expect. A large fire soon blazed upon the hearth of the best house it contained, and his subjects being convened, I was paraded round it, to refute the assertion of a wandering callender (fakir) from Jumbo in the Himalaya mountains, who, it seems, had persuaded the credulous Wakhanis that the Firingis were a nation of dwarfs.

The valley of the Oxus from Ish-kashm, where we first came upon the river, to Kundut, varies from a few hundred yards to a mile in width. As we drew near the fort and hamlet of Shah Turai, the ground became more and more level, and the river, dividing into many channels, meandered over a sandy bed, studded with numberless islets, which were thickly covered with an undergrowth of red willow-trees. In passing through one of these copses, our dog started a hare, the only living thing we saw between Ishtrakh and Kundut.

The houses at Kundut are clustered about the fort like so many cells in a bee-hive. We discovered that the holes in their roofs, besides giving vent to the smoke, perform the office of sun-dials, and when the sun is shining indicate the hour of the day. Before the housewife begins to prepare the family meal, she looks not up at a clock, but round the walls or upon the floor for the spot on which his golden light is streaming. The seasons also are marked by the same means; for when the sun's rays, through this aperture, reach one particular point, it is seed time.

Taking leave of Shah Turai, we resumed our journey up the valley, but had not proceeded far when the barking of dogs and the sight of yaks, camels, and sheep, roaming over the plain, told of a pastoral people being in the neighbourhood, and soon after we came upon a Kirghiz encampment. Anxious to see this nomade race, we struck off towards their beehive-looking tents, but the fierce dogs prowling round kept us at bay until we managed to out-howl them, and succeeded in making ourselves heard by their masters. As we entered among the kirgahs or tents, the spaces between them were seen to be thronged by ewes, children, and dogs. The horde consisted of 100 families, and possessed about 2,000 yaks, 4,000 sheep, and 1,000 camels; not the ugly-looking camel of Arabia, but that species known as Bactrian, and which, to all the useful qualities of the former, adds a majestic port that no animal but the horse can surpass. This was the first year of their abode in Wakhan, and the only instance of the Kirghiz having made this district their winter quarters. They had been solicited to do so by the Uzbeks of Kunduz, with whom the Kirghiz profess to be connected by blood. The two people are evidently of the same stock, though the effects of location, or, in other words, the difference between a temperate and a rigorous climate is observable in the well-proportioned frame of the Uzbek and in the stunted growth of the Kirghiz.

The arrival of strangers was an important event to the horde. Each kirgah poured forth its male inmates, and all clustered round our little party to hear the news of Kunduz. More rugged, weather-beaten faces I had never seen; they had, however, the hue of health. Their small sunken eyes were just visible, peeping from beneath fur-caps, while the folds of a snug woollen *comforter* concealed their paucity of beard. The clothing of most of them consisted of a sheep's skin, with the wool inside; but some wore good coloured cotton chupkuns. Snuff was more in demand with them than tobacco; but to satisfy the craving desires of such voracious snuff-takers would have required a larger stock of *Irish blackguard* than we had brought of charcoal. On presenting my box to the chief of the horde, he quietly emptied half its contents into the palm of his hand, then opening his mouth and holding his head back, at two gulps he swallowed the whole. Our boxes were soon emptied, for none of them were contented with a pinch or two for the nose. In this bad habit the Uzbeks likewise indulged, but not to the extent of their relatives the Kirghiz. The latter have invariably bad teeth; many even of their young men are nearly toothless. This they attributed to the coldness of the water they are obliged to drink, but I should imagine that the snuff had a good deal to do with it.

We now asked permission to rest awhile in one of their kirgahs, and were immediately led up to one of the best in the encampment. Its outside covering was formed of coarse dun-coloured felts, held down by two broad white belts about five feet above the ground. To these the dome or roof was secured by diagonal bands, while the felts which formed the walls were strengthened by other bands, which descended in a zig-zag direction between those first mentioned and the ground. Close to the door lay a bag filled with ice—the water of the family. On drawing aside the felt which screened the entrance, the air of tidiness and comfort that met our eyes was a most agreeable surprise. In the middle of the floor, upon a light iron tripod, stood a huge Russian caldron, beneath which glowed a cheerful fire, which a ruddy-cheeked, spruce damsel kept feeding with fuel, and occasionally throwing a lump of ice into her cookery. She modestly beckoned us to be seated, and continued her household duties unembarrassed by the presence of strangers. If unable to praise the men of the Kirghiz for their good looks, I may, without flattery, pronounce the young women pretty. All have the glow of health in their cheeks, and though they have the harsh features of the race, there is a softness about their lineaments, a coyness and maidenly reserve in their demeanour, that contrasts strongly and most agreeably with the uncouth figures and harsh manners of the men.

The kirgah had a diameter of fourteen feet, a height of eight, and was well lighted by a circular hole above the fireplace. Its framework was of the willow-tree, but between it and the felt covering, neat mats, made of reeds, the size of wheat-straw, and knitted over with coloured worsted, were inserted. The sides of the tent, lined with variegated mats of this description, not only looked tasteful, but imparted a snug and warm appearance to the interior. Corresponding to the outside belts were two within of a finer description, and adorned with needle-work. From these were suspended various articles appertaining to the tent and to the field, besides those of ornament and the sampler. Saddles, bridles, rings, thimbles, and beads, all had here their appropriate places. One side of the kirgah had the family's spare clothes and bedding. In another, a home-made carpet hung from the roof, making a recess in which the females dressed, and where the matron kept her culinary stores and kitchen apparatus. The opposite segment was allotted to the young lambs of the flock. A string crossed the tent to which fifty nooses, twenty-five of a side, were attached, to each of which a lamb was fastened. While we were present, they were taken outside to their dams, and after a time again brought back into the kirgah.

Three yaks are able to carry the tent and all its contents. One takes the *oostakhan*, literally the bones or frame-work, another the felts, and a third its furniture; besides which, a seat is found upon them for the feeble or young of the family. In one kirgah which we entered, the children were conning their lessons under the eye of an aged mullah. Some were learning to write, by tracing letters upon a black board with a bit of chalk, while others were humming over the torn leaves of well-thumbed copies of the Koran. Mutilated as was the condition of their books, they were nevertheless highly valued, if we might judge from the strong wooden box appropriated to their preservation. Where the thirst for instruction appeared to be so keen I could not help wishing there had been better means for its gratification and a safer guide than the Koran.

Continuing our march, a ride of twenty-four miles brought us to Kila Panj, where we crossed the Oxus, and then held on along its right bank to Issar, a village within sight of the fort. Kila Panj is so called from five small rocky hillocks in the neighbourhood, upon all of which there were formerly tenements One of these hillocks rises immediately from the stream, its surface is covered with houses, and it is crested by a fort in tolerable preservation. A murder was committed in this place seven years ago, and although the criminal had up to this time escaped punishment, vengeance, as the sequel of my narrative will show, at length overtook him; but, unfortunately, in a manner more calculated to excite to other atrocities than to satisfy the ends of justice. It appears that the chief of Wakhan, Mohamed Rahim Khán, had suffered greatly from the exactions of the Badakhshi ruler Kokan Beg, and at length, rendered desperate, refused to pay tribute. Immediately Kokan Beg carried fire and sword into his territories. The Wakhanis were eventually worsted, and took refuge in Chitral; but their chief threw himself into Kila Panj, and defended it until an amicable arrangement was agreed to by the two leaders, on which Kokan Beg, confiding in the honour of his opponent, entered his castle, and was immediately slain. The Badakhshies, disheartened at the loss of their leader, withdrew, and the exiled Wakhanis returned to their homes. From that time the loyalty of Mohamed Rahim Khán was considered more than doubtful, and though nominally tributary to Kunduz, he was virtually independent. Sometimes, indeed, to ward off a threatened visit from Murad Beg, he would send him an inconsiderable tribute. Distance and poverty had hitherto been his security; but even these would not much longer have availed him, had it not been for the military movements of Bakhara on the Kunduz frontier. When Murad Beg placed in the hands of Mirza Baddi, our letter of introduction to Mohamed Rahim, he observed that he would not be answerable for our reception in Wakhan, since its chieftain had for two years discontinued communicating with himself, which looked like rebellion.

The valley of the Oxus continued level, about a mile wide, grassy in some places, and though far from fertile, improved in appearance as we proceeded. By the bank of the river and among the willow copses, there was considerable herbage; but the mountains offered none, nor did the plain in their neighbourhood. The river flowed slowly, its velocity scarcely exceeding three miles and a half an hour. Where we crossed it, the stream was split into two channels, one of which, twenty-seven yards broad, was two feet deep; the other was wider by ten yards, but so shallow that our dog crossed it without swimming. The mountains forming the valley had decreased in height at Issar; those on the Chitral side were, however, still lofty. Before entering Issar, we passed a mineral spring about 800 feet up the mountain on the right bank of the river. The ground over which it ran had a ferruginous appearance, but the water was tasteless—its temperature was 116°.

The valley of the Oxus may be said to terminate at Issar, to which point from Ish-kashm, in latitude 36° 42' 32" N., its direction is E. by N. ½ N. The latitude of Issar is 37° 02' 10" N., and its height above the sea 10,000 feet. Here the main valley divides into two, which, when a little beyond Kila Panj, bore respectively E. 20° S. and N. 40° E. The former, we were told, conducted into Chitral, Gilgit, and Kashmir, and the latter across the table-land of Pamir to Yarkand. I had now to ascertain, if possible, which of the two streams I was to trace. One of them, it was certain, must lead to the source of the Oxus, but which of the two was a question of difficulty. The Kirghiz had unhesitatingly told us that the object of our search was to be found in a lake upon the "Bam-i-duniah," or *Roof of the World*, in Pamir, and that the road to it was up the durah [1] or Sir-i-kol; but though the northerly direction of that valley and of the countries to which it led was, when compared with the Mastuch, as the Chitral durah is sometimes called, almost sufficient evidence in favour of Sir-i-kol, I thought it prudent to visit the junction of their respective waters. To my eye the stream of Sirhad, as the river from Mastuch is frequently called, appeared the larger, but the Wakhanis held a different opinion. That from Pamir was divided into several channels, and frozen, so that its aggregate volume could not be well ascertained; though from a clearing in its principal stream I inferred its velocity to be double that of the Sirhad, while its temperature was five degrees lower, being 32°, and that of the other 37°. It seemed a singular circumstance, but certainly confirmatory of the superior height of the source of the river of Pamir to that of the other stream, that it should be sheeted with ice to the very point of their junction, whilst the Sirhad was unfettered by the frost, and had a slower current and a higher temperature. According to my informant, the Pamir branch in summer brings down much more water than the Sirhad, though the latter has many tributaries and the former but two trifling rills—those of Langer Kish and Zerzumen.[2] Among the rivulets that pay

---

[1] *Durah*, a narrow mountain valley or ravine.

[2] An employé of Government in the Great Trigonometrical Survey of India known as the Mirza, started from Kabul for Badakhshan in October 1868, and marching eastwards, followed the course of the Kokcha river and passed into the valley of the upper Oxus. Meeting that river at Ish-kashm, he continued due east until Panja in Wakhan was reached. Up to this point his route and that of the narrative are nearly identical. From Panja onwards he followed the southern branch of the Oxus, correctly judged by Wood to be the larger one, and traced it to another lake called Pamir Kul, at a level of about 13,300 feet, or 2,300 feet lower than the

tribute to the Sirhad is Pir-khar, a name of note in the geography of these regions, since Macartney, with his usual discernment, had supposed it to be the fountain head of the Oxus; and we see how closely he approximated to the truth. Indeed, none but those who have travelled in the countries he mapped, almost entirely from native information, can duly appreciate the labours of that talented and deeply to be regretted officer.

Since crossing the pass of Ish-kashm, we had seen the ruins of three Kaffir forts, which the natives believe to have been erected by the Guebers or Fire-worshippers, one called Sumri, in the neighbourhood of Kundut; another in the vicinity of Ishtrakh, named Kakah; and the last, Kila Zanguebar, close to the hamlet of Issar. I have elsewhere mentioned the repugnance with which a Badakhshi blows out a light. Similar lingering remnants of Zoroaster's creed are to be detected here. A Wakhani considers it bad luck to blow out a light by the breath, and will rather wave his hand for several minutes under the flame of his pine-slip, than resort to the sure, but to him disagreeable, alternative.

Before reaching Issar, I had sent Abdal Ghani forward to inform Mohamed Rahim Khán of our arrrival, and to deliver the Mír's letter, together with sundry trifling presents in my own name. The chief, who lived about ten miles up the Mastuch valley, did not make his appearance till the second day, and when he did, he was equipped for a journey to Kunduz, and not, as we expected, for the purpose of guiding us to Pamir. It appeared, however, that this journey to Kunduz had been contemplated for some time back, and doubts as to the reception he should meet with from Murad Beg had alone kept him from

---

Sirikul, from whence the northern branch flows. This fully accounts for the fact of its not being frozen when seen by Wood, though the northern stream was then covered with ice.

It is impossible to say which of these two deserves to rank as the chief source of the river; the northern stream has the loftier and nobler source in the lake discovered by Captain Wood, whilst the southern is undoubtedly the longer of the two branches. The account of the Mirza's journey, as given by Major Montgomerie, R.E., of the Great Trigonometrical Survey of India, is a record of the most wonderful patience and perseverance in the duty which he had undertaken, under great hardships and difficulties. His route is the same as that by which the Chinese pilgrim Hwen Thsang travelled twelve and a half centuries ago.

undertaking it before. He had now procured a few Bactrian camels from his new neighbours the Kirghiz; a chuppow on Shakh Durah had enabled him to add a number of slaves to his present, and with this propitiatory offering he was on the eve of starting, when Abdal Ghaní reached his residence. On finding Mohamed Rahim Khán had no intention to accompany us, I spoke my mind plainly to him; any affectation of ignorance on my part as to the real state of things would have been perfectly useless, since what had been only whispered in Kunduz was notorious here; and the disaffection of the chief was openly encouraged by his people. It is true the Mír, with proper caution, had made no mention in his letters of the suspicions to which the Wakhan chief's conduct had given rise; but, on the contrary, professed the fullest confidence in his loyalty. He was directed to accompany us in person with twenty horsemen, to protect our party from the Kirghiz, and he was told that his honourable treatment of us would be considered by the Mír as kindness shown to himself, for, said Murad Beg, "they are my guests;" and the Uzbek did not omit to add, that were a hair of our beards injured, he would annihilate his power in Wakhan—"*Beikh Mekushum,*" literally, he would uproot him. I argued the point at great length with the chief, and pointed out to him, that if he really intended a visit to Kunduz, it would be a wiser course first to execute the Mír's commands, and by so doing entitle himself to a favourable reception, rather than by spurning his authority on such an occasion to add to his resentment. The letter, as he saw, described me as an honoured guest of the Mír, and that it therefore behoved him, for his own sake, to be exceedingly careful how he acted in opposition to his wishes. We were, moreover, foreigners, in all transactions with whom, as he must be well aware, the Mír was particularly jealous of his honour, and would be certain deeply to feel and to resent conduct that could not fail to lower him in the estimation of strangers. Mohamed Rahim was on the point of yielding, when Abdal Ghaní drew me aside, and declared in the most positive terms, that if the chief accompanied us, he, the Mír's Yesawal, would not. Knowing, as I did, that he had been fully instructed in

Murad Beg's wishes on the subject, I was greatly astounded at this announcement, but restraining my indignation, I merely told him that as he was no doubt fatigued, and could not partake of the feelings which actuated me to undertake the journey, I conceived the arrangement he proposed was judicious, and that he had permission to remain. This did not satisfy the Yesawal. He now motioned to the chief to go out of doors with him. What passed between them I know not, but on their re-entering the house the whole affair was arranged— Mohamed Rahim was to go on to Kunduz, and the person who was to be his representative during his absence, was to accompany us. In vain did I try to persuade the chief that this arrangement would highly incense the Mír. Backed by the Yesawal, and urged on by his own dogged resolution, Mohamed Rahim laughed at my admonitions, and with his half savage escort of armed, skin-clad followers, set out for the plains, from which he was doomed never to return. No sooner was he gone than Abdal Ghaní stigmatized him as every thing that was vile; said that he had even been so mean as to refuse a feed of barley for his horse, and that he trusted the Mír would not only punish him, but chuppow Wakhan, and make slaves of every soul it contained.

Mohamed Rahim's *locum tenens* was now called upon for the mounted guard, but he could only furnish two horses and five men on foot. No others would volunteer to be of the party, and the vice-governor lacked authority to compel them. In this extremity I turned my thoughts to the Kirghiz, and though these were the very people whose aggression we feared, I resolved to adopt towards them a policy not often unsuccessful with barbarous nations—namely, the reposing implicit confidence in those you dread. I sent a messenger down to their encampment with a letter to their chief, requesting that he would permit a few of his young men to be of our party to Pamir, for that the Wakhanis were not much to be trusted, and were, besides, ignorant of the road. I promised a handsome chupkun to each man, and the latter was backed by the present of a *mukhmul*, or velvet pelisse, for himself. The arrival next day of five mounted and armed Kirghiz gladdened our hearts;

they joined us at Langer Kish, a village at the entrance of the Sir-i-kol-durah, to which in the interim we had removed.

The Kirghiz, like the Kazaks, are a pastoral and nomadic race, inhabiting the steppes of central Asia, and both are termed Mongolian by the writers on the varieties of the human species. The Kazaks range the low-lying plains between the vast empires of Russia and China. The Kirghiz domain is the table-land of Pamir, which, buttressed by Tibet, slopes northward upon Kokan, having the Chinese territories to the east, and the rugged country that feeds the rivers Oxus and Sirr to the west. Their language does not differ, or only in a trifling degree, from that spoken in Kunduz. They acknowledge allegiance to Kokan, and pay tribute to its ruler; but with China and Tibet they are constantly at feud, or, what is much the same thing, rob all parties from either country whom they can overpower. They are, if what we have heard of them in Wakhan be true, notorious plunderers, pusillanimous, and faithless. No one trusts a Kirghiz escort; and they repay this want of confidence by rifling every Yarkand caravan they can master. A horde, at the instigation of the Kokan chief, sometimes migrates to Tibet for the sole purpose of waylaying the Yarkand trader. The Chinese, therefore, as might be expected, detest the race, and their authorities consider them all equally criminal, and put them to death wherever found. The Kirghiz, on the other hand, hold the subjects of the celestial empire in abhorrence, pronouncing them Kaffirs and bad men. Such inveterate thieves are the Kirghiz, that robberies often occur, not only in a horde, but in its smallest sub-divisions. If one man be robbed, he retaliates on his next door neighbour. Their Bais, or chiefs, have little power over them for good or evil. In consideration of their age and blood, some deference to their opinions is shown, but nothing more.

In stature the Kirghiz are under the middle size. Of a Kyl numbering seven men whom I measured, the tallest stood five feet five and a half inches—the shortest five feet two inches. Their countenance is disagreeable: the upper part of the nose sinks into the face, leaving the space between their deep-seated and elongated eyes without the usual dividing ridge; the brow immediately above the eye is protuberant, but slants back more abruptly than in Europeans; their cheeks, large and bloated, look as if pieces of flesh had been daubed upon them; a slender beard covers the chin, and with those individuals who have a more luxuriant growth of hair, both beard and whiskers have a close natural curl; their persons are not muscular, and their complexion is darkened by exposure in all weathers, rather than by the sun. This description does not apply to the Kirghiz women, whom, as I have before said, are rather good-looking. They resemble the Hazara females in their small and delicate form, and, like them, too, seem more calculated for a genial clime than for the stern one they inhabit. Though Suni Mohamedans, they go unveiled, and have quite as much liberty as women have with us. They are modest, but like most of their sex, have a prying curiosity and a craving for dress. At our request they took their ornaments off, and permitted us to examine them. Beads of black and red coral were in the highest estimation, though some had them of stained glass. Others wore gems rudely set in silver, brass ornaments, and fanciful decorations carved out of the pearl oyster shell. Both sexes wore round hollow brass buttons about their clothes. All these articles were obtained from the Chinese. The high head-dress of the women resembles a white paste-board crown, and when the coquette ties a coloured band in front, her look is queenly. They appear to make good wives. All we saw were attentive to the comforts of their domestic circle, and if the thimble was not on the finger, it, and the other implements of knitting and sewing, were seen hanging from the walls of the kirgah. Slaves are not common among this people, though they have, like European families, maid servants. With the Kirghiz, a daughter is more desired than a son. Their flocks and herds, though large, do not require many men to manage them; and as they never cultivate the earth, but are continually on the march, an excess of profitless mouths is not desirable where food is not over-abundant. But for a daughter a large sum is obtained—often as much as £40, if she be not above fifteen years of age. On a husband's death the wife goes to his brother, and on his decease becomes the property of the next of kin, failing which she returns to her father's kirgah. Should a stranger take the widow to wife, a blood feud is inevitable. Both sexes, but especially the women, suffer from cutaneous disease.

The Kirghiz may be said to subsist chiefly on milk and its various preparations, the produce of their herds and flocks. What flesh they consume is obtained by their matchlocks; and the number of horns that strew Pamir bear evidence to the havoc they make among the wild flocks of the mountain. These horns, being of a remarkably large size, supply shoes for the horses' feet, and are also a good substitute for stirrup irons. The shoes are nothing more than a semi-circular piece of horn placed on the fore part of the hoof. When the horse is in constant work, it requires renewal at least once a week. I had been led to entertain much too high an opinion of Kirghiz horses. They are rough-coated, ill-looking animals, incapable of standing great fatigue. A Kattaghan galloway of Kunduz will do double the work of a Kirghiz pony. The horse of the Kazak is quite another animal. What his useful qualities may be I know not; but for beauty, as far as it consists in his shaggy coat, he is unique. Neither goats nor the common cow are domesticated by the Kirghiz, the continued cold of winter being too severe for them to thrive. I have already mentioned the yaks and camels; the latter is a very handsome animal. In their own native region it may be a question which is the most useful; but, like man, the camel adapts himself to circumstances, and consequently is by far the most valuable, being equally well calculated to move across burning sands or frozen steppes. The Kirghiz, as well as the Uzbeks, keep brood mares, according to their means, and the acidulated milk of these animals yields them in spring the intoxicating liquor called *kimiz*. If the milk be taken from the mare in the evening, it is churned till sunrise, by which time it is ready for drinking. A spoonful will produce inebriety, but their *kashuk* or spoon is much more capacious than the largest upon our tables. They assert that when the intoxicating effect has worn off, the appetite is increased and the general health improved. I was told that when this fermented beverage is in season, the encampment of a horde is a scene of the grossest vice and sensuality; that the men give loose to their passions without restraint, and that the barriers of consanguinity are disregarded. The charge is a grave one, and I therefore should add that it was brought against them by men who were not friends to the Kirghiz.

Their principal men affix the title of Bai to their names, as Kurban Kuli Bai, for example. It has the same signification as Khán with the Afghans; that is, a nobleman. Their influence is more patriarchal than despotic, and seldom otherwise exercised than in collecting tribute for the government, and supporting the interests of their respective hordes. The total number of Kirgahs under Kokan is estimated at 100,000.

They were converted from the Shamanian superstition to Mohamedanism early in the seventeenth century. The former belief, if I may credit Abdal Ghaní, is not yet thoroughly eradicated; though in our intercourse with the people, they seemed like all proselytes to erring creeds, to be filled with the most abject reverence for their new doctrines.

In summer the hordes split into parties, and fix themselves in the shallow valleys of the Table-land and in the Alpine glens, where pasturage and water are abundant. Lake Sir-i-kol is one of their most favourite haunts; and in that joyous season its waters are margined by groups of kirgahs. As the departure of the water-fowl gives signs of approaching winter, the Kirghiz seek a somewhat lower station; and again and again shifting their ground, as the weather becomes more severe, at length reach the spot destined for their winter's encampment. This is usually a rough valley, partly sheltered by snowy mountains, among which their yaks may roll and trample, while the other less hardy animals pick up a scanty subsistence on the spots of ground in the plain which the wind has cleared of snow, or on the borders of its ice-bound streams. Most of the Kirghiz annually drive their flocks down the inclined plane of Pamir to Kokhan, and camping near that city, procure by barter various articles of use or ornament for their next migratory campaign.

The Kazaks resemble the Kirghiz in personal appearance, if we may give credence to the latter, except that their necks are thicker and their ears more pendent. The same authority gives them a character of great simplicity; and if all the laughable stories which the Kirghiz tell of them be correct, they are in truth the *Johnny Raws* of Central Asia; though even when so viewed, their ingenuousness and freedom from guile render their character infinitely more winning than that of the people who make merry at their expense. Among the stories told by the Kirghiz of these "children of the desert," is that of a Kazak who, on his first visit to Bokhara, saw a man on the top of a lofty minaret, giving the *Azan*, and reminding the faithful that the hour of prayer had arrived, and calling upon every one to kneel and pray. The Kazak, ignorant of the language and usages of Mohamedans, pitied the Mullah in his forlorn situation, and remarked as he passed along, " Poor man, why climb up where it is so difficult to come down ?" Next year the honest Kazak revisited the holy city, and at the same hour again heard the same sound issuing from the tall turret ; he looked up, and, espying the identical individual of the bygone year, gave utterance to his astonishment with a vehemence and grotesqueness of expression which has never been forgotten.

Another story is that of a chief, who, with his people, wishing to become children of circumcision, sent a messenger to Kokan to purchase prayers for the horde. Unfortunately for the interests of Mohamedanism, the person to whom this grave commission was entrusted, fell into the hands of a droll, merry fellow, one who well knew the people with whom he had to do. A jar carefully covered, containing a swarm of bees, was delivered to the dull Kazak, with instructions to his chief not to open it till all the head men of the horde were assembled. He was further told to select the largest tent for this purpose, to close it up from the gaze of the vulgar, and when all present were undressed, to place the jar upon a fire and remove its covering. The chief conformed most exactly to the directions, and all the party accordingly suffered as the wag intended. The chief himself, literally stung to madness, swore that never again should a Mussulman's prayer issue from a Kazak kirgah.

Q

CHAPTER XXI.

Quit Langer Kish.—Enter Durah Sir-i-kol.—Cold bivouac.—March on the frozen river.—A meeting.—Willows.—Snow encampment.—Horns of the wild sheep.—Snug quarters.—A mutiny.—Difficult travelling.—Accident upon the river.—Kirghiz at prayers.—Source of the river Oxus.—Lake Sir-i-kol.—Height of Mountains.—Sources of many streams.—Sounding the Lake.—Effects of a rarefied atmosphere.—Pulsations upon Pamir.—Snow line.—Scarcity of wood.—Himalaya and Hindú Kosh chains.—The Kutchkar, or wild sheep.—The Rass.—Return to Langer Kish.

AFTER mustering our escort before the door of the Aksikhail of Langer Kish, we mounted our sturdy hill ponies, and having received the "God-speed" of the half savage Wakhanis, struck into the durah of Sir-i-kol. While awaiting the Kirghiz' arrival, we had made sundry alterations in our dress, which, however expedient, were certainly not to the improvement of our personal appearance; and as we moved out of the village in single file, I could not help smiling at my Esquimaux-looking body-guard. The Munshi, in particular, was so hampered up with worsted cloaks, that his arms were all but useless; and his short legs had scarcely action enough to keep him on his horse. In addition to the load of clothing with which each had burdened his steed, the animals carried eight days' food for their riders and for themselves, as well as some firewood.

The mountains forming the defile were not very lofty, nor were their sides precipitous; they appeared to have been broken down to abrupt declivities, either by frost and the vicissitudes of weather, or by subterranean convulsions; and amid their dislocated fragments ran the snow-wreathed stream we had come so far to trace.

About three hours after starting we arrived on the brink of a deep chasm that crossed our track, in passing over which we met with considerable delay. Its slippery sides constituted the principal difficulty, and it was not without risk that we got the horses across. The Yarkand caravan is frequently interrupted at this place, and its merchandise is obliged to be transferred from the camel's back to that of the yak. After getting clear of the ravine, we pushed on at as rapid a pace as the depth of snow permitted; and some time before the day closed in, selected a spot on which to bivouac for the night. It was the summit of an unsheltered knoll, free from snow, the only place within sight which was so; in return for which exemption it was swept by every breath of wind that moved either up or down the durah. It was, however, calm when we alighted. The wooden saddles of our steeds and the bags of charcoal were disposed in a circle, within which, with our feet to the fire, each man took his station. The kettle soon sang upon the red embers, and the koor-geens having been opened, we had begun to feast and make merry, when an ill-natured gust came howling down the valley, and destroyed at once our fire and our good humour. The latter we soon recovered, but all our coaxing failed for a long time to rekindle the former. The patient labours of the Kirghiz were at length successful, and before long the tea-cup had gone its rounds, infusing a warmth into our frames, and a glow into our hearts, that made us, I dare say, happier than many a party who were at that moment quaffing their claret, and surrounded with all the luxuries of civilised life. But all happiness is comparative, and I must confess that when at the best we were not lying upon a bed of roses, nor was the moaning wintry wind particularly soothing to the ear, nor the biting cold very grateful to the person. The feet were the great sufferers; they were like lead, and when it is so with the extremities, it is no use caring for the body. So peeling stocking after stocking, we toasted our feet into a comfortable burning warmth, and having settled the necessary dispositions for the night, each made his own arrangements to pass it as best he could. Thanks to my good horse and his furniture, I got through it tolerably well, but Abdal Ghaní and two Afghans suffered so severely that I was compelled to send them back to Langer Kish in the morning. Our thermometers were only graduated down to + 6° of Fahrenheit; and as the mercury had sunk into the bulb, it was not in my power to register the exact degree of cold; it was, however, intense, and the highly rarefied state of the atmosphere caused it to be the more severely felt. The height of this halting-place was 12,000 feet above the sea.

In the early part of next day we continued our route through a narrow, rough valley, resembling in its principal features the portion traversed the preceding day; but towards noon we descended to the river, and, taking to its icy surface, held on till nightfall. The change was indeed agreeable, for though the snow on the elevated table ridges, of which the sides of the river are here formed, rarely exceeded two feet in depth, our horses were frequently engulfed in wading through the *drift* which was collected on the margins of these plateaux. The river in this day's march held its course for upwards of a mile, through a narrow strait not more than forty yards across in its widest part, and walled throughout the whole distance by perpendicular banks eighty feet high. On emerging from this gut the ravine opened, and resumed its old character.

In the afternoon, a party of men were descried watching us from a height, about a mile in advance. A halt was immediately called, and after the Kirghiz of our party had reconnoitred the strangers attentively, a scout was sent forward to observe them more narrowly, while we dismounted and prepared our fire-arms. Much to our satisfaction, the spy made the signal for friends, on which we pushed forward to meet them. They were a party of Kirghiz, who had left Langer Kish three weeks before us, charged with letters from Mohamed Rahim Khán to their brethren on the Khoord, or Little Pamir. Having executed their commission, they were now on their way to Wakhan. We found that it was to these men we had been indebted for the comparative ease with which we had hitherto journeyed. Their tracks in the snow had been carefully followed by our party, who were thus saved the disheartening toil of forcing a path through an unbroken, though imperfectly, frozen surface. After parting with these strangers, we arrived at a copse of red willows; and as no other opportunity of procuring firewood would offer between it and the head of the Oxus, we halted, and cut down, or rather dug out from under the snow, as much fuel as our already jaded horses could carry. The bushes were stunted, the tallest not much exceeding the height of a man, and they extended for a quarter of a mile along the banks of the river, in a patch of swampy ground. It was dark before we reached the spot which our guides had selected for the night's bivouac; but we were now on the Kirghiz ground, with every inch of which they seemed familiar. Quitting the river, they struck into a lateral defile to our left, and after winding up it for another hour, pointed to a cold, ugly looking spot, buried three feet deep in snow, as our quarters for the night. We remonstrated, at which the Kirghiz laughed, and, seizing their wooden shovels, soon drew from the soil below an ample store of firing, in the shape of sheep's and camels' dung. The eligibility of the place for a night's lodging was now past dispute; no other recommendation was necessary; and what with the fire we were thus enabled to keep up through the night, and the high and warm snow-walls that soon encircled our wintry habitation, we had all great reason to thank our escort for bringing us to such a favoured spot.

The unmounted portion of our party did not reach the camping ground till near midnight, and then so exhausted and way-worn as to render it evident that they would not be able to proceed on the morrow. It was therefore determined that they should be left behind us, to hunt in this neighbourhood till our return, and to look after a *cache* of provision, which was here formed. The height of this station above the sea was 13,500 feet.

On the following morning we retraced our steps to the river, the icy surface of which offered an admirable road. For a great portion of this day's march, the bottom of the valley was bare of snow, or but partially spotted with it, and this was the more remarkable from its lying so deep, further down the durah. We saw numbers of horns strewed about in every direction, the spoils of the Kirghiz hunter. Some of these were of an astonishingly large size, and belonged to an animal of a species between the goat and sheep, inhabiting the steppes of Pamir. The ends of the horns projecting above the snow, often indicated the direction of the road; and wherever they were heaped in large quantities and disposed in a semi-circle, there our escort recognised the site of a Kirghiz' summer encampment. Our keen-sighted guides again pitched on an old haunt for a resting-place, and to their practical sagacity we were indebted for a repetition of the comforts of the preceding night. We here found ourselves to be 14,400 feet above the sea.[1]

When about to resume our journey on the following day, a majority of the escort murmured at proceeding further, and coolly requested to be left behind. I endeavoured in a good-humoured tone to reason with the defaulters; failing in this, I next tried the efficacy of upbraiding them with their unmanly conduct; but to such a rascally set shame was unknown, and though I managed to work myself into a towering passion, it produced no corresponding effect on the knaves. The more violent my language, and the more bitter my taunts, the more doggedly did they adhere to their resolution. With those, therefore, of the party who remained true, we were fain to set forward, ere disaffection should have further thinned our ranks. Two of the Kirghiz were among the faithful; and as the object of our search was reported to be only twenty-one miles distant, we cared little about the strength of our party, so that it contained a person qualified to lead us to the goal. The cause of this secession soon became apparent. The snow track which I have mentioned, and in which we had hitherto conveniently enough trodden, struck off, towards the close of the preceding day's march, over the hills on our left to the plain of Khoord Pamir, which lay beyond them, after which we had to force our own way up the main defile, and this labour the coward deserters would not face.

We had no occasion to remark the absence of snow this day for every step we advanced it lay deeper and deeper; and near

---

[1] Probably the Ovis Poli, a name given by Mr. Blyth in honour of Marco Polo, who first mentioned the animal. Reference to his description of Wakhan will show that he also noted the Kirghiz habit of marking the path by these enormous horns when snow was on the ground.

as we had now approached to the source of the Oxus, we should not have succeeded in reaching it had not the river been frozen. We were fully two hours in forcing our way through a field of snow not five hundred yards in extent. Each individual of the party by turns took the lead, and forced his horse to struggle onward until exhaustion brought it down in the snow, where it was allowed to lie and recruit whilst the next was urged forward. It was so great a relief when we again got upon the river, that in the elasticity of my spirits I pushed my pony to a trot. This a Wakhani perceiving, seized hold of the bridle, and cautioned me against the *wind of the mountain*. We had, indeed, felt the effects of a highly rarefied atmosphere ever since leaving Wakhan; but the ascent being gradual, they were less than what would be experienced in climbing an abrupt mountain of much less altitude.

As we neared the head waters of the Oxus the ice became weak and brittle. The sudden disappearance of a yabu gave us the first warning of this. Though the water was deep where the accident occurred, there fortunately was little current, and, as the animal was secured by his halter to a companion, he was extricated, but his furniture and lading were lost. The kind-hearted Khirakush to whom the animal belonged wrapped him in felts, took off his own warm posteen, and bound it round the shivering brute. Had it been his son instead of his yabu, he could not have passed a more anxious night as to the effects of this ducking. The next morning, however, the yabu was alive and well, and the good mule-driver was most eloquent in his thanks to Providence for its preservation.

Shortly after this accident we came in sight of a rough-looking building, decked out with horns of the wild sheep, and all but buried amongst the snow. It was a Kirghiz burial-ground. On coming abreast of it, the leading horseman, who chanced to be of that tribe, pulled up and dismounted. His companion followed his example, and wading through the deep drift they reached a tombstone, the top of which was uncovered. Before this they knelt, all cumbered as they were, and with their huge forked matchlocks strapped to their backs; and offered up prayers to the ever-present Jehovah. The whole of the party involuntarily reined in their horses till the two men had concluded their devotions. The stillness of the scene, the wild and wintry aspect of the place, with the absence of all animated nature save these devotees and ourselves, were not unimpressive to a reflecting mind. They forcibly told us that man must have something beyond this life on which to rest his hopes, and that the sight of a brother's grave should remind him of his own fleeting existence; and that, when surrounded with difficulties and perils, he should appeal to that Being in whose hands he believes his destinies to be.

After quitting the surface of the river we travelled about an hour along its right bank, and then ascended a low hill, which apparently bounded the valley to the eastward; on surmounting this, at five o'clock in the afternoon of the 19th of February, 1838, we stood, to use a native expression, upon the *Bam-i-Dúniah*, or "*Roof of the World*," while before us lay stretched a noble but frozen sheet of water, from whose western end issued the infant river of the Oxus. This fine lake lies in the form of a crescent, about fourteen miles long from east to west, by an average breadth of one mile. On three sides it is bordered by swelling hills, about 500 feet high, whilst along its southern bank they rise into mountains 3,500 feet above the lake, or 19,000 above the sea, and covered with perpetual snow, from which never-failing source the lake is supplied. From observations at the western end I found the latitude to be 37° 27″ N. by mer. alt. of the sun, and longitude 73° 40′ E. by protraction from Langer Kish, where the last set of chronometric observations had been obtained; its elevation, measured by the temperature of boiling water, is 15,600 feet—as my thermometer marked 184° of Fahrenheit. The temperature of the water below the ice was 32°—the freezing-point.

This, then, is the position of the sources of this celebrated river, which, after a course of upwards of a thousand miles in a direction generally north-west, falls into the southern end of the sea of Aral. As I had the good fortune to be the first European who in later times had succeeded in reaching the sources of this river, and as, shortly before setting out on my journey, we had received the news of her gracious Majesty's accession to the throne, I was much tempted to apply the name of Victoria to this, if I may so term it, newly re-discovered lake; but on considering that by thus introducing a new name, however honoured, into our maps, great confusion in geography might arise, I deemed it better to retain the name of Sir-i-kol, the appellation given to it by our guides.[1] The description of this spot given by that good old traveller Marco Polo, nearly six centuries ago, is so correct in all its leading points, that I have deemed it right to subjoin a considerable portion of it.[2]

The hills and mountains that encircle Sir-i-kol give rise to some of the principal rivers in Asia. From the ridge at its

---

[1] Probably so called by the guides, as Sir Henry Rawlinson has suggested, because the valley leading to it is known as the Durah-i-Sirikol; but this name, as applied to the lake, is not recognised by later native travellers, some of whom designate it as *the lake of Great Pamir*, and others as *the lake of Sikander*, i.e. *Alexander*. In future maps it might with advantage bear the appellation given it by its first discoverer, not only without causing geographical confusion, which he feared, but actually tending to remove it.

[2] Leaving the province of Balashan (Badakhshan), and travelling in a direction between N.E. and E., you pass many castles and habitations on the banks of the river belonging to the brother of the king of that place, and after three days' journey reach a province named Vokan (Wakhan). Upon leaving this country and proceeding for three days, still in an E.N.E. course, ascending mountain after mountain, you at length arrive at a point of the road where you might suppose the surrounding summits to be the highest land in the world. Here, between two ranges, you perceive a large lake, from which flows a handsome river that pursues its course along an extensive plain covered with the richest verdure. Such, indeed, is its quality, that the leanest cattle turned upon it would become fat in the course of ten days. In this plain there are wild animals in great numbers, particularly sheep of a large size, having horns three, four, and even six, palms in length. Of these the shepherds form ladles and vessels for holding their victuals; and with the same materials they construct fences for enclosing their cattle and securing them against the wolves, with which they say the country is infested, and which likewise destroy many of the wild sheep or goats. Their horns and bones being found in large quantities, heaps are made of them at the side of the road, for the purpose of guiding the travellers at the season when it is covered with snow. For twelve days the course is along this elevated plain, which is named *Pamer*. So great is the height of the mountains that no birds are to be seen near their summits; and, however extraordinary it may be thought, it was affirmed that, from the keenness of the air, fires when lighted do not give the same heat as in lower situations, nor produce the same effect in dressing victuals.—"Travels of Marco Polo," translated from the Italian by Wm. Marsden. London, 1818.

east end flows a branch of the Yarkand river, one of the largest streams that waters China, while from its low hills on the northern side rises the Sirr or river of Kokan, and from the snowy chain opposite both forks of the Oxus, as well as a branch of the river Kunar, are supplied. When the lake is swollen by the melted snow of summer, the size of the infant river is correspondingly increased, and no great alteration takes place in the level of the lake itself.

The aspect of the landscape was wintry in the extreme. Wherever the eye fell one dazzling sheet of snow carpeted the ground, while the sky overhead was everywhere of a dark and angry hue. Clouds would have been a relief to the eye; but they were wanting. Not a breath moved along the surface of the lake; not a beast, nor even a bird, was visible. The sound of a human voice would have been music to the ear, but no one at this inhospitable season thinks of invading these gelid domains. Silence reigned around—silence so profound that it oppressed the heart, and, as I contemplated the hoary summits of the everlasting mountains, where human foot had never trod, and where lay piled the snows of ages, my own dear country and all the social blessings it contains passed across my mind with a vividness of recollection that I had never felt before. It is all very well for men in crowded cities to be disgusted with the world and to talk of the delights of solitude. Let them but pass one twenty-four hours on the banks of the Sir-i-kol, and it will do more to make them contented with their lot than a thousand arguments. Man's proper sphere is society; and, let him abuse it as he will, this busy, bustling world is a brave place, in which, thanks to a kind Providence, the happiness enjoyed by the human race far exceeds the misery. So, at least, it has always appeared to me.

In walking over the lake I could not but reflect how many countries owe their importance and their wealth to rivers the sources of which can be traced to the lonely mountains which are piled up on its southern margin. This elevated chain is common to India, China, and Turkistan; and from it, as from a central point, their several streams diverge, each augmenting as it rolls onwards, until the ocean and the lake of Aral receive the swollen tribute, again to be given up, and in a circuit as endless as it is wonderful to be swept back by the winds of Heaven, and showered down in snowy flakes upon the self-same mountains from which it flowed.

How strange and how interesting a group would be formed if an individual from each nation whose rivers have their first source in Pamir were to meet upon its summit; what varieties would there be in person, language, and manners; what contrasts between the rough, untamed, and fierce mountaineer and the more civilised and effeminate dweller on the plain; how much of virtue and of vice, under a thousand different aspects, would be met with among them all; and how strongly would the conviction press upon the mind that the amelioration of the whole could result only from the diffusion of early education and a purer religion!

Pamir is not only a radiating point in the hydrographical system of Central Asia, but it is the focus from which originate its principal mountain-chains. The plain along the southern side of which the lake is situated has a width of about three miles; and viewed from this elevated plateau the mountains seem to have no great elevation. The table-land of Pamir is, as I have already stated, 15,600 feet high, or sixty-two feet lower than the summit of Mont Blanc; but the height of 3,400 feet, which I have assigned to the mountains that rise from this elevated basis, is a matter of assumption only. Where nothing but snow meets the eye it is not easy to appreciate heights and distances correctly; and it is therefore not improbable that the dimensions thus assigned to Sir-i-kol may be subsequently found incorrect. Covered as both the land and water were with snow, it was impossible to tell the exact size; the measurements given were obtained from the Kirghiz, who were familiar with the spot, assisted by my own eye. I regret that I omitted to take the necessary trigonometrical observations for determining the altitude of the southern range of mountains. I estimated their height on the spot, and noted down the impression at the moment; but though I had fully intended to have made the measurements on the morrow, it quite escaped me in my anxiety to fix the geographical position of the lake, nor did I discover the omission until our arrival in Wakhan.

The Wakhanis name this plain Bam-i-Dúniah, or "Roof of the World," and it would indeed appear to be the highest table-land in Asia, and probably in any part of our globe. From Pamir the ground sinks in every direction except to the south-east, where similar plateaux extend along the northern face of the Himalaya into Tibet. An individual who had seen the region between Wakhan and Kashmir informed me that the Kunar river had its principal source in a lake resembling that in which the Oxus has its rise, and that the whole of this country, comprehending the districts of Gilgit, Gunjit, and Chitral, is a series of mountain defiles that act as water-courses to drain Pamir.

As early in the morning of Tuesday the 20th February as the cold permitted we walked out about 600 yards upon the lake, and, having cleared the snow from a portion of its surface, commenced breaking the ice to ascertain its depth. This was a matter of greater difficulty than it at first sight appeared, for the water was frozen to the depth of two feet and a half, and, owing to the great rarity of the atmosphere, a few strokes of the pick-axe produced an exhaustion that stretched us upon the snow to recruit our breath. By dint, however, of unwearied exertions and frequent reliefs, we had all but carried the shaft through, when an imprudent stroke fractured its bottom, and up the water jetted to the height of a man, sending us scampering off in all directions. This opening was too small to admit our sounding-lead, and had of necessity to be abandoned; besides, a wet jacket where the thermometer is at zero is a much more serious affair than where it is at summer-heat. We resolved to be more circumspect in our next attempt, and diligent search having revealed to us a large stone upon an islet in the lake, it was forthwith transported to the scene of our labours. When, judging by the depth of the first shaft, we concluded the second to be nearly through, the stone was raised and upheld by four men immediately above the hole. A fifth man continued to ply the axe, and at the first appearance of water the stone was dropped in and went clean through the ice, leaving an aperture its own size, and from this larger orifice there was no rush of water. The sounding-lead was immediately thrown in, when, much to my surprise and disappointment, it struck bottom at nine feet, and we had prepared and brought with us from Langer Kish a hundred fathoms of line for the experiment.

The water emitted a slightly fetid smell and was of a reddish tinge. The bottom was oozy and tangled with grassy weeds. I tried to measure the breadth of the lake by sound, but was baffled by the rarity of the air. A musket, loaded with blank cartridge, sounded as if the charge had been poured into the barrel, and neither wads nor ramrod used. When ball was introduced the report was louder, but possessed none of the sharpness that marks a similar charge in denser atmospheres. The ball, however, could be distinctly heard whizzing through the air. The human voice was sensibly affected, and conversation, especially if in a loud tone, could not be kept up without exhaustion: the slightest muscular exertion was attended with a similar result. Half a dozen strokes with an axe brought the workman to the ground; and though a few minutes' respite sufficed to restore the breath, anything like continued exertion was impossible. A run of fifty yards at full speed made the runner gasp for breath. Indeed, this exercise produced a pain in the lungs and a general prostration of strength which was not got rid of for many hours. Some of the party complained of dizziness and headaches; but, except the effects above described, I neither felt myself, nor perceived in others, any of those painful results of great elevation which travellers have suffered in ascending Mont Blanc. This might have been anticipated, for where the transition from a dense to a highly-rarefied atmosphere is so sudden, as in the case of ascending that mountain the circulation cannot be expected to accommodate itself at once to the difference of pressure, and violence must accrue to some of the more sensitive organs of the body. The ascent to Pamir was, on the contrary, so gradual that some extrinsic circumstances were necessary to remind us of the altitude we had attained. The effect of great elevation upon the general system had indeed been proved to me some time before in a manner for which I was not prepared. One evening in Badakhshan, while sitting in a brown study over the fire, I chanced to touch my pulse, and the galloping rate at which it was throbbing roused my attention. I at once took it for granted that I was in a raging fever, and after perusing some hints on the preservation of health which Dr. Lord, at parting, had kindly drawn out for me, I forthwith prescribed for myself most liberally. Next morning my pulse was as brisk as ever, but still my feelings denoted health. I now thought of examining the wrists of all our party, and to my surprise found that the pulses of my companions beat yet faster than my own. The cause of this increased circulation immediately occurred to me; and when we afterwards commenced marching towards Wakhan I felt the pulses of the party whenever I registered the boiling-point of water. The motion of the blood is in fact a sort of living barometer by which a man acquainted with his own habit of body can, in great altitudes, roughly calculate his height above the sea. Upon Pamir the pulsations in one minute were as follow:—

	Throbs.	Country.	Habit of body.
My own	110	Scotland	spare
Gholam Hussein, Munshi	124	Jasulmeree	fat
Omerallah, mule-driver	112	Afghan	spare
Gaffer, groom	114	Peshawuree	spare
Dowd, do.	124	Kabuli	stout

The danger we incurred in sleeping literally amongst the snow, in the middle of winter, at the great elevation of 15,600 feet, did not occur to me at the time; we were most fortunate in having done so with impunity. Fatal accidents from this very cause are of frequent occurrence in the Himalaya, as we learn from the late Capt. Alexander Gerard's narrative.[1] But, indeed, that drowsiness, which cold engenders, and which ends in death, has been made familiar to us all by the interesting voyages of Capt. Cook. The misfortunes that befel Dr. Solander and his botanising party in Tierra-del-Fuego is as touchingly told an incident as any in that attractive work.

---

[1] See "Narrative of a Journey from Cawnpoor to the Himalaya Mountains," by Major Sir William Lloyd and Gerard. Madden and Co., London.

Our escape is, under Providence, to be attributed to the oceans of tea we drank. The kettle was never off the fire when we were encamped; indeed, throughout the whole of our wanderings, except when feasted in Jerm, the Munshi and myself lived almost entirely upon it. We used the decoction, not the infusion, and always brewed it strong. Another preservative was the firing we kept up and the precaution of sleeping with our feet towards it.

The height of the snow-line in this parallel is above 17,000 feet. As I visited Pamir in the winter season I could not myself have ocular demonstration of this interesting fact; but that the ice upon the lake is broken up, and the hills in its neighbourhood clear of snow, by the end of June, are facts in which my informants, the Kirghiz, could not possibly be mistaken. At that season, it is said, the water swarms with aquatic birds, which, as the winter approaches, migrate to warmer regions: many are killed by the cold. The lake is a favourite resort of the Kirghiz, and no sooner is the snow off the ground than its banks are studded with their kirgahs. A spot better adapted to the wants of a pastoral community cannot well be imagined, and the hordes that frequent it seem fully to appreciate its advantages, since they are never weary of expatiating upon them. The grass of Pamir, they tell you, is so rich, that a sorry horse is here brought into good condition in less than twenty days; and its nourishing qualities are evidenced in the productiveness of their ewes, which almost invariably bring forth two lambs at a birth. Their flocks and herds roam over an unlimited extent of swelling grassy hills of the sweetest and richest pasture, while their yaks luxuriate amid the snow at no great distance above their encampment on the plains.[1]

After getting a clear and beautiful meridian altitude of the sun on the 20th, we saddled, and casting a last look at Lake Sir-i-kol, entered the defile leading to Wakhan. As we increased our distance from Pamir, the hillocks on each side

---

[1] We find Marco Polo, who seems to have allowed little to escape him, commenting also upon the wonderful properties of the forage grown in this lofty region.

gradually rose in altitude, till at the end of twenty-one miles we had descended by an inclined plane 1200 feet, and the mountains on our left hand were of that height. That which most forcibly strikes a traveller in these regions is the total absence of wood—the nakedness of the country. There are no timber-yielding trees indigenous to the Hindú Kosh, in which appellation I include the range from its first rise in Pamir to its termination at Koh-i-baba, a remarkable mountain to the northwest of Kabul. In making this assertion I should except the Archa, a dwarfish fir, which never equals in size its congeners of the Himalayan forest. It serves, however, for the building purposes of the natives, and is too valuable to be used as fuel. The poplar is seen by the sides of most rivulets, but never in great numbers, and always in localities which indicate that man has placed it there. The same may be said of fruit-bearing trees, except the almond and pistachio-nut, which are evidently natives of the lower portions of the Hindú Kosh, and more especially of the secondary ranges on the northern face of the chain. The willow of many varieties, loving a cold, moist soil, is found margining every stream, and in Durah Sir-i-kol this hardy plant was seen at an altitude of 13,000 feet. There, however, and long before that height was attained, it should be termed a bush rather than a tree. Fruit-bearing trees, of the plum species, were found at Langer Kish at 10,800 feet above the sea. The height to which the ground is cultivated by man I could not ascertain, the snow being upon its surface, though, from the nature of the soil upon Pamir, I can see no reason why a hasty harvest should not be reaped even there. But the Kirghiz abstain from agricultural pursuits; and it is certain the Wakhanis, for such a purpose, would not venture so high. The fuel in use throughout these mountains is a scrubby description of furze-bush, which has but little of woody fibre in it; and in the higher districts the fire-places are adapted solely to this description of fuel. The willow also is used for firing; and when the more affluent burn charcoal, it is prepared either from the archa or the almond-tree. That obtained from the latter is much the best.

In speaking of the Hindú Kosh range of mountains in contradistinction to the Himalaya, it may be well to define both chains. The latter, as is well known, bounds Hindustan on the north, and after crossing the river Indus extends westward to the valley of Panchshir and the meridian of Kabul. The other chain I have before described. They are connected by numerous lateral ridges, and evidently belong to the same great system of the Himalayan-Tartaric mountains, which extend both to the east and west beyond the limits to which my experience reaches. Hindú Kosh is their northern wall, Himalaya is the southern one. The former, however, would appear to be the superior ridge, since it divides the waters of Central Asia from those which flow south. It is one continuous chain; while, on the contrary, the Himalaya is pierced by both the Kuner and Indus rivers; and no stream that has its rise in this range runs towards the north.

On arriving at the station where we had left the hunters we were agreeably surprised to find they had been successful in the chase, and had slaughtered a *Kutch-kar*, or wild sheep. It was a noble animal, standing as high as a two-year-old colt, with a venerable beard, and two splendid curling horns, which, with the head, were so heavy as to require a considerable exertion to lift them. Though in poor condition, the carcase, divested of offal, was a load for a baggage-pony. Its flesh was tough and ill-tasted; but we were told that in autumn, when the animal is in prime condition, no venison is better flavoured. The *Kutch-kar* is gregarious, congregating in herds of several hundreds. They are of a dun colour, the skin more resembling the hide of a cow than the fleece of a sheep. There is another animal peculiar to Pamir, named *Rass* by the Khirghiz: it differs from the *Kutch-kar*, having straight spiral horns, and its dun colour being of a redder tinge; but this species we did not meet with.[1]

---

[1] The following is the measurement of a pair of horns of the Ovis Poli or Rass, forwarded to the Royal Society by Captain Wood.

	Ft.	in.
Length of horn following curvature	4	8
Size round the base		14¼
Distance apart at tips of horns	3	0

In the opinion of Mr. Blyth the Rass referred to in the narrative is probably the Markbur, an animal also found in the hills of Badakhshan, as the description of the horns agrees with specimens of those of the latter animal, while the true Rass (Ovis Poli), the horns of which were forwarded, and

The only other quadrupeds we observed were wolves, foxes, and hares; and of birds we saw but one. It was, however, a regal bird; a fine black eagle, which came sailing over the valley, flapping his huge wings as if they were too heavy for his body.

On the evening of the fourth day after quitting the source of the Oxus we were again housed in Langer Kish, which, considering the nature of the ground, was tolerable travelling, the distance being upwards of seventy miles.

---

of which dimensions are given above, appears to have been confounded with the species described under the denomination of Kutchkar. The great sheep of Pamir has within the last few years been shot in the Western Thian Shan by M. Severtzoff.

CHAPTER XXII.

Wakhan.—Population.—Mohamed Rahim Khan.—Sources of revenue.—Slave dealing.—Its evil tendencies.—Descendants of Alexander the Great.—Physical characteristics of the Wakhanis.—Their dress and appearance.—Vanity of the sex.—Domestic Animals.—Crops and seasons.—Houses.—Stoves.—Fires.—Pine slips.—Matrimonial squalls.—Roshan.—Shagnan.—Darwaz.—Wandering Fakír.—A singing entertainment.—Spring.—Changed aspect of the landscape. —The Edd.—Arrival at Kunduz.

THE district of Wakhan embraces the main valley of the Oxus, from Ish-kashm upwards, and the durahs of Sirhad and Sir-i-kol. Population is confined to the two first regions, the last, as the preceding narrative will have shown, being, throughout the greater portion of the year, a dreary, uninhabitable waste. The total number of souls ruled by Mír Mohamed Rahim did not exceed one thousand: were its poor soil and scanty pasture turned to the best advantage, it might possibly supply with food five times that number. At present it does not produce sufficient grain for its own consumption, the deficiency being imported from countries lying lower down the valley of the Oxus. In former times, when a considerable trade passed through Wakhan, the Mír drew a small revenue by taxing in kind the Yarkand Kafilas, for which he escorted them from the southern limits of his territories to the east end of lake Sir-i-kol, where the Chinese frontier begins. This was an exaction on the part of Mohamed Rahim, since, for this very protection, the chief of Kunduz previously levied fifteen rupees on each camel-load. However, the allegiance of the mountain chief has always been dubious, and though nominally a feudatory of Kunduz, he is virtually independent. The merchants might indeed have remonstrated against this exaction, but they knew their own interest better.

R 2

Another source of income to the ruler of Wakhan is from his slaves. It is disgusting to see the subterfuges and hypocrisy, to which men resort to circumvent their neighbours.

The laws of their Prophet do not admit the making of slaves, but the Mohamedans get over the difficulty by calling their victims proselytes. The beautiful moral axiom that we must not do evil that good may accrue is quite overlooked, and the Sunis of Tartary affect to have reasoned themselves into the pious belief, that in enslaving their heretical brethren they perform an acceptable service to God and to Mohamed.

Avarice gets the better of controversy, and we find the Wakhanis who are of the Shiah belief assuming, in their intercourse with Kunduz, the tenets of an opposite sect; cursing the son-in-law of the Prophet, and lauding to the skies the three first caliphs. By such detestable means they compound with their conscience, and steel their minds to enslave the natives of the Shakh durah, a mountain defile immediately north of Wakhan, who are of their own creed. With the Uzbeks they are Sunis, at home Shiahs; but as some apology for them, it should be remembered that the detestable doctrines of the latter sect not only pardon but enforce dissimulation. The unhappy wretches who are thus enslaved are bartered with the Uzbeks of Kunduz for horses, and are again sold by them to Shah Kittore, the Chitral ruler, at an advance of fifty per cent.

The chief of Wakhan traced his ancestry to Alexander the Great, a descent, whether fabulous or true, of which he was not a little vain. Mohamed Rahim considered his illustrious lineage a fact which none dare dispute, and indeed his neighbours spoke with equal confidence of his high claim. This honour, as other travellers have remarked, is not confined to Wakhan, but is one to which the rulers of Badakhshan, Darwaz, and Chitral, are also aspirants. The representative of Badakhshan we have already described; but on subsequent inquiry in Jerm, we discovered his only title to Grecian lineage rested on an intermarriage with the royal family of Chitral, the blood of which is supposed to be particularly noble, and therefore as a matter of course must flow from Hazrat Zekunder, whom, be it observed, the Mohamedans have canonised. Shag-

nan and Roshan, two mountain districts in the valley of the
Oxus immediately south of Darwaz, demand for their rulers
the same classic lineage; but the Mullahs, who alone are given
to antiquarian research, assert that their right to such a
splendid ancestry rests on no better foundation than does that
of the fallen house of Badakhshan. Among a rude and half
savage people, not given to chronicle their doings, and with
whom books and men to read them are equally rare, we would
search in vain for valid evidence, either in support or refutation
of these pretensions. Being, however, on the spot, I deemed
it right to inquire into this prevailing tradition, which the
Honourable Mr. Elphinstone, and subsequent travellers, have
upon more remote information given to the public; and I will
add a few words on the physical appearance of these true or
pseudo Greeks. Of fifteen Wakhanis whom we measured, the
tallest stood 5 feet $7\frac{1}{4}$ inches; the shortest, 5 feet $1\frac{3}{4}$ inches.
The men are much tanned by exposure to all weathers; they
have nothing peculiar in their facial line, nor in the colour of
their eyes and hair, but in every feature bear a strong resemblance to Tajiks. They wear chupkuns of wool, with
posteens of untanned sheep-skins. Those who can afford it
have turbans, but the greater number are content with caps
fitting close to the head. Their garments being tattered and
sadly out of repair, give them a savage, reckless air; nor does
their appearance belie their disposition. The women wear long
white woollen gowns, and those who can procure it tie a piece
of cotton cloth about the head. They are by no means backward in expressing their wishes on the all-important subject of
dress. Among the articles which we had brought with us for
barter, were a few handkerchiefs made from the silk called
lub-i-ab, the produce of worms reared on the banks of the Oxus.
These and ornamented chupkuns were intended as presents for
the chiefs. But the daughter of a miller with whom we were
lodging chanced to espy one of the smart handkerchiefs, and as
a matter of course asked for it. She was refused; but next day
resumed her suit, and by way of temptation, handed me a lump
of sicee or Chinese silver, weighing about a quarter of a pound.
The young woman had set her heart upon the handkerchief,

but it was not deemed prudent to gratify her taste for finery; and as for the silver, I feigned as great a contempt for the precious metal as the unsophisticated girl had shown. To these poorly clad mountaineers coarse fabrics were more useful, and of such, both in bartering for our food and in presents, we had occasion to distribute a considerable quantity. The flocks of the Wakhani constitute his riches, or rather enable him to endure the ills to which his bleak high-lying valley exposes him. The skin and fleece of the sheep supply him with every article of dress, in preparing which, both women and men find their winter's employment. The women clean and spin the wool, while the men weave it into cloth. The valuable wool of Tibet, from which the costly shawls of Kashmir are fabricated, or at least a wool that has all its good qualities, is yielded by the goat of Wakhan.

The Wakhan dogs differ much from those of India, and bear a strong resemblance to the Scotch colly. They have long ears, a bushy tail, and a frame somewhat slender, and more calculated for swiftness than strength. They are very fierce, make excellent watchers, and will fight dogs twice their own weight. Their prevailing colours are black, or a reddish brown; the latter often mottled. The breed is from Chitral, and so highly are their game qualities valued, that the Sind Amirs, who are great followers of the chase, have their packs improved by importations from this country. The double-humped camel I had always supposed to be the native of Uzbek Tartary; but we here learned that it is bred only among the Kirghiz of Pamir and Kokan.

The principal crops in Wakhan are peas and barley. Wheat is likewise grown, but only to a very limited extent. In April the seed is put into the ground, and in July the harvest is reaped. The land requires to be irrigated, and to yield even a moderate crop must be richly manured. The strong wind that blows with little intermission throughout the winter and spring, down the valley of the Oxus, is unfavourable to vegetation.

The houses resemble those in Badakhshan, except that, instead of the central fire-place, they have large stoves after the Russian fashion. These occupy an entire side of the house, and throw out so general a warmth, that when once you have fairly domesticated yourself under a Wakhani's humble roof, you are unwilling to quit such comfortable quarters. The smoke is somewhat annoying; but the nearer you lie to the floor, the less of it you inhale. To me a wood-fire is more agreeable than a coal one. I loved to hear its cheerful crackling sound, and to feed it during the long hours that we were compelled to remain in-doors was my delight; not that we needed its warmth, but the sight of its long tongues of flame, frisking and roaring under the good wife's enormous pot, induced a contented and happy state of mind, to which a knowledge of the good things it contained might probably no little contribute. It is not uncommon for six families to live together; not in separate apartments as in Badakhshan, but in one, or at most two rooms. As night draws on, the Wakhani pulls down a dry branch of the willow tree out of the many bundles suspended beneath his rafters, and putting one end of the branch to his breast, while the other is held by his wife's foot, takes his knife from his girdle, and with both hands sheaves from off the rod as many lengths as he conjectures will last through the evening. These resinous slips are then deposited above the lintel of the inner door; and they answer all the purposes of an oil lamp or candle.

By the 1st of March we had reached Ish-kashm on our return to Kunduz, and put up in a house, where we had ample opportunity of learning that the matrimonial state is not all sunshine even among Mohamedans; upon whom, in such matters, their Prophet's intended kindness has entailed much misery. Of all the trials which assail a human being in his course from infancy to the grave, I should think a good perfect specimen of a scold of a wife must be the greatest. If a man, whose mind is harassed by contact with the world, have a happy fireside of his own, he soon forgets the rubs of the business day in the comfort in store for him at home. But if he comes into a house where a vixen of a wife galls his very soul with bitter taunts and reproaches, what chance is there for him? Of this calamity, the house in which we lodged at Ish-kashm offered a very striking example. Our host, a young, good-looking, merry fellow, was tethered to a perfect termagant of a wife. She was a manumitted slave of Afghan extraction. He knew nothing of her temper before marriage, but on being introduced to the father foolishly agreed to take his daughter to wife; and as the poor fellow dolefully expressed himself, "On that ill-fated day she seized me by the throat, and has held fast ever since. But," added he (in a half whisper, and by the motion of his hand warning us that his better half was not far distant,) "never mind, never mind, I am making love to a young woman in the next village, a pretty gentle soul, and when the affair is all settled I will break the matter to my wife. If she heard of my intentions now, my life would not be safe. Did she only bite I could live with her, for teeth can be extracted; but, oh the tongue! the tongue! there never was a husband yet could get rid of that." The lady was called *Gool dustah*, or the nosegay; and with reference to this sweet name, the good-humoured facetious husband gave loose to his wit, till he had almost convulsed us with laughter.

It is a mistake to suppose that with Moslems the women have no power. They have, to the full, as much influence in their own house as our fair countrywomen; and not a few, especially in Afghanistan, have become honourably conspicuous by the wisdom with which they guide their husbands' affairs. The wife of Jabar Khán, brother to the late ruler of Kabul, was a well known instance. For a long time she had the entire management of his estates; and since her death the worthy Nawab's exchequer has not been so well filled, nor his influence with Dost Mohamed and the Afghans what it formerly was.

Ish-kashm is the southern entrance to the districts of Roshan, Shagnan, and Darwaz. The season of the year rendered it impossible for me to visit those countries; but I deem it right briefly to give such particulars regarding them as I was enabled to collect. All the three are situated in the valley of the Oxus; and below Wakhan, which, as the reader must already be aware, is the uppermost peopled district on that river. They are passed through by the traveller who descends the stream in the order in which I have named them. They are all strong countries, accessible only at midsummer, and even then the passes are treacherous. Five years ago, during an expedition into Shagnan, Murad Beg in the middle of summer lost nearly one hundred troopers in a snow-fall. When the Oxus is frozen, the best entrance to them is by the river from Ish-kashm, by way of Gharan, and the ruby mines. There is said to be a lake in Shagnan, half a day's journey in circumference, which drains the country on the left bank of the Panj, as the Oxus is here called. A stream sufficient to turn two mills runs from this lake into the river. The three countries abound in stone-fruit, and the mulberry is also plentiful in them all. Their crops are wheat and barley. The Kirghiz camel is the beast of burden; the cow and sheep, both of the usual description, constitute their stock. Horses are not numerous. In Roshan and Shagnan the inhabitants are Shiahs, their dress is similar to that of the Wakhanis, and they occupy the same description of houses. Shagnan now contains about 300 families, but before it was chuppowed by Murad Beg, it could boast of nearly one thousand. Roshan is more populous, and still holds about the last-mentioned number of families. The two districts pay a joint tribute to Kunduz of fifteen slaves, and receive presents in return, of nearly equal value. Their language is a dialect peculiar to themselves. Darwaz is independent of Kunduz, and the intercourse between them is confined to the exchange of presents. This country is exceedingly mountainous, and its dizzy paths can only be traversed by footmen. Cotton is grown on what little soil there is. Made into cloth, it forms an article of export; in return for which they receive grain and gunpowder. All its villages are situated on the banks of the Oxus. The Shah or King keeps up some show of state, and a large force—large at least when compared with the troops of his weaker neighbours. The natives of Darwaz are Tajiks, and most of them Suni Mohamedans. Their language is Persian. To the north-north-east of this state is the district of Karategein, which vacillates in its allegiance between Kokan and Kunduz.

On the 2nd of March we passed, by the Kotul of Ish-kashm, out of the valley of the Oxus, into that of the Wardodj, a tributary of the Kokcha. Here we met an Indian fakír wending his solitary way to Wakhan, where he intended remaining until the summer sun should open the passes to

Shagnan. Scantily clad in the skin of a tiger, or of some other wild beast, these devotees pass unharmed. No one would injure a Callender. He is a welcome guest at every hamlet, and, like the Gaberlunzie of Scotland, in a former age, he is the grand newsvender in regions rarely visited but by himself.

Once again in Badakhshan, Abdal Ghaní resumed the authority which he had wisely permitted to lie dormant during our abode in Wakhan. The Aksakál (or elder) was directed to convene the people, and organise a singing entertainment for the amusement of the Mír's Yesawal. We were present, and partook of the festivity. The villagers assembled in a large barn-like tenement, with benches round its four sides: a cheerful fire in the centre of the room illumined the countenances of the audience, whilst, in the open space around it, a Chitral youth exhibited the dance of his country, with great strength and activity, and not without some grace. Four men sang in chorus to the sound of the tambourine; and although perhaps the scientific amateur might have discovered a want of taste in the music, the deficiency was compensated for in our opinion by the spirit and correctness with which each performed his part. The hands of the singers were constantly in motion, and their countenances showed that they felt the full force of the words they uttered. Towards the conclusion all present joined in chorus, and the song finished with a sustained shout which somewhat reminded me of the good honest cheer from the one-shilling gods of an English theatre.

As we approached the bottom of the Wardodj valley, everything wore the joyous air of spring. The change was delightful. When we passed up snow lay everywhere. Now the plough was in the field; wild flowers were sparkling amongst the withered herbage of the bygone year; and around the edges of the stones tufts of young grass were everywhere to be seen. The sheep, let loose from their sheds, were remunerating themselves for the dry and scanty fare of their winter's quarters. The streams were all unlocked, and we encamped in the open air. The raven, the jay, the lark, and the *bulbul*, or Badakhshan nightingale, were all upon the wing. Numerous insects, too, aroused from their long sleep, began to show themselves:

among them were butterflies, and a most beautifully painted species of gad-fly.

The effects of winter were evidenced by deep furrows in the bottom of the valley. Now that the snow had thawed we could in many places discern the extensive destruction the frost had caused on the steep flanks of the mountains. From these "elder born of time" large fragments had been detached, and, judging from their position, the force with which they had been washed into the plain must have been immense. The mountain chains of Badakhshan are formed of the older rocks, but they are largely traversed by immense masses of a very impure limestone. It is in this latter formation that the deposits of lapis-lazuli occur. Bordering the Kokcha, mica slate, richly impregnated with iron ore, abounds; and here also asbestos and antimony are occasionally found. The Kokcha, like every other tributary of the Oxus, is fertile in gold.

On the 5th we debouched into the valley of the Kokcha, at Khyrabad. Here a danger of a new kind arose, and it was well for us that it had not shown itself at an earlier period. Our sojourn in Jerm had been, it seems, fatal to the too tender heart of Abdal Ghaní—a damsel in Khyrabad having completely captivated the Mullah. He now proposed marriage, and taking her on with our party to Talikhan. To the union the young lady gave an extremely willing assent; but the very idea of going, as she expressed it, to "the grave of the Badakhshi," the fens of Kunduz, made both her and her parents absolutely shudder. The matter was referred to the Mír of Jerm, and I also was called into council. The Yesawal, in very decisive terms, stated that for him again to leave his adorable mistress was quite out of the question. I was constrained, therefore, to dispense with his further services, which, fortunately, were no longer indispensably necessary to our journey; and as I could not conveniently stand bride's-man on this interesting occasion, I made the blushing fair a present; and leaving Abdal Ghaní displaying all the raptures of a successful lover, we continued our journey.

The weather was cloudy, with a drizzling rain. Still the air was delicious, and gentle showers at the opening of the season could not fail of doing much good to the soil, already renovated by the snow with which it had so long been covered. We again passed through Fyzabad,

> "Where many a garden flower grows wild,"

and, on entering the beautiful lawn at the gorge of its valley, I was enchanted at the quiet loveliness of the scene. Up to this time, from the day we left Talikhan, we had been moving in snow; but now it had nearly vanished from the valley, and the fine sward was enamelled with crocuses, daffodils, and snow-drops.

As we pushed briskly along the Kokcha for the plain of Argu, we could see that the Turk of Badakhshan, true to the habits of his race, had already driven forth his flock, and pitched the kirgah where the pasturage was the sweetest and the best. In one spot several agricultural families had set themselves down, and were employed putting their wheat into the ground. The field they had selected, doubtless for some good reason, was the face of a sloping hill, and not the level arable land in the bottom of the valley. Several donkeys, with salt from Akbolak, passed us here on their way to Jerm.

The plain of Argu still wore its snowy robe, but the southern side of the pass of Taishkhan, though much higher, was uncovered. Here the entire face of the mountain was studded with almond bushes. The fruit of the past year still clung to many of them, while the beautiful bell-blossoms mingled lilac and purple—the germ of this year's growth—shot through the withered leaves which still partially clothed them. The almond, like the mulberry and the pistachio, flowers before its leaves appear.

The 8th of March was the Edd-Kurbani, or the Sacrifice, the day on which Abraham offered up Isaac, or, according to Mohamedans, his brother Ishmael. In Mussulman countries this day is one of great rejoicing; and here the men devote it chiefly to the pleasures of horse-racing. But it is the women who profit most by the Edd-Kurbani. In the valley of Meshid, which we crossed on that day, a large party of females had congregated at one end of the little village, and were in high merriment, enjoying the pleasures of a swing. As we drew near, the principal performer ceased her airy circle, but kept her seat, and from beneath a silk handkerchief eyed the intruders. Seeing that our presence checked their festivity, we turned away, and immediately the young lady was again careering in mid-air, amid the flaunting of kerchiefs and the admiration of her fellows. All household drudgery ceases on this day. The husband puts on his best clothes, repeats the fatha, or opening verse of the Koran, and goes *to run his horse;* whilst the wife has the double gratification, first of putting on her smart things, and next of showing them off to her female friends.

It snowed as we passed along the plain of Kila Afghan; but the flakes became rain-drops as we descended the other side of Latta-band, and we arrived late at night in Talikhan, soaked to the skin. Our reception was less cordial than it had formerly been, and I could gather from the altered manner of our host that our influence at court was on the wane.

Saddling next morning long before daybreak, we passed rapidly across the Talikhan plain, and without waiting to bait our horses at Khana-a-bad, pushed on for Kunduz, where we arrived about seven o'clock on the evening of the 11th, just as Dr. Lord was seating himself to his solitary meal.

I had been absent exactly three months; and those only who have been separated for so long a period, in countries as wild as these, from a most kind and valued friend, can appreciate my pleasure at the meeting. We each of us had much to communicate to the other; and it was deep in the morning before our conference ended.

CHAPTER XXIII.

Start for Hazrat Imam.—Marching.—Hazrat Imam.—Patients.—Dogs.—Hunting of pheasants.—Murder of the Wakhan chief.—Fertility of the banks of the Oxus.—Mortality of Kunduz and Hazrat Imam.—Uzbek females.—Sharwan.—Kila Chap.—Ford the Kokcha.—Site of Barbarrah.—Plain of Turghi-i-Tippa.—Jan Kila.—Ford the Oxus.—Said.—Return towards Hazrat Imam.—Inhospitable reception.—Find shelter in an old shed.—Arrive in Hazrat Imam.—Death of the Mír's son.—Death of the Mír.—Kunduz.—Philanthropy of Moghul emperors.—Robbers.—Khulm.—Samarcand.—Export of skins.—Furs.—Mohamedan saint.—Moorcroft.—Kunduz.

I NOW learned from my friend, that in addition to the disease in his eyes, the general health of Mohamed Beg had become precarious, and also that his eldest son was alarmingly ill. On the very day of our arrival, Dr. Lord had been summoned to Hazrat Imam on their account; and the arrangements for the journey having been already made, we started next morning, leaving Atma, the Mír's Dewan Begi, to report my safe arrival to Murad Beg, and to inform him that I had travelled not only unmolested, but honoured throughout his wide dominions.

A ride of nearly six miles brought us to the river of Khana-a-bad. It was not here the same rapid stream which had well-nigh unhorsed the Munshi on a former occasion; but, deep and turbid, it moved sluggishly on between low banks of the richest loam. The taller horses were able to ford the river, but the yabus were obliged to swim. Climbing its right bank, we entered a spacious plain, carpeted with the finest grass, over which we continued for the further distance of thirteen miles, and then dismounted at an abdan, or reservoir,[1] where we pitched our tent for the night.

Travelling, as we now did, with the appendages of civilization

---

[1] In Turkistan these reservoirs are arched over with burnt bricks.

about us, if a small tent may be so denominated, we had to pack up before mounting, and were thus detained longer on our camping ground after daybreak than had been usual in my late trip to the eastward. There is something extremely pleasant in our mode of travelling in India: the care with which all the arrangements are made, and the attention which is invariably paid to various items of luxury and comfort, among which not the least important are *shade, cool* water, and a frothy glass of Hodgson's or Bass's *beer*. The larger tents and the heavy baggage are sent forward over night, and pitched by sunrise, or a little after; so that the European, after a cool morning's ride, can sit down to breakfast immediately on his arrival—the little tent in which he passed the night being brought up to the ground in the course of the day. In the sultry plains of Hindustan this is a safe and very agreeable mode of journeying; but delightful though it be in summer, it cannot in the winter season bear a comparison with the off-hand, free and easy style of travelling practised by all classes in Afghanistan, where your lodging is under the felts of a Kyl or the roof of a farm-house, and where rude hospitality, a good fire, and friendly converse, make ample amends for poor fare and the total absence of form and ceremony. When once you have seen your horse well provided with corn, and have carried your saddle-bags into the house, there is nothing more to do but chat and eat and be at your ease. You are not only more independent, and more the master of your own actions than the traveller who creeps across the plain encumbered with baggage and attendants, but you escape a thousand causes of worry to yourself and others. If when you are roughing it, hardships do occur, as they sometimes will, the buoyancy of spirits which the keen air and light atmosphere of high lands bestow, enables you to bear them without repining.

Resuming our march, the path for three miles continued along the plain, after which we wound for another five through a ridge of grassy hills, on emerging from which we came in sight of Hazrat Imam, and debouched into the valley of the Oxus. An hour's ride from this point over a rich, well-cultivated country brought us to the end of our journey.

Hazrat Imam is about the same size as Kunduz; and its fort, though not so large, is more judiciously constructed. The ditch was full of water, and a wooden bridge in good repair kept up the communication with the town. The market-place is an open square, lying immediately under the south-west bastion of the fortress.

Dr. Lord, after seeing his patients, prescribed moderate exercise for the Mír's son, who, poor lad, with little originally the matter with him, had by the unskilful treatment of a native practitioner been brought to the brink of the grave. They had deferred calling in my friend until the time had gone by when his advice would have been useful. The spirits of the young man were much depressed; but it was thought that country air and the excitement of the chase might dissipate the languor which, independent of bodily infirmities, preyed on his mind; and the result was more favourable than could have been anticipated.

A large party of well-mounted horsemen were accordingly assembled next day at the gate of the fort: a mongrel pack of dogs were in attendance. When joined by the sick prince and his younger brother, we struck north over the country for the Oxus, the banks of which were to be the scene of our sport.

Though I have spoken in somewhat disparaging terms of Mohamed Beg's pack of hounds, there were some dogs in it which could not but have found favour even in the eyes of an English sportsman. These were the *tazi;* a breed which for strength and symmetry, vie with our greyhound, and in beauty surpass it; the spaniel from Kulab, and others of mixed blood, but possessing keen scent, and some of the qualities of our pointers.

On nearing the river the party broke up into small knots, each seeking its own amusement. The objects of our search were pheasants, a goodly number of which were bagged in the course of the day. As soon as a bird was put up, the nearest horseman set off at full speed in the direction of its flight which was nine times out of ten a straight line. Few escaped us, for we went along at a pelting pace, and two flights are as many as the pheasant can take without a long rest. When the dogs were kept back by the stiff reedy grass, which was generally the case, the bird was struck down by the horse's feet.

While at Hazrat Imam, we were shocked to hear that Mohamed Rahim Khán of Wakhan had been murdered by Murad Beg. Atma, who was present when the crime was committed, gave us, on our return to Kunduz, the following particulars :—

The Wakhan chief on his first arrival at Kunduz was well received; but when, instead of the arrears of tribute, a meagre present was offered, Murad Beg was so enraged, that he instantly placed him in confinement, and he was arraigned in the Mír's durbar on the very day that Abdal Ghaní arrived. Murad Beg, who had predetermined the chief's death, inquired of the Yesawal, as if casually, whether his party had been well treated in Wakhan? "No," was the lying reply. "Kaffir," exclaimed the enraged Uzbek, turning to his victim, "and is it thus you set me at defiance : *kutta chob bizun*, strike him with a club." A courtier present, whose father had been killed in Wakhan, required no second bidding; he darted out of the presence-chamber, and returning with a large wooden billet, felled the unhappy man at a single stroke, bespattering with his brains the dresses of those near him. "*Koob kurde! Koob kurde!*" "Well done! well done!" shouted the savage ruler from his musnud.

I soon became weary of remaining inactive at Hazrat Imam, and Dr. Lord having obtained permission for me to visit the Oxus, on the 17th of March, accompanied by Gholam Hussein, I started for its fords. The country was so thickly peopled for the first twenty miles, that frequently a dozen villages were in sight from one spot, each marked by its own little clump of trees. These hamlets, seen from a distance, brought to my recollections the *Tandas*, or farm-steadings of Sind; but the little white mosque with its blue-stained tiles is wanting here. The soil is darker in colour, and of a better quality than Sind can boast, where the cracked, sun-glazed surface of the ground is for the most part a poor, alluvial deposit, interspersed occasionally with tracts of richer land.

The Uzbeks, who follow agricultural pursuits, pitch their

S

kirgahs in localities which most people would avoid. Though the green-sodded hills around invite them to encamp where the air is pure and the breeze healthy, they prefer the swamp and its miasma, and will not purchase health at the price of a certain degree of extra labour. It is no doubt convenient to them to reside in the midst of their cultivated fields; but the very circumstances which cause the extreme fertility of those fields render them deadly to man; to those, at least, who have not been gradually seasoned to the region; nor can any advantages which the husbandman obtains by residing on the low grounds be worth the risk which he incurs. Since the year 1830, Badakhshan and the countries subject to or rather "chuppowed" by Murad Beg, on the northern bank of the Oxus, have been depopulated to stock the plains of Kunduz and Hazrat Imam. The aggregate of foreigners thus forcibly planted in these unhealthy marshes from that year to the present time, is estimated by the Uzbeks at 25,000 families, or, in round numbers, 100,000 souls; and I question whether of these 6,000 were alive in 1838; so great had been the mortality in the short space of eight years. Truly may the proverb say, "If you wish to die, go to Kunduz." Twelve months antecedent to our visit, a great portion of the inhabitants of Kulab were brought from their own hilly country down to Hazrat Imam. Dr. Lord and myself walked over the ground which their straw kirgahs had covered, and where some still stood; but silence and the numerous graves around told us the fate of their former inmates.

In the case of these unhappy people, the mind predisposes the body to disease; for a free mountaineer when forcibly transported to labour in these fens, considers himself a doomed man; pines for the cooling breezes of his own Alpine home, and gradually droops. The energy of his character subsides, and is succeeded by a gloomy indifference, that unnerves the frame, and prepares it to receive the germ of maladies so prevalent in this unhealthy region. The Uzbeks, inured to the country, suffer less than others.

As we passed their villages, the women in groups were standing in front of the tents, or walking among the Zird Alu trees, now partially in blossom. It had been raining for several days, and they seemed delighted to catch as much sunshine as the fitful clouds would spare them; none of them wore veils. In appearance they do not differ from the Kirghiz, except that they are of a larger frame.

Leaving to our right the hill of Khaja Tow, a principal feature in the landscape, we came upon the canal of Sharwan, which irrigates the whole district of Hazrat Imam. In crossing it, the water reached up to our horses' girths; its width was forty feet, and the current ran at the rate of about two and a half miles an hour. Two hours afterwards we arrived on the Oxus, at the castle of Sharwan, where the water enters the canal from the river. The fort overlooks the Oxus: upon the opposite bank of which was a party of ten gold seekers, searching its sand for the precious metal. Sharwan is more a castellated dwelling-house than a place of strength, and is fortunate in being exempt from the pestilential climate of Kunduz and Hazrat Imam. Immediately south of it, between Khaja Tow and the still more remarkable mountain of Koh Umber, lay a beautiful tract of the most delicious pasture, over which the flocks of Murad Beg were roaming. The grazing ground comes close up to the Oxus, and on its northern verge stands Sharwan.

After a ride of another twelve miles, we dismounted at Kila Chap. Before we reached it night had set in, and our guide could no longer conceal his fears of the wild tenants of the jungle through which the road led; nor was his anxiety without a cause, for we learned at Kila Chap that beasts of prey were numerous, and among them the lion.

Kila Chap is faced by a high hill on the opposite bank of the Kokcha, called I-khanam, and the next morning, after fording the river, we ascended it to take the bearings. I could hardly recognise in the muddy banks and soil-tinged stream my old friend of the mountains; so different was its appearance here to that which it presented in Badakhshan.

From the summit of I-khanam we had a glorious view of the surrounding country. At the foot of the hill was the junction of the two rivers. From the point of confluence the Kokcha could be traced to its exit from the mountains on the south, while the eye followed the Oxus westward, till distance concealed its brick-coloured stream. To the east and south, the pinnacles of snowy mountains shot up into the clouds, whilst a lower ridge, but also snow-clad, encircled the horizon to the north. Immediately below I-khanam, on its east side, the ground is raised into low, swelling ridges. Here, we were informed, stood an ancient city called Barbarrah, and there is a considerable extent of mud-walls standing, which the Tajiks think are vestiges of the old city, but which are evidently of a comparatively modern era. The appearance of the place, however, does indicate the truth of their tradition, that an ancient city once stood here. On the site of the town was an Uzbek encampment; but from its inmates we could glean no information, and to all our inquiries about coins and relics, they only vouchsafed a vacant stare or an idiotic laugh.

The whole of this day's march, a distance of twenty-eight miles, was over a splendid pasture-ground as the eye ever saw. From the river on our left to the mountains on the right, was stretched out one sheet of verdure, dotted over with sheep, herds of horses, and droves of cattle. This plain is named Turghi-i-Tippa. We several times came on the remains of a canal, which, though filled up, evinced by the height of its two parallel ridges and their width apart, its truly gigantic proportions. At the close of the march, when descending to Jan Kila, which stands down in the bed of the Oxus, and on its left bank, we saw where this canal left the river; and here its depth, to reach the level of the stream at this season, must have been at least eighty feet. Such a work could only be executed under a despotic government, or by a wealthy and civilized people.

On the morning of the 19th, accompanied by seventeen mounted Uzbek spearmen, we forded the Oxus abreast of Jan Kila,.and opposite the village of Said, which is on the right bank. On our way down to the water's edge, the dogs of the village were seen, just outside the fort, gnawing the bones of a bullock, which during the night a lion had killed for his own repast. At the ford the stream was divided into three channels, the two first of which were easily passed, but the last, though not dangerous, required some generalship in crossing. In all wide-spread rivers the direct line across is never the best ford. Looking attentively on the surface of the water, a slight ripple of a horse-shoe form may generally be detected stretching from bank to bank. The ford is here, and in passing it you must be careful to keep in the deep still water some distance above the ripple, for where the water is shoal, the current shoots down with a velocity against which no horse could stand. A man on foot could not have forded the river at Jan Kila. Three horses abreast is a safer way of passing than in single file. There was something exciting in crossing the last stream. When we had gained the upward curve or horn of the crescent near the opposite shore, it was doubtful whether the leading horses would hold their own. They could make no way against the stream, which fell to the right and left of the line, like waves thrown from off the bow of a steam-boat. It was an anxious moment, since the slightest indecision on the rider's part or any stumbling of his horse, must have annihilated the line. At length, the well-trained steeds began to step out, and, once in motion, slowly but gallantly did they breast the stream till we gained the bank. This largest channel had a width of 200 yards and a velocity of four miles an hour; the centre one was about half the breadth, and had a current of about three miles; the water in the one which we first entered was almost stagnant. The bottoms of all were pebbly.

The Oxus can be forded in the winter season from Hazrat Imam to the frontiers of Darwaz. Westward, the accession of large tributaries renders the stream too powerful to be crossed on foot, while the mountains to the eastward, by narrowing its bed, are productive of a similar result. Within these limits the best ford, both for permanence and good footing, lies immediately under the castle of Sharwan. Guns have there been conveyed across by the Kunduz Mír. Even in the summer season the Oxus in this neighbourhood has been crossed by a troop of Murad Beg's mounted banditti. The riders swam upon mussuks, and guided their horses across. The chuppow on which they were then bent is said to have been eminently successful. In Darwaz the river is bridged, and between it and Shagnan one or two rude description of boats are in use, but no vessel is employed upon the Oxus for commercial purposes, nor indeed at the ferries above the confluence of the Serai river.

Said stands on the permanent bank of the Oxus, and not in its bed like Jan Kila. To reach it we had a march of five miles through a heavy reed jungle abounding in game of every variety. Deer were numerous, and a splendid pair of antlers were procured from one which a villager shot. Pheasants, also, were plentiful, as they are in many other parts of the valley of the Oxus. The method of taking game is to fire the jangal, and when an animal breaks cover he is speared by the horsemen or pulled down by dogs. Upwards of two hundred head of deer are slaughtered annually at Said. I had intended to have remained a few days to see the sport, but when we were about to take the field on the morning following our arrival, the heavens looked so much like rain, that I deemed it prudent to re-cross the river, lest we should be kept prisoners here longer than was convenient.

Said is the frontier province of Murad Beg's dominions, north of the Oxus. The hills in its neighbourhood afford an inexhaustible supply of mineral salt. The village contains a population of about 100 families.[1]

At Jan Kila I found a note awaiting me from Dr. Lord, the contents of which induced me at once to return to Hazrat Imam; so, crossing the plain of Turghi-i-Tippa, we arrived on the banks of the Kokcha about nine o'clock at night. As it had been raining all day it was not judged prudent to attempt fording the swollen stream until daylight. We now looked about for some shelter, the rain still pouring. The flinty hearts of the Uzbeks, who were here encamped, were assailed in vain. Keeping by the stream for a few miles upwards we reached a considerable village; but there we fared no better. We went the round of nearly every house in the place, were threatened at many, and spurned, abused, and driven from the doors of all.

---

[1] Said or Sayád is in Kuláb. Captain Wood is the only European known to have set foot in this little known territory.

Even a cow-house we were not permitted to enter. Our guide, an officer in the service of Mohamed Beg of Hazrat Imam, told them we were guests of Mohamed Beg, to which the Uzbeks replied, "They were subjects of Talikhan, and cared neither for the blind Mír nor his brother." Towards midnight, when these uncouth and inhospitable boors had gone to rest, we stealthily re-entered the village and took possession of an empty house in its suburbs. There was a deep puddle on its floor, but groping round the walls we discovered raised benches, and upon these we lay till day-dawn. When morning broke we found ourselves in an oil-mill shed, cradled in its seed-bins. Having no one to thank for hospitality we left the village before a kirgah was opened. Fording the river, now considerably swollen, we breakfasted at Kila Chap, and that evening by sunset were again in Hazrat Imam.

Dr. Lord's patients were both improving in health; but this was not enough for the friends of the Mír, who had fondly imagined that a single dose of the firingí's *patent* medicine would open the eyes of the blind chief, and set the crippled son on his legs again. From the first, Dr. Lord held out no hopes to the Mír that he could restore his sight; but he did not hesitate to tell him that his son only required careful treatment to ensure recovery; adding, however, that if his advice was not strictly followed he would not be responsible for the result. The day after my arrival a deputation waited on the doctor to tell him that a lad, suffering as the Mír's son now did, had been completely cured by immersion in an oil-bath, and that Mohamed Beg wished the young Mír to be similarly treated. As it was vain to reason with them, Dr. Lord peremptorily required implicit obedience to his prescriptions or permission to quit the place. After some little deliberation the native Galen prevailed, and his *hot* and *cold* nostrums were preferred to the lights of modern science. The poor youth died; but whether his death was hastened or delayed by the *book-bound* ignorance of Mohamedanism, let others judge. Thanks to the comfortable doctrine of predestination, *Wakhut receed*, "his time had come." Neither the firingí Tabeeb[1] nor

---

[1] English doctor.

his rival of Peshawúr suffered in Uzbek estimation by this melancholy event.

Among the Uzbeks the temper of a medical man is sadly tried, for he can seldom, if ever, depend on his prescriptions being faithfully followed. The people eat so enormously that to adhere to any course of diet is a task to which very few among them are equal. For instance, we discovered that the Mír of Hazrat Imam, when suffering from indigestion and undergoing a course of medicine for relief, was gorging himself every morning with sour milk, hard-boiled eggs, and rich pillaus. Three times did Dr. Lord put him to rights, and as often did the man's indiscretion bring on a relapse. But the Peshawari physician was more summary in his treatment—kill or cure seems to have been his motto. He does not, however, appear to have been very successful in his practice, for soon after our departure from Turkistan we heard of Mohamed Beg's death.

As on our arrival at Kunduz we were informed that the Passes of Hindú Kosh were still blocked up with snow, and that none of them could be attempted with safety for at least another fortnight. Dr. Lord asked and obtained permission to visit Khulm in the interim; and on the evening of Saturday, the 24th, we set out for that city. Our first march was a short one; seven miles brought us to the western side of the Kunduz plain, where, on the summit of the high grassy plateau which there forms its boundary, we dismounted and pitched the bechoba. Next day a ride of another five miles in a west-south-west direction, over a plain like a bowling-green, took us to the base of a range of hills, crossed by a path on which a wheeled carriage could travel. At the bottom of their western slope stands a water cistern, a dome-covered building, and a guard-tower—remnants of Mongol munificence, evincing, by their usefulness rather than their beauty, the philanthropic spirit of the monarch who erected them. It is such as these—edifices raised for the wayfaring man's accommodation, water-tanks stored for his use, and canals dug to irrigate lands otherwise infertile, that make us sympathise with the fallen fortunes of this once powerful dynasty, which can boast of many generous and enlightened men. The character of Akbar, for instance, will not suffer by being compared with that of any sovereign in Europe with whom he was contemporary. We slept this night at another of these abdans; for during the palmy days of Baber's line the emperors of Hindustan had post-houses not only

"From Agra to Lahore of Great Moghul,"

but across the India-Tartaric Caucasus to Balkh. Here we found some of Murad Beg's soldiers on guard, as the road was infested by banditti from Bulgewar, on the opposite bank of the Oxus, headed by Kutty Khán, a relation of the Kunduz chief. The guard sent out patrols and saw us down into the plain of Yang Arekh unmolested by their free-booting relatives. Although thus far attentive to the guests of their prince, these troopers showed us little courtesy, and it was not without difficulty that we succeeded in establishing our right to have quarters in their guard-tower.

A slight rise in the ground hid Khulm from our view until we crested the ridge which is within half a mile of the town. The fields around it were green as emeralds, while all beyond was desert. Entering the eastern gate, or that called Badakhshan, we wound through its suburbs to the bázár, which, though inferior to that of Kabul, is infinitely superior to the one in Kunduz. The hum of voices, the well-covered stalls, the predominance of Tajik features, and the rosy cheeks of the young, were what we had not of late been accustomed to, and each in turn came in for its share of our commendation. The orchards looked beautiful in their fresh livery of leaves and blossoms; the mulberry plantations for the rearing of silk-worms were kept clean and neat, the trunk of the tree being pruned down to the height of from four to six feet to increase its foliage. The fruit was now (April 6) well-formed, though not a leaf was yet open. Nearly a month before this time the plum-trees in the orchards of Kunduz had began to blossom.

From a Khaja, a descendant of the former rulers of Kashkar, whom we met at Khulm, we learned that the palaces of Samarcand are still in good preservation; that the halls in which Timur revelled, and the colleges where his grandson, the celebrated Ulug Beg, studied, yet exist. The town is in ruins, but a considerable population, attached to the place, still inhabit the ancient Maracanda. By the Khaja's account, Kokan is little, if at all, inferior in size to Bokhara.

I was surprised at the camel-loads of skins that passed the Khulm custom-house for the Bokhara market. We were told by the Hindu who collects the revenue for Murad Beg that the annual export is nearly 200,000 skins. They are principally those of lambs, wolves, and foxes, but nothing comes amiss. All the fur-yielding animals of the surrounding mountains are eagerly sought after, and even the skins of dogs and cats are not rejected. Lambs'-skins are bought at from twenty-four to thirty shillings per hundred, and bring a profit of about cent. per cent. in Bokhara, the expense of carriage not being deducted. In Khulm the water-spouts in the caves of the houses are formed of the shoulder-blade bones of sheep, a trifling fact in itself, but one which, taken in connection with the above, is singularly illustrative of Uzbek commerce.

A very superior and handsome fur, called Dalkhafik, is met with in Kabul. The animal that yields it must be diminutive, for its skin rarely measures more than four inches by ten. It is used to line posteens. One hundred and twenty-two skins are required for one cloak, and the price of each being two shillings, the article is costly, and only worn by rich Soudaghurs (merchants), and wealthy chiefs. The animal is a native of the Hazara and other mountains around Kabul. I believe it to be the marten of commerce.

The old town of Khulm is distant five miles from Tash Kurghan ("stone fort"), or the new town, which was built in the time of Kalich Ali Beg, whose memory is still deservedly celebrated in Turkistan. It stands immediately without the gorge of the Khulm river, up the course of which its orchards extend. The ruins of the old town occupy more ground than the new; but it is now quite forsaken, except its fortress, within which a few Arab families have taken up their abode. The valley of the Oxus here bears a striking resemblance to that of the Indus south of Kalabagh. Both are destitute of verdure —the soil, a whitish clay, fertile when irrigated, but yielding nothing spontaneously except the tamarisk bush and a few dwarfish and useless jungle trees. The *beds* of both rivers are, however, abundantly productive, and along their margins, when cleared from the wood and gigantic grass which are native to them, every plant may be reared that is adapted to the climate. In fact, wherever their waters reach they carry *plenty* with them, for whether conducted in canals or diffused by inundations, water, assisted by man, will clothe the desert with verdure, and rear an oasis in the wilderness.

One evening, when at dinner in Khulm, a Mohamedan saint introduced himself and was told to be seated. Wine stood upon the table, of which he was requested to partake. He looked highly offended, and said little until the dinner was removed and the servants retired. The Pír's countenance then brightened up at once, and he exclaimed, "Now, hand hither the wine cup! Do you think that I, who have disciples everywhere, from Balkh to Herat, know so little of the world, as to throw away my bread, by indulging in *shrab* (wine) in the presence of Mussulmans? No, no; between ourselves, such restrictions are unnatural and absurd; but you would not have those who live by them let the people know that they think so."

Mazar, where the last of Moorcroft's party died, is thirty miles west of Khulm, and was now visited by Dr. Lord in the hope of procuring any books or manuscripts of the unfortunate travellers which might still be in existence. Nor were his labours without their reward, since with the aid of the Mutawali, or priest, superintendent of the shrine, he succeeded in getting possession of every book which was in Mazar belonging to the party, even to the daily cash account-book. But among them were no manuscript details of their journey, and it is now pretty certain that none exist independent of those from which Professor Wilson compiled his late work.

Being so near to Maimana and Andhko, in which districts many of the Turkoman horses sent to India are bred, we naturally expected to pick up a few choice animals; but we were disappointed. We purchased the only good horse which was shown us, and though it was generally known that we wanted more, we re-entered Kunduz on the 10th of April, without any further addition to our stud. In crossing the plain to the west of Kunduz, herds of antelopes were seen in the distance, gazing at us or scampering off in affright beyond the reach of vision. Throughout this excursion, I was struck with the admirable adaptation of this country to the wants of a pastoral people. West of Khulm, the valley of the Oxus, except on the immediate banks of the stream, appears to be a desert; but in an opposite direction, eastward to the rocky barriers of Darwaz, all the high-lying portion of the valley is at this season a wild prairie of sweets, a verdant carpet enamelled with flowers. Were I asked to state in what respects Kabul and Kunduz most differ from each other, I should say in their mountain scenery. Throughout Kabul the hills are bold and repulsive, naked and bleak, while the low swelling outlines of Kunduz are as soft to the eye as the verdant sod which carpets them is to the foot.

CHAPTER XXIV.

Quit Kunduz.—Death of Mirza Badi.—Shor-Ab rivulet.—Plain of Narin.—Hindú Kosh.—Inderab.—Patriarchal manners of a Tajik chief.—Reflections.—Movements of pastoral tribes.—Arrangement for entering Afghanistan.—Thermal springs.—Crossing the Pass of Khawak.—Khawak fort.—Panchshir valley.—Scenery and inhabitants.—Uzbek dislike of pistols.—Arrive in Kabul.—Friendly reception by Nawab Jabar Khán.—Public feeling.—Dost Mohamed Khán.—A new acquaintance.—Conclusion.

On the 11th of April we attended Durbar and received permission to quit Kunduz. Our arrangements were soon made, and a little after midnight we left, without regret, that metropolis of thieves. Old Mirza Badi saw us some miles on our journey, and then with friendly warmth pressing our hands, he consigned us to the care of God and departed. Poor old man, in the usual course of nature a few years more and the grave would have claimed its own; but life is held cheap in Turkistan, and at no long period after this he fell a victim to animosity and avarice. The circumstances of his murder I have already mentioned.

After getting well clear of Kunduz, we struck south-southeast over an elevated plain, and at the close of an eighteen miles' ride, entered the valley of Shor-ab, or the "Salt-water." This stream drains the mountains of Eshk Meshk, and is strongly impregnated by the salt they contain, from which circumstance it derives its name. After pursuing the course of this rivulet for twelve miles, the yabus of the Kafila were too exhausted to proceed any further, and we accordingly halted. The little valley of Shor-ab is fringed by grass-clad hills rarely exceeding 300 feet in height, along the base of which in every nook stood an Uzbek encampment.

The next day rain delayed us until noon; nevertheless we accomplished by eight o'clock at night one and thirty miles, the general direction of our march being still to the south. Our encamping ground was a sweet spot at the head of the Narin plain, in lat. 36° 5′ 13″ N. The surface of the country had now roughened. To the eastward the Eshk Meshk (probably Isk-Kimish) mountains reared their snowy crests, whilst in other directions the prospect was bounded by lesser and near-lying ridges. Towards the close of this day's journey, we left the little rivulet, flowing from east-by-north, in which direction lay the mountain whence it came. Soon afterwards we crossed the Baghlan, a tributary of the Kunduz river. Westward the country sometimes opened into plains, having their largest axis in that direction.

The following day we traced the river of Baghlan to its source, on reaching which, the Hindú Kosh, only ten miles distant, met our gaze. At the bottom of the pass lay the secluded valley of Inderab, beyond which the snowy mountains rose like a wall, without any intervening ridge to veil their majesty or detract from their bulk. The eye at a glance caught the mighty buttress, from its blackened base to its hoary summit. The snow-line on its mural face was clear and well defined.

As we descended into Inderab, a horseman overtook us, who proved to be Tora Khán, the chief of the valley. He courteously requested us to make his house our home. He had been to Kunduz on business, and though only a short time absent from his people, it was pleasing to see the affectionate manner in which they greeted his return. Every man we passed ran up to the Mír, and taking him familiarly by the hand inquired after his health. The plough was left standing in the fields, and some individuals, who discovered him from their distant cottage-doors, came at full speed to congratulate him on his safe return. The Tajik chief spoke kindly to all. Of some he inquired how certain fields were looking; of others he asked if the last hunt had been successful. More than once he bawled out, and astonished an honest ploughman who had been too mindful of his furrow to perceive his chieftain's approach. How enviable must his feelings have been! It was delightful to us thus unexpectedly to find ourselves in this small but apparently most happy community, where natural affections had their flow, and where its chief was loved rather than feared. Locked up among mountains, the Inderabis know little of what transpires in the country around them. Changes that rend kingdoms disturb not the tranquillity of this secluded district. Now that Kunduz is all powerful north of the mountains, Tora Khán yields a willing obedience, and pays his tribute to its chief; but should Kabul ever regain the provinces she has lost, not only he, but every Tajik who now feels the iron grasp of Murad Beg, would welcome the change.

It is instructive to remark the difference which climate and circumstances everywhere produce on the character and habits of man. The Mír of Inderab, though verging to corpulency, was active both in mind and body. Had he been brought up in India, he would, instead of leading the bustling life he now does, have been, in all probability, a lazy Patan—one of those portly personages, the retainers of the native princes in Hindustan, who, bristling with arms, seem only to relish life in court, in camp, or on a journey. See them at home when the kammerband is ungirdled, and the showy turban replaced by a dirty skull-cap, and they are the very personification of idleness. For hours will they sit on their carpet, or loll upon a *charpœ* (bedstead) in the open air, in seeming unconsciousness; or, if they do give signs of thought and life, it is only to exclaim "Tobah! Tobah!" and to change their position.

A small colony of Sauleh-aulengis is settled in Inderab, whom Tora Khán assured us were among the most industrious and well-behaved of his Ryots. In their own valley, on the opposite side of the mountains, they are notorious freebooters. Here, however, there is no opportunity of levying black-mail; and, with the orderly habits of an honest community ever before their eyes, the Sauleh-aulengis have "ceased from evil, and learned to do good!"

Circumstances constrained us to remain four days with the chief, whose residence proved superior to what we had anticipated. The building was a facsimile, on a small scale, of Dost Mohamed Khán's new houses in the Bagh-i-shah at Kabul.

Our entertainment was such as left us no grounds for quarrel with Tajik hospitality.

The greater number of the inhabitants of Inderab are agriculturists. A portion are, however, pastoral. In early spring their flocks are driven down upon the Oxus. As that season draws to a close, they range the lower hills. Summer advances, and they move towards Hindú Kosh. When autumn is well through, they have eaten their way up to the neighbourhood of the snow line; but the first fall of snow is the signal for a retrograde movement, and the men at once commence providing fuel and provender for winter consumption.

On the 18th, accompanied by Tora Khán, we left Inderab for the Pass of Khawak, by which, and the Panchshir valley, we had decided on entering Afghanistan. Khawak is at the top of the Panchshir valley, and is the source both of its stream and of that of Inderab. It is the most eastern of the Turkistan passes, and by nature one of the most accessible; but the lawless habits of the Panchshiris have long closed it to both traveller and merchant. The power of Kabul is set at nought, and we could not expect that because we were the guests of its ruler we should fare better than others. Superstition was our only safeguard; and Dr. Lord had accordingly arranged for Mír Baba of Koh Daman, a holy man of great influence in these regions, to meet us at the pass, and escort us down the valley.[1]

Following up the stream which wound, in its stony bed, along the foot of the stupendous wall to our right, we arrived at the foot of Khawak, distant twenty-nine miles from Inderab, on the afternoon of the 22nd. Six miles before reaching this halting-ground, we came on two thermal springs, gushing out from the side of a grassy hill, 400 yards to the left of the path, at a place called Sir-ab. Their temperatures were respectively 108° and 124° of Fahrenheit.

Preparations were now made to pass the snowy mountains, and that evening a large party of our host's peasantry were sent forward with the baggage. The horses, stripped to their felts,

---

[1] It is the generally received opinion that this is the pass crossed by Alexander when coming from Bactria, and also by Tawmir on his advance to India.

accompanied them. It was a clear frosty night, and we were not without hope of their gaining the other side of Khawak before the next day's sun should have loosened the frozen surface of the snow. In the morning we followed, mounted from Tora Khán's stud. When the snow became too soft for the horses, they were to be sent back. After being about an hour on the road, Ibrahim the Sindi, was seen stealing back among the hills towards our last night's encampment; and, as he had charge of a chronometer, I suspected something was wrong, and went after him. It appeared that he had only forgotten his sword. Vexed at this detention, I now endeavoured to overtake my companions; and, in my anxiety to do so, unluckily lost the road. After blundering on for some time to the right and left, I at length discovered the path, and pushed the pony at a glassy steep to reach it. When near the top, the animal lost its footing and fell. Both of us were soon at the bottom of the hill, though the speed with which the pony descended considerably exceeded mine. He did not wait for his rider; for before I could get upon my legs he was off at an easy trot, but much too fast for me to think of following him. Stripping off my fur-coat, I now slowly and carefully scrambled up the ice-sheeted hill, on surmounting which I found myself upon the track of Dr. Lord's party.

Fatigued with the late adventure, I had trudged wearily on for about half a mile, when a party of Inderabis were espied on their return from the pass, sitting round a fire with their steeds picketed hard by. Exchanging a few civil words with the party, I asked and obtained permission to try the paces of the best looking of their horses; when kicking him under the flanks, I set off along the track of those who preceded me. Chase was forthwith given, but this time I won the race, and distanced my pursuers, who appeared quite at a loss to understand my somewhat suspicious looking procedure. My intention was to return the horse by one of the Mír's attendants, but I did not like to ask for the loan of the animal, being pretty sure that it would have been denied me. Two miles beyond the spot where the horse had been obtained, I encountered Tora Khán, who had seen Dr. Lord well up the pass, and was now returning home. He told me to dismount, as the snow could bear the horse but little further; so making the animal over to one of his attendants, I bade the Mír farewell, with my warmest thanks for the great kindness he had shown us, and parted from him just in time to escape the angry accusation of my pursuers. From this spot the view extended far up the pass, the road to which was one glistening sheet of frozen snow. The rise was remarkably uniform, not a ridge occurring in the whole ascent to vary the sameness of its surface. Far in the distance, towards the summit of the mountain, I discerned sundry little dark spots, each of which was some individual of our party, dragging his weary body upwards. On starting off on foot, I stepped out at a good pace, but soon learned by experience that short steps were not only the more pleasant method of walking up hill, but the speediest in the end. In the course of a few hours I overtook Dr. Lord, supported between two mountaineers, and in a state of great exhaustion. His plan had been to walk fast, and when tired to sit down and draw breath. I now communicated to him my system, which, though slow, was sure. The effect was surprising, and the doctor and myself were the first of our party to crown the pass.

While the laggards were coming up, we managed to make a fire, and found by the boiling point of water, that the height of Khawak was 13,200 feet. Having seen all the party, both men and horses, over the crest of the pass, we commenced its southern descent; but had not proceeded far when firm footing began to fail the horses. The depth of snow was about four feet; and most of the animals, after floundering till exhausted, sunk in it up to their bellies. It was no use in attempting to move them further that day, but it was necessary to take some precautions to prevent their being frost-bitten during the night. We therefore spread their felts compactly together on the surface of the snow, and with the aid of tent-poles, lifted the animals upon them, and their weight being thus more equally disposed, the snow sufficed to bear them up.

East-by-south, ten miles and a half from the top of the pass, is the fort of Khawak, 9,300 feet above the sea, in latitude 35° 37' 36" N. This place we reached on the same day that we crossed the pass, but three more elapsed before we got the horses to it. Mír Baba, on whose holy protection our safety depended, had not yet arrived, and we felt uncomfortable at his non-appearance. Fifteen miles, however, and a rough road, still separated us from the inhabited part of the valley; and we trusted to gain intelligence of the Pír's locality before his thievish disciples heard of ours.

Between the top of the pass and the fort of Khawak a lead mine was pointed out to us; but the depth of snow upon the ground prevented our visiting it. In the grave-yard of the little fort nine miners are interred, who had been attacked and slain while at work, by a party of the neighbouring Kaffirs. There were ten in all; but one escaped, though badly wounded.

While detained at Khawak snow fell every day; but the cold was not severe. On the 28th a messenger arrived, reporting the near neighbourhood of our protector, on which we quitted the fort, and that evening gave ourselves into the keeping of the holy man. By this messenger we also received letters from Captain Burnes, briefly mentioning that circumstances had constrained him to make arrangements for quitting Kabul, and desiring us to hasten our return.

On the last day of April we cleared the valley of Panchshir, and that night slept at a fort in Koh Daman, the residence of Mír Baba. The length of the Panchshir valley, its sinuosities included, is seventy miles; its general direction being south-west and north-east. It is said to contain seven thousand families, all of which, except those at Khawak, are resident within forty-five miles of its entrance. Probably there is no district throughout Kabul better peopled than this; and I certainly have seen none where signs of prosperity were more abundant. The valley in most places is about a mile and a half wide, and it nowhere exceeds twice that breadth. Numerous streams from the north and south join its main river, and it is up the banks of those that the inhabitants have placed their dwellings. The valley is naturally sterile. Everything here is artificial. Panchshir, like all the cultivated valleys of Afghanistan, owes its productiveness and its beauty to man; there being scarcely a tree but what has been planted by his

T 2

hand. There is little land fit for cultivation, but the whole of that was in crop. The orchard and mulberry plantations furnish the staple support of its inhabitants. Though limited in range, the scenery of Panchshir is soft and beautiful. Its rugged, red-tinged surface is dotted over with castellated dwellings, whose square corner towers and solid walls rising on every knoll are relieved by the smiling foliage of fruit trees, and the lively green of the garden-like fields which surround them.

Yet this fair scene is chiefly peopled by robbers, whose lawless lives and never-ending feuds render it an unfit abode for honest men. It is astonishing how soon, where crime is general, the moral perceptions and the kind feelings of the heart are lost and blunted. In most other countries atrocious crimes are the result of evil passions strongly excited; but in the Kohistan blood is too often shed without provocation, and in the mere wantonness of cruelty. Some time ago a Kasid coming up Panchshir, with letters for Tora Khán, was asked to part with his shoes (*kamaches*). He refused, and was put to death. One of our own attendants, attempting to come up the valley, was sent back naked. He afterwards arrived under Mír Baba's protection.[1]

In the quarrels which perpetually occur in this region, where blood had been shed, and castles demolished, never, as far as I could learn, has a mulberry plantation been destroyed. Such an act would complete the ruin of a family; and, if often repeated, as it assuredly would be, were the system once introduced, must desolate the valley; mulberry flour being the staff of life in the Kohistan.

Since the reign of Timur Shah, the Panchshiris have been virtually independent of the many rulers who have successively occupied the Kabul *ghuddi*. Prior to that period they were governed by nine Kháns, revered the king's authority, and

[1] In Ibn Haukal's account of Khorasan, written eight centuries ago, we find Panjhir mentioned as "a place in the hills inhabited by ten thousand men, chiefly robbers and thieves," a description thoroughly in accord with that of the narrative; and it is evident that, since the days of the Arab geographer, but little change has taken place as regards the unenviable notoriety of the dwellers in this valley.

peaceably paid their taxes. Now every man is for himself, and the valley has consequently become a scene of turbulence and unnatural warfare. They acknowledged Dost Mohamed Khán as their ruler, but added nothing to his exchequer. It is calculated that, in the event of a religious or a national war, this valley could send out 10,000 armed men. On such occasions their domestic feuds lie dormant for the time, to be revived when peace returns. The same unity of action would have shown itself had Dost Mohamed attempted to force a tribute from them; but though able to cope with the limited means of the ex-Amir of Kabul, they will doubtless be coerced into submission by the disciplined battalions of Shah Shuja. It is, however, more than questionable whether, for some years to come, the tribute realised will defray the expense of its collection, either in this region or among any of the hill-tribes in Afghanistan.

The Panchshiris have the reputation of being good soldiers. Their arms are the musket and the long knife-like sword of the Afghans. All the muskets which we examined bore either the King's or the Company's mark on the lock. In Kunduz a matchlock is preferred to a flint-lock; but south of Hindú Kosh it is otherwise. The Uzbeks detest the very sight of pistols; but an Afghan or Tajik covets their possession. Dr. Lord once presented a brace of pistols to one of the young princes in Kunduz. Next day they were returned by the father, with the remark that if the doctor wished to make his son a present, he should give him something useful. A matchlock from the bázár, about one-tenth of the value of the pistols, gave unbounded satisfaction.

Leagues similar to those existing between the Kaffirs and Badakhshis are formed here. These are in force during the summer, at the close of which season the hostages are returned. Yearly, when the passes open, the leagues are renewed. Sometimes this pacific compact is broken; but this does not happen so frequently as to do away with all confidence between the contracting parties. When the truce ceases hostilities commence. In the stealthy advance and the night attack the cunning of the Kaffir gives him the advantage; but in open day the musket of the Panchshiri is more than a match for the Kaffir spear.

The Panchshiris, like the rest of the Kohistanis, are Tajiks. They are Suni Mohamedans, and not being very old in the faith, are the more violently bigoted to it. Before Baber's time they are said to have been Kaffirs; and it is also stated that the Sauleh-Aulengis became Mussulmans about the same era. We saw a few weavers amongst the former people; but their clothing is principally procured from the bázár of Kabul. Amidst the anarchy which prevails in this valley there are two dignified exceptions. These are the brothers Khanjan Khán and Mohamed Shah Khán, who tranquilly rule over about 500 families, at the beautiful village of Barak.

At eleven o'clock at night, on the 1st of May, after a weary ride of upwards of fifty miles, we re-entered Kabul. Finding that Captain Burnes had left the city we called on the Nawab, from whom we received our letters and a hearty welcome. He was in bed when we arrived, but got up at once, and came out to us in *déshabille;* nor would he, in spite of all we could say, return till he had seen all our wants supplied. Not to disturb his servants, Nawab Jabar Khán placed refreshments before us, with his own hands; and then, having called up a trusty person to wait on us, this truly hospitable and excellent man went back to his zenana.

The non-arrival of the baggage detained us a few days in Kabul, during which we had ample opportunity of observing how far recent events had influenced the public mind. The Kuzilbash, or Persian party, numbering many of the most respectable citizens of Kabul, rejoiced at what had occurred; but the mass of the people, Afghan and Tajik, were at no pains to conceal their discontent. Annoyed at Dost Mohamed's reception of Vikovitch, the Russian emissary, and disquieted by the departure of the British agent, they looked to the Mír as the sole cause of their troubles, and thought of Shah Shuja and redress. The resistance, passive and open, which our army experienced throughout the late campaign, and which, by the last accounts from India, has not yet altogether ceased, shows that we are no longer regarded by the Afghans as their friends. Can it well be otherwise? The conquest and occupation of their country by *British* troops, not to mention the brilliant affairs of Ghizni and Kelat, will no doubt diffuse a knowledge of our names from the Indus to the Caspian; but in substituting the dread of our arms for the respect which, throughout Asia, was before voluntarily accorded to the British character, I question whether our present gain may not ultimately prove a loss.

Before finally quitting Kabul, we waited on its ruler, who was residing in the house we ourselves had formerly occupied in the Bagh-i-Shah. Dost Mohamed Khán was engaged at chess when we entered the apartment; and while the interview lasted he affected to be more intent upon the chess-board than on the political game, which we well knew was the uppermost in his mind. His manner was at first cold; but this we could perceive was more feigned than real, as he soon assumed his usual tone of cordiality; and after some conversation upon recent events, he uttered, when we arose to depart, a pious ejaculation, and bade us a kind farewell.

From Kabul we marched to Jelalabad. During the few days of our stay at the former place, we had made the acquaintance of a young Frenchman, of pleasing manners, and gentlemanly address. He gave out that he had travelled among the Kaffirs of Hindú Kosh, and was anxious to make another journey through their country. I had long felt a desire to visit these people, and agreed to accompany him, provided I had Captain Burnes's permission. For this I applied, and arranged with the Frenchman that I would remain at Jelalabad till an answer arrived; where, if it were favourable, he was to join me. In the interim I ordered presents for the journey, to the amount of about 10*l.* These consisted of looking-glasses, beads, needles, thread, &c. At parting, I requested a sight of my new acquaintance's journal; but to this he demurred, and, in lieu of it, presented me with what he called *extracts*. This was not so satisfactory a document: however, the strange adventures he professed to have met with among the Kaffirs were so plausibly told, that I had no suspicion of his falsehood, until the day before we entered Jelalabad, when Gholam Hussein asked me whether I believed the Frenchman's story,—"Yes, certainly," was my reply: on which the Munshi exclaimed, *Tumam durrohg,* " it's all a lie," and brought forward a discharged servant of the Frenchman, who satisfactorily proved that his master had never been nearer to Kaffiristan than Jelalabad, at which place he had gathered the strange stories he was in the habit of relating as his own adventures. This man introduced himself to me as a sailor; and among other stories of the sea, related at great length the incidents of a cruise in the Pacific, in a French vessel commanded by an Englishman. Some months afterwards I discovered, that for all he knew of nautical matters he was indebted to Mr. Masson's library, from which he had borrowed a work, entitled "A Whaling Voyage in the Pacific."

From Jelalabad we embarked on rafts of inflated skins, and dropped down with the stream to Peshawúr. Here we rejoined Captain Burnes, now ordered to Lahore, where events soon transpired, the remote tendencies of which, though they cannot yet be defined, must be pregnant with interest to Great Britain and the East.

THE END.

www.ingramcontent.com/pod-product-compliance
Lightning Source LLC
Chambersburg PA
CBHW032020220426

43664CB00006B/311